Enhancing the Quality of ABAP® Development

 **PRESS**

SAP PRESS is a joint initiative of SAP and Galileo Press. The know-how offered by SAP specialists combined with the expertise of the publishing house Galileo Press offers the reader expert books in the field. SAP PRESS features first-hand information and expert advice, and provides useful skills for professional decision-making.

SAP PRESS offers a variety of books on technical and business related topics for the SAP user. For further information, please also visit our website: *www.sap-press.com.*

Sigrid Hagemann, Liane Will
SAP R/3 System Administration
2003, approx. 450 pp., ISBN 1-59229-014-4

Helmut Stefani
Archiving Your SAP Data
A comprehensive guide to plan and execute archiving projects
2003, 360 pp., ISBN 1-59229-008-6

A. Rickayzen, J. Dart, C. Brennecke, M. Schneider
Practical Workflow for SAP
2002, 504 pp., ISBN 1-59229-006-X

Horst Keller, Joachim Jacobitz
ABAP Objects. The Official Reference
2003, 1094 pp., 2 Volumes and CD Set
ISBN 1-59229-011-6

Frédéric Heinemann, Christian Rau
SAP Web Application Server
The complete guide for ABAP and web developers
2003, approx. 600 pp., ISBN 1-59229-013-2

Ben Meijs, Albert Krouwels,
Wouter Heuvelmans, Ron Sommen

Enhancing the Quality of ABAP® Development

Galileo Press

Bonn • Boston

Editor: Florian Zimniak
Copy Editor: Nancy Etscovitz, UCG, Inc.,
Boston, MA
Cover Design: Silke Braun

Printed in Germany

ISBN 978-1-59229-030-7
1st edition 2004, 2nd reprint 2007

Contents

3 Correctness   73

4 Stability   145

5 Exceptions and Error Handling 219

6 User-Friendliness 245

7 Performance 267

8 Maintainability — 331

9 Checking Robustness and Troubleshooting — 379

Preface

Although the ABAP programming language is widely used throughout the world, there is no account or study that defines the optimal use of this language. This book is intended to fill this gap. It is one of a series of books with guidelines for using the ABAP language written by people from our company—Ctac. Despite its being a relatively small company, Ctac has established a singular position in the first ranks of the Dutch SAP market as an entirely SAP-focused consultancy firm. It takes special pride in the ABAP skills that exist in-house. Former colleagues have documented their experiences with the ABAP language in earlier books, which were published for a relatively small audience in the Netherlands. Since the last book (published in 1997), the time was ripe for a completely fresh and updated approach. Originally, we had no intention of writing this book for an international audience. However, that was before we met Andreas Blumenthal— vice president of the department NetWeaver Development Tools ABAP who is responsible for the development of the ABAP language—on the TechEd Conference in Basel in 2003. In a sudden burst of enthusiasm, we asked him whether he would be willing to write a foreword for the book. Instead, he suggested that we write a book proposal for SAP PRESS and offered us the necessary support. We soon followed his advice, and submitted our proposal, which was accepted in January 2004. Thus began a long and demanding journey.

We're very pleased with the final outcome, which would not have been possible without the support of certain contributors. We're most grateful to our colleagues at Ctac for their interest in our work and their encouragement, especially Theo Bolta, for affording us the necessary time to complete this project. We also would like to thank Patricia Ellman for helping us to convert our rough drafts into an acceptable and readable English. Last but not least, the excellent support provided to us by the people at SAP PRESS has been critical for the completion of this book: in particular, Florian Zimniak, who guided us through the whole process with a positive attitude and wit; and Nancy Etscovitz, who made the manuscript—with its technical bend—suitable for an international audience.

's Hertogenbosch, Netherlands
September 2004

Ben Meijs
Albert Krouwels
Wouter Heuvelmans
Ron Sommen

1   Introduction

This book deals with the quality of customized ABAP developments. It has been written from the perspective of SAP customers who need additional ABAP software on top of the standard software. The goal of this book is to provide practical guidelines for managing and improving the quality of ABAP software. We hope that these guidelines will be a valuable addition to the large amount of material that has already been published on the ABAP language.

Since the 1990s, the development of ABAP software has become serious business. The fourth generation programming language (4GL) ABAP was originally developed by SAP in the 1980s as an addition for the R/2 product—SAP's successful ERP product at that time. Actually, the original users of the ABAP programming language were supposed to be end users who could use it themselves to make output lists, for example. The R/2 standard software was still developed in Assembler.[1] However, the ABAP language was never really used as initially intended because the 4GL turned out to be too complex for ordinary users. Because a high level of skill was required, the language demanded that dedicated programmers use it.

But this was only the beginning. Since the 1980s, the ABAP language has undergone a complete transformation. The extent to which it is used changed drastically with the introduction of SAP's client-server product R/3 in the 1990s. This successor of the R/2 product has almost entirely been developed in ABAP. Although several more recent SAP products were developed in Java, you cannot deduce that the ABAP language is gradually becoming obsolete. The fact that it now also supports object-oriented developments is sufficient evidence that it's continuously being adapted to meet modern requirements. Moreover, an enormous number of development tools have been created in support of the language. Today—since SAP's customers also have the ABAP development tools at their disposal—numerous developers worldwide dedicate themselves to the development of ABAP applications.

The maturity of the language itself is not always reflected in the way it is applied by ABAP developers outside SAP. Not surprisingly, it has been difficult to keep up with the pace in which the tool itself has progressed. On various occasions, this has resulted in the following problems:

▶ Invoices cannot be sent to customers because they contain the wrong data.

▶ Wrong output forms are sent to customs and tax authorities.

---

1   Assembler is a low-level programming language that was used by SAP to build the earliest versions of its software.

▶ Interface data can be processed only with a considerable amount of overhead activity.

▶ Programs require too much processing time, sometimes more processing time than is available.

▶ Program dumps suddenly occur for no obvious reason.

▶ Planning activities are hindered because of wrong information.

▶ Operational (logistical) processes are delayed.

▶ Relatively small changes in customized programs require more time than planned.

To some extent, such problems are part of a normal learning curve. All ABAP developers outside of SAP (including ourselves) have had to address such problems at one time or another. Moreover, these problems are not specific to software developed in ABAP. For example, various studies on the quality of software development show that, unless specific measures are taken, a relatively large amount of the total development time is consumed by rework:[2] tracing programming bugs and executing repair activities just to keep the existing functionality intact. Although such studies probably haven't been made specifically for ABAP developments (except, perhaps, by SAP itself), there's little reason to believe that the outcome would be much different. Perhaps, such problems are part of the normal evolution of a programming language: similar things have happened before with a language such as COBOL. It's not unlikely that the ABAP language is going through the same phases of its lifecycle. Regardless, experience with everyday use of ABAP developments shows us that there is considerable room for improvement. It's fair to say that the pioneering phase is over now, and the next phases in the evolution of the ABAP language will be more demanding.

In light of the increasing variety of customized ABAP applications being developed and the high demands placed on them, the need for an active assessment of the quality of ABAP development is apparent. The first signs are already visible: for instance, various organizations have established some standards for ABAP development. However, there is more to quality management than having standards. Standards don't improve anything if they're not actively applied and monitored. This is exactly what still seems to be missing in many places. Another area where we see additional room for improvement is the way that ABAP developments are often tested. Note that in various other parts of the software developing industry, developments are often tested by specialized testers, that is, by people who have been specifically trained for this job. Conversely, testing customized

---

2 Refer to Jenkins, David F.: "Put Better Programs into Production in Less Time with Code Reviews" (see Appendix D).

ABAP programs is often considered an end-user activity. If you ask a user to test an ABAP development, you should expect that only the outer behavior of the delivered software will be checked; it would be unreasonable to expect a more thorough test or check of the software. The main drawback of this type of approach is that it tends to lead to the acceptance of software if it just *looks* okay. However, many programming deficiencies cannot be traced this way, let alone prevented.

Even so, the market is shifting in the right direction. The average level of ABAP skills found in the market is considerably higher than, say, ten years ago. The amount of experience gained over the last fifteen years by developers who work for SAP partners or SAP customers has been substantial. The basic organizational measures needed in order to support ABAP developments are known to most organizations. A great deal of information is being published in various sources on the Internet and in publications such as the *SAP Professional Journal*. However, this information is often widely disseminated. As far as we know, there aren't any books available that deal with the quality management of ABAP software. We hope to fill that gap with this book. In short, it contains practical experience with the use of the ABAP language, the most commonly associated pitfalls, and guidelines to prevent these pitfalls.

All these guidelines have been derived from our own experiences with ABAP development since the end of the 1980s. Most of this experience comes from working with SAP's R/3 product, but the guidelines should be useful in any area where the ABAP language is used. We hope that they can serve as a kind of well-documented common sense for making proper ABAP developments. This book is not intended as an introduction to ABAP programming; rather, it presupposes some previous experience with ABAP programming.

As we mentioned in the first paragraph, it is worth pointing out that we have written the book from the perspective of SAP customers who make their own ABAP developments. We assume this perspective to be somewhat different from that of SAP's own developers. Of course, the same development tools are available for any ABAP developer. But ABAP developers working for a SAP customer have to meet objectives other than those of SAP's own developers: *implementing* standard software is not the same line of business as *creating* standard software. When implementing software is the main objective, developing additional software is *just* part of the implementation process. Nevertheless, the origin of a program isn't relevant where quality is concerned. Depending on the program's use, even a single poorly designed program can do considerable damage. The fact that many SAP customers have hundreds or even thousands of customized ABAP developments in place is reason enough to stress the importance of quality management of ABAP developments and give it the recognition and the place that it deserves, namely, as part of the regular development process.

Although this book was not primarily intended as training material, it could be used as such. The primary prerequisite to understanding this book is a basic knowledge of ABAP programming. We particularly assess good and bad ABAP programming habits. In doing so, we'll use code examples both in the text and in various appendixes. Therefore, the book should, initially be useful for ABAP developers. However, others—such as consultants and IT managers—will also benefit from this book: first, because the quality of ABAP developments is improved not only by the introduction of programming guidelines but also by organizational measures; and secondly, because improving the quality of ABAP developments also requires the awareness of those other than just developers; for example, key users, consultants, and IT managers should also know that quality doesn't just *happen*.

1.1   The Technical Quality of ABAP Software

Now that we've explained why we think that specific material about the quality of ABAP developments is critical, it's time to explain what we mean by *quality*. Quality means more than just user satisfaction—if we used this definition, a program could be defined as having quality merely by *seeming* to do what it was intended to do. Clearly, meeting the user's expectations is important, but it's not enough.

Instead, we must stress that a program isn't complete if it doesn't also have sufficient *technical quality* or *robustness*. Technical quality is the difference between a quick-and-dirty program and a genuinely well-written program, regardless of whether the program meets the user's expectations. We think that the importance of the technical quality of ABAP developments is particularly underrated. A well-developed program not only meets the user's expectations; it also ensures that its output is correct. A well-developed program should be immune to wrong input or use in the wrong circumstances; it should not be affected by changes in the surrounding SAP implementation; it should perform well, and remain predictable and easy-to-use under every possible circumstance; and, lastly, it shouldn't be difficult to change—a small change should require only a few lines of code and minimal effort.

Unlike functional requirements, requirements of robustness are more generic, in the sense that they have little to do with specific functionality. The people who make specifications for a new program are often unaware of such generic requirements, or don't consider them to be important. Therefore, they will discuss such requirements only briefly or only if asked to do so, or not at all. It is implicitly assumed that the developer will handle the technical quality of a program because no one else is qualified to do so. Most of what an ABAP program should do in order to achieve a technically acceptable quality level is not transparent to the user, that is, it remains hidden behind the user interface, waiting for a disaster to happen, unless the individual ABAP developer and the development organization can ensure the robustness of their ABAP developments and guarantee their quality.

From here on, we will completely focus on the technical quality of ABAP software and not on the question of whether an ABAP program meets the functional requirements. We assume that ABAP software is usually developed according to functional requirements, simply because there is a clear distinction between a supplier—the ABAP developer—and his or her customer—the user. This distinction ensures that at least the functional part of a program's quality will be explicitly checked and accepted. The customer who needs the functionality to be developed will automatically feel responsible for checking and approving the functionality. Knowing the required functionality makes the customer sufficiently qualified to check the developed functionality. A technical background is not required.

While a program's *functional* quality is more or less ensured due to this kind of customer-supplier-relationship, a program's *technical* quality is not. The fact that there is a customer who knows the functionality does not ensure that the technical quality of a program is properly assessed. Because most elements that determine the technical quality of a program are hidden, only a thorough examination of the program code and the use of various testing tools would reveal any deficiencies. Such checks cannot be executed by someone with an inadequate technical background. Consequently, there is usually no one else except the developer who can ensure a program's technical quality. Note that this emphasizes where the responsibility of an individual ABAP developer lies. Even without the backup of a development organization, the individual developer should primarily consider it his or her own responsibility to deliver ABAP software of a certain quality level.

1.1.1 Aspects of Technical Quality

To further elaborate on technical quality, we need to distinguish the following aspects:

▶ Correctness
▶ Stability
▶ User-friendliness
▶ Performance
▶ Maintainability

These aspects are explained in more detail below:

▶ **Correctness**

The term *correctness* refers to the quality of the data produced by a program. The output generated, or the updates performed, by a correctly designed program are accurate and consistent with the results of other programs. Incorrect output is usually the first, and relatively obvious, kind of error found in ABAP programs.

▶ **User-friendliness**

The term *user-friendly* refers to the usability of the program. It must have a familiar look-and-feel and behavior; it must be easy to navigate through its screens; and it must offer support to the user whenever this is required. Like correctness, a lack of user-friendliness is usually apparent in relatively early stages of a program's use.

▶ **Performance**

The term *performance* also needs little explanation. An online program should respond to the user quickly, if possible, say, within a second. A background program has much more time available, but there will always be time limits determined by the hardware, operating system, and DBMS used. Since ERP environments need shared resources, the suboptimal development of just one program may not directly harm the overall system performance, however, the suboptimal development of many programs will definitely have a considerable impact. Performance problems usually don't reveal themselves immediately. Instead, they lie in wait for data volumes to increase. And, along with such an increase, performance problems gradually build up as well.

▶ **Stability**

The term *stability* refers to the degree to which a program behaves predictably from a technical point of view. In contrast to performance problems, the negative effects of poor stability can reveal themselves at any time, such as immediately after a program has been implemented, and also, after a couple of months of normal use. An unstable program typically ends abruptly, with a program dump or a technical error message, or, it simply stops. To some degree, preventing stability problems is just a matter of proper programming. But, it also requires a proper understanding of the technical environment of a program.

▶ **Maintainability**

The term *maintainability* refers to the degree to which program changes can be applied easily by developers other than the original author of the program. This is determined by the readability of existing source code and the extent to which later reuse of part of the code is possible. Maintenance may not be necessary until one year after a program's introduction. However, because most programs will be maintained at some point, this aspect of technical quality should be accounted for from the very start.

1.1.2 Standards and Guidelines

Basically, there are two ways to safeguard the aforementioned aspects of technical quality: by applying *guidelines*; and by adhering to *standards*. Since we use these terms throughout the book, we should briefly explain how we interpret them. Note, however, that the difference between the two terms is not very strict; sometimes, you can use them interchangeably:

1. **Applying Guidelines**
   For most pitfalls related to ABAP programming, there are a limited number of appropriate solutions. So, if the pitfall can be described, corresponding and objective guidelines can also be given in terms of actual *Do's and Don'ts*. Most aspects of the technical quality—particularly the aspects *correctness*, *stability*, and *performance*—can be ensured by following guidelines.

2. **Adhering to Standards**
   Standards make programs predictable for both end users and developers. It is easier for end users to work with programs that have a standardized look-and-feel, standardized behavior, and standardized help and navigation facilities. Developers other than the author of a specific program can more easily read and modify the program if the same naming conventions and the same basic structuring principles are applied as in other programs. Standards are particularly useful for the quality aspects *maintainability* and *user-friendliness*.

1.2 ABAP Objects and Unicode-Enabling

Throughout this book, we'll periodically refer to the terms *Unicode-enabling* and *ABAP Objects*. We do this because of how they collectively benefit the technical quality of ABAP code. Once, in a SAP presentation about ABAP Objects, we happened upon the following statement: "Unicode-enabled ABAP Objects is the best ABAP available up to now."[3] One of the goals we set ourselves when writing this book was to find out why Unicode-enabling and ABAP Objects have a synergistic effect, and to present our findings in this book. This objective doesn't completely match our original goal. Initially, we just wanted to describe, on the basis of practical experience, what measures can be taken to manage and improve the technical quality of ABAP software.

---

3 This statement was derived from the presentation "Why use ABAP Objects?" held at the SAP TechEd Conference in Basel in 2003 (see also Appendix D).

However, the objective of specifically describing the benefits of Unicode-enabled ABAP Objects code forced us to confront another challenge. With the exception of SAP's own developers, the vast majority of ABAP developers have had limited opportunities to work with Unicode-enabled ABAP Objects. Therefore, we checked the details that we didn't yet know; we discussed what kind of examples would best describe the benefits of ABAP Objects and Unicode-enabling; and we created and tested corresponding sample pieces of ABAP code and argued why such code prevents the inappropriate use of more traditional ABAP language elements. Needless to say, we checked all pieces of sample code ourselves.

We will introduce these two topics in the following sections. Then, whenever necessary, we'll refer to them in the remainder of the book.

1.2.1 ABAP Objects

Now, we'll briefly introduce the main aspects of the object-oriented language elements in ABAP. Then, we'll focus on the basics of object-orientation; how object-oriented concepts are implemented in ABAP Objects; and where the benefits of ABAP Objects can be found.

Basics of object-orientation

An introduction to any object-oriented programming language isn't complete without at least a brief explanation of the most important concepts of object orientation,[4] such as classes, objects or instances, attributes, methods, events, and subclasses. (If you're already familiar with these concepts, you may prefer to skip this section.)

Object-oriented programming languages are based on the assumption that building software is a one-on-one implementation of a model of reality. A *class* is the central concept in such a model. A class represents a series of objects from real-life that, to some degree, can be dealt with in a generic way. In a business environment, this usually pertains to objects such as materials, customers, suppliers, or sales orders, but, in fact, any kind of object could be relevant. Actually, the only prerequisite for distinguishing objects is that you need to find some generic way of processing data for the same type of object. The term *object* or *instance* refers to an occurrence within a class: one particular customer, material, and so forth.

All objects in a class share the same characteristics—the same *attributes* and the same *methods*. All objects of the class of employees will usually share attributes such as address, salary group, and date-hired. In addition, all objects of this class

---

4 We have included various references to articles and books on object orientation in Appendix D.

will also share methods to calculate an employee's age, and to determine the remaining amount of sick leave, and so forth.

A particular object doesn't always belong to just one class. It may have additional attributes and require specific logic that it shares with only part of the main class to which it belongs. To make such a distinction, the concept of a *subclass* is introduced. A subclass can inherit all the functionality of the main class and have its own variation of the main functionality. For example, a finished product may, to a certain extent, be defined and treated as any other material, but also require specific characteristics and logic that are relevant for only finished products. Hence, the class of finished products could be defined as a subclass of the class of materials.

In fact, anyone who has worked with SAP applications will already think in terms of classes and objects, although most users may not immediately be aware that they are doing this. As such, these concepts aren't difficult to understand. So, why are these concepts important for ABAP programmers? Probably because object-oriented programming requires you to think in a different way. Developers who worked with the procedurally-oriented version of the ABAP language may experience difficulties with the mindshift required to think in this new way. When using procedural ABAP, a developer is accustomed to thinking of concepts such as programs, function groups, or subroutine pools. The main drawback of such concepts is that they're technical concepts—they don't immediately correspond to objects from real life. Whether you need to create a function is based on experience, intuition, or technical reasons, but it isn't a one-on-one implementation of a model of reality. However, whether you need to create a specific class depends primarily on the model of reality used and not on technical considerations. For example, only properly modeled classes will improve the reusability of software. Therefore, it makes little sense to create a class from scratch in the same way in which you would create a program. So, if you seriously intend to use ABAP Objects, we recommend that you first familiarize yourself with the basics of object orientation.

Basics of ABAP Objects

Now that we've described the most important concepts of object-orientation, we'll discuss how to implement these concepts in ABAP Objects. We'll discuss the following: class definitions, class implementations, object instances, subclasses, and interfaces. Although we're aware that it may seem a bit strange to do so in an introductory chapter, we have also included some examples of sample code. These examples are merely intended to show you what ABAP Objects look like and to explain the most important terms.

The basis of an ABAP Objects implementation is a *class definition*. This definition expresses *what* functionality is represented by a class. It doesn't say anything about *how* this functionality is implemented. The implementation is defined separately. In the following example, we collected the most important ABAP terms that can be found in a class definition. To simplify matters, we used only *local* classes here and in the rest of this section. To achieve optimal reusability, you would typically define *global* classes.

```
CLASS lcl_class_example DEFINITION.

  PUBLIC SECTION.

    EVENTS:         an_event.

    METHODS:        constructor     IMPORTING itp_matnr TYPE matnr
                                    EXCEPTIONS mara_not_found,
                    display_mat.

    CLASS-METHODS:  display_number_instances.

    DATA:           tp_mtart        TYPE mtart.

  PROTECTED SECTION.

    DATA:           wa_mara         TYPE mara.

  PRIVATE SECTION.

    METHODS:        get_description IMPORTING value(itp_matnr) TYPE matnr
                                    EXPORTING etp_maktx        TYPE maktx.

    CLASS-DATA:     tp_instances_cnt TYPE i.

    DATA:           tp_maktx        TYPE maktx.

ENDCLASS.                    "lcl_class_example DEFINITION
```

As you can see, the keywords used in this code are different than those used in procedural ABAP. The first thing that you may have noticed is that the class definition is explicitly subdivided into three SECTIONS: a PUBLIC SECTION, a PROTECTED SECTION, and a PRIVATE SECTION. Each of these sections of a class definition represents another degree of visibility for the *outside world* (i.e., all the functionality defined in other classes or programs, function modules, etc.) of what is defined in the particular section:

- The *public section* contains the class elements that can be seen *and* used by the outside world.
- The *protected section* contains the elements that can be seen and used by the class itself and its subclasses.
- The *private section* contains the elements that can be used by only the class itself.

To some degree, this distinction resembles the difference between global data and local data in traditional ABAP. *Local data* is visible only in the procedure in which it is defined. *Global data* is available for the entire program in which it is defined and, on various occasions, even for other programs. However, you should note that the unrestricted availability of global data is not simply a powerful feature of traditional ABAP, but also introduces some important weaknesses (see Section 3.4). Contrary to local and global data, the strict and explicit definition of both data *and* logic in the PUBLIC SECTION of a class allows the developer to determine precisely which part of the class can be used elsewhere.

Within each of the three sections, you see the basic elements that can be defined in a class:

- DATA is defined in much the same way as in procedural ABAP.
- EVENTS represents a new concept. In object-oriented programming languages, an *event* is a kind of signal that triggers the start of functionality. The actual functionality is defined elsewhere. Note that an event and the corresponding actions are completely decoupled. We won't elaborate on this concept any more. To a certain extent, the decoupling principle is also used in case of class-based exception events (see Section 5.3).
- METHODS should be fairly easily to comprehend. They represent pieces of logic that can be compared with procedural ABAP counterparts such as function modules and subroutines. They share most kinds of interface parameters with function modules (defined in IMPORTING, EXPORTING, CHANGING, and EXCEP-TIONS parameters). However, in contrast to both function modules and subroutines, methods have no TABLES parameters.

Then, you will have noticed the terms DATA and METHODS on the one hand, and CLASS-DATA and CLASS-METHODS on the other. We will now explain the difference:

DATA and METHODS refer to the data and logic that is available for each single real-life object that is *instantiated*: each material, each order, each order line, and so forth. Perhaps, you could compare this with the level of one internal table entry, since this is usually the level at which such real-life objects are processed in procedural ABAP. Because of this strict relation to one instance of a class, you can define a method as a property of exactly one specific material, order, and so forth.

CLASS-DATA and CLASS-METHODS, on the other hand, can be used only in the context of the class, not in the context of a single instance. A *class-method* is also referred to as a *static method*. In fact, because a static method is independent of a specific instance, its behavior most resembles that of a subroutine or function module.

While the definition part of the class only shows the outside characteristics, the actual behavior is entirely encoded in the class IMPLEMENTATION, as is done in the following piece of code. All the statements in-between the METHOD and END-METHOD statements represent this behavior. In this case, four methods are encoded:

```
CLASS lcl_class_example IMPLEMENTATION.

  METHOD constructor.

    ADD 1 TO tp_instances_cnt.

    SELECT SINGLE * FROM mara INTO wa_mara
          WHERE matnr = itp_matnr.

    IF sy-subrc NE 0.
      RAISE mara_not_found.
    ELSE.

      tp_mtart = wa_mara-mtart.

      CALL METHOD me->get_description
        EXPORTING
          itp_matnr = wa_mara-matnr
        IMPORTING
          etp_maktx = tp_maktx.

    ENDIF.
  ENDMETHOD.                      "constructor

  METHOD display_mat.

    WRITE: / wa_mara-matnr,
            tp_maktx.

    RAISE EVENT an_event.

  ENDMETHOD.                      "display_mat
```

```
METHOD display_number_instances.
   WRITE: / tp_instances_cnt.
ENDMETHOD.                      "display_number_instances

METHOD get_description.
   SELECT SINGLE maktx FROM makt
          INTO etp_maktx
          WHERE spras = sy-langu
            AND matnr = itp_matnr.
ENDMETHOD.                      "get_description
ENDCLASS.                       "lcl_class_example IMPLEMENTATION
```

Most of the code will seem familiar if you're used to traditional ABAP, but some things should be noted, in particular:

▶ The interface parameters of the methods are not visible in the implementation of the class as when subroutines are defined. The interface parameters were already defined the class definition.

▶ One (object-oriented) event is raised (with the RAISE EVENT command). Note that the associated logic is not located at the same place. Also a traditional EXCEPTION is raised as in a function module (RAISE mara_not_found.).

▶ Method get_description was defined in the PRIVATE SECTION of the class definition of this implementation. Therefore, this method can be used only by another method of the same instance of this class.

▶ The term me in the statement CALL METHOD me->get_description refers to the current instance. The term super is used in a similar way, that is, to refer to a method of the superclass.

As we mentioned when we compared class-methods or static methods with regular methods, you usually don't apply the functionality of a class on the class level but on the level of a *class instance*, or *object*. The biggest mindshift that an ABAP developer will probably need to make is to appreciate that each single object can have data and logic (methods) of its own. The consequence for the ABAP language is that it must provide various commands that uniquely refer to one instance and the elements (data, methods, and events) contained in it. You cannot, for example, execute a method belonging to one particular instance by just referring to the method's name: you first have to refer to the exact instance that you're dealing with.

Let's start with the object itself. Each single object has a lifetime of its own: this life starts and ends at specifically defined moments. Before you can use a particular object's functionality (i.e., its data and the associated logic), you have to create the object. In addition, you need to be able to refer to one particular object.

With respect to the latter, the ABAP language provides reference variables for pointing to individual objects, as is defined here:

```
DATA: rf_object     TYPE REF TO lcl_class_example.
```

Once you have the reference variable, you must have the means to create the actual object itself. For this purpose, the CREATE OBJECT command is used, as is done here:

```
CREATE OBJECT rf_object
   EXPORTING
       itp_matnr = tp_matnr
   EXCEPTIONS
       mara_not_found = 1
       OTHERS         = 9.
```

An important *side-effect* of using the CREATE OBJECT command is that the logic contained in the *constructor* method of the class is automatically executed. For this reason, the constructor method is typically used for all kinds of initialization logic. Other methods of the class have to be called explicitly. Performing a call of a method that belongs to a specific instance is done by first referring to the object (by using the corresponding reference variable); then, the required method must be mentioned. A single arrow (->) represents the link between the object and the name of the method:

```
CALL METHOD rf_object->display_mat( ).
```

Compare this with a call of a static method: in that case, you first use the name of the class instead of the reference to the individual object, and then the name of the method, with a double arrow (=>) in-between:

```
CALL METHOD lcl_class_example=>display_number_instances( ).
```

If you have to use a public attribute of a particular object, you can use the same kind of indirect reference:

```
WRITE rf_object->tp_mtart.
```

Ending the life of a particular object is done by removing the reference to the object:

```
CLEAR rf_object.
```

Actually, this means that the object itself still exists but you can no longer refer to it (an automatic *garbage collector* removes the objects without a reference). Unlike other object-oriented languages such as Java, ABAP Objects does not (yet) have a *destructor* method.

An important characteristic of object-oriented programming languages is the potential for a class to inherit existing functionality that is defined elsewhere. However, the extent to which this kind of inheritance is possible varies. One way of explicitly inheriting functionality is by defining a subclass of an existing class. The functionality that is defined in the public or protected section of a class can be passed on to another class. Consider the definition of the following superclass, in which the methods constructor and do_a_method are part of the public section:

```
CLASS lcl_example_superclass DEFINITION.
  PUBLIC SECTION.
    METHODS:         constructor,
                     do_a_method IMPORTING itp_parameter TYPE any optional.
    DATA:            tp_public   TYPE c.
  PRIVATE SECTION.
    DATA:            tp_variable_super TYPE c.

ENDCLASS.                        "lcl_example_superclass DEFINITION
```

The same two methods are defined in the definition of this subclass:

```
CLASS lcl_example_subclass DEFINITION
                    INHERITING FROM lcl_example_superclass.
  PUBLIC SECTION.
    METHODS:         constructor IMPORTING itp_parm      TYPE c,
                     do_a_method REDEFINITION,
                     my_own_method.

  PRIVATE SECTION.
    DATA:            tp_variable_sub TYPE c.

ENDCLASS.                        "lcl_example_subclass DEFINITION
```

Note that the class definition is introduced with the addition INHERITING FROM, followed by the name of the superclass. This actually makes the class a subclass. Secondly, note that in the definition, method do_a_method has the addition REDEFINITION. This means that this method can be called by the same name on the level of both superclass and subclass, although the actual implementation on the two levels varies. The prerequisite is that both the method of the superclass and the method of the subclass share the same interface parameters.

In the implementation of both the superclass and its subclass, the same two methods are implemented:

```
CLASS lcl_example_superclass IMPLEMENTATION.
  METHOD constructor.
    tp_variable_super = 'X'.
  ENDMETHOD.                     "constructor
```

```
    METHOD do_a_method.
    ENDMETHOD.                          "do_a_method
ENDCLASS.                               "lcl_example_superclass IMPLEMENTATION

CLASS lcl_example_subclass IMPLEMENTATION.
    METHOD constructor.
      CALL METHOD super->constructor.   "must be called here
      tp_variable_sub = 'X'.
    ENDMETHOD.                          "constructor

    METHOD do_a_method.
      CALL METHOD super->do_a_method.   "can be called here
      tp_public = 'X'.
    ENDMETHOD.                          "do_a_method

    METHOD my_own_method.
    ENDMETHOD.                          "my_own_method

ENDCLASS.                               "lcl_example_subclass IMPLEMENTATION
```

Note that it is mandatory to execute the constructor method of the superclass first in the constructor method of the subclass. Additional logic can then be added immediately following this call. Also note that it is optional to first call the method carrying the same name of the superclass in the implementation of other methods such as do_a_method. The reference to the superclass is made by using the reserved keyword super.

In ABAP Objects, inheritance through subclasses has a strictly hierarchical nature. This means that each class can be a subclass of just *one* superclass, but can itself have *more than one* subclass. Multiple inheritance (that is, inheriting the behavior from *more than one superclass*), which is sometimes found in other programming languages, is not possible in ABAP Objects. However, there is an alternative that comes close to multiple inheritance, namely, the use of an INTERFACE definition.

An INTERFACE definition is an entirely different concept when compared with the interface parameters of a method or a function module. Like a regular class definition, an INTERFACE defines the outer behavior of the associated functionality. Note that, unlike the definition of a regular class, an INTERFACE is not subdivided into a public, protected, and private section, as you can see in the following code:

```
INTERFACE lif_interface_1.

    METHODS:        do_a_method             EXPORTING etp_data TYPE any.

    DATA:           tp_variable     TYPE  c.

ENDINTERFACE.                       "lif_interface_1
```

The difference between an interface and a regular class is that an interface merely stops after its definition, whereas a class must actually be implemented: it has an IMPLEMENTATION. Therefore, an interface is just a description of *what* certain functionality should do; it doesn't define *how* this functionality is implemented. Instead, the actual implementation of an interface is done in a class, or in various classes, such as in the following code. In fact, this class definition *inherits* the definition of two different interfaces. So, some form of multiple inheritance does actually take place here:

```
CLASS lcl_class_example DEFINITION.

  PUBLIC SECTION.

    INTERFACES:  lif_interface_1,
                 lif_interface_2.

    METHODS:     constructor.

ENDCLASS.                         "lcl_class_example DEFINITION
```

In the implementation of a class, all methods of all the interfaces that were included in the definition must be implemented. This means, that each of these methods must be encoded in the implementation of the class. Note that the name of the interface should be part of the names of *inherited* methods and variables, as in the following class implementation:

```
CLASS lcl_class_example IMPLEMENTATION.

  METHOD constructor.

  ENDMETHOD.                       "constructor

  METHOD lif_interface_1~do_a_method.
    lif_interface_1~tp_variable = 'X'.
  ENDMETHOD.                       "lif_interface_1~do_a_method

ENDCLASS.                         "lcl_class_example IMPLEMENTATION
```

When the implemented functionality that corresponds with an interface is actually used, the name of the interface keeps coming back in method calls and variable use (in Section 8.3.2, we'll show you how this can also be solved more elegantly):

```
DATA: rf_object      TYPE REF TO lcl_class_example.
CREATE OBJECT rf_object.
CALL METHOD rf_object->lif_interface_1~do_a_method( ).
WRITE rf_object->lif_interface_1~tp_variable.
```

The Impact on the Quality of ABAP Code

The specific qualities of ABAP Objects are demonstrated in several aspects of robustness. First, the correctness of the data that is processed is improved. In Chapter 3, we point out that ABAP Objects help to keep data in memory more consistent than is possible using traditional ABAP constructs (see Section 3.4.8). This should particularly help to reduce the number of errors caused by the incorrect use of global data.

Second, ABAP Objects helps developers to avoid introducing implicit logic in their code. The errors that this may lead to can be particularly hard to analyze and solve. When using ABAP Objects, the Syntax Check warns against certain ABAP language elements that have implicit behavior. Therefore, you can view ABAP Objects as a much more distilled and *clean* version of the ABAP language than procedural ABAP.

Third, you can make the exception handling in your programs more flexible by making it class-based (see Section 5.3).

Finally, some specific characteristics of ABAP Objects should be emphasized that can help to make software more maintainable. We'll provide some examples to demonstrate this (see Section 8.3).

1.2.2 Unicode-Enabling

The *Unicode Standard* is a character coding system designed to support the worldwide electronic interchange, processing, and display of written texts of most modern languages and technical disciplines. SAP has incorporated the Unicode standard in its software in the SAP Web Application Server (Web AS) as of Release 6.10. You can make an entire SAP system Unicode-enabled (that is, on the level of database server, application server, and individual ABAP programs), or, you can make just a single ABAP program Unicode-enabled. This last option is the main reason why we mention Unicode-enabling here. Unicode-enabling is not just a way to make ABAP programs platform-independent. Besides using ABAP Objects, making ABAP programs Unicode-enabled is another way of enhancing the quality of your ABAP programs.

But first, we want to introduce the basics of Unicode. Before Web AS Release 6.10, the SAP software used character sets from coding systems such as ASCII and EBCDIC. In such coding systems, every character is represented by one byte, which is why they're also referred to as *single-byte* coding systems. Since one byte equals 256 (2^8) bit combinations, single-byte coding systems can be used to uniquely distinguish only the characters of a limited number of languages. For example, a single-byte coding system cannot display all characters of East Asian languages. Therefore, for some time Asian countries have used double-byte coding systems, in which every character equals two bytes. However, such Asian language-specific coding systems usually aren't compatible either. In general, incompatibility problems arise in situations where software has to work with data that has been encoded according to a coding system other than the one supported by the software. This could cause, for example, unreadable output on a screen where texts of various languages are displayed simultaneously. In the case of ABAP software, many statements that deal with character-based data in some way could make false interpretations. Also consider the exchange of data between two systems that could lead to misinterpretations. Or, imagine having to migrate hardware and an operating system that presupposes the EBCDIC standard to hardware and an operating system working with the ASCII standard. All existing programs would have to be checked for possible incompatibility problems.

In Unicode, each character is, in general, mapped using 16 bits (=2 bytes), which offers a maximum of 65,536 bit combinations or different character interpretations. This should be sufficient for interpreting the characters of most modern languages.

The Impact on the Quality of ABAP Code

Making an entire SAP system Unicode-enabled will not immediately be an obvious choice for many SAP customers. Consider, for example, the extra disk capacity that such a change would require (in principle, each single character would require twice the space as before). However, a more interesting option for most SAP customers is to make their ABAP programs Unicode-enabled. This is particularly interesting from the point of view of the quality of the ABAP software, because:

▶ A clear distinction must be made between characters and bytes in the definition of variables. Types X and XSTRING are specifically used to refer to byte (hexadecimal) variables.

▶ The potentially dangerous use of ABAP commands that implicitly assume that one character equals one byte is prevented. If a reference to the internal length of a character is required, the addition IN CHARACTER MODE or IN BYTE MODE can be used to define exactly which assumption is valid (in statements such as CLEAR, CONCATENATE, FIND, REPLACE, SHIFT, and SPLIT).

- Some commands can only be used for processing characters (CONDENSE, CONVERT TEXT, OVERLAY, and TRANSLATE).

- Operations on text files that are usually used for interface processing (such as OPEN DATASET) are no longer allowed on the basis of an implicit assumption about the coding system used. The coding system (and code page) used must explicitly be specified.

In short, the restrictions placed by Unicode-enabling on ABAP code strongly reduce the number of possible bugs and make the programs more efficient. In Section 4.2.1, we show some examples of non-Unicode-enabled code that would not pass the syntax check in a Unicode-enabled program.

ABAP programs can be Unicode-enabled by setting the Unicode attribute. ABAP programs that have been made Unicode-compliant will also run on a non-Unicode-enabled system. In contrast, ABAP programs that haven't been made Unicode-compliant will run only on non-Unicode- enabled systems and not on Unicode-enabled systems. We obviously recommend making all ABAP programs Unicode-compliant because of the associated quality improvements of existing programs. In Chapter 4, we'll show you some situations where Unicode-enabling is beneficial (see Section 4.2.1). In Chapter 9, we'll also discuss the tool that you should use to check for Unicode complicance (see Section 9.1.4).

1.3 The Structure of This Book

This section describes the main contents of the individual chapters. The chapters have been set up according to the distinctions we made between the main aspects of technical quality (correctness, user-friendliness, performance, stability, and maintainability). Some additional chapters have been added for more general topics (organization, exception- and error-handling, checking robustness and troubleshooting).

The point of view chosen is that of an SAP customer who implements customized functionality on top of SAP standard functionality. All situations described, all typical errors discussed, and all solutions proposed should be regarded from this viewpoint.

- **Chapter 2: Organization**
  The basic conditions for improving the quality of ABAP developments are determined by the quality of the surrounding organization. An IT organization must cope with two contradictory main requirements: on the one hand, the SAP production system should be kept as stable as possible, while, on the other, new development should also be implemented as quickly as possible. In this chapter, we describe the basic requirements for properly organizing the development of ABAP software. After introducing these requirements (in Sec-

tion 2.1), they are further discussed on the basis of the complicating factors that can have an impact on the quality of ABAP software: the fact that developments take place in an ERP functionality (in Section 2.2); the use of multi-system landscapes (in Section 2.3); the co-existence of various different applications in a system landscape (in Section 2.4); and finally, the co-existence of various SAP production systems (in Section 2.5).

▶ **Chapter 3: Correctness**

This chapter describes the pitfalls that ABAP developers must face in order to secure the accuracy of the output of their programs. The most common violations of the correctness of a program are mainly discussed in chronological order of relevance. These violations occur when selecting data (in Section 3.2); processing data (in Section 3.3); and performing database updates (in Section 3.5). A special topic is the management of data in memory during processing (discussed in Section 3.4). We particularly argue why the introduction of ABAP Objects makes it easier to control the data in memory (in Section 3.4.7). We end this chapter with a discussion of the correctness of interface data (in Section 3.6).

▶ **Chapter 4: Stability**

This chapter addresses the technical stability of ABAP programs. Here, we focus on various ways to prevent programs from suddenly producing dumps, raising technical error messages, or simply stopping. We start with basic internal program deficiencies that cause instability (in Section 4.2). In this context, we show some examples of Unicode-enabling that are particularly helpful in improving the stability of ABAP software (in Section 4.2.1). Then, we address the risks of dynamic programming (in Section 4.3). Next, we show that instability is not only caused by internal program deficiencies but also by changes in the program's outer environment (in Section 4.4). And finally, we'll argue why basic choices about the circumstances in which programs have to operate (in the foreground; in the background; in the update task; in batch data communication) can also lead to instability (in Section 4.5).

▶ **Chapter 5: Exception and Error Handling**

This chapter about exception and error handling does not represent a separate aspect of technical quality but is directly related to the aspects presented earlier in Chapter 3 and Chapter 4: an important way to make programs more *correct* and *stable* is by introducing proper exception handling. After emphasizing the importance of exception handling (in Section 5.1), we discuss the available ways of actually implementing exception handling in ABAP programs (in Section 5.2). We devoted a separate section (Section 5.3) to the introduction and benefits of class-based exception handling. This section provides another example of why the use of ABAP Objects is beneficial.

▶ **Chapter 6: User-Friendliness**

The third main aspect of the technical quality of an ABAP program pertains to the communication with the end user. The main question underlying this chapter is: How can you make your ABAP programs more predictable, logical, easy to understand, and easy to handle for a user? In short, our answer is basically through standardization. We explain this in Section 6.1. In the following sections, we give various examples of how standardization can be implemented. First, we deal with guidelines for standardizing the look-and-feel and behavior of your programs (in Section 6.2). The second series of guidelines deals with the ease of navigation and the degree of support offered (in Section 6.3).

▶ **Chapter 7: Performance**

This chapter discusses the most important ways of enhancing the performance of ABAP programs. We start off by pinpointing the places in SAP's client-server architecture where an ABAP program can cause performance bottlenecks (in Section 7.1). Then, we deal with each of these potential bottlenecks in turn, discussing the ABAP constructs that have the most negative impact, and presenting guidelines to minimize this impact. We discuss the four bottlenecks in descending order of importance: we deal with processing on the database server (in Section 7.2); with the data traffic between the database server and the application server (in Section 7.3); with processing on the application server (in Section 7.4); and, finally, with the data traffic between the application server and the client (in Section 7.5).

▶ **Chapter 8: Maintainability**

The last aspect of technically well-written ABAP code is its maintainability, that is, the degree to which changes can be applied easily and quickly. In an SAP system, there are two ways of looking at maintainability: from the point of view of the standard software; and from the point of view of the customized software. First, we briefly discuss how to introduce changes to the standard software (in the form of user exits, enhancements, BADIs, or modifications of the standard source code) in such a way that later maintenance of the standard software is least affected (in Section 8.1). Then, we concentrate on the maintainability of your own ABAP software (in Section 8.2). In that section, we not only focus on guidelines to make your own programs easily recognizable and well-structured. We also specifically discuss the most important ways of reusing existing standard SAP components in order to make later maintenance easier. We conclude this section with some practical tips and tools. Finally, we show you additional benefits of ABAP Objects for the maintainability of your own software (in Section 8.3).

▶ **Chapter 9: Checking Robustness and Troubleshooting**

All previously discussed topics are summarized in this chapter, but now, from a different perspective: by introducing the most practical ways of checking your ABAP developments on their robustness. This chapter contains two main sections. We first discuss how to approach the testing during the normal development cycle (in Section 9.1). Here, we emphasize that checking the quality of developments is done best by involving colleagues (in Section 9.1.2) rather than by doing all the checks yourself. In support of colleague checks, simple checklists are the first valuable tool. To support such checks, we have added checklists for all the main quality aspects (in Section 9.1.3). In addition, there's a wide variety of standard SAP tools that you can use. We explain which SAP tool is best suited for performing which kind of test (in Section 9.1.4).

The second part of this chapter addresses troubleshooting or solving production incidents (Section 9.2). To some extent, incidents require another kind of testing and a different use of the available tools. We discuss troubleshooting on the basis of three types of incidents that deal with correctness (Section 9.2.2), stability (Section 9.2.3), and performance (Section 9.2.4). This is the final chapter.

Now, let's get started.

2 Quality of the Development Organization

2.1 Introduction

The technical quality of an ABAP program is primarily determined by the skills of the developer who designed the program; however, this is not the only factor that determines quality. To ensure that ABAP developments have at least an acceptable level of quality, you must also consider the quality of the development organization. You could argue that the quality of ABAP developments is also achieved by keeping development cycles short; by ensuring that maintenance activities don't usurp most of the development time; and by overseeing that the stability of the production environment is not undermined by the introduction of new developments. But, you could also look at how the quality of ABAP development is achieved from another perspective—not all incidents and disturbances in a production environment are caused by poor programming. Neither does the speed at which production incidents are resolved, nor the frequency at which the maintenance of existing developments are carried out, depend only on the availability of experienced developers. All these aspects that determine the level of quality are primarily implemented via organizational measures. In this chapter, which is intended for IT executives in SAP development organizations and also ABAP developers and consultants, we show you which organizational measures must exist in order to ensure quality in your ABAP developments.

2.1.1 What You Need to Organize to Facilitate ABAP Developments

The biggest challenge for most organizations that have implemented ERP functionality, such as SAP's R/3 system, is twofold. On the one hand, the goal of IT organizations is to make the existing functionality as reliable and as stable as possible. On the other hand, these IT organizations must implement changes to existing and new developments as quickly as possible. You will note that these two main objectives are somewhat contradictory.

In order to properly support ABAP developments, you will have to organize the following measures: establish guidelines for ABAP programming; document ABAP development standards; provide sufficient and accurate real test data; and, lastly, set up version management in order to enable the controlled co-existence of several versions of the same software. None of these topics sounds critical, but everyone will agree that they are necessary to ensure a certain quality level. In an environment where hundreds or even thousands of development objects are added to the standard SAP software, you can't afford to lose control. Three of the four topics just mentioned (testing, documenting, and version management) will be addressed at several points in this chapter (guidelines for ABAP programming are addressed in the remainder of this book).

2.1.2   Factors That Complicate the Organization of Developments

Various factors can complicate the management of ABAP developments, for example, the basic complexity of an ERP environment. To a certain degree, ERP functionality is inherently complex and SAP's R/3 system is no exception. Additional ABAP developments are hardly ever developed in complete isolation. Most customized ABAP programs reuse existing standard development objects. In addition, the same ABAP development environment (i.e., SAP Web Application Server) that SAP uses for its standard applications is also used for customized ABAP developments. Although there are excellent tools that can help you navigate through the development environment, you will find that there is still much to learn. We discuss the impact of using ERP functionality in Section 2.2.

In addition to the basic complexity of an ERP environment, the second factor that complicates ABAP developments (and paradoxically facilitates these developments) is that these developments are usually made in a system landscape, consisting of several SAP systems. An example of such a landscape is a three-system landscape that consists of a development, an acceptance, and a production system. In Section 2.3, we address the necessity of such a multi-system landscape, despite the fact that it introduces additional complexity.

The third complicating factor is that frequently it's not just SAP's R/3 system that has been implemented. Apart from the ERP functionality in the R/3 system, many large but also medium-sized enterprises have also implemented other SAP (or non-SAP) software applications, such as a separate Management Information system, for example, SAP's BW, a CRM system, and so forth. These multi-application landscapes introduce another set of problems, which we address in Section 2.4.

The fourth and final source of complexity is that not just one, but several SAP system landscapes can be implemented. Large multinationals, for example, sometimes prefer to implement an SAP R/3 system in the form of a roll-out scenario. Such a scenario starts in one central place where all the core functionality is developed; then, this core functionality is gradually implemented in other sites. In Section 2.5, we discuss the impact of several SAP R/3 production systems.

2.2   The Impact of Using ERP Functionality

In most cases, implementing SAP functionality implies that, at the very least, SAP's R/3 system is being used. The highly integrated R/3 system is still SAP's most frequently used product. Therefore, because R/3 is such a complex ERP system, you must manage this complexity very carefully. Consequently, you need to spend more time organizing such basic tasks as testing and providing documentation than you would for a less complex application.

The inherent complexity of ERP functionality that spans the size of an R/3 system is twofold. From a functional point of view, there are many highly-integrated application components. A good example of the high degree of integration in SAP R/3—and a highly appreciated benefit—is that most financial postings are automatically generated on the basis of postings in logistical application components such as purchasing, inventory management, and sales and distribution.

From a technical point of view, there are many development objects and relations among these objects. The SAP R/3 system consists of thousands of components and provides numerous kinds of functionalities. In order to give you an idea of how large SAP R/3 actually is, here are some figures: the system contains a little less than 35,000 database tables, about 8,000 ABAP programs, and over 6,000 function modules that were released for customer use (out of a total of almost 200,000). Note that these figures pertain to only three particular types of objects, of which a SAP system is constructed. In total, there are more than 20 different types of building blocks, the most important of which are shown in Figure 2.1. Moreover, all of these objects can be interrelated. An ABAP program will often refer to several database tables, function modules, or external subroutines, just to mention a few. In all, we counted over 70 kinds of such interrelationships (not all of these were actually depicted). Nevertheless, given the size and complexity of this ERP functionality, you can well appreciate why at least a basic understanding of both the technical fundamentals of the SAP software and the functionality offered in the application components is warranted.

This section addresses the impact of using the complexity of an ERP product in your organizations. Because neither of the following topics will probably be among your favorites, you might as well organize the associated activities properly in order to minimize their impact. First, in Section 2.2.1, we discuss the effects that ERP complexity has on testing. Then, in Section 2.2.2, we address the fundamentals of documenting ABAP developments.

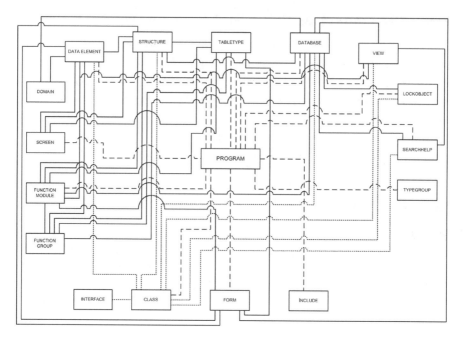

Figure 2.1 The Technical Complexity of an SAP System—Numerous Relations Among Objects

2.2.1 Testing the Quality in a Complex Environment

ERP complexity has the following effects on testing activities for customized ABAP developments:

▶ Testing even a relatively small piece of new or changed functionality can, nevertheless, be relatively complex: in an ERP environment, hardly any piece of new functionality is developed in complete isolation. Consequently, the high degree of integration forces the developer to consistently check all relations during testing. This often makes a test's scope wider than any one person can handle as both in-depth technical and functional knowledge are required. There is simply too much that needs to be known. Therefore, the ABAP developer alone cannot be responsible for the complete functional testing of ERP developments.

▶ Test data used in an ERP environment can often be used only once. The exact state of the database before starting a test cannot be reestablished. For update programs, this is often apparent; however, this can also apply to report programs. For example, you might test a report with test data that is continuously being changed by other people working with the same system. This makes testing akin to shooting at a moving target. In many cases, test data must be recomposed before each individual test can be executed.

Reusing Test Data

Testing is made somewhat easier by some additional test tools. If you developed your own update programs, you can record test data once with the Computer-Aided Test Tool (CATT or its successor eCATT), and reuse this data as often as you like. Furthermore, test input of function modules can be stored and reused, and for reports, selection variants can be stored. SAP also includes a unit-test option in the SAP Web Applicaton Server (Web AS) Release 6.40. Still, for the majority of your customized ABAP developments, you need to organize your test data yourself.

Limitations of Current Test Approaches

Most development organizations know that testing is critical in an ERP environment. In large projects, in particular, testing activities are usually divided into several detailed tests, such as "Unit Test" (conducted by the developer), "Integration Test" (performed by key users and *functional specialists*—consultants who specialize in the customization of SAP systems), and "Acceptance Test" (done by end users). Smaller developments are tested by the ABAP developer, and then, by the end user.

However, when it comes to testing ABAP developments, we think that the current approach has limitations. It ignores the fact that more than half of the development effort is usually spent establishing an acceptable level of robustness or technical quality of the development. This is the difference between the effort required for a 'quick-and-dirty' development and the effort that a technically complete development requires. In order to verify the technical quality of ABAP programs, a separate test activity is rarely explicitly distinguished. It is simply left up to the developer to address. The goal of most of the testing performed by those other than the developer is not to increase the technical quality of an ABAP program, but rather, to verify the external behavior of an ABAP development: if a program *seems* to behave fine, it is supposed to *be* fine. What this means is that only half of what ABAP code actually does is tested by someone other than the developer.

Recommendations

To improve the quality of ABAP developments, we recommend the following: assign someone (i.e., the ABAP developer) with the primary responsibility for testing the technical quality; and determine what your development organization can do to actively support quality checks.

Responsibility for Testing

The robustness of ABAP developments cannot be tested by just one person, but someone has to have the ultimate responsibility. In our opinion, this is the ABAP developer. Only the developer can be expected to test the technical quality of all aspects of a newly developed functionality before handing it over to others. There is another and more practical reason to shift most of the testing responsibility to the developer: it is easier for an ABAP developer to acquire sufficient functional knowledge than it is for a functional specialist—let alone an end user—to acquire sufficient ABAP knowledge. Only someone who understands the full implications of how program source code is actually generated can test the code properly. Therefore, we expect the quality of ABAP developments to be the primary responsibility of ABAP developers themselves.

Organizational Measure to Support Quality Checks

In terms of organizational measures, there is more to be done than just assigning responsibility for the undertaking of these measures. If the technical quality of developments is really deemed important, it does not suffice to make the developer solely responsible for these quality checks. A separate assessment of the technical quality of a development during testing can be arranged relatively easily. Large organizations may choose to create a separate Quality Assurance (QA) team to conduct this quality check. However, this doesn't mean that small or medium-sized organizations can't focus on technical quality. Activities such as a "peer review" can bring some relief with relatively little effort. We'll revisit this subject in Chapter 9.

2.2.2   Documenting ABAP Developments

Next to testing, documenting is probably one of the least sexy topics to discuss with a developer. No one will say that documenting customized ABAP developments isn't necessary. Yet, most organizations seem to struggle with this organizational measure, and not simply because this task is so disliked by ABAP developers. Typical complaints of documentation include:

▶ The documentation isn't there
▶ It's scattered over network directories
▶ It isn't current
▶ It isn't relevant

This section highlights the basic dilemmas that IT management often encounters regarding development documentation. The first question is: Why, when, and for whom is development documentation relevant? The other questions include:

What kind of documentation is essential? In which places can documentation be stored? And what benefits and pitfalls are associated with these places? We provide some recommendations for dealing with documenting ABAP developments at the end of this section.

Documentation about customizing settings, or project-related documentation describing design decisions made, are beyond the scope of this book, although some of our discussions regarding documentation may be applicable.

Why Documenting Is Important in an ERP Environment

The primary reason why documenting customized SAP developments is so important is simply because there usually are so many of them, which is a direct result of the inherent complexity of an ERP environment. Just try to imagine how many developments objects were actually added in your own ABAP development environment. The chances are that your first estimates will be too low. This should come as no surprise. If ABAP developers require time to become familiar with the large number of objects and interrelations in an SAP system, it stands to reason that people other than those directly involved—including the IT staff responsible—won't be aware until much later. For example, not all customized developments will be immediately apparent (visible) to end users. More prominent development objects, such as online reports and interface programs, and perhaps the print forms won't be overlooked. However, as we indicated in the introduction of this section, there are many more development objects, many of which should be documented because of their importance. Even smaller objects that are transparent to the end user can have an impact on standard functionality; for example, consider user exits, modifications, copy requirements, condition-based formulas, function modules, and ABAP Dictionary objects.

When to Define Documenting Standards

For various reasons, organizing documentation standards is preferably done *before* starting developments: first, because in most organizations, many ABAP programs are made by external developers (i.e., consultants) who need to be instructed; and secondly, because implementing ERP software that is the size of an R/3 system is a one-time experience for most organizations. At the time of a Go-live, most project members have other concerns, and creating documentation usually doesn't have top priority.

Now, we must emphasize the following points:

▶ SAP has already spent considerable effort in supporting implementation projects with the SAP Solution Manager: part of its functionality is specifically intended for documenting design decisions and customizing settings. This does not mean, however, that the shortcomings described below, and their proposed corresponding solutions, are no longer relevant.

▶ Most organizations that have already implemented SAP won't have the Solution Manager at their disposal and will have used their own tools.

▶ Note that not all kinds of documentation are included in our discussion. Instead, we have chosen to primariliy focus on development documentation for customized developments.

What Documentation Is Relevant for ABAP Developments?

If we consider only ABAP developments, we must ask ourselves "What documentation is relevant for ABAP developments?" First, it is important to focus on *when* it is used and by *whom*. In our opinion, the documentation is used primarily for maintenance; and, it is used primarily by developers. Now, imagine the position of a developer handling a maintenance request for an ABAP program with which he or she is not familiar. What kind of questions would the developer have? Perhaps, the following:

▶ What is the *purpose* of the developed program? Why does it exist?

▶ What is its *main functionality*?

▶ Is there some kind of *dependency* from other programs, which make, for instance, a certain order of execution mandatory?

▶ Does the program contain important *update functionality*? If so, is there a fallback scenario in case an update fails? Can the program be restarted?

▶ What is its *maintenance history*?

▶ Why were specific *technical choices* made?

While more information than this can sometimes be helpful, let's not overrate its added value. The average ABAP developer will hardly need more than what is mentioned here. Moreover, checking the source code will be one of the first tasks performed by a developer in handling this request.

Why the Original Specification Is Not Useful as Documentation

In development organizations, there is the tendency to consider a functional specification as sufficient documentation. Although this can be conceived as both a logical and practical conclusion, nevertheless, it is far from adequate.

To start with, the original specification for ABAP functionality will, in all probability, not be current. Most development is typically implemented in several iterations, adding or changing bits and pieces along the way. Changing the original specification at the same pace would be counterproductive. Therefore, unless strict procedures are in place, it's unlikely that even after immediately releasing a program for actual use in the production environment, the original specification would still be accurate.

However, there is an even more fundamental reason for not using the original functional specification as a prototype for maintenance activities to come. A typical functional specification will contain a detailed prescription for the proposed code, that is, what the code *yet to be made* should do, often making it look like detailed pseudo-code. That is not the type of information that is most relevant *after* initial development. Being confronted with a maintenance request for an unknown program, most developers are helped most with such limited contextual information as purpose, main functionality, and relationship to other functionality. Note that this may suffice for 90% of the objects developed. Finding more details is always possible by simply checking the source code carefully. This definitely gives the most reliable, accurate, and current information.

A third reason why specifications will often not sufficiently support maintenance activities is simply because either they just can't be found or they can't be found quickly enough. This brings us to the next question "Where is it best to store documentation?"

Where to Store ABAP Documentation?

Knowing what to document is important, but of even greater importance is knowing *where* to store your documentation. In most SAP environments, there are three available options:

▶ **Inline**: comment lines and comment blocks in the source code

▶ **Online**: in a separate document that is stored together with the source code

▶ **Offline**: separated from the source code, and stored in one or more documents outside the SAP system—in network directories, on an intranet, or in other tools

As you'll learn, each of these options has its own benefits and limitations:

▶ **Inline**
Inline documentation consists of comment lines that are directly added to the ABAP source code in the ABAP editor (for example, using Transaction SE38) (see Figure 2.2). Therefore, both the advantages and the limitations don't require an extensive explanation. Comments that are added to the source code can be particularly helpful because the help they offer is instantly accessible. However, because of the space restrictions and the limited formatting possibilities, you should word your comments as concisely and succinctly as possible.

```
REPORT  <report>.
*$*$-------------------------------------------------inline documentation
*$*$ Company  : Ctac Netherlands
*$*$ Author   : Wouter Heuvelmans
*$*$ Date     : 03/22/2004
*$*$ SAP rel. : 620
*$*$ Transport: CIDK900110
*$*$ Purpose  : Short description of the program.
*$*$----------------------------------------------------------------*
*$*$----------------------------------------------------------------*
*$*$         M O D I F I C A T I O N S                               *
*$*$----------------------------------------------------------------*
*& Changed By  : Wouter Heuvelmans
*& Date        : 03/24/2004
*& SAP rel.    : 6.20
*& Transport   : CIDK900208
*& Purpose     : Short description of the modification.
*&---------------------------------------------------------------*
*& Changed By  : Wouter Heuvelmans
*& Date        : 03/27/2004
*& SAP rel.    : 6.20
*& Transport   : CIDK900214
*& Purpose     : Short description of the modification.
f*&---------------------------------------------------------------*
.
TYPES: ty_buf(70)            TYPE c,
       BEGIN OF ty_at_name,
         at(2)               TYPE c,
         syst(2)             TYPE c,
         nr(4)               TYPE n,
       END OF ty_at_name.

DATA: tp_path(60)            TYPE c,
      tp_at_fname            TYPE ty_at_name,
      tp_fname_slash(1)      TYPE c. " '/' or '\'
```

Figure 2.2 Inline ABAP Documentation

These circumstances make inline documentation most appropriate for introductory comments such as a summary of the main functionality; references to the author and to those who have maintained the program; and the reasons for maintenance. This kind of general information is typically placed in comment blocks above the source code. Therefore, the most important information is immediately visible for each developer working on ABAP code.

Secondly, extra remarks in-between the source code are often useful. This is particularly true for comments explaining the technical choices made in comment lines or comment blocks just before the code. In general, comments merely describing the functionality of the code ("Here we fetch the data from the material master") have less added value for the next developer working on the code. Therefore, be careful to add such comments for other purposes than that of describing the main logic of the code.

Because it's so easy to make inline documentation, there is no reason for not doing so. Moreover, checking the completeness of inline documentation can easily be made part of an overall checklist used as a final step in the procedure of taking ABAP functionality into production.

▶ **Online**
The next possibility for documenting ABAP sources in an SAP system is also available via the ABAP editor (Transaction SE38). There is a standard facility for creating a separate text document that is tied to the source code instead of being placed within it. This facility is available for most (if not all) development objects (see Figure 2.3).

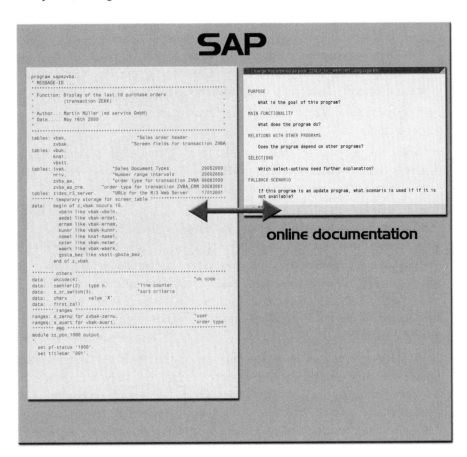

Figure 2.3 Online ABAP Documentation

SAP's online editor offers some very practical benefits:

▶ You can predefine standard headings in templates. For example, you can ensure that such headings correspond with the main functions of development documentation: purpose, functionality, dependencies on other functionality, and reference to fall-back scenario.

▶ Online documentation enables you to add hyperlinks to the documentation of other development objects. For example, you can add hyperlinks when you need to mention important dependencies on other functionality.

▶ For module pool programs, you can also create online documentation. First, you must create an online document via the menu path **Tools · Hypertext** or directly via Transaction SO72. You can link the created document to a program and screen by establishing the relation in table TTCDS. Consequently, you can make your own context-sensitive documentation available throughout an entire SAP system. Users can also access the documentation via the standard menu option **Help · Application Help**.

▶ A practical advantage is that online documentation can be made language-dependent.

▶ When online documentation is added to an ABAP report, the documentation is visible, not only to ABAP developers, but to those users working with the report via the standard menu option **Help · Application Help**.

The documentation of other ABAP development objects, such as function modules and database tables, will not be visible to the end user. However, this doesn't mean that adding online documentation to such objects isn't useful. The user of the documentation—the next developer working on the object—is not restricted. For example, most of SAP's standard function modules that have been released for customer use in the SAP R/3 system are accompanied by detailed online documentation on their functionality and the use of the interface parameters.

An obvious drawback of the online documenting facility is the limited editing options that it offers. The SAP Editor can be used for texts only, and it leaves little room for formatting, which may account for why the online editor isn't applied as often as one would expect. Other possible reasons for not using this facility may be the lack of standards and procedures for documenting; or perhaps, it's because examples in standard SAP software aren't widely available. SAP's own developers don't consistently apply the online documenting facility themselves either—only a limited number of standard reports have been documented with it. But, given that SAP has tools at its disposal that aren't available to the average SAP customer, that would be a rather poor excuse for not using this facility.

Despite its limitations, the online documenting facility is suitable for both end users and ABAP developers for most of the development information usually needed and for perhaps as much as 90% of the objects developed. Just a limited amount of information will suffice for most developments. Moreover, most customized developments pertain only to reporting functionality. Therefore, it should be clear that we consider this facility to be vastly underrated.

▶ **Offline**
The biggest advantage of storing documentation outside an SAP system is the possibility of using existing and familiar end-user tools. Much project-related documentation and user documentation is made offline for other purposes during an SAP implementation. Using the same offline tools for making development documentation is often considered convenient.

The organization of offline development documentation is usually based on the organization of development activities themselves, that is, per project and project phase. It is perfectly understandable during project-based development for project-related documents to be stored as offline documents in network directories with names like "Projects in process" or "Finalized projects." Doing the same with development documentation is less understandable. To see why, just imagine what would happen when a specific ABAP program is developed and changed in subsequent projects by various developers; most likely, the corresponding documentation will end up being scattered over various network directories. In that case, let's just hope that a powerful search engine is available.

The fundamental limitation of using offline tools for documenting ABAP developments is that storing a document outside your SAP system implies losing the direct link between the object to be described and its documentation.[1] Therefore, it must be controlled in another way (see Figure 2.4). Unless your development organization is prepared before the actual development starts, tracing and maintaining documentation that is stored offline will be much more difficult than using the online documenting tool. Unfortunately, this constraint of the offline option is often ignored until the number of developments has grown substantially, and the point of no return is reached.

---

1 Strictly speaking, such a link can be made, but the required functionality is rather laborious and hardly ever used. As of Release 4.6C, you can attach an offline document to a business object such as a sales order or an invoice. Perhaps, this option will become available for development objects as well.

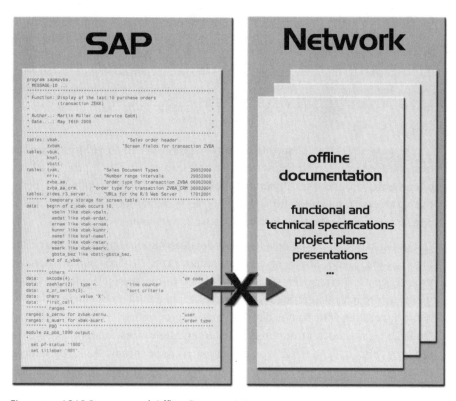

Figure 2.4 ABAP Programs and Offline Documentation

How to Keep Offline Documentation Available

In a limited number of situations, however, maintaining development documentation offline will be the most practical solution. For example, complex functionality such as interface programs may require more extensive documentation including diagrams. So, what if documentation can be made only offline? How can the link between the documentation and the ABAP Workbench object be established, so that a basic task like tracing back documentation by the name of a developed program or vice versa won't become too big an obstacle?

For various reasons, establishing such a link is not as easy as it seems. First, the name of a developed program is often not even mentioned in offline documents, so, for example, the programmer receives the documentation but there is no mention of the name of the program. In order to circumvent this restriction, you can name offline documents with the identical name of their respective ABAP object. This brings us to the second restriction—some offline documents are available before the development object is created. So, how can a document name be made identical to the object name if the object doesn't exist?

The only way to establish the unique reference between offline documentation and the object developed is by taking procedural measures such as establishing strict naming conventions for ABAP developments (and adhering to them), so that the official name for each new development exists *before* the developer creates the object. An alternative is to rename offline documentation after a development has been completed. As you can see, both alternatives require that you adhere to rather strict procedures.

Recommendations

You may want to consider the following recommendations if you need to establish some minimal documentation standards for your own developments. Applying these recommendations should make your life somewhat easier:

▶ Use inline and online documentation options in SAP wherever possible, at least for limited amounts of documentation that can directly be related to developed functionality. This will help you to avoid the worries over extensive procedural measures designed to keep offline documentation in sync with your developments.

▶ Use offline documentation only if using inline and online documentation isn't feasible. In our opinion, the only good reason for doing so is the complexity of customized developments, for example, in case of interface programs. Under such circumstances, extensive use of offline documenting tools is justified. However, most customized developments will not be that complex.

▶ If you maintain documentation offline, find a way to store development documentation independently from other types of project-related documentation. Keep various versions of documentation for the same ABAP program available together, preferably in one document.

▶ If you maintain documentation offline, think of a way to directly retrieve it! If possible, use the exact name of the object developed for naming offline documents, since this will make tracing documents easier, even if standard search engines are available.

▶ Documenting can hardly be called a favorite activity. Therefore, focus on the minimally required information for future maintenance. Don't confuse a functional specification with standardized development documentation. Fundamental information, such as purpose, main functionality, and relationships to other functionality, is, in most cases, sufficient. Being able to quickly determine a program's purpose during maintenance will often suffice. Detailed specifications aren't required for that purpose. Finally, in order to spend your documenting time most efficiently, you may want to focus primarily on the most critical functionality such as update programs (i.e., programs that perform updates to the SAP database).

▶ Ensure that you document customized functionality that is indirectly used by an end user (e.g., enhancement projects, BADIs, function modules, database tables).

▶ Describe the minimum guidelines in a handbook for your development staff.

2.3 The Impact of a Multi-System SAP Landscape

This section addresses the second complicating factor that an ABAP development organization will have to deal with—the impact of a multi-system landscape when it is required to support a central SAP system. Regardless of its size, any organization that implements ERP functionality—such as SAP R/3—will need to work with various versions or instances of the same ERP application. This is a fundamental necessity; implementing only one system instance would make development or maintenance activities virtually impossible. The most important possibilities and limitations for developing and testing customized software are determined by the chosen system landscape. To ensure that we've covered everything regarding multi-system landscapes, first we'll deal with some basic topics (see Section 2.3.1). If you're already familiar with these topics, you may prefer to skip them and start with the advantages and disadvantages of the system landscapes that are used most often (see Section 2.3.2).

2.3.1 Basics of a Multi-System Landscape

If you aren't familiar with the specifics of a multi-system landscape, this section may serve as an introduction. It discusses the purposes of a system landscape; the use of SAP clients; and, the basic measures required to keep a multi-system landscape synchronized.

Requirements of a Multi-System Landscape

Most organizations will continuously execute activities for their SAP production system. During such implementations, all the people involved must, to a certain degree, be able to do their job without being hindered by others: technical system specialists must be able to install new standard software versions (e.g., hot packages or upgrades); the ABAP developers must be able to do their programming; functional specialists may need to test out new customizing settings in a separate environment; key users will have to test and officially accept newly developed or changed software and customizing settings; project members will need to perform integration tests to determine whether all changes work together properly; and finally, the end users must be trained.

In the ideal world, each of these requirements is supported by a separate environment. However, in reality, less conflicting requirements are typically supported by the same environment. Basically, there are two ways to create a new environment—either by installing the SAP software on physically separate hardware (a *system instance*), or, by subdividing one SAP system into various *logical* environments. In very large organizations, one SAP production system is sometimes supported by as many as five additional systems, all acting as part of the same system landscape.

Using SAP Clients

The term *client* is used either broadly to mean a separate SAP logon environment, or, more specifically to refer to the primary key field of most SAP database tables. Various SAP clients can be defined within one SAP system instance in order to distinguish among several logically separated environments. Any user who tries to access an SAP system must enter a specific SAP client on the logon screen. If the required user master doesn't exist *in* the client mentioned, access is denied. After a successful logon, all subsequent actions (i.e., customizations, user authorizations, etc.) performed will automatically be tied to that logon client.

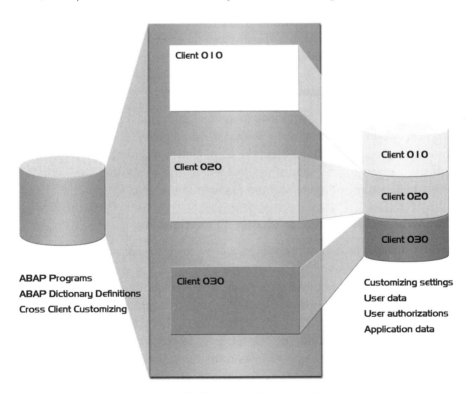

Figure 2.5 Client Independent Data (left) an Client Dependent Data

In Figure 2.5, we distinguish two forms of data: client-dependent data (on the right) and client-independent data (on the left). Defining various clients in one SAP system offers the advantage that, apart from the user master data and authorization data, various other kinds of data can also be treated separately, such as most of the customizing settings and the application data (master and transaction data). We refer to these kinds of data as *client-dependent* data.

Technically, the client is not an *environment,* but merely the primary key field (called `mandt`) of most of the SAP database tables (and also of properly designed database tables made by customers themselves). All programs applied by a user employ the logon client to select and update data in the SAP database, even without the ABAP code having to explicitly reference this key field. Therefore, although to the average user, working *in* a client may seem like working in a completely separate environment, this division of clients is only virtual. The client-dependent data of all clients in the same SAP system is physically stored in the same database tables.

Conversely, data such as the source of ABAP programs and the ABAP Dictionary definitions applied are, by definition, *client-independent*. Although created and started from within one specific client, they are stored and used independently from this client. In addition, a relatively small part of the customizing settings (the *cross-client* customizing settings) is also client-independent. Consider, for example, the customizing of condition tables.

Synchronization of a Multi-System Landscape

Having more systems and clients available in one landscape requires various forms of synchronization throughout the landscape (see Figure 2.6). Two kinds of synchronization must be distinguished: the continuous synchronization of pieces of new or changed functionality (from the left to the right); and the periodical *refresh* of an entire environment (from the right to the left).

The Introduction of New or Changed Functionality

New or changed functionality requires new or changed customizing settings, or new or changed ABAP developments. Transferring such changes between environments is supported by SAP's *Transport Management System* (TMS). The main benefit of the TMS is that it enables SAP customers to isolate changes in ABAP code or customizing settings.[2] Each isolated piece of functionality can be established individually, released for transport, exported from the source client, imported and tested in the target client (in another system), accepted, and imple-

---

2 As of Release 4.6C, you can also group customizing settings that support an entire process in Business Configuration Sets (BC Sets).

mented in the SAP production system. Note that the pipeline from initial development to production is fixed. The clients involved in the transport mechanism form a kind of chain, starting in a client in the development system (on the left) and ending in a client in production (on the right). The number of times that an individual transport must be explicitly released and transferred depends on the number of systems in the landscape.

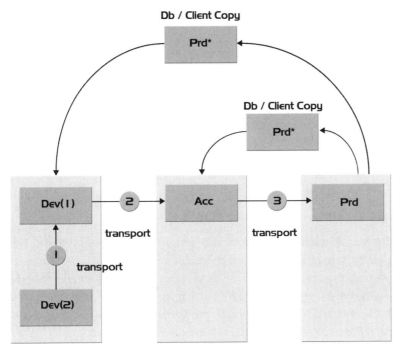

Figure 2.6 Transports and Data Synchronization Within a Three-System SAP System Landscape

Periodical Refresh of the Data in the Development Environments

Not only new or changed functionality must be synchronized in a system landscape (from development to production). The implementation of new or changed functionality is an ongoing process. In order to reflect the data of the production system as closely as possible, the development system must also have a periodical *refresh* of test data on the basis of production data.

Occasionally, such a refresh may also include customizing settings and ABAP software. Implementation activities usually require testing various pieces of alternative functionality. However, these aren't always transferred to the production system. Consequently, the development systems in the landscape may become somewhat *polluted* with unused and incomplete functionality.

Making a refresh of a development system is done by making either a *client copy* or a full *database copy* of the production system. A full database copy is relatively easy because everything is replaced: all the data, the programs, and the customizing settings. In this case, you need to safeguard only the work-in-progress and the version management data on the development system where the copy is imported. A client copy, on the other hand, allows you to copy specific types of data. You can copy client-dependent customizing settings (the rest of the data within that client is eradicated), or, other types of data, such as client-independent customizing settings (user data and application data can be added as well). Repository data (i.e., all Workbench objects like ABAP programs or ABAP Dictionary definitions), however, cannot be included. Compared with a full database copy, the advantage here is that transport requests and version management data are not deleted. However, the drawbacks of a client copy are the main reason why this option is rarely used: technical circumstances can cause the import of large volumes of data to be interrupted; and the consistency of the imported data is not ensured. The frequency for the need to make a refresh varies—some companies rarely make a production copy, whereas other companies makes production copies on a monthly basis.

2.3.2 Basic Variants of an SAP System Landscape

The SAP R/3 system landscape consists of two or more separate SAP systems. This section deals with some basic variants that are commonly found in SAP systems. We'll address only the most frequently used variants. To assess and compare the basic possibilities and limitations of different landscapes, we'll also discuss the variant with just one SAP system, although this variant will rarely be used. Next, we'll introduce the two- and three-system landscapes.

One SAP R/3 System

Despite being the cheapest alternative, an SAP system landscape with only one SAP system—logically subdivided into two or more clients as shown in Figure 2.7—is rarely used. This should hardly come as a surprise, because the shortcomings of a one-system landscape are significant for both production and development.

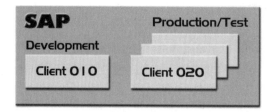

Figure 2.7 A One-System SAP Landscape

Because an ABAP program will run independently from the client in which it is started, technical problems caused by one program in one specific client can affect the options for working in all clients. For example, think of a program, which is started for test purposes in the *Development* client, that causes an endless loop. This could result in performance problems, or, worse, downtime for all the users of the *Production* client as well. So, in order to ensure the stability of the production environment in a one-system landscape, you must avoid making any changes to your ABAP code during office hours (or better still, by not applying any changes at all). If, however, you do make changes to your ABAP code, you can limit the risks by applying changes first to copy versions of the production program. Still, this will provide only temporary relief; it won't resolve the problem. For example, you won't be able to copy and test ABAP code in user exits and modifications separately.

Security problems can further exacerbate this situation. Because data from different clients is stored in the same database tables, it is fairly easy for an experienced ABAP developer to make his or her programs manipulate the data in clients other than the logon client. Therefore, although a single SAP R/3 system landscape is the least expensive alternative, it can hardly be called a viable option because of its many restrictions.

Two Systems

Many medium-sized and smaller companies using SAP R/3 software have a system landscape that consists of two physically separated SAP systems for production and development. On the development system, at least two clients are installed: one for executing all developments, and another for acceptance or quality assurance testing (see Figure 2.8). An additional *sandbox* client is often added to test customizing settings.

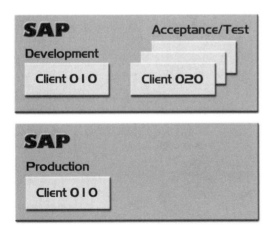

Figure 2.8 A Two-System SAP Landscape

A two-system landscape offers some practical advantages for ABAP development:

▶ Apart from implementing the actual developments in a separate client in the development system, ABAP developers are often allowed to use the test data of another client in the same SAP development system for acceptance purposes. This makes a two-system landscape relatively quick and flexible for developments.

▶ You can minimize the extra effort that is required to exchange and monitor the transport of new program versions and customize settings from the development to the SAP production system.

However, a two-system landscape also has some serious disadvantages. Inevitably, each separate system's master and transaction data will be out of sync. This will affect testing particularly in the development system. The only way to provide developers with appropriate test data is by making a regular copy of the production system to the development system. However, making such a copy is hindered by several restrictions:

▶ Frequent updates aren't always feasible. Copying production data is often complicated by the fact that a development system usually has less storage space and less processor capacity available than does a production system.

▶ SAP software doesn't support selective client copies between different system instances, in the sense that it won't be able to help you if you accidentally overwrite data that shouldn't have been lost.

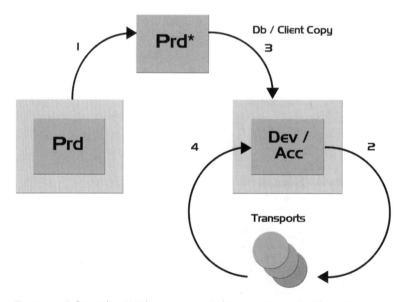

Figure 2.9 Safeguarding Work-in-progress Before Importing a Database Copy

Therefore, you must take several measures yourself in order to secure the most valuable open transports, since these represent the *work-in-progress* in the development system. Figure 2.9 shows how this is basically done: the making of the full database copy (Step 1); the important transports being worked on in the development system are first released and exported (Step 2); the same is often done with ABAP programs used for test purposes and version data of existing ABAP programs; then, a copy replaces the existing system (Step 3); and the transports and other safeguarded data are imported on top of the copy (Step 4). An extra step in the procedure (not shown) is usually to create new *open* transports again for the changes being worked on.

▶ Making a copy of production data may give developers, often hired externally, access to confidential data. The only way to prevent this from happening is by developing additional software; for example, creating software to change the salary data in an HR system immediately after making a database copy.

Despite the associated difficulties, a frequent refresh of the entire development system on the basis of a copy of the production data is a measure often used to ensure at least the basic quality of the development activities. Testing properly in an ERP environment is virtually impossible without having test data that closely resembles the production data. Reducing the amount of testing is not an option; you would end up testing your developments in the production system. Letting developers invent all the test data themselves is definitely not recommended: this is simply too difficult a task in an ERP environment unless you're an experienced functional specialist.

An attractive, but complicated, option is to periodically extract a relatively small but representative portion of master data and transaction data from a production system and make a selective update of the development system with it. However, this is easier said than done. Perhaps third-party tools that support this option for SAP environments are, or will be, available. If not, the only alternative is to develop your own solutions using SAP tools such as the extended Computer Aided Test Tool (eCATT), the Legacy System Migration Workbench (LSMW), or completely customized software. In short, straightforward solutions are not available.

Three Systems

From the standpoint of the ABAP developer, an ideal SAP system landscape consists of three separate SAP systems: a development system, an acceptance (or test, or quality assurance) system, and a production system (see Figure 2.10). Large organizations sometimes have landscapes of more than three SAP systems, but it isn't necessary to discuss these separately: the main characteristics that affect the quality of the support for ABAP developments are comparable with those of a three-system landscape.

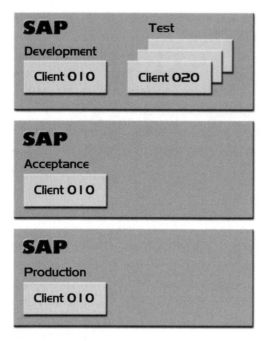

Figure 2.10 A Three-System SAP Landscape

The decision to install a three-system landscape implies the choice to include a separate SAP system into the landscape for acceptance testing. This makes sense only if the size of such an acceptance system allows a complete database copy of the production system to be made. Therefore, an acceptance system is usually made equal in size to a production system. Because a frequent, exact copy of the production system can be made, a three-system landscape offers several benefits over a two-system landscape:

▶ Developers can rely on the exact customizing settings and authorizations used in production during their test activities.

▶ Elaborate testing of complex functionality such as interfaces is better supported, because master data in the acceptance system will be completely identical to the master data in production (exactly the same product numbers will be available, the same supplier numbers, and so forth).

▶ Solving incidents in the production system is better supported, because problems that are raised in the production system can often be simulated with the same data.

In a three-system landscape, copying production data to the acceptance system is more straightforward than it would be in a two-system landscape because a database copy suffices. Consequently, however, disadvantages similar to those of a two-system landscape are introduced. And, because the frequency of making the production copy is higher in a three-system landscape than it is in a two-system landscape, coping with these disadvantages requires more Standard Operating Procedures (SOPs):

▶ Authorizations for developers in the additional acceptance environment will have to be provided liberally (i.e., enabling developers to do anything they need or want to do). Only then can the use of extensive testing options—options that are integral to standard acceptance procedures and indispensable for debugging programs (i.e., in the case of production incidents)—be provided.

▶ Some form of *after-treatment* on confidential data copied from a production system may be necessary.

▶ Open transports (for customizing settings and developments) in-between the acceptance system and the production system must be secured before a copy is made and then, restored afterwards.

A typical drawback of complex landscapes is the proliferation of transports and the different versions of ABAP Workbench objects (for more information, see Section 2.3.3). Usually, this makes the control activities involved and the required procedural measures more extensive. The effect this sometimes has on developers is the tendency to release newly-developed functionality prematurely for transport to the acceptance system, in order to be able to test the new functionality under optimal circumstances. Although that is not necessarily a problem, the increase in the number of transports between development and acceptance will make the monitoring of transports more difficult. Therefore, you should consider the possibility that there might be additional side effects at throughput times.

Choosing an Adequate Landscape

Typically, choosing a specific SAP system landscape is determined primarily by the costs involved—part of the costs are fixed (for the hardware); and another part of the costs are variable (for the extra time and effort needed to keep extra systems up and running).

In addition, you must distinguish what goals you have in mind for the landscape. Do you consider the stability of your production system to be so critical that you want to allow the maximum level of support to resolve production incidents? Have you implemented extensive interfacing (i.e., ABAP programs that process or send interface data) on top of your SAP functionality? Do you want to be able to test all interfaces under optimal conditions? In either case, you must have a production copy available. This could be realized either in a two-system, or a three-system landscape. Businesses that rely on SAP functionality to support their core processes usually choose to make a production copy, whereas businesses that rely solely on SAP functionality for administrative purposes choose not to make a copy.

Do you also want to ensure the maximum flexibility possible for all development activities? Do you anticipate several simultaneous and ongoing implementations? In such circumstances, a logical next step would be to install separate development and acceptance systems in the landscape.

2.3.3　Pitfalls of Monitoring Transports

A common problem of a multi-system landscape occurs with the monitoring of those transports to be exchanged between the different systems in the landscape. Typically, the transports that are required to bring about changes in functionality must be implemented in chronological order. This may not be simple for the following reasons: first, many transports may have to be monitored; secondly, various transports may refer to interrelated objects; and third, these interrelationships aren't directly visible in the TMS. If you don't transfer transports in the correct order, the transports will be rejected in the destination client. In the worst-case scenario, the corresponding symptoms may be identical to those described in Chapter 4—a program may suddenly result in a program dump, or prompt you with a technical error message.

Here is a relatively straightforward example of a version conflict. We'll discuss the causes of version conflicts in the sections that follow.

Example of a Version Conflict in One Object

When executing transports, you must always check the order in which changes are applied. The order in which the changes are applied must always be the same as the order in which the associated transports are deployed. Let's illustrate what happens when these processes are not in sync (see Figure 2.11). In this example, a program undergoes the standard transport procedure in a three-system landscape. After its first version (*Version A*) is created in the development system (at *Moment 1* on the time axis), it is released and transported to the acceptance test system (*Moment 2*); and after some additional testing, it is transferred from there to the production system (*Moment 3*)—business as usual.

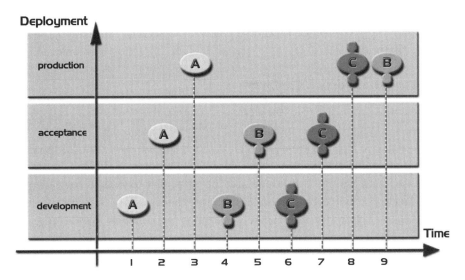

Figure 2.11 Version Management Problems Within a Three-System SAP Landscape

After some time, another developer is asked to change the program (*Moment 4*). This developer's modification is established in *Version B*, and transported from the development system to the acceptance system (*Moment 5*). However, although it is approved there, for some reason, it isn't transferred to the production system. This leaves *Version A* of the program still active in the production system.

Meanwhile, additional modifications are applied to the program in the development system by yet *another* developer who is unaware of the program's maintenance history. This results in *Version C* of the program in the development system (*Moment 6*). At this point, each system in the landscape contains another version of the same program and, therefore, a potential problem is in the making. Note that the third (or last) developer can only see the version of the program that is present on the development system. While working in the development system, the developer is *not* warned that he or she is about to change a program for which another change hasn't yet arrived at its final destination (the production system). If Version B was still a work-in-progress in the development system, a warning *would* have been issued. However, that is no longer the case. So, without knowing, the third developer implements Version C, although Version B is still only halfway along the pipeline.

This last developer's modifications are transported to the acceptance system (*Moment 7*), immediately agreed upon, and implemented in production (*Moment 8*). Consequently, Version C has actually overtaken Version B on its way to production. Shortly thereafter, the transport that contains Version B in the acceptance system is also transferred to production (*Moment 9*). At this moment, the damage is done; the older Version B overwrites Version C, and causes the last modifications to be lost.

Main Causes of Version Conflicts

The previously discussed example describes a version conflict that is caused by transferring changes in one program in the wrong chronological order via the landscape. In real-life situations, the conditions that lead to version conflicts are usually more complex. Suppose that Figure 2.11 described a situation in which changes were applied to two interrelated development objects: a program (C), and a function module (B), which is called in the program. In addition, let's assume that, in order for the change in the program (C) to work properly, the change in the function module (B) must also be implemented. Implementing the program change and not implementing the change in the function module can cause three types of errors. These errors, in ascending order of their level of severity, are as follows:

▶ The least disturbing error is the rejection of a transport import. After checking the cause, a second attempt to import the missing transport will usually help you to resolve the problem.

▶ The import of the transport is accepted, but a typical stability problem could occur; for example, if the parameters used by the program don't match the function's interface, this could result in a program dump.

▶ The worst-case scenario is that the transport is accepted, but no visible error is generated; nevertheless, the data produced by the program could be wrong.

Now, let's recall the large number of development objects and the even larger number of possible interdependencies that may exist between different development objects in an SAP system (as we discussed in Section 2.2). In such circumstances, it is more than likely that, at some point, you'll have to deal with several interrelated transports. Therefore, you need to know which interdependencies exist in the transports being processed at any moment in time. Unfortunately, SAP's transport management system offers little help here: it doesn't check these interdependencies. Therefore, you'll have to perform this check yourself to ensure that interrelated changes have been transferred in the correct sequence to the next client.

The main cause of version conflicts is the combination of a large number of transports, a multitude of possible interrelationships between development objects, and the need to check these interdependecies manually. In a multi-SAP system landscape, the possibility for such conflicts is not merely hypothetical. Any organization using various SAP systems, on various sites, and simultaneously working with many employees on several projects, is exposed to this risk. In fact, most organizations that have worked with a SAP system for a reasonable duration may already have experienced disturbances of their production systems due to a version conflict. In short, as the complexity of the system landscape increases, so, too, does the probability for version conflicts.

How to Prevent Version Conflicts

Clearly, you should realize that applying changes consistently throughout your system landscape is not possible without putting in place additional checking mechanisms. A fully-controlled implementation of a change cannot rely solely on SAP's transport mechanism. You also need to consider the following checks:

▶ When you start changing a development object, you must know whether the object itself, or a related object, already exists somewhere in the pipeline.

▶ When transferring transports, you must ensure that *all* related transports have been transferred.

▶ You must also verify that the transports have been transferred in the correct *sequence*: in terms of both the underlying object dependencies (changes to basic objects first) and the chronological order in which changes were applied.

You can implement the aforementioned checks in two ways: by additional customized developments, or by additional procedural measures. For example, a message can be raised when an ABAP program (or any other ABAP Workbench object) is *touched* in the development system that is still a *work-in-progress* somewhere else in the landscape. Several organizations have developed additional software for this purpose (as we have ourselves). Because such customized software will afford the best protection against disturbances in your system landscape, we wholeheartedly recommend this option. If you're not in a position to develop customized software, extensive procedural measures are the only alternative you have. In that case, you must check each transport for interdependencies meticulously before it is released.

2.4   The Impact of a Multi-Application Landscape

In the previous section, we discussed system landscapes that support the implementation of just one application. In that context, we referred to SAP's R/3 system in particular. However, many organizations implement more than just one application. Often, medium-sized and large organizations have various interrelated applications in place instead of just one application (see Figure 2.12 for example). Besides several legacy applications, SAP's Business Warehouse (SAP

BW) application may be employed, as well as a separate Supply Chain Management (SCM), and a Customer Relationship Management (CRM) application.

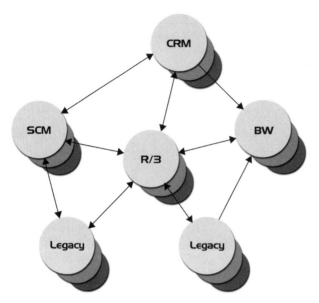

Figure 2.12 A Multi-Application SAP System Landscape

This circumstance definitely adds to the complexity of the overall landscape. No longer will there be just one system landscape supporting a production application; instead, each individual application requires a landscape of its own. Therefore, the basic issues that we addressed for a multi-system landscape also apply to a multi-application landscape.

2.4.1 Requirements

Besides what you must do to manage a *one-application* system landscape, the interaction in a *multi-application* system landscape requires that you take additional measures. Most likely, the applications in such a landscape will exchange data with each other. The completion of a specific business process may even include the consecutive use of functionality of more than one application. A SAP BW system, for example, may have to be fed with detailed transaction data from the SAP R/3 system. After processing the detailed data, the SAP BW system may, in turn, have to feed forecasting data to the SAP R/3 system. This scenario requires that you should execute the different steps in a fixed sequence.

If you manage a multi-application landscape, you should consider the following requirements and recommendations:

▶ Establishing the test data of a single application may depend on the data of another application; for example, you might need to establish a link with the acceptance system of an SAP R/3 system.

▶ A test scenario for a process that uses the functionality of more than one application requires more effort than does a test scenario in just one application.

▶ Because each application will have its own release management, each upgrade or each hot package installation can change the individual application's behavior. This further compounds the efforts required to test the interfaces with the surrounding applications.

▶ The release versions of various SAP applications can, to a certain degree, be interdependent. For example, an SAP BW application cannot be upgraded individually without checking the constraints of the actual SAP R/3 release. All major changes—such as upgrades of interrelated SAP applications—must be timed carefully.

▶ In all cases where interfacing between the individual components in the landscape is involved—even the introduction of a minor change in production—will have to be timed accurately. Consider, for instance, the change of the length of one field in a BW table (an *infocube*), which must be filled on the basis of SAP R/3 data. Such a minor change can be made only by transferring the two associated transports in both applications simultaneously.

▶ Note that automatic checking of the consistency of interrelated objects, in order to prevent version conflicts between the development objects of different applications, may no longer be possible (as we proposed in Section 2.3.3). Only extensive manual procedural measures will suffice.

2.5   The Impact of Several SAP R/3 Production Systems

Very large organizations, such as multinationals, don't always implement just one SAP R/3 system. Each single division or regional headquarters within the organization may need to manage its own production SAP R/3 system (and the corresponding landscape). Given the desire to standardize the administrative procedures throughout the enterprise and keep the overall implementation costs under control, such implementations are usually executed in a roll-out scenario. This means that the *core* functionality for the entire enterprise is developed first, on top of standard R/3 functionality. On the basis of the core system, subsequent implementations are then executed for individual subsidiaries. This scenario is depicted in Figure 2.13. Note that you could also use the same scenario in other SAP applications.

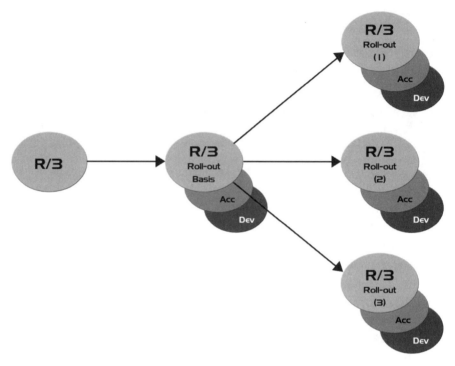

Figure 2.13 A Roll-Out Scenario with Three SAP Production Systems

2.5.1 Drawbacks of a Roll-Out Scenario

Depending on how a roll-out is actually executed, it may have some specific drawbacks. The most realistic scenario is the one in which local organizations are allowed to have a certain degree of freedom to implement their functionality. Usually, some variation of the core functionality is feasible. However, this introduces another complicating factor. In this type of scenario, all R/3 systems can end up all being similar, and yet no two systems will contain exactly the same functionality. In other words, each single implementation of the application will be a separate system in its own right, and should be treated as such.

This is particularly true for maintenance activities. For example, think of yourself as a project manager who must plan the implementation of a support package or a release upgrade throughout all the system landscapes. What kind of consecutive actions would you need to execute? First, you would have to plan the upgrade activities required for the core system:

1. The upgrade of SAP's standard software must be installed on the core system.

2. All the technical problems directly caused by the technical upgrade must be processed to make the existing functionality work as it did before. You will have to adjust user exits and make direct modifications to the standard software applied in the core functionality in order to align the core again with SAP's new standard software.

3. All other customer-specific developments—such as online reports, forms, and interfaces—will have to be adjusted. This will generate a number of transports in the system landscape surrounding the core system, which will also have to be imported and processed in all the other systems.

At this point, only the kernel of the company's functionality will still work as before. Now, you must repeat the same process for each of the actual implementations that was initially based on the core system:

1. In each of these R/3 implementations, the same technical upgrade must be executed.

2. The transports for the alignment of the core must be processed.

3. Despite these measures, you cannot ensure that the existing functionality will work as it did before. Therefore, depending on the number of modifications applied on top of the core, you may have to repeat the entire process.

All the aforementioned upgrade activities require that you do all the monitoring of your own developments yourself—both on the core system and on each of the local systems. Ultimately, the question you might ask yourself is whether you're still working with a roll-out scenario or separate implementations. A roll-out scenario like this will have delivered most of its benefits in the first implementation. With regard to maintenance, there is less difference with a regular SAP R/3 implementation. Because the cost of maintenance forms the larger part of the overall implementation cost, you may not have gained as much as you hoped.

2.5.2 Recommendations

To a certain degree, you can limit the complications generated by the roll-out on different systems. You do this by reserving a so-called *namespace* for all the developments, the core system, and, perhaps, also a separate namespace for each of the local SAP R/3 implementations. This results in better SAP software support during a software upgrade or the processing of hot packages: the software reduces the load of required monitoring activities that you have to handle. Figure 2.14 shows what the process would look like for the entire landscape:

1. A software upgrade (or import of a hot package) of the core system is executed.

2. Transaction SPAU (SPDD for ABAP Dictionary objects) shows all the standard SAP objects that were changed in the core system. This ensures a 100% check on the changes you implemented. Of course, actually checking and adjusting the changes that were originally made is still entirely up to you. All reprocessing of modifications will lead to repair requests.

3. The additional ABAP developments may also have to be changed, however, they won't result in repairs, but in ABAP Workbench requests.

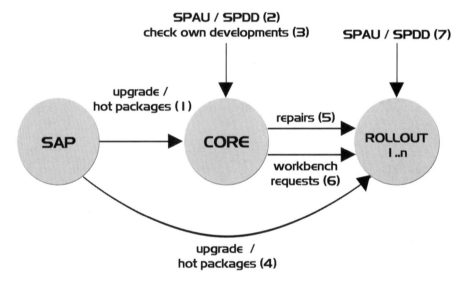

Figure 2.14 Complexity of the Upgrade Process in a Roll-Out Scenario with Several SAP Systems

The same procedure is repeated on each of the local R/3 implementations:

4. The software upgrade on the local SAP R/3 implementation is executed.

5. All repairs generated by adjustments to existing modifications to the standard software or to the core system are imported.

6. All Workbench requests generated by other adjustments to customized ABAP software are imported.

7. Because all developments made on the core system have their own namespace, they will also be regarded as foreign developments in a local implementation. Therefore, they automatically become part of the standard processing via the SPAU or SPDD list.

2.6 Summary

In this chapter, we highlighted the most important issues that you should consider when you're attempting to establish a framework for ABAP developments. We discussed these issues based on the four main factors that will complicate the management of your developments: the basic complexity of ERP functionality; the necessity to use a multi-system landscape for one production application; the complications added when various production applications must be supported; and, finally, the additional complications that arise when several production versions of the same application are generated.

The very fact that you're dealing with ERP software should encourage you to implement some basic measures: first, you must determine where to place primary responsibility for testing developments and how best to organize your documentation as effectively as possible.

Secondly, we saw that optimal support of one production application requires a multi-system landscape. This landscape, in turn, requires some essential organizational measures in order to ensure both the stability of the production system and the flexibility of the development process. We particularly stressed the importance of frequently refreshing test data in other systems in the landscape, and the pitfalls associated with version management of your developments.

Finally, particularly large organizations can require that you take certain measures to address specific problems. Often, these large organizations must deal with many applications and sometimes with various production versions of the same application. We discussed the specific synchronization problems that can arise, and how best to address these problems.

3 Correctness

The term *correctness* refers to the quality of a program's output: the output generated, or the updates performed, by a program should be accurate and consistent with the results of other programs. You must ensure that your ABAP code selects, processes, and updates data correctly. Therefore, you must ask yourself the following questions: Are the ABAP statements that affect the data used properly? Is the program logic capable of handling unexpected data? In other words, does the ABAP code really work? Can it be safely transferred to the productive system? You may argue that correctness is simply part of implementing functional requirements, however, we think of correctness as an aspect of technical quality, which we consider to be part of the developer's responsibility.

3.1 Typical Correctness Categories

There are various reasons why ABAP developments don't always work correctly. The first category of errors has little to do with the ABAP language itself. These errors are caused by the developer's basic lack of skills. These are the kind of errors that may be allowed for an inexperienced developer, but would make an experienced developer question whether he or she chose the right profession.

The second category of errors can be characterized as the short-sighted kind, that is, wrong assumptions are made about the data from an SAP system to be processed. These assumptions are often based on a lack of understanding or a wrong interpretation of customizing settings. Often, the way in which a company's hierarchical structure is modeled in an SAP system is not considered during ABAP developments. However, you cannot develop additional ABAP functionality without having a basic knowledge of SAP functionality.

The third category of errors has to do with common misunderstandings about the ABAP language. Several widely used ABAP statements and ABAP Dictionary object types were specifically designed to make the developer's life easier. The implicit nature of some of these language elements, however, often contributes to their being poorly understood.

You will find examples of these three kinds of errors in the different topics covered in this chapter. These correctness issues include: selecting data; processing data; managing data in memory; database updates; and exchanging data with external systems.

3.2 Selecting Data

So, how do you avoid errors when selecting data from the SAP database? In this section, we provide you with guidelines to help you avoid selecting too much data, too little data, or simply the wrong data.

3.2.1 Selecting One Unique Row

Now, we'll show you an example of what can happen when the wrong assumptions are made about the organizational structure modeled in the SAP system. In this case, the data selected from the SAP database is affected adversely. The assumption is that only one organization unit of a certain kind exists. However, in practice, such an assumption often expires sooner than expected, that is, the assumption becomes invalid and obsolete when a second organization unit of the same kind is modeled in the SAP system. Consequently, existing ABAP code will have to be changed.

The report to which we refer performs calculations using the standard price from the material valuation table mbew. Let's assume that one company code (one financial entity) and two plants (two factories) have been modeled in the SAP organization structure. The same materials are used in the two plants, but with different prices. (In other words, the report was originally written on the assumption that the company would have only one plant. This assumption became obsolete when a second plant was later introduced.)

Consequently, the wrong prices for the materials were inadvertently selected by the report. Let's look at the piece of ABAP code that causes this:

```
LOOP AT ta_materials INTO wa_materials.

* Get standard price for this material
  SELECT SINGLE stprs
         INTO   tp_standard_price
         FROM   mbew
         WHERE  matnr = wa_materials-matnr.
  IF sy-subrc <> 0.
    ...
  ENDIF.

ENDLOOP.
```

Exactly one price per material should be selected from internal table ta_materials. For that purpose alone, the use of a SELECT SINGLE is appropriate. However, the problem here is that its WHERE clause leaves room for selecting more than one row. A table row can be identified uniquely only by using all primary key fields. But, in this example, key fields bwkey and bwtar are missing in the WHERE clause. The `bwkey` key field is the field that is directly related to a plant. As soon as prices are created for the materials used in a second plant, `bwkey` can have two values. Therefore, this code does not ensure that the correct price is selected. In fact, you would not even be able to accurately predict which of the two database rows would be selected.

Having to select exactly one database row without knowing all selection criteria is a common challenge (or problem) for most ABAP developers. Because of the complexity of an SAP database, it is not easy for users or analysts to specify exactly how the selection of data should be done. Adding to this complexity is the fact that not all key fields of database tables are always mentioned on the screens of an SAP system, thereby making it harder to know the underlying database tables. Consequently, the ABAP developer is the person who must typically cope with such matters. This is one of the reasons why you need to have more than just programming skills to be a fine ABAP developer. You also need to have a basic knowledge of the functionality of a SAP system and the way it has been implemented for a specific organization.

We refer here to the problem caused by the last ABAP code example, with the wrong `SELECT` statement in it; the report that selects the wrong material prices because the `SELECT` statement is not specific enough. The wrong database row is selected because of a missing key field in the `WHERE` clause of a `SELECT SINGLE` statement. The developer could have prevented the error in the ABAP code by simply executing an extended syntax check. Then, the following warning is given:

```
Syntax check warning
This warning is only displayed in SLIN.
 In "SELECT SINGLE ...", the WHERE condition for the key field "BWTAR"
does not test for equality. Therefore, the single record in question may
not be unique.
```

Interpreting the error message as a reference to a strictly technical problem is wrong. Avoiding the syntax warning is possible. An ABAP programmer can suppress the extended syntax check warning, or change the ABAP code using the `UP TO 1 ROWS` addition. Neither of these two options is correct because the actual problem is not solved: the wrong database row can still be selected.

```
LOOP AT ta_materials INTO wa_materials.

* Get standard price for a material
  SELECT stprs
         INTO tp_standard_price
         FROM mbew
         UP TO 1 ROWS
         WHERE matnr = wa_materials-matnr.
```

```
  ENDSELECT.
  IF sy-subrc <> 0.
    ...
  ENDIF.
ENDLOOP.
```

Despite being syntactically correct, this does not actually solve the basic problem: the selection of one correct database row. Although the full and unique key of table `mbew` is not used, the code still expects to select one database row.

If you cannot uniquely identify one row, there are several options. First, you can force the user to determine the missing part of the unique key, for instance, by making him or her enter the missing values as parameter values on the selection screen.

If that isn't feasible, because you shouldn't expect the user to know how to do this, there is another alternative. It is a fallback option, because it doesn't really solve the problem, however, it does identify the problem for the user when it appears. It involves verifying the assumption that only one database row meets the selection criteria. If this assumption is wrong, appropriate measures can be taken, for example, raising an error message and stopping the program. This second option is illustrated below. Suppose that only the value of the `bwtar` key field is missing and users cannot be prompted to enter this value.

```
LOOP AT ta_materials INTO wa_materials.

* Get standard price for a material
  SELECT stprs
         INTO TABLE ta_standard_price
         FROM mbew
         WHERE matnr = wa_materials-matnr
           AND bwkey = pa_bwkey.

  IF lines( ta_standard_price ) > 1.
* Too many rows found => take appropriate action
  ELSEIF lines( ta_standard_price ) < 1.
* Nothing found => take appropriate action
  ELSE.
* This is ok, so proceed.
  ENDIF.
ENDLOOP.
```

There are numerous other examples of tables with key fields whose values aren't easy to determine. Think, for instance, of other tables for organizational units, or tables in the *Logistics Information System* (LIS). Because additional examples are provided when we discuss performance issues (see Chapter 7), we won't go into greater detail here.

3.2.2 Complex WHERE Conditions

Note that SELECT statements can be complex. In particular, you should avoid using combinations of AND, OR, and NOT if possible. Consider the following, relatively straightforward piece of code, which selects material data from the material master mara:

```
SELECT * FROM mara INTO TABLE ta_mara
       WHERE matnr IN so_matnr
         AND mtart EQ co_mtart_raw
         AND meins EQ co_meins_raw
         OR  mtart EQ co_mtart_products
         AND meins EQ co_meins_products.
```

If you take another look at this code, you'll notice that the selection appears a bit odd. All conditions placed after the OR, in this case, the last two lines of the WHERE clause

```
         OR  mtart EQ co_mtart_products
         AND meins EQ co_meins_products.
```

will be interpreted independently from the conditions placed before the OR.

The first condition in the WHERE clause (matnr IN so_matnr) was probably intended to be used in combination with all other conditions, but *is*, in fact, used in combination with the first two AND conditions only. Although this code is syntactically correct, you would expect the query to resemble the following:

```
SELECT * FROM mara INTO TABLE ta_mara
       WHERE
           ( matnr IN so_matnr
         AND mtart EQ co_mtart_raw
         AND meins EQ co_meins_raw )
         OR
           ( matnr IN so_matnr
         AND mtart EQ co_mtart_products
         AND meins EQ co_meins_products ).
```

The correct use of parentheses is not only useful to keep the syntax readable. It is also essential to make the selection correct, because of the effect that it has on the interpretation of the query by the database server. Therefore, keep SELECT statements simple, readable, and as clear as possible. If you split up complex statements into separate statements, you may improve performance as well.

3.2.3 Validity of Selected Data

The next selection problem that we want to address has to do with the validity period of selected data, that is, a lot of data in the SAP system is valid only during a limited period of time. At the end of its validity, data is either explicitly flagged for deletion, or new data is created, with a new validity period. Because handling time-related data is a frequent cause of confusion, we will devote more time to discuss it here.

Validity Period

A good example of a database table that is defined to contain time-related data is table a004 in the SAP R/3 system. It contains condition records for the sales organization, distribution channel, and material number. Part of the table's contents is shown below in Figure 3.1. It contains three condition records of type k004 available for material PM-1000, sales organization 1000, and distribution channel 10. Each condition has its own validity period. It starts on the **Valid on** date and ends on the **Valid to** date. Note that the validity periods listed in the three rows do not overlap. The first condition is valid up to, and including, 07/25/2000. The second condition is used as of 07/26/2000.

Cl.	App	CnTy	SOrg.	DChl	Material	Valid to	Valid on	CondRecNo.
100	V	K004	1000	10	PM-1000	07/25/2000	12/01/1999	0000012138
100	V	K004	1000	10	PM-1000	08/01/2000	07/26/2000	0000013758
100	V	K004	1000	10	PM-1000	12/31/9999	08/02/2000	0000015859

Figure 3.1 Condition Records and Their Validity in Time

Suppose that you would need to make a program that selects exactly one condition record from table a004. How would you make your code in such a way that takes into account the restriction that the data in the table is time-related? The condition record should be valid on a specific date. In attempting to do this, the following piece of ABAP code is not correct.

```
SELECT * FROM a004
       INTO TABLE ta_condition_a004
       WHERE kappl = pa_kappl
         AND kschl = pa_kschl
         AND vkorg IN so_vkorg
         AND vtweg IN so_vtweg
         AND matnr IN so_matnr.
```

The resulting internal table `ta_condition_a004` will contain all three records instead of only one record (when using the contents shown in Figure 3.1). Selecting the one condition that is valid must be done by explicitly using the validity dates **Valid to** (`datbi`) and **Valid on** (`datab`) in the `SELECT` statement. That is still difficult to do as is demonstrated by the selection below, which is still incorrect.

```
SELECT * FROM a004
      INTO TABLE ta_condition_a004
      WHERE kappl = pa_kappl
        AND kschl = pa_kschl
        AND vkorg IN so_vkorg
        AND vtweg IN so_vtweg
        AND matnr IN so_matnr
        AND datbi GT pa_valid
        AND datab LT pa_valid.
```

To understand why this code is still inaccurate, imagine what would happen if the selection parameter `pa_valid` contains date 07/26/2000 (or any other of the **Valid on** or **Valid to** dates in Figure 3.1). If the value of the **Valid to** date (`datbi`) or the **Valid on** date (`datab`) exactly matches the selection date (in parameter `pa_valid`), no entry is selected due to the `GT` and `LT` operators used. Therefore, the correct code should look like this:

```
SELECT * FROM a004
      INTO TABLE ta_condition_a004
      WHERE kappl = pa_kappl
        AND kschl = pa_kschl
        AND vkorg IN so_vkorg
        AND vtweg IN so_vtweg
        AND matnr IN so_matnr
        AND datbi GE pa_valid
        AND datab LE pa_valid.
```

So far, the selection parameter `pa_valid` has been used in the example as a selection-screen parameter. The selected date can also depend on other data in the system; for instance, the document date in a sales order. Below, field `wa_vbak-audat` has replaced the selection-screen parameter `pa_valid` as the selection date:

```
SELECT * FROM a004
      INTO TABLE ta_condition_a004
      WHERE kappl = pa_kappl
        AND kschl = pa_kschl
        AND vkorg = wa_vbak-vkorg
        AND vtweg = wa_vbak-vtweg
        AND matnr = wa_vbap-matnr
        AND datbi GE wa_vbak-audat
        AND datab LE wa_vbak-audat.
```

Another considerably more complex scenario occurs when a selection period, and not just one specific selection date, is used. For example, this is a common scenario that you would encounter in SAP's Human Resources (HR) system. The validity of data in most SAP HR-related tables is often not delimited by a date range of only one specific HR-table. Selecting an employee's current salary, for instance, wouldn't simply mean selecting this year's salary data (valid from the January 1st to December 31st). In addition, you should also check the salary data against the employee master, which also contains period-related data (date hired, date fired). This comparison might reveal that the employee left the company last month. This results in selections in which, say, data from table pa0001 (Organizational Assignment) must be checked against a date range in another HR table. However, note that these kinds of comparisons can often result in the selection of more than one table row.

Now, let's look at the next figure (Figure 3.2), which shows the effect of a selection period on the data selected. Condition records 1 to 6 are available, but only conditions 2, 3, and 4 fall within and 5 would, at least partially, overlap the selection period.

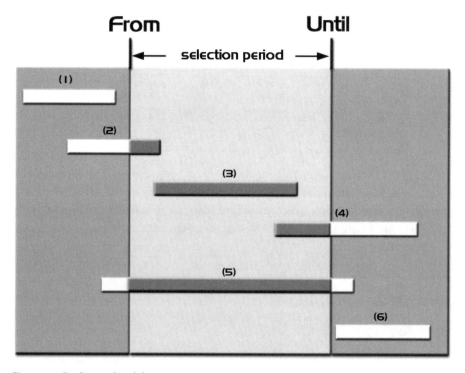

Figure 3.2 Dealing with Validity

You should understand how to deal with the validity period of condition records when making a query that uses a selection period. A condition record must be selected if its own valid-*from*-date lies before or on the *end*-date of the selection period, and if its valid-*to*-date lies after, or on the *start*-date of the selection period. Or, in ABAP code:

```
SELECT * FROM a004
    INTO TABLE ta_condition_a004
    WHERE kappl = pa_kappl
      AND kschl = pa_kschl
      AND vkorg IN so_vkorg
      AND vtweg IN so_vtweg
      AND matnr IN so_matnr
      AND datbi GE pa_datab
      AND datab LE pa_datbi.
```

Note that the selection period is not established in a select option, but in two separate selection parameters (pa_datab and pa_datbi) for the start date and end date, respectively. In order to make the right selection, you must refer to either the start date or the end date of the selection period. If an end user is allowed to use a select option, any date range can be entered: a period, various periods, or a series of specific dates. Consequently, a more complex condition may have to be implemented. Simply referring to the select-option in the WHERE clause, as is done below, would not be correct:

```
SELECT * FROM a004
      INTO TABLE ta_condition_a004
      WHERE kappl = pa_kappl
        AND kschl = pa_kschl
        AND vkorg IN so_vkorg
        AND vtweg IN so_vtweg
        AND matnr IN so_matnr
        AND datbi IN so_date
        AND datab IN so_date.
```

We recommend that you avoid this type of coding and adhere to using two separate selection parameters for the start date and end date of the selection period. To summarize, we recommend always using parameters instead of select-options to represent a selection date or selection period.

Delete Flag

Other well known examples of fields that affect the validity of data are *delete flags* and *status fields*. These fields are used for both master and transaction data. Selections often include an explicit reference to such a field in order to prevent outdated data from being processed. The following code shows you an example of a selection on the material master with its delete flag (mara-lvorm):

```
SELECT * FROM mara
    INTO TABLE ts_mara_sel
      WHERE matnr IN so_matnr
        AND lvorm = abap_false.
```

3.2.4 Selections Based on Database Views

As we already mentioned, when you correctly select the data from a database table, this implies that you have exactly specified what data is asked for—no more, no less. In keeping with this discussion, we now turn our attention to some basic misunderstandings regarding the use of database views.

Implicit Selection Conditions

The first thing you should do when using a database view is to check its *implicit selection conditions*. You will find an example below in Figure 3.3. An implicit selection condition has the same effect as a WHERE clause in ABAP source. The advantage of an implicit selection condition is that it only has to be defined once, that is, in the ABAP Dictionary instead of in various ABAP sources. The disadvantage of an implicit selection condition is that it will remain hidden for all ABAP sources that refer to the database view—a fact that is easily forgotten. If you don't consider this fact, you can wind up with selections that return less data than is required.

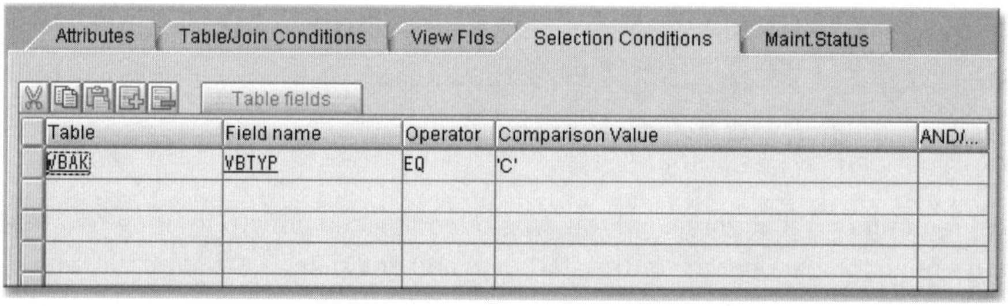

Attributes	Table/Join Conditions	View Flds	Selection Conditions	Maint.Status	

| Table fields | | | | |
Table	Field name	Operator	Comparison Value	AND/...
VBAK	VBTYP	EQ	'C'	

Figure 3.3 Implicit Selections in Database Views

Misunderstandings About Joins (1)

The second thing to remember when using database views is that they represent *inner joins*. A lack of understanding of inner joins is another source of problems when database views are used in SELECT statements. To understand why, we will first briefly summarize the nature of inner and outer joins, as shown schematically in the following Figure 3.4:

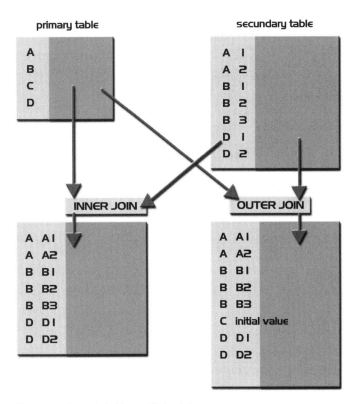

primary table

secundary table

Figure 3.4 Inner Join Versus Outer Join

An *inner join* combines only those rows that are actually present from different database tables. In the example above, the row in the primary table (upper left) with key value C is not represented in the inner join (lower left), because the secondary table (upper right) does not contain any corresponding rows with key value C. Under the same circumstances, an *outer join* (lower right) will include partially filled rows. In this case, a partially empty row is created with key value C.

Both types of joins are useful, however, each in only specific situations. Database views are an example of inner joins. They are used for database selections on database tables that are interrelated and frequently used in combination.

Imagine a report that derives its data from the MARAV database view—the view that combines data from the material master table MARA and corresponding language-dependent descriptions from the table MAKT. For each material, more than one description in MAKT may exist, but this is *optional*. Therefore, if you assume that the data to be selected from the MARAV view is always complete, subsequent processing may fail.

To illustrate this, consider the following situation. An American enterprise has a European subsidiary. Headquarters in the U.S. uses its own non-SAP system; headquarters in Europe uses an SAP system. In the European SAP system, product sales data is maintained in several languages. The language in which a product has a material description depends largely on the nationality of the customers to whom the product is sold. If a product is sold to Italian customers only, its material description will be only available in Italian.

Every month, sales data per product must be reported from the European SAP system to headquarters. The report must generate output that, among other things, includes material numbers and their descriptions in English. The report starts with a selection from the `marav` database view:

```
SELECT matnr maktx
       INTO TABLE ts_marav
       FROM marav
       WHERE matnr IN so_matnr
         AND spras = pa_spras
         AND ..........
```

Imagine what would happen if the *English* language was selected (that is, if selection parameter `pa_spras` contained value E) and a material description for one of the selected products sold was available only in Italian. In these circumstances, the product would not be selected because no row with a material description in English (key field SPRAS = E) is available in database table MAKT, although the product itself would be present in the database view MARAV. Consequently, its sales totals would not be reported either.

To ensure that all materials are selected, it is preferable to use an explicit SELECT on database table MARA for the materials, and a separate SELECT on table MAKT for the corresponding descriptions:

```
SELECT matnr
       INTO TABLE ts_matnr
       FROM mara
       WHERE matnr IN so_matnr
         AND ...
IF sy-subrc = 0.
  SELECT matnr maktx
         INTO TABLE ts_makt
         FROM makt
         FOR ALL ENTRIES IN ts_matnr
         WHERE matnr = ts_matnr-matnr
           AND spras = pa_spras.
ELSE.
  ...
ENDIF.
```

Of course, this still doesn't ensure that all required material descriptions in English will be selected, but, at least the report will be able to explicitly check whether data from the database table MAKT is missing and respond with an error message, for example.

Another way to avoid this problem is to define an outer join in the source code:

```
SELECT mara~matnr
       makt~maktx
       INTO TABLE ts_materials
       FROM mara
       LEFT OUTER JOIN makt
            ON makt~matnr =  mara~matnr
           AND makt~spras =  pa_spras
       WHERE    mara~matnr IN so_matnr.
```

Using the correct ABAP code, however, is not the primary lesson to be learned here. To use database views properly, it is far more important that you understand the SAP data model and the relationships between the database tables. If *optional* relationships exist between tables, as is the case for MARAV, there is no guarantee that all the data that you need will actually be selected by using a database view. In other words, the relationship between tables MARA and MAKT in database view MARAV is optional because it is not guaranteed that there is a row in MAKT for any specific language. Consequently, if you need to select rows from table MARA that do not have related rows in table MAKT, using database view MARAV is not be the right solution.

The MARAV represents an example of a frequently used database view. Another example of a database view is KNA1VV, which is based on tables KNA1 and KNVV. It represents a customer data per sales organization. A third example is database view LFA1M1, based on tables LFA1 and LFM1, which represents a vendor data per purchasing organization.

The aforementioned pitfalls (i.e., implicit selection conditions in a database view and misunderstandings about joins) should in no way discourage you from using database views for selection purposes. They can still be worthwhile, but only under certain circumstances and for specific purposes. We will mention two such examples.

First, a database view is useful if the completeness of selected data is ensured. A database view that combines sales order item data and sales order header data, for example, would, by definition, be complete: for every sales order item, there is always a sales order header available. Standard SAP functionality for maintaining sales order data ensures that this information is complete. It does not allow sales orders items to be created without sales order headers. In other words, the relation between sales order item and header is not optional.[1]

The second and opposite situation in which a database view can be useful is when the selected data does not *have* to be complete. Think of our initial example again that used database view MARAV. If you needed only the sales data of products sold to English-speaking customers, the same code would have been perfectly appropriate!

Similar examples could be the selection of all customers for one sales organization, based on view KNA1VV, or the selection of all vendors for one purchasing group, based on view LFA1M1.

Misunderstandings About Joins (2)

In addition to avoiding selecting too little data, you should also avoid selecting too much data. A join can result in multiple occurrences of the base table if the relationship between the two tables is one-to-many, which is the norm for the majority of relationships in large databases. Let's now recall the example based on the marav database view.

```
SELECT matnr maktx
     INTO TABLE ts_marav
     FROM marav
     WHERE matnr IN so_matnr.
```

If a description exists in three different languages, the contents of field matnr will be repeated three times (with different descriptions in field maktx) by this SELECT statement in the result set ts_marav.

In principle, this is not a problem, however, there is one exception—if the program using this piece of code does not anticipate a situation where multiple entries might occur. Therefore, you must check the probability of this exception.

Note that this example shows some similarities to the problem discussed in relation to the SELECT SINGLE statement (see Section 4.2.1). Try to avoid making assumptions about the future use of functionality as much as possible. Typically, you would encounter this type of problem in organizations that are gradually extending their SAP implementation by adding a new plant, sales office, company, or any other type of organizational unit. The problem primarily occurs when only one organizational unit (company, plant, sales organization) was implemented initially, but other units (companies, plants, sales organizations) are added later. This often results in double entries being processed by existing reports and transactions.

---

1 If we look at it from the other side, however, the relation is optional: a sales order header can sometimes have no sales order items.

Misconceptions About the FOR ALL ENTRIES Option

The FOR ALL ENTRIES option was added to the ABAP syntax before the option to use inner joins was introduced. This option is still often used to improve performance, instead of an inner join. Consider the following typical example of its use, in which two consecutive SELECT statements are executed:

```
* Select orders for specific material and order type
  SELECT matnr auart vbeln posnr
        FROM vapma
        INTO TABLE ts_vapma
        WHERE matnr IN so_matnr
          AND auart IN so_auart.

* Use this result to read the detail data from VBAP: Order Item data.
  SELECT matnr vbeln kwmeng vrkme
        FROM vbap
        INTO TABLE ts_orders
        FOR ALL ENTRIES IN ts_vapma
        WHERE vbeln = ts_vapma-vbeln
          AND posnr = ts_vapma-posnr.
```

Two possible errors are affiliated with this type of ABAP code. First, you'll notice that it is not anticipated that the first SQL statement might not find any data in table VAPMA. This would result in an empty internal table ts_vapma. By itself, that is not a problem, however, the FOR ALL ENTRIES option in the second SELECT statement will react rather adversely, because it interprets the SELECT statement to mean that there is no existing WHERE condition. Consequently, the second SELECT statement will force the database server to perform a full table scan and the entire database table's contents will be copied to internal table ts_orders.

You can prevent this error from occurring by explicitly checking the contents of the internal table before starting the second SELECT statement:

```
  IF NOT ts_vapma[] IS INITIAL.
    SELECT matnr vbeln kwmeng vrkme
          FROM vbap
          INTO TABLE ts_orders
          FOR ALL ENTRIES IN ts_vapma
          WHERE vbeln = ts_vapma-vbeln
            AND posnr = ts_vapma-posnr.

  ENDIF.
```

Another error that can occur is the result of a hidden time bomb located in the first source code, which is due to another particularity of the FOR ALL ENTRIES option—the result set ts_orders will, by definition, be filled with a new row only if a unique combination of field values is selected. If you encounter the same combination of field values in several rows of the database table, the corresponding row from the database table will be skipped.

To see the result, look at the following example in Table 3.1. The material number (matnr), the fields order number (vbeln), the quantity sold (kwmeng), and the sales unit of measure (vrkme) are selected from the database table vbap. In this example, a small portion of data in table vbap is represented. In SAP standard functionality, the same material number can occur in several items of the same sales order. As you can see, for Order 8221 and Material 100–200, two identical combinations of values for the selected fields are found.

Material (Matnr)	Order (Vbeln)	Quantity (Kwmeng)	Unit (Vrkme)
100–200	8200	6,000	PC
100–200	8200	4,000	PC
100–200	8219	2,000	PC
100–200	8221	5,000	PC
100–200	8221	5,000	PC
100–200	8226	3,000	PC

Table 3.1 Database Table vbap

Performing the SELECT statement, including the FOR ALL ENTRIES option in the aforementioned code, would result in the following contents of the internal table ts_orders (see Table 3.2):

Material (Matnr)	Order (Vbeln)	Quantity (Kwmeng)	Unit (Vrkme)
100–200	8200	6,000	PC
100–200	8200	4,000	PC
100–200	8219	2,000	PC
100–200	8221	5,000	PC
100–200	8226	3,000	PC

Table 3.2 Internal Table ts_orders

Only one of the two rows is selected. Consequently, five pieces of material 100–200 will be missing if total values are calculated.

In order to prevent this kind of error, we recommend that you always include all primary key fields in the resulting table when using the FOR ALL ENTRIES option. For the database table vbap, this implies that field posnr should also have been selected into the table ts_orders, as is done below:

```
IF NOT ts_vapma[] IS INITIAL.
  SELECT matnr vbeln posnr kwmeng vrkme
         FROM vbap
         INTO TABLE ts_orders
         FOR ALL ENTRIES IN ts_vapma
         WHERE vbeln = ts_vapma-vbeln
           AND posnr = ts_vapma-posnr.

ENDIF.
```

3.2.5 Authorizations

Because one of the goals of SAP software has always been to support complex organizations, security is a key factor in all SAP developments. The extensive authorization system allows organizations to implement detailed user profiles in order to prohibit unauthorized access to data.

When implementing an authorization check into a custom development, you should note some specific characteristics of the SAP authorization functionality's behavior, in particular, that your development work does not stop after implementing an authorization check in ABAP code, for example:

```
AUTHORITY-CHECK OBJECT 'F_BKPF_BUK'
                ID 'BUKRS' FIELD wa_t001-bukrs
                ID 'ACTVT' FIELD '03'.
```

In addition, you should make some concerted effort to find the correct exception handling in the event of unauthorized access. In principle, two scenarios are possible: needing to reuse standard SAP exception handling, or developing your own.

Reusing Standard Authorization Functionality

In the first scenario, that is, if standard ABAP code already contains its own authorization logic, hidden in global class methods, functions, or logical databases, the corresponding exception handling cannot be influenced. Consider, for example, a situation whereby a custom-made report is developed that uses the logical database KDF (Accounting documents per vendor). If, during the selection of data by the report, an authorization check fails, an error message like the following example (see Figure 3.5) is returned by the logical database directly to the user. The custom-made logic cannot change this.

Figure 3.5 Authority Check Has Failed

Other logical databases such as BRM (Accounting Documents related to purchasing) would not return an error message, but an information message instead. After sending out this message, it would then process the data to which the user is entitled.

The fact that standard authorization functionality can show varying behavior is something to keep in mind, in particular, when testing custom-made functionality on top of standard functionality. So, if authorization checks are relevant, ensure that you include a test on the same functionality using various user profiles.

Defining Your Own Authorization Functionality

In the second scenario, an authorization check is included in a custom-made program. In that case, you can do all exception handling yourself. The drawback is that you run the risk of either processing unauthorized data, or excluding data that should have been processed.

In this situation, you should include exception handling with an information message, such as does the logical database BRM, which we already mentioned. In this way, the user will get the information to which he or she is entitled, and, simultaneously be notified that some of the data he or she has selected has been skipped over. In addition, the user can automatically be directed to Transaction SU53, which displays the authority checks that were just made. This is exemplified in the following screenshot:

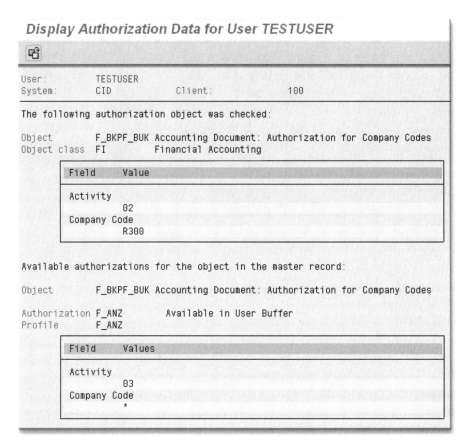

Figure 3.6 Authority Check Results

3.3 Processing Data

3.3.1 Processing Quantities and Amounts

One of the more annoying programming habits is the sloppy treatment of amounts and quantities. A figure like "one thousand" is meaningless until its context is further clarified. One thousand dollars is not the same as one thousand Euros, or one thousand Yen, or one thousand pieces of soap. To be meaningful, an amount of money must be associated with a type of currency. Similarly, a quantity of a material requires a unit of measure in order to be properly understood.

One of the basic errors made in ABAP programming is to assume that a unit of measure or currency can be fixed. This makes it impossible for the outcome of a program to vary with the data processed. If the data processed does not always contain exactly the same unit of measure or currency, the program will simply fail.

Imagine a company that sells its products worldwide. Its customers may be represented in several countries. In that context, an overview of financial documents per customer must be reported. Now imagine a developer who has been told by the end user that all customers always pay their invoices in the same currency. This hypothetical developer then carried this assumption over into an ABAP report, including the piece of coding for totaling the amounts below. The code processes the contents of the financial document items table in SAP R/3 (the bseg) into an internal table ta_bseg, like this:

```
LOOP AT ta_bseg INTO wa_bseg.

* The amounts have already been multiplied by -1 for creditlines
  ........

    AT LAST.
      SUM.
      FORMAT COLOR COL_TOTAL.
      WRITE / wa_bseg-dmbtr NO-ZERO UNDER wa_bseg-dmbtr.
      ULINE.
    ENDAT.

ENDLOOP.
```

As you probably already know, the SUM command doesn't distinguish between currencies; it merely performs a summation. In this case, all amounts are totaled at the AT LAST event, regardless of currency code. This could cause meaningless totals if dollars, yen, and pounds were mixed up. Although a first test might not reveal any deficiencies, you'd be ill advised to leave the program in this precarious state. In a more thorough test, or perhaps later in the productive system, things may have changed.

This kind of problem can easily be avoided. All SAP applications use the *reference field* concept. Database tables that contain fields for amounts or quantities will also refer to an associated currency or unit of measure. Selecting the associated reference field, along with the required quantity or amount field, will suffice. In the following example in Figure 3.7, the reference field linked to the amount (bseg-dmbtr) is currency code t001-waers. Double-clicking on field dmbtr in the display of the table definition with Transaction SE11 will reveal this, as shown in the screenshot below:

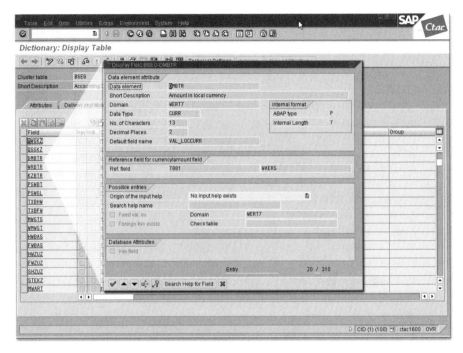

Figure 3.7 Attributes of the Table Field

Typically, we recommend that you check the reference field explicitly. In this case, you could, for example, have incorrectly presumed that the amount in field `bseg-dmbtr` refers to the currency in field `bkpf-waerk` instead of `t001-waers`.

The simplest way to handle quantities and amounts in reports is by using the ABAP List Viewer (ALV) technique. To use the ALV, you must provide the reference fields associated with quantity and amount fields (although you can still refer to the wrong reference fields). In addition, the ALV will automatically perform calculations of subtotals per reference currency or unit of measure.

However, it may not always be possible to use the ALV, and therefore, we have included the following example. The same summation as before is now performed explicitly:

```
LOOP AT ta_bseg INTO wa_bseg.

  AT NEW bukrs.
    SELECT SINGLE waers FROM t001 INTO ltp_waers
          WHERE bukrs = wa_bseg-bukrs.
  ENDAT.

  wa_tot_amt_01-waers = ltp_waers.
  wa_tot_amt_01-dmbtr = wa_bseg-dmbtr.
```

```
  COLLECT wa_tot_amt_01 INTO ta_tot_amt_01.

AT LAST.
  FORMAT COLOR COL_TOTAL.
  LOOP AT ta_tot_amt_01 INTO wa_tot_amt_01.
    AT FIRST.
      WRITE: / 'Total Amount in local currency'(001).
    ENDAT.
    WRITE: wa_tot_amt_01-dmbtr UNDER    wa_bseg-dmbtr
                              CURRENCY  wa_tot_amt_01-waers,
          wa_tot_amt_01-waers.
    NEW-LINE.
  ENDLOOP.
ENDAT.

ENDLOOP.
```

There is also a third alternative. If you explicitly want to represent amounts in one currency, you can convert various currencies into one currency. SAP provides several standard functions for this kind of conversion. Function Module UNIT_CON-VERSION_SIMPLE and other functions from function groups SCV0 and SCVU can be used for conversions between quantity fields of type QUAN. For the conversion of currency type fields (CURR), the functions CONVERT_TO_LOCAL_CURRENCY and CONVERT_TO_FOREIGN_CURRENCY are available in function group SCUN. All function modules mentioned have been released by SAP for customer use.

3.3.2 Rounding Problems

In this section, we discuss another weakness during processing, namely, rounding problems. Some of these rounding problems are caused by the misinterpretation of ABAP computation statements and data definitions in the ABAP language. Others are less tied to the ABAP language; rather, they are due to a lack of common sense. Examples of both of these types of rounding problems are discussed below.

General Rounding Errors in ABAP

Here, we discuss some general rounding errors, resulting from either the incorrect use of variables with a limited number of decimal places, or the wrong implementation of a calculation. Three particular topics are addressed: the number of decimal places; (incorrectly) splitting up calculations; and the order of performing various calculations.

General rounding errors often occur because of defining too few decimal places for a variable that is used to contain an intermediate value. See what happens in the following example. The code performs a calculation of monthly costs based on the distribution of annual costs. On the basis of the intermediate result, a total annual cost is calculated again. This is done twice—first using an intermediate variable with two decimal places, and then, using a variable with six decimal places.

```
DATA: tp_beginvalue   TYPE p DECIMALS 2 VALUE '100000.00',
      tp_endvalue      TYPE p DECIMALS 2,
      tp_monthvalue_2 TYPE p DECIMALS 2,
      tp_monthvalue_6 TYPE p DECIMALS 6.

* Intermediate field 2 decimals => rounding differences
   tp_monthvalue_2 = tp_beginvalue   / 12.
   tp_endvalue     = tp_monthvalue_2 * 12.              "99,999.96

* Intermediate field 6 decimals => no rounding differences
   tp_monthvalue_6 = tp_beginvalue   / 12.
   tp_endvalue     = tp_monthvalue_6 * 12.              "100,000.00
```

If the intermediate monthly value is stored in a packed field with 2 decimal places (tp_monthvalue_2), the total of the twelve individual values no longer exactly adds up to the original annual amount. If an intermediate variable with more decimals is used (tp_monthvalue_6), the problem is avoided. As an alternative solution, you could calculate the rounding difference as a separate figure and distribute this (0.04) over a period of 12 months.

In the previous paragraph, we used a calculation with an intermediate result. However, if possible, you should avoid using intermediate results. The following example shows why not splitting up a calculation into separate statements will make it more accurate. First, a calculation in two steps is made, based on an intermediate result with three decimal places (tp_average). The same calculation is then executed in one step.

```
DATA: tp_average TYPE p DECIMALS 3,
      tp_result  TYPE p DECIMALS 3,
      tp_total   TYPE p DECIMALS 3 VALUE '444.555',
      tp_sum     TYPE p DECIMALS 3 VALUE '999.999'.

* Calculations with type P fields
* - Intermediate result with 3 decimals
   tp_average = tp_sum / tp_total.
   tp_result  = 12 * tp_average.                        "26.988

* - Without intermediate result
   tp_result  = 12 * ( tp_sum / tp_total ).             "26.993
```

The reason that the first end result, based on the use of an intermediate variable, is less accurate is caused by its intermediate result. The intermediate value in the variable tp_average is rounded to three decimal places before the calculation continues. This means that the remainder of the calculation will therefore be less accurate as well.

A third example shows the importance of the order in which calculations are processed. To influence the order of consecutive calculations, the correct use of parentheses plays an important role. A tip that might be helpful is to consistently place a multiplication equation before a division equation. As the following example shows, this is particularly important for calculations with integers.

```
DATA: tp_result_i    TYPE i,
      tp_sum_i       TYPE i               VALUE '500',
      tp_total_i     TYPE i               VALUE '1000'.

* Calculations with type I fields
* First divide, then multiply
    tp_result_i  = 12 * ( tp_sum_i / tp_total_i ).      "12

* First multiply, then divide
    tp_result_i  = ( 12 * tp_sum_i ) / tp_total_i.      "6
```

To a lesser extent, the same applies to calculations with other numeric fields of type f (floating point).

```
DATA:   tp_result_f  TYPE f,
        tp_total_f   TYPE f VALUE '444.55500000000000',
        tp_sum_f     TYPE f VALUE '999.99900000000000'.

* Calculations with type F fields
* - First divide, then multiply
    tp_result_f  = 12 * ( tp_sum_f / tp_total_f ). "26.993258426966293

* - First multiply, then divide
    tp_result_f  = ( 12 * tp_sum_f ) / tp_total_f. "26.993258426966296
```

What you should extract from this example for future reference is that there are ways to prevent rounding from having an effect on the accuracy of calculations: first, by using the correct data types; and, secondly, by using these data types in the right order. You should also note that calculations in which decimals are involved (as is the case with most amount and quantity fields) will be most accurate if fields of type p (packed) are used. These packed fields have the highest possible accuracy of 31 decimal places.

Rounding Before Totaling

The last topic about rounding that we want to address in this section does not deal with the correct use of the ABAP language, but rather, the importance of using common sense. Consider the following real-life situation. A truck with valuable goods is not allowed to cross the U.S. border. The reason? The customs officer has found a difference of 1 lb. between the overall totals mentioned on two different documents. The total weights differ, but they should have been identical.

We should first mention that the two calculations are based on the same weight field in the company's SAP system. The weight is stored in ounces, whereas the total on both documents must be displayed as a rounded amount in pounds. In addition, you need to know that the way the total weight calculation must be presented on the two forms is different. In Document 1, intermediate subtotals in pounds must also be presented per commodity code (based on the fact that various products can have the same commodity code). In Document 2, just an overall total weight is required. Now, let's look at the corresponding code of the two programs below (the variable `tp_weight_total` is used in both programs):

Document 1: Rounding per commodity code (`stawn`)

```
CLASS customforms IMPLEMENTATION.
  METHOD calculatetotal.
    SORT ta_document_data BY stawn.
    LOOP AT ta_document_data INTO wa_document_data.
      AT END OF stawn.
        SUM.
        tp_weight_total = tp_weight_total + wa_document_data-weight.
      ENDAT.
    ENDLOOP.
  ENDMETHOD.                      "calculate total
ENDCLASS.                  "customforms IMPLEMENTATION
```

Document 2: Rounding at the end

```
CLASS customforms IMPLEMENTATION.
  METHOD calculatetotal.
    SORT ta_document_data BY stawn.
    LOOP AT ta_document_data INTO wa_document_data.
      AT LAST.
        SUM.
        tp_weight_total = wa_document_data-weight.
      ENDAT.
    ENDLOOP.
  ENDMETHOD.                      "calculate total
ENDCLASS.                  "customforms IMPLEMENTATION
```

The cause of the difference in the end totals lies in the intermediate rounding that is done in the program for Document 1. There, the variable `tp_weight_total` is recalculated several times on the basis of rounded (!) subtotals. The individual amounts (in `wa_document_data-weight`) are summed and a subtotal is calculated for each commodity code (field `stawn`). On the other hand, in the second program, the variable `tp_weight_total` is calculated only once, at the very end.

Therefore, if the number of different commodity codes processed is high, the difference between the total weights on the first and the second document will steadily grow. It is very easy to imagine what can happen if the totals must also be presented in pounds, without decimals. To illustrate this, we show you two calculations in the following table: the total in the second column is based on intermediate results without rounding; the total in the last column is based on rounded subtotals.

Commodity code	Not rounded	Rounded
22030010	101.400	101
39059090	105.400	105
39235090	109.400	109
Total	316.200 = 316	315

Table 3.3 Rounding Differences

The conclusion is similar to the one in the previous paragraph: try to avoid rounding until the final result must be presented. Rounding too early in a program will make all dependent results less accurate. This applies not only to totals, but also to other dependent results such as calculated percentages.

3.3.3 Misunderstandings About Control Statements

The way in which the ABAP language works is not always accurately understood. In particular, some control statements will frequently cause confusion among ABAP programmers, the main reason being that the functionality of many control statements is defined implicitly. Although implicit functionality makes statements intuitively attractive, it also makes them relatively hard to learn. Consequently, control statements are sometimes applied inappropriately. We have chosen two particular statements—the ON CHANGE OF statement and the LOOP AT statement—to illustrate this point.

The ON CHANGE OF statement

Most developers know that the ON CHANGE OF statement can prove dangerous when not used correctly. Troubleshooting problems created by the wrong use of the ON CHANGE OF statement can often be very time-consuming. Associated errors will typically seem to appear at random and be equally hard to detect. Moreover, such errors may be hard to reproduce. The same program that produces inexplicable errors in a productive system may perform smoothly in a development system.

A specific misinterpretation of the ON CHANGE OF command is to compare it with the AT NEW kind of command. While the context of the AT NEW command is very strictly defined (looping at sorted internal tables, referring to the sorting order), the context of an ON CHANGE OF command is not. It simply compares the contents of the comparison field with its former contents, at the exact location where it is executed. If the two values don't match, the condition is true. In making this comparison, the ON CHANGE OF command behaves completely independently from, for example, a LOOP statement, or a method-, subroutine-, or function call. There is a relation only with the internal session running and with the exact location in the source. You can use this command at any location in an ABAP program.

Now, let's look at some code. It was applied in a function module that collects customer invoices and, on that basis, produces a corresponding interface file, one per selected customer. While processing the invoices of a specific customer, the available stock for the materials listed in the invoices had to be calculated. The calculated totals then had to be added to the output file. The developer chose to limit the number of times to do this using the ON CHANGE OF statement.[2]

```
REPORT /ctac/r_create_interfaces.
..
    LOOP AT ta_customers INTO wa_customers.
      CALL FUNCTION '/CTAC/CREATE_INTERFACE'
        EXPORTING
          itp_kunnr = wa_customers-kunnr.
    ENDLOOP.

FUNCTION /ctac/create_interface.
  DATA: lwa_interface TYPE ty_interface.

* Table ts_invoices is filled first with invoice data
* for the customer.

* Routine to fill interface file format in internal table
  LOOP AT ts_invoices INTO wa_invoices.
    ON CHANGE OF wa_invoices-matnr.

* Calculate total material available stock
      CALL FUNCTION '/CTAC/MATERIAL_STOCK_CALC'
        EXPORTING
          itp_matnr = wa_invoices-matnr
        IMPORTING
          etp_stock = lwa_interface-stock
          etp_unit  = lwa_interface-unit
        EXCEPTIONS
```

---

2 Of course, there are better ways to achieve this, but this kind of ABAP language construction is used often and should therefore be discussed.

```
          not_found = 1
          OTHERS    = 2.
      IF sy-subrc <> 0.

    ENDIF.

  ENDON.
*
    lwa_interface-vbeln = wa_invoices-vbeln.
    lwa_interface-matnr = wa_invoices-matnr.
    APPEND lwa_interface  TO ta_interface.

    AT LAST.
* Create the interface file per SOLD-TO partner
       CALL FUNCTION '/CTAC/CREATE_INTERFACE_FILE'
          TABLES
             tta_interface = ta_interface.
    ENDAT.

  ENDLOOP.
ENDFUNCTION.
```

One problem that was raised by executing this code was that sometimes the stock quantity and unit of measure in the first entry of a produced interface file were missing. A pattern in the occurrence of the error could not be found, nor could it be reproduced in the development environment. After extensive debugging in the production environment, with the exact data that had originally caused the error, the ON CHANGE OF statement was found to be the culprit: in exceptional cases, its condition was not met and therefore, function /CTAC/MATERIAL_ STOCK_CALC was not executed.

A sample of the data producing the error might have looked like the following example in Figure 3.8. On the basis of the contents of internal table ts_custo-mers, function /CTAC/CREATE_INTERFACE_FILE will be called three consecutive times, for customers 10001, 10002, and 10003, respectively.

TS_CUSTOMERS

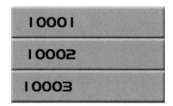

Figure 3.8 Internal Table ts_customers

Now, let's look at the contents of the internal table `ts_invoices` in Figure 3.9 for each of the three customers processed and the effect that each row processed has on the corresponding *old* and *new* value of the `ON CHANGE OF` statement.

TS_INVOICES(10001)

Invoice number	Material number		Old Value	New Value	On Change
90000001	1234		...	1234	YES
90000001	1001		1234	1001	YES
90000001	1001		1001	1001	NO
90000003	9101		1001	9101	YES
90000004	9101		9101	9101	NO

TS_INVOICES(10002)

Invoice number	Material number		Old Value	New Value	On Change
90000007	1234		9101	1234	YES

TS_INVOICES(10003)

Invoice number	Material number		Old Value	New Value	On Change
90000005	1234		1234	1234	NO

Figure 3.9 Internal Table ts_invoices

For customer 10001, the `ON CHANGE OF` condition is false for the third and fifth entry in the internal table `ts_invoices`: no new material is encountered, therefore, no material stock is calculated. However, this is what the programmer had in mind. For customer 10002, nothing eventful occurs. For customer 10003, however, the `ON CHANGE OF` condition is false for the first row processed. The material number found is the same number that appeared in the previous row, the last one processed for customer 10002. Consequently, the function that calculates the material stock is not executed and local workarea `lwa_interface` remains empty.

In this case, the programmer's misconception was probably due to the fact that he or she expected the comparison field's value, used in the `ON CHANGE OF` statement, to be reset for every new function call. Instead, it simply ignored everything else that occurred and continued to compare an old value with a new value. For this reason, the use of the ON CHANGE OF statement is not appropriate within functions or subroutines. You cannot predict when the command is called exactly. There is no way to ensure that the ON CHANGE OF command is executed for each entry processed. This makes dependent results unpredictable.

Note that the ON CHANGE OF command is not allowed in an ABAP Objects context, that is, within a method implementation. You can avoid the complications in procedural ABAP by not using the ON CHANGE OF statement. In that case, you explicitly program the comparison yourself, using private data in a class. An example is given below:

```
FUNCTION /ctac/create_interface.
  DATA: lwa_interface TYPE ty_interface,
        ltp_matnr_old TYPE matnr.

* Table ts_invoices is filled first with invoice data
* for the customer.

* Routine to fill interface file format in internal table
  LOOP AT ts_invoices INTO wa_invoices.
    IF wa_invoices-matnr NE ltp_matnr_old.
      ltp_matnr_old = wa_invoices-matnr.

* Calculate total material available stock
  ..

    ENDIF.
*
  ..
  ENDLOOP.
ENDFUNCTION.
```

The LOOP AT <itab> statement

The second implicit control statement that causes confusion is the LOOP AT <itab> command, in particular, if it is combined with an AT FIRST, AT NEW, AT END, and AT LAST condition. We will show its effects in two examples to explain why such constructs should not be used.

Defining level breaks during internal table processing with a LOOP statement is simplified using AT events. Although the introduction of the ALV (based on the use of Enjoy controls or function modules) has limited its necessity, it can still be used, for example, for calculations:

```
REPORT /ctac/r_at_new_1_err.
TYPES: BEGIN OF ty_rec,
          bukrs TYPE bukrs,
          auart TYPE auart,
          aufnr TYPE aufnr,
          posnr TYPE co_posnr,
          wemng TYPE co_wemng,
          amein TYPE co_aufme,
          count TYPE i,
       END  OF ty_rec.

  DATA: ta_orders TYPE STANDARD TABLE OF ty_rec,
        wa_orders TYPE ty_rec.
..
  SORT ta_orders BY bukrs auart aufnr posnr.
  LOOP AT ta_orders INTO wa_orders.
    AT END OF auart.
      SUM.
      tp_average = wa_orders-wemng / wa_orders-count.
..
    ENDAT.
  ENDLOOP.
```

In this example, the timing of the calculation of the variable `tp_average` is correct. However, this would not be the case if the internal table `ta_orders` were sorted differently, for example:

```
  SORT ta_orders BY auart bukrs aufnr posnr.
  LOOP AT ta_orders INTO wa_orders.
    AT END OF auart.
      SUM.
      tp_average = wa_orders-wemng / wa_orders-count.
..
    ENDAT.
  ENDLOOP.
```

Consider the effects of the code if table `ta_orders` would have the following contents.

Company code (bukrs)	Sales document type (auart)	Order number (aufnr)	Order item number (posnr)	Quantity of goods received for the order item (wemng)	Unit of measure (amein)	Counter (count)	Expected	Actual
3000	RM01	701675	1	30,000	PC	1	No	No
3000	RM01	701676	1	40,000	PC	1	**No**	**Yes**
4000	RM01	702285	1	30,000	PC	1	Yes	Yes

Table 3.4 Unexpected Loop Behaviour of Internal Table ta_orders

Company code (bukrs)	Sales document type (auart)	Order number (aufnr)	Order item number (posnr)	Quantity of goods received for the order item (wemng)	Unit of measure (amein)	Counter (count)	Expected	Actual
1000	SD01	7000000	1	51,000	PC	1	Yes	Yes
3000	US02	902879	1	11,000	PC	1	No	No
3000	US02	903003	1	23,000	PC	1	Yes	Yes
3000	US03	S-3000-10	1	30,000	PC	1	Yes	Yes

Table 3.4 Unexpected Loop Behaviour of Internal Table ta_orders (Forts.)

Initially, you would expect the AT END OF auart event to depend on the sorting order of the auart field. According to this logic, the AT END OF auart event would occur at the end of the third row, that is, the last row in which the auart field is equal to RM01. Instead, the AT END OF auart event already occurs in the second row. This is caused by the value change of the bukrs field in the third table row. The AT END OF auart event must be interpreted as AT END OF auart or any of the preceding fields. It depends on the field sequence that is defined in the internal table.

This example emphasizes that processing internal tables using AT events should be allowed only if the sorting order is fixed. The optimal way to ensure that the sorting order is fixed is by using sorted tables, with a sorting order that is identical to the sequence of the sort fields in the table definition.

Now, let's look at a second example. The amounts calculated had to be interfaced to another system. The problem was that the amounts calculated were sometimes too high (as explained below). During the processing of selected data in an internal table, intermediate values were cleared for every sold-to partner (kunnr):

```
LOOP AT ta_customer_data  INTO wa_customer_data
            WHERE amount <> 0.

  AT NEW kunnr.
   CLEAR tp_amount.
  ENDAT.

ENDLOOP.
```

Now imagine what the code would do when the internal table ta_customer_data depicted in Table 3.5 would be filled as below. The AT NEW condition is skipped if the first occurrence of the kunnr field contains a value amount = 0. Because the condition is not always true, errors will seem to occur at random at first.

Customer number (kunnr)	Invoice number (vbeln)	Amount (amount)	AT NEW event executed?
10001	900000001	100.00	Yes
10001	900000006	200.00	No
10002	900000003	0	No
10002	900000009	300.00	No
10003	900000010	400.00	Yes

Table 3.5 Unexpected Behaviour of the AT NEW event for Internal Table ta_customer_data

The third entry of the internal table shown above will be skipped. It does not meet the WHERE condition (it contains an amount equal to 0). In the interim, the AT NEW condition—checking whether a new customer is encountered—will have been tested and found to be true anyway. As both the third and subsequent fourth entry contain the same customer number, the AT NEW condition for the fourth entry will *not* be considered true (the customer number did not change from the third to the fourth entry). Consequently, all statements to be triggered when the AT NEW condition is true are not executed for the fourth entry. In this case, the subtotal in tp_amount is not cleared, so you should be able to predict what happens. Instead of being initialized for customer 10003, tp_amount will keep the subtotal calculated for 10002 (that is, 300.00 in this case). The subtotal calculated for customer 10003 will be added on top of that. As a result, it will be too high.

In summary, for all kinds of LOOP processing, we recommend that you don't use AT FIRST, AT NEW, AT END, or AT LAST if you use the LOOP AT <itab> WHERE construction. In fact, the Extended Syntax Check will warn against it.

3.3.4   Misunderstandings About Interactive Reporting

In this section, we address those correctness issues that deal with interactive reporting. Interactive reporting is powerful, yet easy to implement. It enables the user to fetch detailed data about one item in an overview, start a new process for one or more selected items, or display the same overview in another format. Sometimes, interactive reporting techniques are even used for dialog functionality for programs that update database tables.

The obvious advantage of interactive programming is its integrated reporting functionality: printing, downloading, basic navigation, and look-up functionality are all available with minimal effort. The use of ABAP List Viewer (ALV) functions has further enhanced these possibilities: sorting, summing, suppressing fields, or interfacing with external applications have become standard options.

Possible errors affiliated with interactive reporting are caused by the implicit character of interactive statements such as HIDE, GET, CURSOR, or MODIFY LINE, and the effect they each have on global data. Another real concern is the misuse of interactive statements. Examples reflecting each of these scenarios are discussed in the following paragraphs.

The AT LINE-SELECTION command

It is common practice to use the **F2** key or double-click feature in the SAP system, for example, to display more details. By using the reporting event AT LINE-SELECTION, you can process this data with the values of a selected line. See if you can find a common error in the example below:

```
LOOP AT ta_data INTO wa_data.
  WRITE: / wa_data-field1,
           wa_data-field2.
  HIDE : wa_data-field1.
ENDLOOP.

AT LINE-SELECTION.
  CALL METHOD rf_object->more
    EXPORTING
      itp_value = wa_data-field1.
```

In this code, some CLEAR statements are missing. This code is an example of a misunderstanding about the use of data in memory (this issue is discussed in more detail in Section 3.4). The reason that clearing is easily forgotten in this particular case is that errors will occur only in an exceptional situation; for example, the situation in which the double-click function is executed when the cursor has not been positioned on a valid line. The value in the hide area is returned to the hidden field only if a line is selected with this hidden data. There is no explicit way of knowing—during the interactive event—whether this condition is met. If the user positions the cursor on a wrong line, the value of the wa_data-field1 field is not changed; it remains the same. The result is that the method is called with the wrong value. The seriousness of the problem depends on what the method called should do; if the method is called to perform a database update, it can cause serious damage.

Now, let's see if you agree with the following listing. The statements that were added are bolded.

```
LOOP AT ta_data INTO wa_data.
  WRITE: / wa_data-field1,
```

```
          wa_data-field2.
   HIDE : wa_data-field1.
  ENDLOOP.
  CLEAR wa_data-field1.

AT LINE-SELECTION.
  CALL METHOD rf_object->more
    EXPORTING
      itp_value = wa_data-field1.
  CLEAR wa_data-field1.
```

Note that it is assumed that the check to verify whether the field contains any data is executed within the method called. The `wa_data-field1` field remains empty if the user presses **F2** while the cursor is outside the user's vision. In our experience, we have encountered some variants of this solution, but most of these other solutions check the position of the cursor during double-clicking. We think the solution proposed here is simpler. Moreover, it works in all situations.

Using Interactive Programs for Dialog Functionality

Interactive programming statements are sometimes used for dialog functionality. Although this may appear to be a nice extension, it can produce some unwanted effects. Sometimes, we encounter customer developments that use the formatting option `INPUT` to receive user input. The input is then used to make changes to SAP tables via the `CALL TRANSACTION` functionality. To fully understand its consequences, in terms of the correctness of the data processed, it is necessary to clarify the difference between input in a regular (non-list) dynpro and input in a list screen. We have compared these two types of input in Figure 3.10.

Figure 3.10 summarizes what happens when a user enters data in a regular (non-list) dynpro field. The lower part of this figure shows what happens when list input fields are used. In a regular dynpro, the content of a dynpro field is automatically converted from an external presentation format to the correct internal format. For example, when a user enters "07/06/2004" for a date, this is automatically converted to SAP's internal date format "20040706". By simply using the `INPUT` format option in a list-dynpro, however, you cannot execute this conversion. Instead, you must program the conversion from scratch, including the exception handling. This affects not only the maintainability and stability of the program; it can also cause the wrong data to be processed if conversion routines are programmed improperly. A user might enter an amount in a format that was not considered. This could mean that an amount entered as "123.456" can be interpreted as either one hundred and twenty three plus three decimal places, or as a thousand times more.

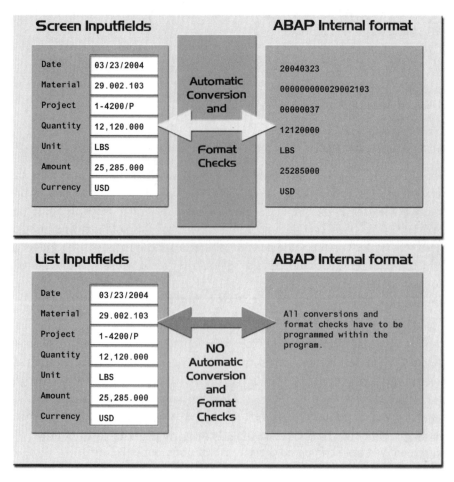

Figure 3.10 Differences in Output Formats

Another check that is not performed automatically in list dynpros (unlike in regular dynpros) is the value evaluation using foreign key relationships, which are checked automatically in dynpro screen fields only. In list dynpros, using the INPUT format, no value check is performed. This means that data that violates the defined foreign key relationships could end up in a database table anyway. Consequently, database inconsistencies can occur. An automatic value check on the basis of a foreign key relationship is executed, for example, when a material number is entered in a sales order item. The system then checks whether this material number actually exists in the materials database table (mara). However, when a material number is entered in a list dynpro because the INPUT statement is used, this value check is not executed. This could lead to the input of invalid data.

What have we learned from these two examples? How to utilize basic interactive possibilities, and the importance of testing robustness. A program should be full proof and *foolproof*. Testing what happens if the unexpected occurs is primarily the developer's responsibility.

3.4   Managing Data in Memory

In this section, we look at the global data concept of the traditional ABAP language. Apart from the many advantages of using globally defined data, several pitfalls are associated with using global data. Global variables are filled once and kept available during the entire session of programs such as reports, module pools, function groups, and subroutine pools. For the duration that a program is in use, its global variables are active or *alive*, during which, global data is not only *visible* for the program in which it is defined; it is also accessible. Externally-called procedures, such as function modules or external subroutines, have access to it.

Contrary to the concept of global variables is the concept of local variables. Local variables are defined within the context of a subroutine, a function module, or a method. They are *alive and visible* only during the procedure.

Many ABAP programmers use global data as often as possible. This is perfectly understandable. It is very practical to have program variables filled once and kept available wherever and whenever necessary. However, in various circumstances, this advantage can turn into a risk—using global data makes source code more prone to error, and if an error is encountered, it is often difficult to detect why the error occurred. This typically complicates maintenance of existing ABAP developments.

In fact, the basic shortcomings of global data in the traditional ABAP language (i.e., before the introduction of ABAP Objects) is its implicit availability. If you want to fill or initialize (refresh or clear) a global variable, you must always do so explicitly. Moreover, you have to time these tasks very accurately. However, initializations are easily forgotten. In the next sections, we'll show you some of the possible complications. We'll start with a straightforward example of global data within one report, then, follow up with more complicated examples, and end with why using ABAP Objects can help you to prevent this kind of problem in the future (see Section 3.4.7).

3.4.1   Availability of Data Within One Program

As we already mentioned, global data must be explicitly initialized. The ABAP programmer must explicitly CLEAR workareas and REFRESH internal tables, defined in the global data area of a program. The lifetime of global data—the time during which it is available for use—cannot really be influenced. Once a program or function pool is loaded into memory, its global data *implicitly* starts its lifetime. It remains active until the main program or session ends. A FREE statement will release the memory space occupied by global data, but it doesn't really end its life.

A programmer can only control the content of global data in two ways: to explicitly assign values to it, and to use the aforementioned commands CLEAR, REFRESH, or FREE. The most common problems are caused either by forgetting to initialize global data, or by timing the initialization incorrectly. Consequently, a program will inadvertently use the wrong values.

During the initial development of an ABAP program, clearing data is usually not difficult. Most issues tend to occur during maintenance, when the program structure is modified, new functions are added, or existing procedures are changed. By then, it is harder to recognize these problems, especially when there is a limited amount of time in which to perform tests.

Here's an example of how to use global data in loop processing (as in Figure 3.11) incorrectly.

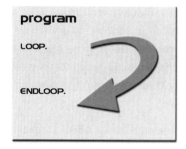

Figure 3.11 LOOP Processing

In the code programmed below, a material description must be selected for each material number processed during a loop. You will probably be familiar with the situation whereby a specific material description is repeated several times in a list, while the associated material numbers keep varying. If you look carefully at method get_material_description, in particular, it shouldn't be difficult to discern why this variation occurs:

```
CLASS lcl_application DEFINITION.
  PUBLIC SECTION.
    METHODS: get_material_description
               IMPORTING itp_matnr TYPE matnr
                         itp_spras TYPE spras
               EXPORTING etp_maktx TYPE maktx.
```

```
  PRIVATE SECTION.
    DATA:    tp_maktx TYPE maktx.
ENDCLASS.                        "lcl_application DEFINITION


CLASS lcl_application IMPLEMENTATION.
  METHOD get_material_description.
    SELECT SINGLE maktx
          FROM makt
          INTO tp_maktx
        WHERE matnr = itp_matnr
          AND spras = itp_spras.
    etp_maktx = tp_maktx.
  ENDMETHOD.                     "get_material_description
ENDCLASS.                        "lcl_application IMPLEMENTATION
```

Note that forgetting a CLEAR statement here will not necessarily lead to problems. In this case, the code will not cause problems if a material description in the logon language is available for each material processed. If, however, a material description is missing, the description of the material processed previously is used. The reason for this is that the corresponding workareas are not cleared. The implementation below is correct. Two alternatives are shown:

```
CLASS lcl_application IMPLEMENTATION.
  METHOD get_material_description.
    CLEAR tp_maktx.
    SELECT SINGLE maktx
          FROM makt
          INTO tp_maktx
        WHERE matnr = itp_matnr
          AND spras = itp_spras.
    etp_maktx = tp_maktx.
* Or
    IF sy-subrc = 0.
      etp_maktx = tp_maktx.
    ENDIF.
  ENDMETHOD.                     "get_material_description
ENDCLASS.                        "lcl_application IMPLEMENTATION
```

Yet another option would be to use a local variable. A local variable is initialized every time a subroutine, function or method is called.

```
CLASS lcl_application IMPLEMENTATION.
  METHOD get_material_description.
    DATA: ltp_maktx TYPE maktx.
    SELECT SINGLE maktx
           FROM makt
           INTO ltp_maktx
          WHERE matnr = itp_matnr
            AND spras = itp_spras.
    etp_maktx = ltp_maktx.
  ENDMETHOD.                        "get_material_description
ENDCLASS.                           "lcl_application IMPLEMENTATION
```

3.4.2   Availability When Calling an External Subroutine

In our second example, global data is used in a report that calls an external sub-routine from another report (see Figure 3.12).

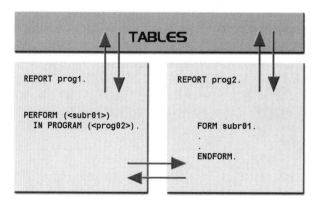

Figure 3.12 Calling an External Subroutine

Look at the SAPscript program /ctac/rvadin01 for printing invoices. From within program RSNAST00, an external routine in /ctac/rvadin01 is called to print each individual invoice. During initial testing, layout and output seemed correct. However, the amounts and values on the printouts increased with each invoice when a range of invoices was printed in the background. For really large ranges, the program sometimes even dumped with the runtime error compute_bcd_overflow, caused by the fact that a calculated total value has exceeded the maximum value for the field in which it must be temporarily stored.

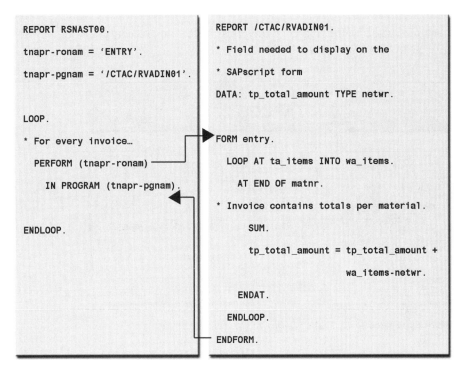

```
REPORT RSNAST00.                      REPORT /CTAC/RVADIN01.

tnapr-ronam = 'ENTRY'.                * Field needed to display on the

tnapr-pgnam = '/CTAC/RVADIN01'.       * SAPscript form

                                      DATA: tp_total_amount TYPE netwr.


LOOP.
                                      FORM entry.
* For every invoice...
                                          LOOP AT ta_items INTO wa_items.
    PERFORM (tnapr-ronam)
                                            AT END OF matnr.
      IN PROGRAM (tnapr-pgnam).
                                      * Invoice contains totals per material.

                                              SUM.

                                              tp_total_amount = tp_total_amount +

                                                              wa_items-netwr.

ENDLOOP.
                                            ENDAT.

                                          ENDLOOP.

                                      ENDFORM.
```

Figure 3.13 Example of Calling the Same External Subroutine Several Times

The problem is caused by global variable tp_total_amount in program /ctac/rvadin01. It is not refreshed as long as the main program RSNAST00 keeps running. Consequently, a new total value is added to tp_total_amount each time /ctac/rvadin01 is called for the next invoice. The error will not occur if it is tested in dialog for one invoice, however, it will occur if several invoices are printed all at once.

Of course, a problem like this should be spotted during testing, but, in practice, it is easily overlooked. The developer should have thought about the right moment for resetting values for tp_total_amount. In this case, resetting all global data should be one of the first actions taken in the program /ctac/rvadin01.

3.4.3 Shared Availability of Data (TABLES)

Here, we have another example of using global data for the wrong reason. In this case, a program calls an external subroutine from another program, while, concurrently, the two programs refer to the same table in the global data area (as shown in Figure 3.14). In an external subroutine call, the global data area of the calling program and the external subroutine called are fully separated. However, there is one exception to this rule: work areas, defined with the TABLES statement, are shared by the two programs. This can lead to problems that are very difficult to analyze and resolve.

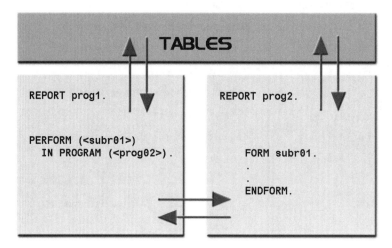

Figure 3.14 Shared TABLES When Calling an Internal Subroutine

In order to understand this scenario, let's look at the following example. It shows an excerpt from two programs. Program 1 selects data from a sold-to party for a sales order. After that, it also needs the country code of the ship-to party, which it finds by calling a subroutine of program 2.

The calling report (program 1):

```
REPORT  /ctac/r_cor_clear_ext1_err                           .
* This program calls a subroutine in the program below,
* using the same TABLES statement.
TABLES: vbpa.

CONSTANTS: co_partner_sold_to TYPE parvw VALUE 'AG'.

DATA     : tp_land1  TYPE land1.

PARAMETERS: pa_vbeln TYPE vbeln OBLIGATORY,
            pa_posnr TYPE posnr  .

START-OF-SELECTION.

  SELECT SINGLE * FROM vbpa
  WHERE vbeln = pa_vbeln
    AND posnr = pa_posnr
    AND parvw = co_partner_sold_to.
```

```
  WRITE: / vbpa-land1. "country of the sold-to

  PERFORM get_ship_to_country
          IN PROGRAM /ctac/r_cor_clear_ext2_err
          USING pa_vbeln
                pa_posnr
       CHANGING tp_land1.
* This VBPA-LAND1 now contains data that was read in the externally
* called routine. But what does the developer expect here?
  WRITE: / vbpa-land1.
```

The report that is called (program 2):

```
REPORT /ctac/r_cor_clear_ext2_err                        .
* This program contains a subroutine, called in another program.
* Both programs use the same TABLES statement.
TABLES: vbpa.

CONSTANTS: co_partner_ship_to TYPE parvw VALUE 'WE'.
* Routine to get country for the ship to partner
FORM get_ship_to_country
          USING value(itp_vbeln) TYPE vbeln
                value(itp_posnr) TYPE posnr
       CHANGING value(etp_land1) TYPE land1.

  SELECT SINGLE * FROM vbpa
  WHERE vbeln = itp_vbeln
    AND posnr = itp_posnr
    AND parvw = co_partner_ship_to.

  IF sy-subrc = 0.
    etp_land1 = vbpa-land1.
  ENDIF.

ENDFORM.                          "get_ship_to_country
```

As you can see, both programs reference table vbpa (customer data) in their global data. This will affect the result of the two WRITE statements that display the contents of the country code (vbpa-land1) in program 1. The first WRITE statement is done before, and the second WRITE statement is occurs after, calling subroutine get_ship_to_country from program 2.

Imagine what would transpire if the country code of the ship-to partner (found by program 2) differed from the country code of the sold-to party (found by program 1). It would have changed in the global data area of program 1 after executing the subroutine in program 2. As such, it isn't a problem, but what if the developer expects to continue using the country code of the sold-to party? *If this becomes a problem, finding the error may be like looking for a needle in a haystack. The* need to test this situation will not be apparent to everyone except perhaps to the developer. Therefore, the only way to avoid this hidden deficiency is by not using the `TABLES` statement in the global data area of an external subroutine. Working with explicit work areas is always preferable. Not using external subroutines is even better. In the context of ABAP Objects, the statement `TABLES` is not allowed. In the last paragraph of this section, we compare subroutines, functions, and methods in terms of their capabilities for memory use.

3.4.4 Availability of Data in Module Pools

Typically, during the development of module pools, ABAP developers encounter two types of problems regarding the use of global data. First, the exact moment when the value of screen variables becomes available will cause confusion. Another misunderstanding stems from the assumption that data, defined in a `MODULE` of a module pool, is local.

When Does Global Data Become Available?

To use global data properly in a module pool, timing is everything. Because of the interactive nature of module pools, you must know exactly how global variables are used in this type of ABAP program.

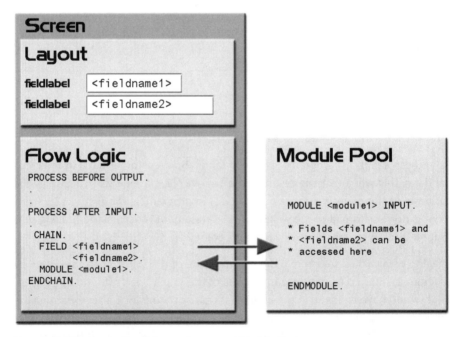

Figure 3.15 Communication Between Screen and Module Pool

You must use an identical name for both a screen variable and its associated global variable, which is used in further processing. However, this can make it seem as if just one variable actually exists, which is not the case. This becomes immediately apparent after a screen variable is filled. At that moment, its value is not yet available for processing. Therefore, the exact order of the statements used in the module pool is critical.

Look at the following example. On the screen below (Figure 3.16), a user enters an order number and order item. Some additional information must be displayed: the order type of the order header, the material number, and the material description of the order item.

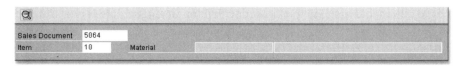

Figure 3.16 Screen Processing Sequence (1)

After pressing the **Enter** button, the output is displayed (see Figure 3.17).

Figure 3.17 Screen Processing Sequence (2)

As you can see, the order type is not yet visible on the screen. It is not displayed until the user presses **Enter** again (see Figure 3.18).

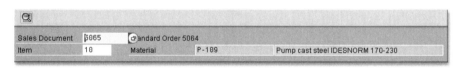

Figure 3.18 Screen Processing Sequence (3)

Now the user enters a new order number of another order type ("Rush Order"). He or she probably expects to see this change reflected after pressing **Enter**. What happens next is that the material number and its description change as expected, but the order type remains the same as before (see Figure 3.19).

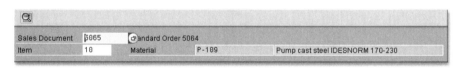

Figure 3.19 Screen Processing Sequence (4)

Again, the user must press **Enter** to display the correct order type (see Figure 3.20).

Figure 3.20 Screen Processing Sequence (5)

This strange behavior is caused by the screenflow below. We should mention that the global variable vbap-vbeln is used within module get_ordertype_9000 to select the order type. Note that the associated screen variable is also called vbap-vbeln.

```
PROCESS AFTER INPUT.

    MODULE get_ordertype_9000.
    CHAIN.
      FIELD: vbap-vbeln,
             vbap-posnr.
      MODULE get_material_9000 ON CHAIN-REQUEST.
    ENDCHAIN.
```

As predicted, the fact that the order type is lagging behind is caused by bad timing. The value of screen variable vbap-vbeln has not yet been passed on to global variable vbap-vbeln when module get_ordertype_9000 is called. That will not happen until module get_material_9000 is called. Then, variable vbap-vbeln occurs in a field statement for the first time, so that is when the screen variable and the global program variable are synchronized.

The next two pieces of code are therefore correct:

```
    CHAIN.
      FIELD: vbap-vbeln,
             vbap-posnr.
      MODULE get_ordertype_9000.
      MODULE get_material_9000 ON CHAIN-REQUEST.
    ENDCHAIN.
```

Or:

```
    FIELD vbap-vbeln MODULE get_ordertype_9000.
    CHAIN.
      FIELD: vbap-vbeln,
             vbap-posnr.
      MODULE get_material_9000 ON CHAIN-REQUEST.
    ENDCHAIN.
```

Note that if a screen variable is used, which does not occur in a module pool, it doesn't produce a syntax error. The extended syntax check, however, would display a warning.

Local Data Actually Being Global

The second thing to be aware of is which data is global and which data is local in traditional ABAP. Problems will sometimes occur if data, defined in a module pool, is assumed to be local.

```
MODULE user_command_9000 INPUT.

  DATA ltp_stop TYPE boolean.

...

  ENDMODULE.                    " USER_COMMAND_9000  INPUT
```

Although its place in the code and its name suggests otherwise, variable ltp_ stop is a global variable. It will be visible throughout the entire program, which means that its contents can be controlled everywhere, that is, the contents of this variable can be controlled from every place in the ABAP program, not only between the MODULE and ENDMODULE statements. It must therefore be managed globally. The screenflow (in Figure 3.21) does not do this.

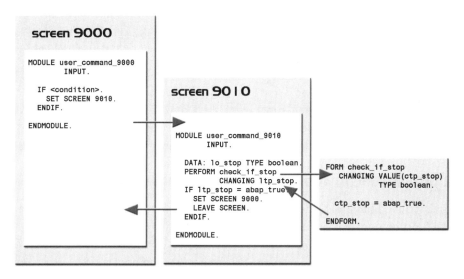

Figure 3.21 Processing the Screenflow

In this example, `ltp_stop` is set to the value of constant `abap_true` in routine `check_if_stop` in specific circumstances. In module `user_command_9010`, this results in leaving the screen and returning to a preceding dynpro. Now, if the user wants to navigate to screen 9010 again and the value in `ltp_stop` is still equal to `abap_true`, he or she will constantly be redirected to screen 9000 instead. In this case, the stop condition should have been defined in the top include of the module pool. Its contents should be cleared explicitly.

Now, we should make some general suggestions about the location of data definitions. Data that is not defined within a subroutine, method or function-module[3] is always global. Contrary to programming languages like Java, in ABAP code, it isn't important where you define the data. Because the data definition is static, there is no inherent difference between the following two pieces of code:

```
IF <condition>.
  DATA: tp_field TYPE i.
ENDIF.
```

And:

```
DATA: tp_field TYPE i.
IF <condition>.
ENDIF.
```

There is one exception to this rule—a data definition must be placed before it is referred to for the first time; otherwise, a syntax error will occur. In order to make ABAP source as readable as possible, you can best define all global data at the top of your program; for example, in a top include. You should define local data at the top of the procedure.

Another thing to keep in mind is that local and global data can have the same name. This can lead to interpretation errors when the wrong field is used. Therefore, we recommend that you consider this before you introduce naming conventions for data declarations. For more information on this maintainability topic, see Chapter 8.

3.4.5 Availability of Data Using Function Modules

Function modules are, by definition, part of a function pool. The global data area of a function pool is available for all functions defined in it, in much the same way as global data is generally available for external subroutines within a subroutine pool. As soon as the first function module from a function pool is called, the complete function pool is loaded into memory and stays there. Just as you did before, you must initialize its global data explicitly.

---

3 Actually, data defined at the events `AT SELECTION-SCREEN` and `AT SELECTION-SCREEN OUTPUT` is also local.

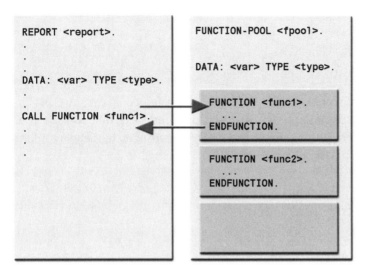

```
REPORT <report>.                FUNCTION-POOL <fpool>.
    .
    .
    .                           DATA: <var> TYPE <type>.
DATA: <var> TYPE <type>.
    .                           FUNCTION <func1>.
    .                               . . .
CALL FUNCTION <func1>.          ENDFUNCTION.
    .
    .                           FUNCTION <func2>.
    .                               . . .
                                ENDFUNCTION.
```

Figure 3.22 Calling Function Modules

Because of the similarity with subroutine pools, you should not be surprised that the same kind of problem is encountered with external subroutines as with function modules. Most issues will occur during initial development, but some issues always manage to slip through the cracks.

The listing below includes within it an example of what could go wrong. The report mentioned calls the same function within a loop construction.

```
REPORT /ctac/r_report.
...
LOOP AT ta_data INTO wa_data.
...
   CALL FUNCTION '/CTAC/_ABC_1'
     EXPORTING
       itp_parm = wa_data-value
     IMPORTING
       etp_parm = tp_value_new.
...
ENDLOOP.

FUNCTION-POOL /ctac/abcd.

DATA tp_value TYPE /ctac/t_dbtab.

...

FUNCTION /ctac/_abc_1.
...
   SELECT SINGLE * FROM /ctac/t_dbtab
```

```
        INTO tp_value
        WHERE value = itp_parm.
    etp_parm = tp_value.

ENDFUNCTION.
```

If no value is encountered in table /ctac/t_dbtab for variable tp_value, the contents of the SELECT statement that was previously executed will be used instead. The standard way to prevent this from occurring is by defining a local variable in the function module, as follows:

```
FUNCTION /ctac/_abc_1.
...
    DATA ltp_value TYPE /ctac/t_dbtab.
...
    SELECT SINGLE * FROM /ctac/t_dbtab
        INTO ltp_value
        WHERE value = itp_parm.
    etp_parm = ltp_value.

ENDFUNCTION.
```

In complex programs with a large call stack, this kind of problem is more likely to happen. A sequence of procedure calls as illustrated below in Figure 3.23 is very common, but far more complex situations will occasionally arise (e.g., a call stack of up to 30 levels deep). SAP R/3 functionality offers several examples, such as a complex price calculation in the Sales and Distribution module or the explosion of a large multilevel bill of materials in the Production Planning module.

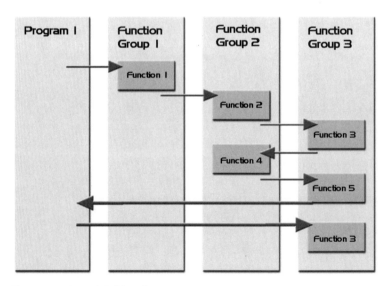

Figure 3.23 Several Call Levels

All ABAP developers who use existing function modules should check the function pool of which they are a part. In Figure 3.23, function modules 2 and 4, and function modules 3 and 5 share the same global data area. As we already explained, not initializing global data in the function modules can lead to serious problems. For that reason, many standard SAP function pools contain a separate function module that is dedicated specifically to clearing global data.

When developing a function module, you should avoid making it too complex. The problems described are less likely as long as you design a function module with a clear interface, and use local data definitions as much as possible.

Therefore, it is perhaps rather difficult to imagine the extensive use of global data in function pools. However, you will find several such examples in SAP R/3. Some function pools use global data intentionally in order to create an internal data buffer, for reuse by other functions of the same function pool. A typical example is function pool smsg. Its function module message_store is used to add a single message to an internal table defined in the global data area of the pool. Function module messages_show will display all messages stored in the internal table.

Although the global data areas of a calling program and a function pool are separated by a clear interface, there are still ways in which to exchange global data that are based on using field symbols. This technique[4] can also be used in external subroutine pools. SAPscript was even based on this technique. Although most of you may be tempted to try out these less known techniques, don't rely on them. Reserve using them only for those situations where all other options have been exhausted. Techniques like these may not be supported anymore in future versions of the ABAP language.

3.4.6 Parameter IDs

So far, we've discussed global data that has been defined as such in ABAP code and is used in a *program session*. We also want to briefly discuss a kind of global data at another level—the level of a *user session*. A parameter ID is an example of this kind of global data. It can be used to hold user-specific data. Sometimes, custom-made ABAP code (i.e., an ABAP program that was not developed by SAP) refers to parameter IDs as well. Parameter IDs can be very useful in interactive reporting. You can use a CALL TRANSACTION statement, for instance, to trigger a display transaction for one line in a list. There are other situations, however, where it is best to avoid using parameter IDs.

---

4 Refer to the online documentation of the dynamic assign statement. SAP describes that this option is for internal purposes only!

Sometimes, ABAP developers use the feature also in programs that use several consecutive and interrelated CALL TRANSACTION statements. In itself, this is a nice thought: a program calls several standard transactions in a row; one of these transactions needs some of the data that the previous transaction has produced. Hence, the program reads the value of the associated parameter IDs to get it.

Unfortunately, it's not that simple. As mentioned, the value of a parameter ID is reserved for a *user session*. Now, several *program sessions* can be started from within the same user session. These can also be program sessions that use the same program. Each of these individual program sessions can change the value of the same parameter ID. Therefore, one particular program session cannot ensure just what are the contents of a parameter ID. This value may not be correct. It may not even have a value. A program test will not likely reveal this deficiency either. Who would think of starting two program sessions of the same program in parallel with the same user?

Imagine, for example, a program that calls two transactions in a row. After the first call, it reads a parameter ID to get the value of an order number. The second transaction needs the order number as its input. Now, this program is started two times in parallel by the same user. This is when things will get mixed up: the first session sets the parameter id; then, the second session sets the same parameter ID, with a different order number. Next, both sessions enter the second transaction using the same order number, resulting in the loss of the first order number. Consequently, one of the transaction calls will be wrong.

In short, don't overuse parameter IDs. They may be appropriate for calling a single transaction from within an interactive list, but using them as a kind of temporary memory in extensive CALL TRANSACTION functionality is not appropriate. There are more optimal ways in which to reuse the results of a transaction call. You can, for instance, read the message table of the CALL TRANSACTION; use a user exit to export data to memory; or, better still, use a BAPI and read its export parameters.

3.4.7 Why ABAP Objects Will Improve Management of Data

We end this section with a short introduction of the memory concept used in ABAP Objects. Based on this concept, we will then explain why the introduction of ABAP Objects brings substantial advantages when compared with the pitfalls that can occur, which we previously addressed. First, we'll compare the memory concept of traditional ABAP programs with the memory concept of function pools. Then, we'll discuss the memory concept used with ABAP Objects.

The Memory Concept of Traditional ABAP Programs

The memory concept of traditional ABAP, shown in Figure 3.24 has two primary basic characteristics:

1. Programs like reports and subroutine pools have their own global data. Global data is implicitly defined as soon as a program is started. Only one *version* of global data is available in memory. This has two basic consequences for the complexity of the ABAP logic:

   ▶ Every time an external subroutine is called, the first thing the subroutine must always do is check and, if necessary, explicitly initialize global data. That is the only way to make a *clean* start if global data has been changed. Undoubtedly, this makes the code of a subroutine more complex.

   ▶ By initializing global data, previously available data is lost, unless additional coding is included to store it beforehand (for example, in an internal table). This is just another reason why the code will be more complex.

2. A program cannot have full control over its *own* global data:

   ▶ Other programs can change global data via shared TABLES statements.

   ▶ Other programs can change global data in other, not preferable ways, using field-symbols.

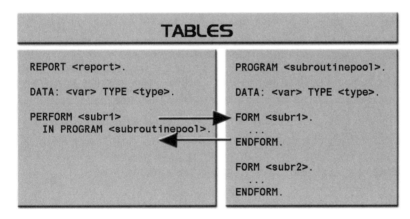

Figure 3.24 Calling External Subroutines

Function Pools

Now, let's see to what extent function pools have brought some relief. The basic advantages of function pools (see Figure 3.25) are twofold:

▶ Sharing global data with another program via the TABLES statement is impossible.

▶ Function modules have a well defined and clear interface.

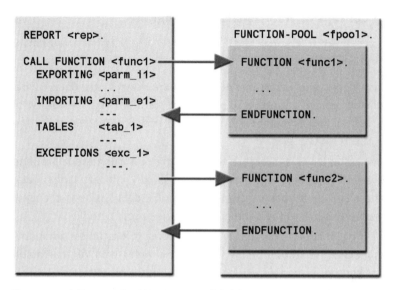

```
REPORT <rep>.                      FUNCTION-POOL <fpool>.

CALL FUNCTION <func1>              FUNCTION <func1>.
    EXPORTING <parm_i1>
          ...                          ...
    IMPORTING <parm_e1>
          ---                      ENDFUNCTION.
    TABLES    <tab_1>
          ---
    EXCEPTIONS <exc_1>
          ---.                     FUNCTION <func2>.

                                       ...

                                   ENDFUNCTION.
```

Figure 3.25 A Function Pool Has Its Own Global Data

Despite those two advantages, however, function pools still suffer from some of the basic drawbacks that we mentioned before:

▶ There are still not supported ways to exchange global data with other programs.

▶ Functions from the same function pool still share one version of the same global data. Consequently:

  ▷ Extensive coding is still required to check and explicitly initialize global data; other functions from the same pool will still use the same global data.

  ▷ Separate solutions are necessary to prevent the loss of data that has to be initialized; this will also make code more complex.

Classes, Methods, and Instances in ABAP Objects

We will now compare the memory concept of ABAP Objects (see Figure 3.26) with the two aforementioned memory concepts. ABAP Objects use terms like *class, instance,* and *method.* To ensure that a basic understanding exists, you can compare the level of definition of a class (pool) with that of a function pool or subroutine pool. Similarly, you can compare a method in a class with a particular function or subroutine in a pool.

Unlike the concept of a class or a method, the concept of an instance cannot be compared with existing concepts. Using instances will prove very beneficial for memory use. Before methods can be called and attributes used (with the exception of *static* methods and attributes), you must create an instance (object reference) of the class.[5] To do so, you have to use the CREATE OBJECT statement. Each instance will have its own data area. Consequently, the method call won't have to determine whether data is already available. Note what direct benefits this brings, when compared with function modules and external subroutines:

▶ Contrary to function modules or external subroutines, extensive checks and initializations of data aren't required. Data of an instance is, by definition, initialized when the instance is created.

▶ You don't have to include additional logic in order to keep existing global data available (alive). Other instances with their own data are still available.

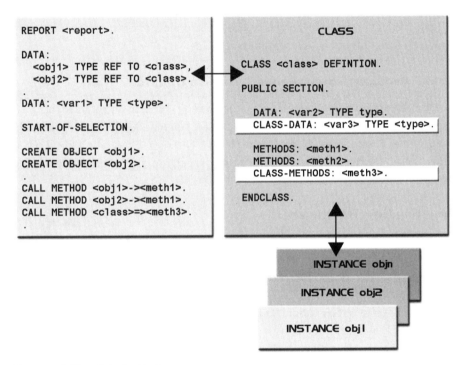

Figure 3.26 Class Data And Instances

Another big advantage of ABAP Objects is that the accessibility of attributes of a class is entirely under the control of the class itself. Data is explicitly defined as either *public* (visible for functionality outside the class), *protected* (visible for all functionality within the class and its subclasses), or *private* (visible for functionality only within the class). In other words, contrary to traditional ABAP, with ABAP Objects, the visibility of data for other functionality is explicitly defined.

---

5 As described in Chapter 1, static methods and attributes are not part of an instance of a class. This means that the CREATE OBJECT statement does not initialize static attributes.

3.5　Inconsistencies in Database Updates

A program error that leads to wrong database updates tends to cause more stress than, for example, a program error that causes wrong list output. This is mainly because it's difficult to spot all possible update errors. Detecting to what extent an affected database is actually corrupt is hard enough at the outset. Not only can a database table have the wrong contents; database rows can even be missing. Sometimes, the errors found can only be corrected using additional repair programs.

In this section, we discuss how to prevent erroneous database updates. Two main topics are addressed: how to prevent a specific row in a database table from being updated simultaneously by several processes; and, how to ensure the consistency between the contents of several database tables.

3.5.1　Avoiding Simultaneous Database Updates

Most programmers are familiar with the locking concept introduced by SAP, based on lock objects and function modules. In general, this type of logical locking is preferable to locking on database level.[6] Now, we'll describe typical problems caused by not implementing—or not properly implementing—the locking concept, and how to avoid them.

Inserting New Table Rows

Inserting a new row in a database table means that a new and unique key value must be created at run time. Below, you'll see an example that demonstrates how this should *not* be done. The test case is based on the flight-reservation system used frequently in SAP material. This particular case shows the addition of new bookings in table sbook. Adding a booking is done in two steps. First, a method is executed that checks free seats and looks for a new booking ID. Then, a second method executes the actual update of table sbook. It uses the booking ID found by the first method. Now, the code below simulates the scenario whereby two customer bookings are added at almost the same moment. Pay special attention to the order of the four method calls involved:

```
* Create two separate travel agencies
      CREATE OBJECT: rf_trv_1 EXPORTING itp_agencynum = pa_trv_1,
                     rf_trv_2 EXPORTING itp_agencynum = pa_trv_2.

* The first travel agency checks for free seats and receives a booking id
      CALL METHOD rf_trv_1->get_free_seats
        EXPORTING
```

---

6 For this purpose, the statement SELECT SINGLE * FOR UPDATE is used.

```
        itp_carrid    = pa_carr
        itp_connid    = pa_conn
        itp_fldate    = pa_date
     IMPORTING
        etp_seatsfree = rf_trv_1->seatsfree
        etp_bookid    = rf_trv_1->bookid.
```

* The second travel agency checks for free seats and receives a booking id

```
     CALL METHOD rf_trv_2->get_free_seats
        EXPORTING
           itp_carrid    = pa_carr
           itp_connid    = pa_conn
           itp_fldate    = pa_date
        IMPORTING
           etp_seatsfree = rf_trv_2->seatsfree
           etp_bookid    = rf_trv_2->bookid.
```

* The first travel agency books the flight

```
     CALL METHOD rf_trv_1->book_flight
        EXPORTING
           itp_carrid = pa_carr
           itp_connid = pa_conn
           itp_fldate = pa_date
           itp_bookid = rf_trv_1->bookid.
```

* The second travel agency books the flight

```
     CALL METHOD rf_trv_2->book_flight
        EXPORTING
           itp_carrid = pa_carr
           itp_connid = pa_conn
           itp_fldate = pa_date
           itp_bookid = rf_trv_2->bookid.
```

In addition, focus on the functionality below. This function determines a new booking ID. To get the next booking ID, it fetches the last ID used in database table sbook and simply adds 1 on top.

```
* Get next free booking id
SELECT MAX( bookid ) FROM sbook
          INTO etp_bookid.
etp_bookid = etp_bookid + 1.
```

An experienced ABAP developer will immediately spot the flaw in the example. Table 3.6 shows the order in which each of the four steps mentioned are executed. The request for the second booking ID starts before the update of the first booking ends. Consequently, the booking ID returned by method get_free_ seats for the second request is identical to the one provided for the first request

(N + 1). After the booking ID for both requests is established, the database inserts for both bookings are done. The first insert in table `sbook` will be successful. But the second insert will fail, because it attempts to use the same booking ID.

Booking 1	Booking 2	Booking ID
Step 1: Check free seats and get booking ID		N + 1
	Step 1: Check free seats and get booking ID	N + 1
Step 2: Insert new booking		
	Step 2: Insert new booking	

Table 3.6 Incorrect Locking

As this example illustrates, the code does not ensure correct updates on table `sbook`. After method `get_free_seats` is called for a specific booking, but *before* method `book_flight` is called, one or more other bookings can get the same booking ID. If that happens, all the associated inserts in table `sbook` will fail, because by that time, an entry with the same booking ID will already exist. But, wait ... it can get even worse! If no proper error handling is implemented, the problem won't even be visible. If we continue with our scenario, the error may not be discovered until the customer ordering the second booking asks for more information.

Fortunately, there is a straightforward solution. It involves the use of SAP's standard number range functionality. This requires the creation of a new number range to identify the bookings in table `sbook` and to call standard function `number_get_next` in each request for a new booking ID. This function ensures that a unique number is created for every request. Contrary to the aforementioned piece of code, it will update (and commit) each new number in the database *before* returning it to the calling program, and in that way, each generated number is returned only once.

Using Lock Objects When Changing Existing Data

Straightforward examples of the implementation of the locking mechanism are available throughout the entire SAP software. During the time that, for instance, a material is changed by an end user session in the SAP R/3 system (using Transaction MM02), the locking mechanism will prevent other sessions from entering the same change transaction for the same material.

In practice, however, using the locking mechanism is not always intuitive. Whether an ABAP program has to run in the foreground or in the background seems to make a difference. Implementing the locking mechanism in online transactions is usually done properly; however, when developing background programs, it is easy to overlook. Somehow, in this context, it seems less intuitive, considering the number of times this happens. Sometimes, even more than one custom-made program is allowed to perform updates on the same database table without locking.[7] The following example shows some of the results that can occur because of this error.

The following program was executed in the background. It uses the contents of a customized table called /ctac/tbk01 to trigger the creation of standard SAP documents. After a document is created successfully, the status of the original entry in /ctac/tbk01 is changed to "processed". The program is scheduled initially to run in one background process. To optimize performance, however, a second background job is scheduled in parallel. It uses exactly the same input parameters:

```
SELECT * FROM /ctac/tbk01 INTO TABLE ta_bk01
            WHERE status = co_to_be_processed.

LOOP AT ta_bk01 INTO wa_bk01.
* Now a function call is executed that will create the document
    CALL FUNCTION '/CTAC/CREATE_DOCUMENT'
      EXPORTING
        ist_bk01       = wa_bk01
      IMPORTING
        est_bapireturn = st_bapireturn
        etp_vbeln      = tp_vbeln.
* Process the result: change status and add document number
    IF st_bapireturn-type = co_success.
      wa_bk01-status = co_processed.
      wa_bk01-vbeln  = tp_vbeln.
    ELSE.
      wa_bk01-status = co_error.
    ENDIF.
* Change the internal table
    MODIFY ta_bk01 FROM wa_bk01.
  ENDLOOP.
* Change the database
  UPDATE /ctac/tbk01 FROM TABLE ta_bk01.
  IF sy-subrc NE 0.
* Error handling here
  ENDIF.
```

---

7 Designing different programs that update the same table is also questionable, but that is not the issue here.

Now, if two background processes execute this code in parallel, too many documents will be created. Table 3.7 illustrates why. The code does not lock the entries selected from table /ctac/tbk01. Therefore, the second run (on the right) will be able to select the same entries as the first run. While program run 1 is processing the data (in Step 2), and *before* it updates the status of the selected entries (in Step 3), program run 2 is selecting the entries a second time (in Step 1).

Program run 1	Program run 2
Step 1. Select the data to be processed from /ctac/tbk01	
Step 2. Start creating the documents	Step 1. Select the data to be processed from /ctac/tbk01
Step 3. Update the status of the selected entries in /ctac/tbk01	Step 2. Start creating the documents
	Step 3. Update the status of the selected entries in /ctac/tbk01

Table 3.7 Incorrect Locking

There are various ways to avoid this, but they all come down to using the SAP locking mechanism. A lock must be set for all entries to be processed immediately after selecting them (in Step 1). The lock can be removed again after the update (in Step 3). If simultaneous execution of a program is not allowed, it is even possible to lock the program itself.

Let's suppose that, in this particular example, parallel processing is actually necessary. In addition to applying the locking mechanism, part of the solution could then include adding a SELECT-OPTION for the key field of table /ctac/tbk01. Based on that, every program run could select its own series of table rows. This would make it less likely that table rows of another program run would be used. The selection logic should then be adjusted accordingly (field /ctac/tbk01-seqnr is supposed to be the key field of table /ctac/tbk01):

```
SELECT * FROM /ctac/tbk01 INTO TABLE ta_bk01
         WHERE status = co_to_be_processed
         AND seqnr  IN so_seqnr.
```

A more advanced technique using parallel processing is described in Chapter 7. Now, let's more fully define SAP's locking concept.

Implementing Lock Objects

When implementing a lock object, you should be able to answer the following questions:

▶ When is the lock set?

▶ What lock mode is used?

▶ When is the lock released?

Each of these points will be discussed below.

Let's address the first question: *When* is the lock set? If the timing of setting a lock is not correct, other processes will have the opportunity to enter the *data* before it is locked. Setting a lock just before the SAVE command, for example, does not help. The following can happen:

1. User 1 starts the transaction including the locking functionality to change data.

2. User 2 starts the same transaction to change the same data.

3. User 1 decides to save the first version of the data: a lock is set, the data is saved, and the lock is released.

4. User 2 decides to save the second version of the same data: a lock is set, the data is saved, and the lock is released.

In this way, the updates made by user 1 are immediately overwritten by the changes of user 2.

What should happen instead is the following sequence:

1. User 1 starts a transaction to change data. The transaction sets a lock immediately.

2. User 2 starts the same transaction to change the same data. The transaction will attempt to set a lock, but this fails. User 2 gets a corresponding message ("Data locked by another user" or something similar to that). He or she will not be able to change the data.

As you can deduce, your basic strategy should be to set a logical lock as early as possible—as soon as the data to be locked is identified.

The next thing to consider is the *type of lock* that you need to set. When calling the function to set a lock object, a lock mode must be indicated. Two basic types of locks are possible: an exclusive lock, or a shared lock. As the term implies, an *exclusive lock* reserves data for one program session at a time. Hereafter, every other program will be denied access to the data. An exclusive lock is best suited for update functionality. In most cases, you won't have difficulties in understanding its impact.

The exact nature of a *shared lock* is harder to explain. You should use a shared lock when multiple read accesses to data are allowed, but a combination of read and change access is not allowed. We don't expect you to understand fully what that means at this point. Let's just use some additional examples.

All the examples consider the combination of display and change functionality for the same data. Also, in all examples, the update functionality will set an exclusive lock. The only variation we have introduced is caused by the choice made for the display transaction. The first option is to not set a lock. The second option is to set a shared lock.

In the basic scenario, the display transaction does not set a lock. The change transaction sets an exclusive lock. The following would typically happen:

1. User 1 starts the display transaction to look at data.
2. User 2 starts the change transaction for changing the same data. The change transaction sets an exclusive lock successfully.
3. User 2 changes the data and saves it.
4. If, meanwhile, user 1 hasn't left the display transaction, the data that is being displayed will be outdated.

Although the aforementioned scenario is fine for most display transactions, let's assume that you're still not satisfied with it. You may want the data that is to be displayed to be always current. In that case, you can make the display functionality set a shared lock. It will, in particular, change the interaction between display and change functionality:

1. User 1 starts the display transaction to look at the data. The display transaction sets a shared lock for the data.
2. User 2 starts the change transaction for the same data. The change transaction attempts to set an exclusive lock, however, this fails because of the shared lock. The user gets a corresponding message and is denied access.
3. User 3 starts the display transaction for the same data. A shared lock is set successfully. The user is given access. User 3 and user 1 are simultaneously looking at the same data.

However, the shared lock works both ways. The change transaction can also be the first to access the data:

1. User 1 starts the change transaction. The change transaction sets an exclusive lock on the selected data.
2. User 2 starts the display transaction for the same data. Now, the display transaction cannot set a shared lock because of the exclusive lock. The user gets a corresponding message and is denied access.

As you can see, the shared lock behaves fairly strictly. Because of this, it is not often used. As mentioned, the exclusive lock will cause less difficulty. We recommend that you apply it in all ABAP programs performing database updates.

The last question you should ask yourself is: When should a lock be *released*? A lock should not be released too soon, as releasing it before data has been updated is not recommended for obvious reasons. Basic update problems can still occur. In general, a lock should remain intact until an update is committed to the database.

A lock is set using an enqueue function module. It can be released again with a dequeue function. Both functions are generated when you create the lock object. Generally, you won't need to use the dequeue function. If you've designed your program to process updates directly in the dialog process, the lock will be released automatically when the program ends. However, if you want the database update to be performed in the update task (Figure 3.27), the lock should not be released before the database update is finalized. You can automatically transfer a lock from the dialog task to the update task. To do so, set the _SCOPE parameter of the enqueue function module accordingly.

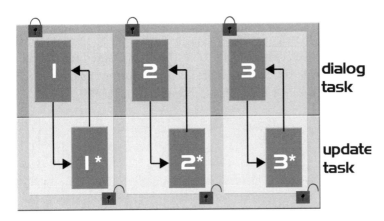

Figure 3.27 Set Lock and Release Lock

Sometimes, you will need to explicitly release a lock (with the dequeue function). Typically, that's the case if you want to release a lock earlier than the program ends. Consider, for example, a program that produces a list, from which the user is allowed to select one line at a time and update the corresponding data. If one specific lock must be released, use generated function dequeue_<lockobject>. If all locks must be released, use generic function dequeue_all. This last option is appropriate, for example, when a transaction switches from change to display mode without leaving the program session.

3.5.2 Keeping Updates of Several Tables Consistent

There are many situations in which SAP customers are satisfied with standard SAP functionality, but want some additional functionality. One of those requirements could be that you want to update customer data along with the data available in the standard software. We'll show you an example of how to integrate a customized update with standard SAP update functionality. We'll focus primarily on the correct definition of a *Logical Unit of Work* (LUW), which is fundamental for the design of update functionality. Basic knowledge of update techniques is assumed.

An Example of a Customized Update

A part of the SAP software where standard and customer-specific functionality are combined often is the Sales and Distribution (SD) module. Therefore, let's use a sales order update as our starting point. Now, we'll add to this a customized update. For this purpose, an SAP customer chose to create a new database table (of course, other solutions such as using append structures to add fields to SAP database tables would perhaps be more appropriate, however, this choice is frequently made).

The relationship between the standard SAP data (order header and order items) and the customer data is depicted in Figure 3.28. The table created for the customer data has a one-to-one relationship with the order header table. For each sales order, there should be one entry in the customer table as well.

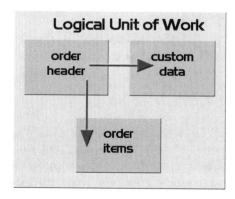

Figure 3.28 One Logical Unit of Work

You must adhere to this one-to-one relationship very strictly. Perhaps not every change, but, at least every creation and deletion of a standard sales order should be accompanied by a corresponding creation or deletion of one row in the customer table.

But, what if this principle is violated? Suppose, for example, that entries in the customer table are inserted or deleted, but the other two tables aren't? To start with, other functionality using the customer table would be inconsistent. It could, for example, reference sales documents that don't exist in the SAP database. Analyzing the errors and removing invalid entries from the custom table would not be easy. This kind of inconsistency does not normally attract attention until errors turn up elsewhere. By that time, the number of erroneous updates may be piling up.

So, it's all or nothing. An update on one of several interrelated tables can be accepted only if the updates to all the other tables are also accepted. In this case, order header, all order items, and the customer data should all be accepted, or all be rejected. If, for instance, the insert of a specific order item fails, then associated insertions of other order items, the order header, or the customer data should all be rejected. To keep updates consistent in accordance with this principle, you must make them part of the same LUW. Related updates form part of the same LUW. Each LUW starts and ends with an implicit or explicit commit or rollback.

The Obvious and Easy Solution

The obvious way to combine an update of customer data with the update of standard sales order data is to implement it in a user exit. Most ABAP developers can figure that out for themselves. In this case, two user exits are available in sales order maintenance, in include mv45afzz (forms userexit_save_document_prepare and userexit_save_document).

The next step is more critical. Unfortunately, not all ABAP developers will immediately understand the impact of the following Open SQL statements if implemented in the user exit userexit_save_document:

```
MOVE-CORRESPONDING vbak TO zt_salesorder_ext.
MODIFY zt_salesorder_ext FROM wa_salesorder_ext.
IF sy-subrc NE 0.
  MESSAGE E100.
ENDIF.
```

This solution is not full proof for those extreme situations whereby a standard sales document cannot be created, which would happen if the update task process fails. In the interim, the customer table would be updated anyway, which would result in an inconsistency between the SAP order data and the customer table. For additional clarification, we'll briefly review SAP's LUW concept.

The Logical Unit of Work (LUW) Concept

As mentioned, the LUW concept means that a group of related data is either updated entirely, or not at all. The LUW concept in ABAP supports this principle. All database modifications, executed between a commit or rollback in one internal session, are part of the same LUW. A new internal or external session is started by either a SUBMIT, CALL TRANSACTION, or CALL FUNCTION STARTING NEW TASK statement. Updates within these procedures start their own LUW. Table 3.8 provides a summary.

Calling Mechanism Used	New LUW	Same LUW
Submit	X	
Batch Input Map	X	
Call Transaction	X	
Call Function starting new task	X	
Call Function in update task[1]	X	
Subroutine		X
External Subroutine		X
Call Dialog		X
Call Function (incl. BAPI)		X
Call Method		X

Table 3.8 Relation Type of Call and Logical Unit of Work

1. Using the CALL FUNCTION IN UPDATE TASK implies creating a new LUW once. All CALL FUNCTION IN UPDATE TASK statements between two explicit COMMIT WORK or ROLLBACK WORK statements form one LUW.

In particular, the asynchronous UPDATE technique warrants your attention. This technique assumes that an update function is called with the IN UPDATE TASK addition. An explicit COMMIT WORK statement is necessary to trigger the actual execution of all UPDATE TASK functions that were called since the last synchronization point.

Ignoring the LUW Concept

Let's now return to our example. The UPDATE TASK failed, with corresponding inconsistencies as a result. They were caused by the implementation of the update on the customer table in the mv45afzz include. The following sequence of actions caused the problem:

1. Standard SAP: `CALL FUNCTION <update order header> IN UPDATE TASK`

2. Standard SAP: `CALL FUNCTION <update order item> IN UPDATE TASK`

3. User exit: `UPDATE <customer table>`

4. Standard SAP: `COMMIT WORK`

   ▶ The update on `<customer table>` is committed.

   ▶ The update process is triggered to execute the first two `UPDATE TASK` functions for the standard SAP data (in one LUW).

All updates up to and including Step 3 (above) are triggered by the same `COMMIT WORK` in Step 4. That doesn't mean, however, that all three updates are actually part of the same LUW. The update of the customer table in Step 3 forms its own LUW. It will be committed anyway, regardless of whether the other updates succeed. Therefore, if an error in the `UPDATE TASK` of the standard SAP updates occurs, it will not lead to a rollback of the update of the customer table.

Including a Customer Update into an Existing LUW

This problem can be avoided. The update of customer data can be handled jointly with the update of the two standard SAP tables. In order to achieve that, you must create an `UPDATE` function that modifies the custom table. That function must be called in the user exit. The addition `IN UPDATE TASK` ensures that just one update task is created for all three consecutive functions. Note, however, that all three functions must be called in the same program session before the `COMMIT WORK`:

1. Standard SAP: `CALL FUNCTION <update order header> IN UPDATE TASK`

2. Standard SAP: `CALL FUNCTION <update order item> IN UPDATE TASK`

3. User-exit: `CALL FUNCTION <update customer table> IN UPDATE TASK`

4. Standard SAP: `COMMIT WORK`

   ▶ Update on `<customer table>` is committed.

   ▶ Triggering the update process to execute the two `UPDATE TASK` functions within one logical unit.

This ends the section on combined updates of standard data and customer data. Remember that other and better alternatives exist for the scenario that was described. Alternatively, customized fields can be added to the standard SAP order header table with an append structure. In that case, the update of the customer data is handled as part of standard SAP functionality.

3.6 Checking the Unicity of Interface Data

Typically, SAP applications are not implemented as complete standalone solutions. Many enterprises have implemented other software systems, custom-made or standard, from SAP or others, ranging from a few systems to over a hundred. Obviously, in such circumstances, some form of data exchange between applications is required. There is little point in addressing all kinds of issues related to interfacing, but we do want to focus on one issue in particular. It isn't related to company size or the number of interfaces; and, its importance doesn't change by using modern SAP technology like BAPI and IDoc functionality. It does not primarily focus on wrong or incorrect ABAP code, but rather on a basic principle for interfacing—to prevent the same data from being processed more than once.

3.6.1 An Example of Incorrect Data Exchange

Imagine the following case: periodically, an interface file containing financial data from a salary system is processed. Based on this, corresponding general ledger postings are created in an SAP R/3 system. Somehow, the same data was processed twice. All resulting general ledger postings had to be corrected manually. You might not be surprised to know what caused this to happen. The data that was interfaced could not be identified uniquely. Neither the file nor the individual postings in the file carried a unique identifier. Therefore, the same file could have been processed even more than twice. As a matter of fact, any file containing data in the expected format would have been processed.

This example shows what to do in order to prevent this kind of situation from happening. Data to be interfaced should always carry a unique identifier. This identifier should exist on one of the two levels mentioned, at least on file level, but also, if possible, on the level of the individual transaction. In addition to that, you will require checking mechanisms on both sides of the interface, that is, in both the sending and receiving system.

3.6.2 Quality Levels for Exchanging Data

In order to exchange data between different systems, SAP distinguishes three quality levels; for example, in the SAP Exchange Infrastructure (SAP XI) component supporting the exchange of data between SAP and other software products:

▶ Best Effort
▶ Exactly Once
▶ Exactly Once In Order

These three quality levels are briefly explained below.

Best Effort

The *Best Effort* quality level refers to a situation in which the data being processed is not unique. Because you cannot check whether this data has already been processed, this quality level introduces a considerable risk. Therefore, you should avoid implementing interfaces of this quality level for purposes other than one-time data uploads (conversions). In all other scenarios, the risk of processing data twice is just too high. The salary interface in the example in Section 3.6.1 was of this lowest quality level, whereas it should have been handled as the *Exactly Once* scenario, which is described below.

Exactly Once

The second level is the *Exactly Once* quality level, which means that a unique identifier is defined on the level of the individual message to be exchanged (i.e., each individual posting in the example). Checking mechanisms in the sending system use the identifier to ensure that the same data (i.e., two messages with the same identifier) is not sent twice. Checking mechanisms in the receiving system use the identifier to prevent the same data from being processed twice. This quality level may be appropriate in many situations.

Exactly Once in Order

The highest quality level is the *Exactly Once in Order* level. It is comparable with the *Exactly Once* scenario, but the additional *in Order* qualification on top means that individual interface messages should also be processed in a certain order. This order should be considered by the checking mechanisms on both sides of the interface.

Imagine, for example, a scenario in which both goods movement messages and stock level messages are received by an inventory management system. This scenario is shown in Figure 3.29. The system has to use both types of messages to update its stock levels. Note that a goods movement represents a *change* in a material stock level, whereas a stock level message represents a *status* at a specific moment in time.

Processing a status message in a receiving system makes sense only if the system can ensure that all preceding changes have been processed. Once a periodical stock level message is received, the inventory management system must first compare it with the corresponding stock level in its own database, calculate the difference, and correct the stock level accordingly. Such a scenario is only feasible if the receiving inventory management system can guarantee that *all* goods movements preceding the stock level message were received and processed. This is only possible if the order of all messages is absolutely and completely controlled.

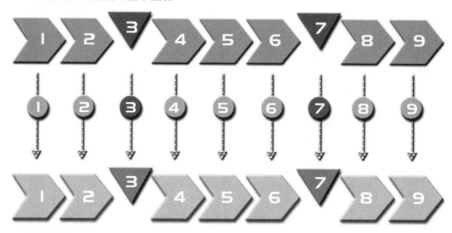

SENDING SYSTEM

RECEIVING SYSTEM

Figure 3.29 Exactly Once in Order

How to Use the Unique Identifier

The checking mechanisms mentioned need to access unique identifiers that have already been processed. When processing a new document, the program you made should be able to establish whether the unique identifier of this new document had been used before. In the case of an inbound scenario (i.e., from outside an SAP system into an SAP system), this means checking whether a specific identifier value already exists in the database of the receiving SAP system. In terms of the initial example, the interface program processing a salary posting must able to verify if the identifier of an individual posting is already there in a general ledger posting. These IDs can also be used for tracking purposes; for example, for tracing back a file that is used for certain entries. This is also necessary to restore backups. You need to be able to see, at any point in time, which files have been processed and which ones have not.

3.6.3 Implementing Data Exchange Scenarios

It is worth pointing out some additional implementation details for the *Exactly Once* and *Exactly Once in Order* scenarios. Adequately identifying the data to be interfaced is not enough. You also must prevent data from being processed more than once, which could happen either on the sending system, or on the receiving system, or in between both ends of an interface. This principle is familiar to the locking mechanism discussed in a previous section (see Section 3.5.1).

Processing Data Twice

The first pitfall is that the system at either the sending or the receiving end of an interface processes the same data more than once. This can best be illustrated with an example. Imagine a program in a receiving system that is responsible for processing an input file. It is part of a job that is triggered every minute. If an exceptionally large file is processed, the program session might still be running after a minute, when the next program session starts. This situation is depicted in Table 3.9. The second program session will process the same file (*File 1*) again, unless, of course, you take the appropriate measures to prevent this from occurring.

Time (hh:mm:ss)	Program Session 1	Program Session 2	Input File Processed
00:00:00	Start session 1		File 1
00:01:00		Start session 2	File 1
00:01:15	End session 1		
00:02:16		End session 2	

Table 3.9 Processing Data Twice

The first thing you can do is to extend the time interval in-between two jobs, but that is not the full- proof implementation that you should be looking for. Instead, we recommend that you use a proper locking mechanism, in much the same way as discussed in Section 3.5.1. Note that such a locking mechanism should be applied in *all* individual systems involved that use some kind of buffering of interface data before actually processing it.

Simultaneous Access of the Same Data by Two Systems

The second thing to consider is the possibility that the sending and receiving systems at both ends of an interface access the same interface file simultaneously. Think of the situation where the sender is still updating the file to be processed, when the receiver has already started to process the file. Technically speaking, this is possible. To exclude this possibility as much as possible, you can implement some kind of locking mechanism yourself (see Figure 3.27). Think of either renaming the file or moving it to a directory *in process* before the receiving program is allowed to actually start processing. Immediately after processing, you should move the file to a directory with *processed* files (or simply delete the file). Note, however, that this may not be 100% full proof.

The Availability of Standard Functionality

Make sure that you always consider the two aforementioned pitfalls. The extent to which you must implement them yourself depends on the available middleware for data exchange. SAP XI, for example, supports most interfacing checks mentioned, but whether you actually use those options is up to you. If you use middleware like the SAP Business Connector, you should develop part of the checking mechanisms separately.

4 Stability

Stability is the degree to which an ABAP program behaves predictably from a strictly technical point of view. Perhaps, it is best explained by highlighting its very opposite, namely, *unstable* behavior. An unstable ABAP program either stops by itself, or must be stopped by the system administrator when the program's behavior causes problems in other parts of the SAP system. In such instances, the *patient* (i.e., the program) usually presents one of the various symptoms that can appear such as program dumps, technical error messages, endless loops, or the blocking of system resources. Sometimes, a program doesn't even respond. Unstable program behavior typically reveals itself suddenly, without warning, long after a program has been used in production, without showing any prior signs of a defect or deficiency.

4.1 Stability Problems

The first cause of stability errors is *wrong or incomplete programming*. Two well known symptoms of arithmetical errors are a division by zero and a field-overflow. Instability symptoms can also be caused by the careless programming of operations on structures, DO and WHILE loops, and recursive calls. We'll discuss several typical problems that can arise in these areas in Section 4.2. You should note how important the Unicode-enabling of your ABAP programs can be to help prevent such problems from occurring.

The second cause of stability errors is the *overzealous use of dynamic programming*. Although the types of problems associated with dynamic programming features are similar to those that are already presented in Section 4.2, the topic is extensive enough to warrant a separate section. Therefore, we address how you can deal with the risks of dynamic programming in Section 4.3.

The third cause of stability errors is *a change in the program's environment*, something that frequently happens in an ERP environment such as SAP's R/3 system. In this context, you should interpret the term *environment* to mean the circumstances, objects, or conditions by which one is surrounded. Each ABAP program contains many references to objects both within and outside its ABAP environment (see Figure 4.1).

This doesn't apply only to references to ABAP Dictionary objects, external procedures (such as function modules and external subroutines), or includes. An ABAP program can also be dependent on native operating-system (OS) commands, technical filenames, user settings, client software, file-encoding systems, and so forth. Section 4.4 is devoted to the fourth cause of stability errors, which is associated with *changes in an ABAP program's environment*.

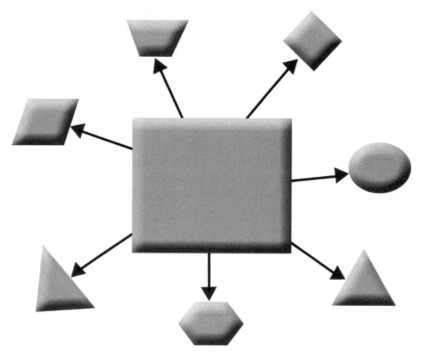

Figure 4.1 References

The fifth and last cause of stability errors is *using an ABAP program incorrectly*. However well-designed an ABAP program may be, it cannot be tailored to meet processing requirements for all potential situations, nor is it possible to prevent an ABAP program from being used in the wrong circumstances. For instance, a program that is designed for processing in the foreground cannot always be used in the background as well. Therefore, you need to be aware of some basic restrictions of the most important processing types. The associated stability problems and strategies to deal with these problems are discussed in Section 4.5.

Exception Handling for Stability Problems

Before we go into greater detail in the next sections, we need to remind you that, in effect, *standard exception handling* for many stability errors already exists: program dumps and technical error messages are generated by standard SAP functionality. In many cases, however, you can make exception handling more elegant. In situations that would typically lead to a program dump, you can implement your own exception handling, thereby ensuring that you can avoid dumps and experience a *smooth landing* after an emergency.

4.2   Programming Errors That Promote Instability

This section addresses several kinds of basic deficiencies in an ABAP program that can all result in program dumps. It is divided into two subsections: Section 4.2.1 pertains to the wrong use of field types; Section 4.2.2 pertains to endless loops in various forms.

4.2.1   Field Types

A primary cause of program dumps is the inability to use fields in a way other than what their field types permit. We'll begin by showing you examples of two basic errors due to deficiencies in arithmetic: division by zero and a field-overflow. Then, we'll discuss type-conflicts, initially via some basic examples, and then, with some examples that are based on the use of structures. In the latter case, in particular, you will notice the importance of making your ABAP program *Unicode-enabled*.

Division by Zero

Let's take a look at the next example. Executing this code will result in a program dump:

```
LOOP AT ts_bseg INTO wa_bseg.

  AT NEW belnr.
    CLEAR: tp_dmbtr_tot, tp_dmbtr_avg, tp_dmbtr_max, tp_recs_cnt.
  ENDAT.

  ADD 1 TO tp_recs._cnt
  IF wa_bseg-dmbtr > tp_dmbtr_max.
    tp_dmbtr_max = wa_bseg-dmbtr.
  ENDIF.
  IF wa_bseg-shkzg = 'H'.
    wa_bseg-dmbtr = wa_bseg-dmbtr * -1.
  ENDIF.
  tp_dmbtr_tot = tp_dmbtr_tot + wa_bseg-dmbtr.

  AT END OF belnr.
    tp_dmbtr_avg = tp_dmbtr_tot / tp_recs_cnt.
    tp_perc      = tp_dmbtr_max / tp_dmbtr_tot.
  ENDAT.
ENDLOOP.
```

The dump information in Figure 4.2 shows that a runtime error was caused by a division by zero. If we scrolled down a few pages, the dump would show that this error was caused by the statement `tp_perc = tp_dmbtr_max / tp_dmbtr_tot`. The reason is that the content of the field `tp_dmbtr_tot` was equal to zero.

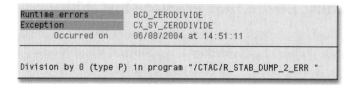

```
Runtime errors        BCD_ZERODIVIDE
Exception             CX_SY_ZERODIVIDE
       Occurred on    06/08/2004 at 14:51:11

Division by 0 (type P) in program "/CTAC/R_STAB_DUMP_2_ERR "
```

Figure 4.2 Dump Information

There are various ways to prevent this from happening. The simplest solution is to add a test to the code before the percentage is computed, in order to check whether the field `tp_dmbtr_tot` is equal to zero. Note that you allow your program to continue only if this field is *not* equal to zero:

```
AT END OF belnr.
  IF NOT tp_dmbtr_tot = 0.
    tp_dmbtr_avg = tp_dmbtr_tot / tp_recs_cnt.
    tp_perc      = tp_dmbtr_max / tp_dmbtr_tot.
    ...
  ELSE.
    WRITE: / gl_text. "or something else to handle this error
  ENDIF.
ENDAT.
```

Alternatively, you can *catch* the error just before it can cause a program dump (see also Section 4.1). By catching an error before it can cause a program dump, you have the added advantage of being able to define your own exception handling. As of SAP Release 4.0, you can use a CATCH statement to define the system-exceptions that you want to be handled, as shown in the following code. In this case, the system-exception `bcd_zerodivide` is explicitly defined as one of the exceptions to be anticipated:

```
AT END OF belnr.
  CATCH SYSTEM-EXCEPTIONS bcd_overflow  = 1
                          bcd_zerodivide = 2.
    tp_dmbtr_avg = tp_dmbtr_tot / tp_recs_cnt.
    tp_perc      = tp_dmbtr_max / tp_dmbtr_tot.
  ENDCATCH.
  CASE sy-subrc.
    WHEN 0.
      ...
    WHEN 1.
      WRITE: / 'Overflow occurred in result!!!'.
    WHEN 2.
      WRITE: / 'Division by ZERO!!!'.
    WHEN OTHERS.
  ENDCASE.
ENDAT.
```

With the SAP Web Application Server (Web AS) Release 6.10, the `CATCH...END-CATCH` command has become obsolete. It should be replaced by a `TRY...ENDTRY` block (with a `CATCH` statement in it), as is done below. System exceptions have now become class-based (see Section 5.3):

```
AT END OF belnr.
  TRY.
    tp_dmbtr_avg = tp_dmbtr_tot / tp_recs_cnt.
    tp_perc      = tp_dmbtr_max / tp_dmbtr_tot.
   CATCH cx_sy_zerodivide INTO gl_oref.
      gl_text = gl_oref->get_text( ).
  ENDTRY.
  IF NOT gl_text IS INITIAL.
    WRITE: / gl_text. "or something else to handle this error!
  ELSE.
    ...
  ENDIF.
ENDAT.
```

Field-Overflow

Another basic arithmetic error is what is termed a *field-overflow*. A field-overflow occurs when a field is defined as being too small for the value that it is supposed to contain at runtime. Imagine having to calculate the total amount of money of a range of financial documents on the basis of the detailed amount in each document. That may not be as easy as it seems if you don't know the maximum value of the total amount. After consulting a functional specialist (i.e., a consultant who specializes in customizing), you could declare the field with a fixed number of decimal places, as is done in the following code:

```
TYPES: ty_dmbtr(4) TYPE p DECIMALS 2.
DATA: tp_dmbtr_tot TYPE ty_dmbtr.
.
LOOP AT ts_bseg INTO wa_bseg.
  AT NEW belnr.
    CLEAR: tp_dmbtr_tot, tp_recs_cnt.
  ENDAT.
  tp_dmbtr_tot = tp_dmbtr_tot + wa_bseg-dmbtr.
  WRITE: / 'Line', wa_bseg-buzei, 'amount', wa_bseg-dmbtr.
  AT END OF belnr.
    WRITE: / 'Docnr       :', wa_bseg-bukrs, wa_bseg-belnr, wa_bseg-gjahr,
           / 'Nr.of recs  :', tp_recs_cnt,
           / 'Tot Amount  :', tp_dmbtr_tot.
  ENDAT.
ENDLOOP.
```

In this case, the total amount field has been defined as a four-byte packed field (type P) with two decimals. In other words, it is assumed that this field's value will not exceed the maximum value of 99,999.99. However, if we learn that the functional consultant was wrong, and the field's value does exceed the maximum stated, the program will cause a program dump with the following message (see Figure 4.3):

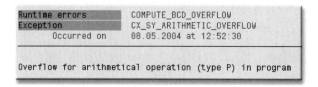

```
Runtime errors      COMPUTE_BCD_OVERFLOW
Exception           CX_SY_ARITHMETIC_OVERFLOW
      Occurred on   08.05.2004 at 12:52:30

Overflow for arithmetical operation (type P) in program
```

Figure 4.3 Overflow in Intermediate Result

There are ways to avoid having to rely on other people's advice. Nevertheless, if you use the traditional way of building lists, the only option you have is to define a variable large enough (i.e., so that it can accommodate very large numbers). Your other alternative is to catch the corresponding system exception BCD_OVERFLOW in a CATCH...ENDCATCH block (up to Release 4.6) or TRY...ENTRY block (as of Web AS Release 6.10).

The best option, however, is to avoid having to program explicit exception handling. Since SAP Release 4.0 there's an alternative to the traditional way of building lists—the ABAP List Viewer (ALV, see also Chapters 3 and 6). Not only does the ALV offer standard facilities for calculating totals and subtotals on demand, it also determines the formats required for all total fields dynamically, that is, at runtime. Therefore, in order to avoid basic field-overflow problems, all you need do is use ALV.

Basic Type-Conflicts

One error that you may frequently encounter is that the system cannot convert data from one format into another. We'll show you how to prevent some basic errors first.

In the following sample code, an external file is being read that contains order line data from a legacy system. The only thing the program has to do is to determine the total quantity for the order lines. The record layout has been defined in the legacy system and is considered to be stable.

```
TYPES:  BEGIN OF ty_itemc,
          vbeln          TYPE vbeln,
          posnr          TYPE posnr,
          kwmeng         TYPE num15,
          vrkme          TYPE vrkme,
        END OF ty_itemc.
```

```
DATA:    wa_itemc       TYPE ty_itemc.
DATA:    tp_total       TYPE num15.

OPEN DATASET pa_dsn FOR INPUT IN TEXT MODE ENCODING DEFAULT.
IF sy-subrc NE 0.
  MESSAGE e000(38) WITH 'Dataset' pa_dsn 'could not be opened'.
ENDIF.

DO.
  READ DATASET pa_dsn INTO wa_itemc.
  IF sy-subrc NE 0.
    WRITE: / 'End of file'.
    EXIT.
  ENDIF.
  tp_total = tp_total + wa_itemc-kwmeng.
ENDDO.

CLOSE DATASET pa_dsn.
```

Executing the program code results in the following dump (see Figure 4.4):

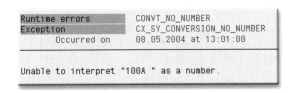

Runtime errors	CONVT_NO_NUMBER
Exception	CX_SY_CONVERSION_NO_NUMBER
Occurred on	08.05.2004 at 13:01:08

Unable to interpret "100A " as a number.

Figure 4.4 Error in Numeric Field

Apparently, one of the order lines contained a quantity field with a non-numeric content. The dump resulted because the system was not able to convert the content of the field wa_itemc-kwmeng to the type definition assigned to it (NUM15). Because this conversion error is also a *catchable* system exception, you can prevent the program dump with the CATCH...ENDCATCH statement (up to Release 4.6), or the TRY...ENDTRY block (from Release Web AS 6.10. onwards):

```
DO.
  READ DATASET pa_dsn INTO wa_itemc.
  IF sy-subrc NE 0.
    WRITE: / 'End of file'.
    EXIT.
  ENDIF.
  CATCH SYSTEM-EXCEPTIONS conversion_errors = 1.
    tp_total = tp_total + wa_itemc-kwmeng.
  ENDCATCH.
  IF sy-subrc NE 0.
    CASE sy-subrc.
      WHEN 1.
```

```
      WRITE: / 'Conversion error occurred', wa_itemc.
    WHEN OTHERS.
  ENDCASE.
 ENDIF.
ENDDO.
```

Or:

```
DO.
  READ DATASET pa_dsn INTO wa_itemc.
  IF sy-subrc NE 0.
    WRITE: / 'End of file'.
    EXIT.
  ENDIF.
  CLEAR gl_text.
  TRY.
      tp_total = tp_total + wa_itemc-kwmeng.
    CATCH cx_sy_conversion_no_number INTO gl_oref.   Inspringen!!!
      gl_text = gl_oref->get_text( ).
  ENDTRY.
  IF NOT gl_text IS INITIAL.
    WRITE: / 'Conversion error occurred', wa_itemc.
  ENDIF.
ENDDO.
```

Another basic conversion error is a *type-conflict* resulting from the wrong inter-pretation of the interface of a function module or subroutine. The following code would result in a corresponding program dump:

```
DATA: tp_day(3)          TYPE c.

LOOP AT ts_bkpf INTO wa_bkpf.
  CALL FUNCTION 'DATE_COMPUTE_DAY'
    EXPORTING
      date = wa_bkpf-budat
    IMPORTING
      day  = tp_day.
ENDLOOP.
```

To better understand what went wrong in this particular example, you'd have to look at the interface definition of the function module date_compute_day. The importing parameter day is defined as a LIKE reference of field scal-indica-tor, which is a character field (type C) with a length of 1 byte. In the preceding example, however, the associated field tp_day is defined as a character field with a length of 3 bytes. The usual syntax check won't detect this discrepancy and will allow you to activate the code. Unfortunately, it will also cause a dump at runtime (see Figure 4.5):

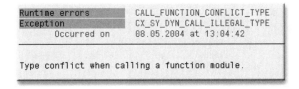

Figure 4.5 Error in CALL

You can predict a program dump, if you execute an extended syntax check. It will mention the following type-conflict error (see Figure 4.6):

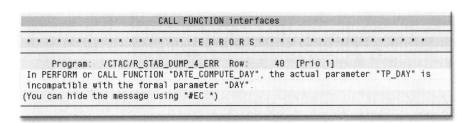

Figure 4.6 Extended Syntax Check

Clearly, we therefore recommend that you execute an extended syntax check on your programs. Try to follow the principle of solving all errors before transferring the program to the next development phase.

Type-Conflicts When Using Structures

Type-conflicts often occur as unintended side-effects that result from using structures combined with offset and length addressing in all kinds of operations, instead of directly referring to the individual fields contained in a structure. Here, we provide you with several examples showing how such type-conflicts can occur. In this context, we will stress just how important it is to make your ABAP programs *Unicode-enabled*. As you may recall, in Chapter 1, we introduced Unicode-enabling.

In general, accessing a structure based on specifying an offset (e.g., +2: start at 2 positions from the beginning of the structure) and a length (e.g., (5): use 5 characters) is a programming technique that you should avoid if possible, however, we realize that sometimes you will have to use it. Figure 4.7 describes such an example. The offset (+21) and length (8) in the last statement in the code refer to a non-character part of the structure's contents, to field e, which has type f (floating-point).

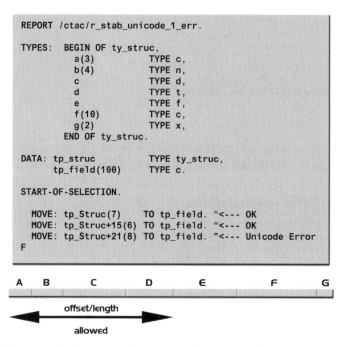

```
REPORT /ctac/r_stab_unicode_1_err.

TYPES:   BEGIN OF ty_struc,
              a(3)             TYPE c,
              b(4)             TYPE n,
              c                TYPE d,
              d                TYPE t,
              e                TYPE f,
              f(10)            TYPE c,
              g(2)             TYPE x,
           END OF ty_struc.

DATA: tp_struc            TYPE ty_struc,
         tp_field(100)      TYPE c.

START-OF-SELECTION.

   MOVE: tp_Struc(7)    TO tp_field. "<--- OK
   MOVE: tp_Struc+15(6) TO tp_field. "<--- OK
   MOVE: tp_Struc+21(8) TO tp_field. "<--- Unicode Error
F
```

```
A   B       C       D       E           F       G

        offset/length

        allowed
```

Figure 4.7 Unicode Error When Using Offset and Length

From this point on, we will refer to Unicode-enabling several times, because of its stability-enhancing effects, particularly in this area. An ABAP program is considered Unicode-enabled if the field **Unicode check active** in the program attributes has been set.

If this piece of code is part of a Unicode-enabled ABAP program, this particular program wouldn't pass the syntax check, because in a Unicode-enabled program, the offset and length specification can include only character-type fields (that is, of type C, N, D, or T) starting from the beginning of the structure. However, the part of the structure that is specified in the last statement (tp_struc+21(8)) doesn't meet this condition.

Conversely, the syntax check in a non-Unicode-enabled program wouldn't interpret this code to be wrong or harmful. This, however, can lead to various errors, although perhaps not immediately. In any case, the content of tp_struc+21(8), which is equivalent to field tp_struc-e, would be interpreted as meaningless. Whether this actually leads to an error depends on what operations are done with the field. Therefore, it may lead to either no error, or to any of the stability errors discussed so far, or to wrong output, as discussed in Chapter 3.

In the sample code in Figure 4.8, subroutine `r001_convert` is called while referring to a specific part of the contents of structure `tp_struc` (with an offset of +50 and a length of 3).

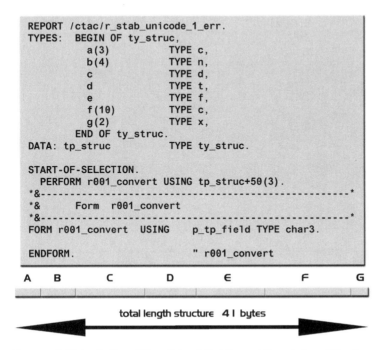

```
REPORT /ctac/r_stab_unicode_1_err.
TYPES:  BEGIN OF ty_struc,
          a(3)              TYPE c,
          b(4)              TYPE n,
          c                 TYPE d,
          d                 TYPE t,
          e                 TYPE f,
          f(10)             TYPE c,
          g(2)              TYPE x,
        END OF ty_struc.
DATA: tp_struc            TYPE ty_struc.

START-OF-SELECTION.
  PERFORM r001_convert USING tp_struc+50(3).
*&---------------------------------------------------*
*&      Form  r001_convert
*&---------------------------------------------------*
FORM r001_convert  USING     p_tp_field TYPE char3.

ENDFORM.                    " r001_convert
```

A	B	C	D	E	F	G

total length structure 41 bytes

Figure 4.8 Unicode Error When Using Offset Beyond Boundaries of Structures

In a non-Unicode-enabled program, ABAP code such as this will deliver unpredictable results, in the same way as in the previous example. This would result in either no errors; one of the runtime errors already discussed in this chapter; or, a correctness error.

In a Unicode-enabled program, you can no longer pass parameters to subroutines via using an offset and length that exceeds the boundaries of the structure. This will return a syntax-error.

The following ABAP code incorporates a structure operation based on the ADD command, which could lead to a type-conflict. Generally, these particular type-conflicts occur when existing ABAP code is changed; for example, when one of the fields in an existing structure is added, changed, or removed. Using the ADD command, the ABAP code in the example calculates a total on the basis of the ten components of the structure. Although the statement on the last line in the code does not explicitly refer to a specific offset and length in the structure, it does make implicit use of the underlying concepts:

```
TYPES: BEGIN OF ty_s2,
          n01(2)               TYPE n,
          n02(5)               TYPE n,
          n03(2)               TYPE n,
          n04(2)               TYPE n,
          n05(2)               TYPE n,
          n06(2)               TYPE n,
          n07(2)               TYPE n,
          n08(2)               TYPE n,
          n09(2)               TYPE n,
          n10(2)               TYPE n,
       END OF ty_s2.
DATA: tp_s2                    TYPE ty_s2,
      tp_total                 TYPE f.
   tp_s2-n01 = 23.
   tp_s2-n02 = 53.
   tp_s2-n03 = 56.
   tp_s2-n04 = 88.
   tp_s2-n05 = 75.
   tp_s2-n06 = 73.
   tp_s2-n07 = 33.
   tp_s2-n08 = 48.
   tp_s2-n09 = 32.
   tp_s2-n10 = 66.
   ADD tp_s2-n01 THEN tp_s2-n02 UNTIL tp_s2-n10 GIVING tp_total.
```

Since the syntax check did not raise any warnings, you would expect the field tp_total to contain a result of 547. Instead, it is 451. The reason why this happens is that the ADD statement at the end of the code considers all the operands tp_s2-n01 and tp_s2-n02 through tp_s2-n10 to be of exactly the same type and length. Also the distance between tp_s2-n01 and tp_s2-n10 is expected to be exactly 10 times the distance found between tp_s2-n01 and tp_s2-n02. This implies that no other fields may be placed in-between. However, that is not the case in the example. Figure 4.9 shows why.

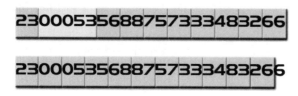

Figure 4.9 Unicode Error Caused by Different Field Lengths in ADD UNTIL Statement

The first line in Figure 4.9 shows both the layout and the contents of the structure. The second line shows how the structure is interpreted by the ADD statement. All components of the structure up to and including tp_s2-n10 are considered equal in size to tp_s2-n01.

Again, the effects for both a Unicode-enabled and a non-Unicode-enabled program would be the same as before: the syntax check for a Unicode-enabled program would not allow this; the syntax check for a non-Unicode-enabled program would; and the results would be unpredictable.

The following example is similar to the previous one, but uses other ABAP commands:

```
TYPES: BEGIN OF ty_s2,
          n01(2)              TYPE n,
          n02(2)              TYPE n,
          n03(2)              TYPE n,
          n04(2)              TYPE n,
          n05(2)              TYPE n,
          n06(2)              TYPE n,
          n07(2)              TYPE n,
          n08(2)              TYPE n,
          n09(2)              TYPE n,
          n10(2)              TYPE n,
       END OF ty_s2.
DATA: tp_s2                 TYPE ty_s2,
      tp_char(10)           TYPE c VALUE 'ABCDEFG',
      tp_field(3)           TYPE n,
      tp_total              TYPE f.
DO 10 TIMES VARYING tp_field FROM tp_s2-n01 NEXT tp_s2-n02.
  ADD tp_field TO tp_total.
ENDDO.
WRITE: / 'Total', tp_total.
```

In this example, field tp_field is defined as a variable with length 3.

The DO loop starts at field tp_s2-n01 and fills tp_field with the contents of the three positions from tp_s2 starting at field n01. Then, the pointer is placed at the beginning of field n02, and field tp_field is filled with the contents of the three next positions from tp_s2 starting at field n02, and so forth. Consequently, an amount consisting of three figures, instead of two figures, is added ten times (see Figure 4.10).

In this case, the program will end with a dump. The tenth time that the DO loop is repeated, field tp_field is not only filled with the content of field tp_s2-n10, but the last position of tp_field is filled with the first position of field tp_char. Because the content of tp_field is not numeric, the ADD command fails, and a program dump is generated.

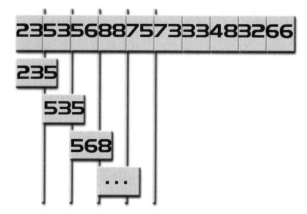

Figure 4.10 Unicode Error Caused by Different Field Lengths in DO VARYING Statement

What we want to emphasize again, however, is that the syntax check on a non-Unicode-enabled program would fail to see this deficiency, whereas the syntax check on a Unicode-enabled program would recognize the problem and issue an error. Moreover, if the Unicode attribute is set for the program, you can use some additional options in loop statements. The addition [RANGE f3] enables you to perform an additional check in order to ensure that the contents of operands f1 and f2 are actually placed within the boundaries as specified by f3.

```
DO … VARYING f FROM f1 NEXT f2 [RANGE f3]
WHILE ... VARY f FROM f1 NEXT f2 [RANGE f3]
```

non-Unicode

```
REPORT   /ctac/r_stab_unicode_6_err.

TYPES:   BEGIN OF ty_struc1,
           a(2)          TYPE c,
           b             TYPE i,
           c(1)          TYPE c,
           d(4)          TYPE x,
         END OF ty_struc1,
         BEGIN OF ty_struc2,
           a(2)          TYPE c,
           b             TYPE i,
           c(1)          TYPE c,
           g(6)          TYPE p,
           f(2)          TYPE x,
         END OF ty_struc2.

DATA:    tp_struc1  TYPE ty_struc1,
         tp_struc2  TYPE ty_struc2.

MOVE tp_struc1 TO tp_struc2.
```

Unicode

```
REPORT   /ctac/r_stab_unicode_6_sol.

TYPES:   BEGIN OF ty_struc1,
           a(2)          TYPE c,
           b             TYPE i,
           c(1)          TYPE c,
           d(4)          TYPE x,
         END OF ty_struc1,
         BEGIN OF ty_struc2,
           a(2)          TYPE c,
           b             TYPE i,
           c(1)          TYPE c,
           g(6)          TYPE p,
           f(2)          TYPE x,
         END OF ty_struc2.

DATA:    tp_struc1  TYPE ty_struc1,
         tp_struc2  TYPE ty_struc2.

MOVE-CORRESPONDING tp_struc1
                TO tp_struc2.
```

Figure 4.11 Move of Incompatible Structures not Allowed in Unicode

A last example of an operation on a structure that we want to mention is a MOVE from an entire structure's contents to another structure (see Figure 4.11). In non-Unicode programs, you're allowed to do this even if the field types of both structures don't match; in a Unicode-enabled program, you're not. Non-Unicode enabled programs can lead to specific types of errors resulting in unpredictable output whereas Unicode enabling prevents these errors from ever occurring.

4.2.2 Endless Loops

An *endless loop* occurs when a piece of ABAP code keeps repeating until the program is cancelled by the end user or a system administrator. Sometimes, a program session that runs into an endless loop results in a program dump due to a lack of system resources. In dialog mode, an endless loop usually leads to a run-time error (i.e., time-out dump) because of a time limit (see Figure 4.12):

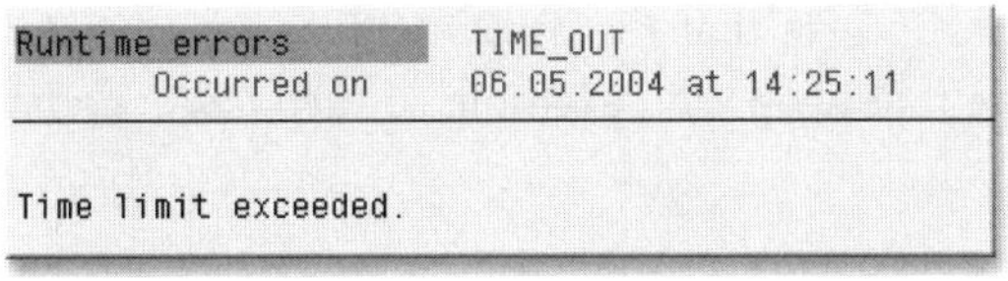

```
Runtime errors        TIME_OUT
         Occurred on   06.05.2004 at 14:25:11


Time limit exceeded.
```

Figure 4.12 Runtime Error

Endless loops don't occur very often. Nevertheless, we'll address them because of the impact they can have on the SAP system. If an endless loop occurs, it can disturb the entire productive system. This usually happens because the program session causing the loop continues to claim system resources, thereby monopolizing one system task. In addition to that, it can disrupt the daily operation.

In this section, we address three possible causes of endless loops: executing a DO or WHILE statement without a guaranteed exit, recursive programming without an ensured way out, and using the SUPPRESS DIALOG statement while processing screens in dialog mode.

Endless DO and WHILE Loops

Like most other programming languages, the ABAP language has several commands at its disposal aimed at looping. Two such commands are the DO and WHILE statements. Both commands require an explicit exit condition to ensure that the loop will come to an end. The primary difference between the two commands is the exact placement of the exit condition: in a DO loop, the exit condition is inserted within the loop itself;[1] in a WHILE loop, the exit condition is part

---

1 Of course, this is not true for statements such as DO n TIMES or DO VARYING.

of the actual loop construction. Some sample code showing both types of loops is shown in the following example:

```
DO.
  IF <condition>.
    Exit.
  ENDIF.
ENDDO.

WHILE <condition>.

ENDWHILE.
```

You can run the risk of an endless loop by specifying a <condition> that is not true in all circumstances. Problems with the stability of an ABAP program usually occur just after changes have been made to the program itself, or to related customizing settings. In such cases, the developer (or the person who has changed the customizing settings) sometimes forgets that the associated loop processing should be changed accordingly. The following is an example of such ABAP code:

```
DO.
  PERFORM check_order CHANGING tp_status.
  IF tp_status = co_finished.
    CASE wa_vbak-auart.
      WHEN co_ordertype_or.
        PERFORM finish_order_or.
        EXIT.
      WHEN co_ordertype_ztx.
        PERFORM finish_order_ztx.
        EXIT.
    ENDCASE.
  ENDIF.
ENDDO.
```

The exit conditions here are no longer true each time that a new sales document type is introduced. Only existing order types are explicitly mentioned in the WHEN statements where the EXIT command is placed. Therefore, introducing a new order type would make it impossible to avoid adding a new WHEN statement and a corresponding EXIT statement.

You can prevent this *time bomb* by always anticipating deviations from the normal program flow. One particular way of doing this has been added to the existing code below:

```
DO.
  PERFORM check_order CHANGING tp_status.
  IF tp_status = co_finished.
    CASE wa_vbak-auart.
      WHEN co_ordertype_or.
        PERFORM finish_order_or.
        EXIT.
      WHEN co_ordertype_ztx.
        PERFORM finish_order_ztx.
        EXIT.
      WHEN OTHERS.
* Add exception handling here
        EXIT.
    ENDCASE.
  ENDIF.
ENDDO.
```

Endless Recursive Calls

A second situation where you specifically need to consider how to prevent endless loops is when a procedure calls itself. This is known as a *recursive call*. In ABAP, a recursive call looks like this:

```
FUNCTION /ctac/do_something.

  CALL FUNCTION /ctac/do_something.
...
ENDFUNCTION.
```

If you need to use this technique, you must ensure that the recursive calling tree will come to a normal end. If a wrong exit condition does not lead to a time-out dump in dialog mode, you can be certain that it will lead to other types of dumps in the background.

To demonstrate the effects of a recursive call, we use the example of a subroutine that is designed to trace the oldest predecessor of a specific material number (see Figure 4.13). It performs this search by finding the *old material number* (in field bismt) in the material master. If the old material number contains a value, this value is used to select the next material master record. If this second material master also contains an old material number, this procedure is repeated again. You cannot know beforehand how many material masters you need to go through in order to find the *oldest* material number of one material. Therefore, you must ensure that the program has enough flexibility to determine this by itself at run-time.

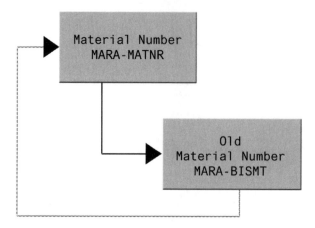

Figure 4.13 Link from Material to Old Material

In order to factor in adequate time to search a chain of previous material numbers, the implemented code must contain the recursive subroutine shown below:

```
REPORT  /ctac/r_stab_process_err9          .

TYPES: BEGIN OF ty_material,
         matnr TYPE matnr,
         bismt TYPE matnr,
       END  OF ty_material.

DATA:  wa_nextmaterial TYPE ty_material.

PARAMETERS     : pa_matnr TYPE matnr OBLIGATORY.

START-OF-SELECTION.

  SELECT SINGLE matnr bismt
         FROM mara INTO wa_nextmaterial
         WHERE matnr = pa_matnr.

  PERFORM next_material USING wa_nextmaterial
                        1.

*&--------------------------------------------------------------------*
*&      Form  next_material
*&--------------------------------------------------------------------*
*         If material contains an old material call this routine again.
*---------------------------------------------------------------------*
FORM next_material  USING     utp_material TYPE ty_material
                              utp_level    TYPE i.
  DATA: ltp_level TYPE i.

  IF NOT utp_material-bismt IS INITIAL.
```

```
   ltp_level = utp_level + 1.

   SELECT SINGLE matnr bismt FROM mara INTO wa_nextmaterial
             WHERE matnr = utp_material-bismt.

   PERFORM next_material USING wa_nextmaterial
                               ltp_level.

  ENDIF.

ENDFORM.                        " next_material
```

The underlying assumption that makes this recursive call work is that every old material number found will actually exist in database table MARA. Now, of course, this assumption could prove to be false, due, for instance, to a typing error made during the maintenance of the material master. And it probably will, since the old material number (field `bismt`) found is not checked against a value table during material maintenance. Therefore, some additional code is required to ensure that the recursive call will always come to a proper end.

```
FORM next_material  USING    utp_material TYPE ty_material
                             utp_level    TYPE i.
  DATA: ltp_level TYPE i.


  IF NOT utp_material-bismt IS INITIAL.
    ltp_level = utp_level + 1.
    CLEAR wa_nextmaterial.
    SELECT SINGLE matnr bismt FROM mara INTO wa_nextmaterial
               WHERE matnr = utp_material-bismt.
    IF sy-subrc = 0.
      PERFORM next_material USING wa_nextmaterial
                                 ltp_level.
    ENDIF.

  ENDIF.

ENDFORM.                        " next_material
```

As you can see, it's imperative to clear the global field `wa_nextmaterial` and to explicitly check the return code after the execution of the SELECT SINGLE on table MARA.

We have added another example below. It doesn't exactly fit the definition of a recursive call, but it's a close enough approximation:

```
LOOP AT <itab> INTO <wa_itab>.

  IF <condition>.
```

```
   APPEND <wa_itab> TO <itab>.
 ENDIF>

ENDLOOP.
```

In this example, an internal table is extended if a specific condition is found true while the table is being processed. If the APPEND statement is executed under only exceptional circumstances, this can be a valid construction. If this is not the case, however, the growth of the internal table may become uncontrollable. Consequently, the runtime error ROLL_IN_ERROR will occur.

Using SUPPRESS DIALOG

You can use the option SUPPRESS DIALOG in the Process Before Output (PBO) event of a dynpro if you want to skip the display of the screen. Consequently, the screen is not shown and the Process After Input (PAI) event is executed directly. This is similar to running a dynpro in the background. It does not often make sense to do this, but the construction is sometimes used in practice. Try to imagine what the result of the following ABAP code will be:

```
PROCESS BEFORE OUTPUT.
  MODULE status_9000.
  MODULE suppress_the_dialog.
*
PROCESS AFTER INPUT.
  MODULE user_command_9000.


*&---------------------------------------------------------------------*
*&      Module  STATUS_9000  OUTPUT
*&---------------------------------------------------------------------*
*       Setting the status for the dynpro
*----------------------------------------------------------------------*
MODULE status_9000 OUTPUT.
  SET PF-STATUS 'SCREEN'.

ENDMODULE.                    " STATUS_9000  OUTPUT
*&---------------------------------------------------------------------*
*&      Module  suppress_the_dialog  OUTPUT
*&---------------------------------------------------------------------*
*       suppressing the dialog if this is needed.
*----------------------------------------------------------------------*
MODULE suppress_the_dialog OUTPUT.
  IF tp_no_dialog = true.
    SUPPRESS DIALOG.
  ENDIF.
ENDMODULE.                    " suppress_the_dialog  OUTPUT
*&---------------------------------------------------------------------*
*&      Module  USER_COMMAND_9000  INPUT
```

```
*&---------------------------------------------------------------------*
*         Handling the okcode that has been pressed by the user
*---------------------------------------------------------------------*
MODULE user_command_9000 INPUT.
  tp_okcode = okcode.
  CLEAR okcode.
  CASE tp_okcode.
    WHEN 'BACK'.
      SET SCREEN 0.
      LEAVE SCREEN.
  ENDCASE.
ENDMODULE.                    " USER_COMMAND_9000  INPUT
```

The unwanted result is that the code will keep running since the condition to leave the screen will never be true. In dialog mode, this will lead to the *time-out runtime error* that we mentioned at the start of this topic on endless loops. In the background, the program can only be stopped by brute force, that is, by canceling the process in the process overview (SM50). The following addition is required (marked bold):

```
MODULE user_command_9000 INPUT.
  tp_okcode = okcode.
  CLEAR okcode.
  CASE tp_okcode.
    WHEN 'BACK'.
      SET SCREEN 0.
      LEAVE SCREEN.
  ENDCASE.
  IF tp_no_dialog = true.
    SET SCREEN 0.
    LEAVE SCREEN.
  ENDIF.
ENDMODULE.                    " USER_COMMAND_9000  INPUT
```

4.3   Risks of Dynamic Programming

As an ABAP developer, you can make your ABAP code more flexible by determining part of the required variables to be used at runtime, in order to influence the working of specific statements. This is what is known as *dynamic programming*. There are several dynamic possibilities you can use, namely:

▶ The names of programs, function modules, methods, and external subroutines can be determined at runtime.

▶ Field-symbols and data references can be used to refer to other variables at runtime.

▶ All parts of an Open SQL statement can be constructed at runtime.

As mentioned, the biggest advantage of dynamic ABAP programming possibilities is that they enable you to introduce more flexibility into your SAP applications. There are various programming problems that would otherwise require many more lines of coding, or even be impossible to solve.

However, that is not the emphasis of this section. Here, we primarily want to focus on the risks inherent in dynamic programming. These risks are a direct result of the nature of dynamic programming. Because of the dynamic programming features of ABAP, you can determine at runtime what the statements are going to do. The syntax check won't be able to check the correct working of these statements, however, *before* the code is actually executed. In other words, some of the warnings that would otherwise have been given by the syntax check are replaced by program dumps at runtime. Therefore, dynamic programming needs to be done very carefully.

This section first describes the use of several ABAP elements that make the data that is being processed dynamic (see Section 4.3.1). The second main topic discussed deals with those runtime errors you should expect when working with all kinds of dynamic calls (in Section 4.3.2). For each of the topics mentioned, we'll present the most common runtime errors and provide you with guidelines on how to either prevent those runtime errors, or catch them just before they can cause a program dump.

4.3.1 Dynamic Data

Dynamic data refers to data that has to be processed, but isn't known yet at design or compile time. SAP provides three ways of handling dynamic data: using field-symbols; using data references; or using dynamic Open SQL. The common goal of each of these options is to enable you to determine at runtime what database or program variables are actually required. This section deals with the stability problems that are associated with each of these options. Because of the complexity of these ABAP elements, a basic knowledge of all topics addressed is indispensable. If you can't remember them all, don't fret. We'll refresh your memory by starting the corresponding topics with a brief summary of the basic options of each element.

Field-Symbols

Field-symbols have been available in ABAP since SAP R/2. They represent a basic feature that is not only used by itself but also serves as a basis for subsequent dynamic ABAP features. Field-symbols enable you to point dynamically to all kinds of variables: not only to single fields but also to structures and internal tables. For a quick understanding, you can interpret a field-symbol as a symbolic reference. It doesn't contain a value as would a *normal* variable. Instead, it points to the place where the value can be found. The place where the value can be found is determined at runtime via using the ASSIGN statement. The following pieces of code show the difference between three basic ways of making a field-symbol assignment. The field-symbol ⟨fs1⟩ is defined first, along with two regular variables:

```
FIELD-SYMBOLS: ⟨fs1⟩ TYPE ANY.

DATA: tp_value      TYPE string VALUE 'Any value is acceptable',
      tp_fieldname  TYPE string VALUE 'TP_VALUE'.
```

The first ASSIGN statement that is made fills the field-symbol ⟨fs1⟩ with a reference to a string. By itself, such an assignment with a specific value doesn't really make sense. You could also do this without using a field-symbol:

```
* 1a Static assign to a literal
ASSIGN 'A very static assignment' TO ⟨fs1⟩.
* ⟨fs1⟩ refers to literal 'A very static assignment'
```

The second ASSIGN statement below is more flexible. This field-symbol now points to another variable instead of referring to a literal value. However, this flexibility is limited. For each change of the field that is referred to by ⟨fs1⟩, you will still need to use additional ASSIGN statements in the code:

```
* 1b Static assign to a variable
ASSIGN tp_fieldname TO ⟨fs1⟩.
* ⟨fs1⟩ contains value 'TP_VALUE'
```

In summary, the aforementioned assignments 1a and 1b are static since they both refer to a value that cannot be changed at runtime. The syntax check can perform the necessary verification:

▶ Does the variable tp_fieldname exist?

▶ Is the type of this variable conflicting with the type of the field-symbol ⟨fs1⟩?

The following assignment, however, is really dynamic; the variable tp_fieldname is now used to contain the name of the variable that will be assigned to the field-symbol. Consequently, the compiler cannot check whether tp_value really exists or has the correct type. An ASSIGN statement like this might be sufficient in order to keep varying the actually assigned values to ⟨fs1⟩:

```
* 2 Dynamic assign to the fieldname in a variable
ASSIGN (tp_fieldname) TO ⟨fs1⟩.
* ⟨fs1⟩ contains value of field TP_VALUE which is 'Any value is
* acceptable'.
```

Now, we'll focus on the associated runtime errors. The first and most typical runtime error that can occur when field-symbols are employed is the one shown in Figure 4.14:

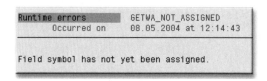

```
Runtime errors       GETWA_NOT_ASSIGNED
       Occurred on   08.05.2004 at 12:14:43

Field symbol has not yet been assigned.
```

Figure 4.14 Field-Symbol Not Assigned

In this program dump message, a field-symbol that has not yet been assigned is referenced. This type of problem can be the result of either an error in the assignment of the field-symbol, or simply an indication that the assignment has not been executed. This error is not a catchable exception.

In order to prevent this kind of error, there are two checks that you can perform before you use a field-symbol. The first check is to determine whether a dynamic field-symbol assignment has succeeded. You can do this by verifying the return-code after the ASSIGN statement:

```
ASSIGN (tp_fieldname) TO <fs1>.
* Check if a dynamic assignment has been successful
IF sy-subrc = 0.

ENDIF.
```

A second possibility is to verify whether a field-symbol has been assigned before referring to it. This is especially useful if the ASSIGN statement takes place at a location in the ABAP code other than where the field-symbol is used. This check can be done using the IS ASSIGNED operand:

```
* Check if a field-symbol has been assigned before actually using it
IF <fs1> IS ASSIGNED.

ENDIF.
```

The second type of runtime error associated with the use of field-symbols is caused by a type-conflict during the assignment of a field-symbol. Usually, a field-symbol without a type definition or with type ANY is used because it implicitly inherits the characteristics of the variable to which it is pointing, including its type. On the other hand, explicit *typing* of field-symbols has some small performance advantages (i.e., it improves the performance of the ABAP program, namely, the processing time). However, this also poses a risk of type-conflicts when a dynamic assignment is made. If the assignment is static, this specific type-conflict is recognized by the syntax check before it can do any damage. If the assignment is dynamic, a syntax check is not effective, and consequently, a run-time error is generated (see Figure 4.15):

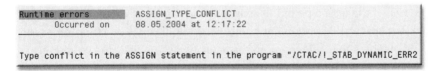

```
Runtime errors       ASSIGN_TYPE_CONFLICT
       Occurred on    08.05.2004 at 12:17:22

Type conflict in the ASSIGN statement in the program "/CTAC/I_STAB_DYNAMIC_ERR2
```

Figure 4.15 Assign Type-Conflict

For example, this message could result from the following piece of ABAP code:

```
FIELD-SYMBOLS: <fs1> TYPE char255.

DATA: tp_value      TYPE string VALUE 'Any value is acceptable',
      tp_fieldname  TYPE string VALUE 'TP_VALUE'.

* Dynamic assign of fieldname to field symbol
ASSIGN (tp_fieldname) TO <fs1>.
```

What happens here is that the assignment wants the field-symbol <fs1> to refer to variable tp_value, which has type STRING. The field-symbol itself, however, expects a reference to a variable of type CHAR255. In the event of a dynamic assignment, neither the syntax check nor the extended syntax check will antici-pate this type-conflict; and, at compile time, neither of these checks will predict that this particular field-reference will occur at runtime. Flexibility, you will learn, comes at a price.

If a field-symbol is fully *typed* by its definition, this runtime exception cannot be caught by class-based exception handling. However, you can use an alternative that forces a type on a field-symbol at runtime. This alternative uses the CASTING option. On this basis, a runtime error will, if it occurs, at least be a runtime error that can be caught, enabling you to replace the program dump with more elegant exception handling. Let's look at the listing below:

```
FIELD-SYMBOLS: <fs2> TYPE ANY.

DATA: tp_value      TYPE string VALUE 'Any value is acceptable',
      tp_fieldname  TYPE string VALUE 'TP_VALUE'.

TRY.
  ASSIGN (tp_fieldname) TO <fs2> CASTING TYPE char255.

  CATCH cx_sy_assign_cast_illegal_cast.
    MESSAGE i000(38) WITH 'cx_sy_assign_cast_illegal_cast'.
```

```
      CATCH cx_root.
        MESSAGE i000(38) WITH 'Other catchable error'.
    ENDTRY.
```

Using a field-symbol without a type, or with the generic type ANY, is recommended only if the data type of the assigned field can be any type. However, you should note that risks for stability come with this flexibility—string processing with field-symbols that refer to non-character fields will lead to runtime errors. The same holds true for calculations with non-numeric field types.

To determine the type of an assigned field at runtime, you can use methods from global class cl_abap_typedescr or one of its subclasses, as is shown below:

```
DATA: wa_vbap       TYPE vbap.
DATA: rf_descr_ref  TYPE REF TO cl_abap_typedescr .

FIELD-SYMBOLS: <fs2> TYPE ANY.

  DO.
* Assign every field of this structure subsequently to the untyped
* fieldsymbol.
    ASSIGN COMPONENT sy-index OF STRUCTURE wa_vbap TO <fs2>.
    IF sy-subrc NE 0.
      EXIT.
    ENDIF.
* Get the type of the field that the field-symbol refers to
    CALL METHOD cl_abap_typedescr=>describe_by_data
      EXPORTING
        p_data     = <fs2>
      RECEIVING
        p_descr_ref = rf_descr_ref.

    CASE rf_descr_ref->type_kind.
      WHEN 'C' OR 'N' OR 'g'.
* Only for these types of fields specific string processing is valid
      WHEN OTHERS.

    ENDCASE.

  ENDDO.
```

Data References

Before the introduction of ABAP Objects, ABAP developers primarily worked with so-called *value-based variables* (see Figure 4.16). A value-based variable contains a value, which is used in the program code by referencing the variable's name.

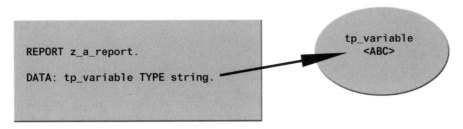

Figure 4.16 Declaring a Variable

In the previous section, we explained how field-symbols can add flexibility to an ABAP program. In a dynamic assignment, you can make a specific field-symbol point to any variable, and this assignment can be changed at runtime. However, note that every variable, which a field-symbol points to, keeps its static behavior. In other words, you must explicitly define the variable in the program itself; the variable's type cannot be changed; and, a piece of memory is implicitly reserved for this variable when the code, in which it is contained, starts its execution.

A more recent step in the evolution of the ABAP language has changed the need for these requirements. In much the same way as you do when creating an object instance in ABAP Objects, you can now create a variable at runtime, using what is known as a *data reference* (see Figure 4.17).

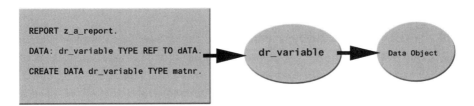

Figure 4.17 Declaring a Reference Variable

In the example in Figure 4.17, the reference variable dr_variable refers to a data object that is created at runtime with the CREATE DATA command (in the same way as an object instance is created with the CREATE OBJECT command in ABAP Objects). This data object can be of any type. Using a data object affords much flexibility to an ABAP program, for example, you can define an internal table dynamically and use it for ALV-functions (see the example code in Section 8.3.2).

Before we go into greater detail about the stability problems related to data references, we'll introduce you to some basic ABAP constructions that use this feature, just as we did for field-symbols. The first option, shown directly below, is not really flexible: the type of the created data is already determined at compile time, by adding it to the data definition of the reference variable.

```
* 1 Static typing of a reference variable
DATA:
    dr_variable_1 TYPE REF TO i.
FIELD-SYMBOLS:
    <fs_1>       TYPE ANY.

CREATE DATA dr_variable_1.

ASSIGN dr_variable_1->* TO <fs_1>.
<fs_1> = 1.
```

The second option is adding the type definition to the CREATE DATA statement, however, this has the same effect—the type is already defined before the code is executed (we should add that this piece of code is actually slightly slower than the first):

```
* 2 Static typing using a reference variable of an anonymous type
*   and postponing typing to the CREATE DATA statement
DATA:
    dr_variable_2 TYPE REF TO data.
FIELD-SYMBOLS:
    <fs_2>       TYPE ANY.

CREATE DATA dr_variable_2 TYPE i.

ASSIGN dr_variable_2->* TO <fs_2>.
<fs_2> = 2.
```

The third option is the most dynamic one. In this option, not only the variable itself, but also the name of the type used for the variable is determined at runtime. On this basis, it is, for example, possible to write very generic Open SQL statements such as the SELECT statement in the following example. We'll elaborate on Dynamic Open SQL in the next section.

```
* 3 Dynamic typing using reference variable of anonymous type
*   and using dynamic type at CREATE DATA statement
DATA:
    dr_variable_3 TYPE REF TO data.
PARAMETERS:
    pa_tabnm      TYPE char255 DEFAULT 'MARA'.

FIELD-SYMBOLS:
    <fs_3>       TYPE table.

CREATE DATA dr_variable_3 type TABLE OF (pa_tabnm).

ASSIGN dr_variable_3->* TO <fs_3>.

SELECT * FROM (pa_tabnm) INTO table <fs_3>.
```

Note that all the aforementioned three options reuse field-symbols to point to the created data. Only a field-symbol can actually point to data; a reference variable cannot. For this purpose, a slightly different variant of the original ASSIGN statement was created for data references: ASSIGN <dataref>->*. This command does what is officially known as *dereferencing*.

So far, we've been looking at references to data that were dynamically created using the CREATE DATA statement. You can also create a reference to statically defined variables using the statement GET REFERENCE OF <data> INTO <reference variable>.

```
DATA:
    tp_variable   TYPE string.
DATA:
    dr_variable_4 TYPE REF TO data.

tp_variable = 'This is a string'.

GET REFERENCE OF tp_variable INTO dr_variable_4.
```

This option can, for example, be useful if the variable dr_variable_4 is part of the interface of a dynamically called function-module. See the documentation available in the SAP system on this subject.

Because the same kind of ABAP construct is used, the problems that are typically associated with field-symbols can also occur here.

Figure 4.18 Invalid Data Type

The runtime error shown in Figure 4.18 occurs whenever the dynamic type used for the CREATE DATA statement does not exist. Fortunately, however, it is a catchable runtime error. Catching it using class-based exception handling would look like this:

```
TRY.
  CREATE DATA dr_variable_3 TYPE TABLE OF (pa_tabnm).

  CATCH cx_sy_create_data_error.
* Error Handling Here
ENDTRY.
```

If a reference variable does not refer to any data object, because the CREATE DATA statement has not yet been executed, the dereferencing ASSIGN statement won't lead to a runtime error. However, the subsequent use of the field-symbol will refer to a data object, thereby raising the non-catchable error GETWA_NOT_ASSIGNED. The following piece of code exemplifies this behavior:

```
DATA:
      dr_variable_1 TYPE REF TO i.
FIELD-SYMBOLS:
      <fs_1>          TYPE ANY.

ASSIGN dr_variable_1->* TO <fs_1>.
IF <fs_1> > 5. "=> RUNTIME ERROR
ENDIF.
```

There are three ways to prevent this from happening. We have combined all three in the next piece of coding:

```
IF dr_variable_1 IS BOUND.
  ASSIGN dr_variable_1->* TO <fs_1>.

  IF sy-subrc = 0.
  ENDIF.

  IF <fs_1> IS ASSIGNED.
  ENDIF.
ENDIF.
```

The check that is executed first—and is the best option—is the check that determines whether a reference variable is already *bound* (that is, already there) before it is dereferenced.

The statement GET REFERENCE can also generate a comparable problem whenever a field-symbol that has not yet been assigned must be referenced. We already showed you how you can verify this check:

```
IF <fs> IS ASSIGNED.
  GET REFERENCE OF <fs> INTO dr_variable_5.
ENDIF.
```

If a dynamic type such as pa_tabnm exists, but doesn't correspond with the static type of a data reference variable, another type of error will occur (see Figure 4.19):

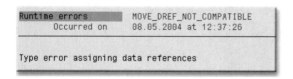

Figure 4.19 Assign Errors

This particular runtime error was caused by the following piece of coding:

```
DATA:
    dr_variable_1 TYPE REF TO i,
    tp_type       TYPE string VALUE 'STRING'.

FIELD-SYMBOLS:
    <fs_1>        TYPE ANY.

CREATE DATA dr_variable_1 TYPE (tp_type).
```

As you can see, field tp_type contains the value "STRING", which is interpreted as the data type. This creates a type-conflict with the static type i, which was already defined for reference variable dr_variable_1.

So far, we've been looking at references to dynamically created data using the CREATE DATA statement. You can also create a reference to statically defined variables by using the statement GET REFERENCE OF <data> INTO <reference variable>. In its basic form, this looks like the following code:

```
DATA:
    tp_variable   TYPE string.
DATA:
    dr_variable_4 TYPE REF TO data.

FIELD-SYMBOLS:
    <fs_4>        TYPE ANY.

tp_variable = 'This is a string'.

GET REFERENCE OF tp_variable INTO dr_variable_4.

ASSIGN dr_variable_4->* TO <fs_4>.
```

Note that the statement marked bold could also refer to a field-symbol instead of tp_variable:

```
GET REFERENCE OF <fs> INTO dr_variable_4.
```

You can now use reference variable dr_variable_4 to get information on the type of the variable to which <fs> is pointing. In the previous section, we showed you how to use this information in order to prevent runtime errors.

The statement GET REFERENCE can lead to several types of runtime errors. First, the field-symbol <fs> must be assigned:

```
IF <fs> IS ASSIGNED.
  GET REFERENCE OF <fs> INTO dr_variable_5.
ENDIF.
```

Another type of error occurs if the type of field-symbol ⟨fs⟩ is not identical to the type of data reference dr_variable_4. The resulting runtime error MOVE_DREF_NOT_COMPATIBLE is not a catchable error. You can avoid this error only by checking the types of both the field-symbol and the reference variable. This is done in the listing below, but, as you can see, it requires a bit of effort:

```
DATA:tp_field      TYPE i,
     dr_variable_6 TYPE REF TO char255,
     rf_descr_ref1 TYPE REF TO cl_ABAP_typedescr ,
     rf_descr_ref2 TYPE REF TO cl_ABAP_typedescr .


FIELD-SYMBOLS:
     ⟨fsa⟩         TYPE ANY,
     ⟨fs_6⟩        TYPE ANY.

* First, check the type of the field-symbol
ASSIGN tp_field TO ⟨fsa⟩.

CALL METHOD cl_ABAP_typedescr=>describe_by_data
  EXPORTING
    p_data     = ⟨fsa⟩
  RECEIVING
    p_descr_ref = rf_descr_ref1.
* Then check the type of the referenced field.You have to create the
* data first, otherwise the method will raise exception 'REFERENCE_IS_
* INITIAL'
CREATE DATA dr_variable_6.

CALL METHOD cl_ABAP_typedescr=>describe_by_data_ref
  EXPORTING
    p_data_ref            = dr_variable_6
  RECEIVING
    p_descr_ref           = rf_descr_ref2
  EXCEPTIONS
    reference_is_initial = 1
    OTHERS               = 2.

IF sy-subrc                   = 0                          AND
   rf_descr_ref1->type_kind = rf_descr_ref2->type_kind AND
   rf_descr_ref1->length    = rf_descr_ref2->length    AND
   rf_descr_ref1->decimals  = rf_descr_ref2->decimals  .

  GET REFERENCE OF ⟨fsa⟩ INTO dr_variable_6.

ELSE.
  MESSAGE i000(38) WITH 'Differences between the types'.
ENDIF.
```

Dynamic Open SQL

Dynamic Open SQL (also called *Dynamic SQL*) allows an ABAP developer to define literally every part of a SQL statement at runtime: the selected fields; the selected database tables; the result set; and the WHERE clause. The most dynamic SQL statement imaginable looks like this:

```
SELECT (ta_fieldlist)
       FROM (tp_tabnm) INTO TABLE <fs>
       WHERE (ta_where).
```

In your everyday work, you won't need this extreme flexibility. It's preferable to use dynamic SQL in only those situations where the dynamic parts of the statement are required. For example, defining a dynamic table name—if the name is known at the outset—makes no sense. However, we expect that the dynamic WHERE clause may be particularly useful, for example, in situations where the most efficient WHERE clause can be determined only at runtime, or the fields to be used in a WHERE clause are known only at runtime. This section presents the most important risks of dynamic SQL that endanger the stability of ABAP programs, and it provides some tips to help you prevent and, if need be, address these risks.

The field list contains the names of the fields to be selected from a database table. If you enter a field name in a field list that doesn't appear in the database table, the following runtime error occurs (see Figure 4.20):

Runtime errors	SAPSQL_INVALID_FIELDNAME
Exception	CX_SY_DYNAMIC_OSQL_SEMANTICS
Occurred on	08.05.2004 at 11:58:41

One of the field names in the SELECT clause was not recognized.

Figure 4.20 Invalid Field Name

The easiest way to prevent this program dump is to catch the error:[2]

```
TRY.
    APPEND 'XYZ' TO ta_fieldlist.
    SELECT (ta_fieldlist)
            FROM (pa_tabnm) INTO TABLE <1_table>
            WHERE (ta_where).
  CATCH cx_sy_dynamic_osql_semantics.
* Error handling here
ENDTRY
```

---

2 Some of the exceptions that are caught here with the TRY statement can also be caught in Releases prior to 6.10 by using CATCH SYSTEM-EXCEPTIONS.

There are various methods that you can use to verify whether all fields in the field list really exist in the table that is referred to in parameter pa_tabnm. Checking table DD03L, which contains all table fields available in an SAP system, is one of these ways. In our opinion, however, catching the runtime error is much easier. Moreover, catching the runtime error is necessary, whether or not other checks are executed beforehand. Because you can never predict all types of errors that may or may not occur, catching the runtime error is the best option. Something that could still happen, for example, is an inconsistency between the definition of a database table in the ABAP Dictionary and the underlying database.[3] On the other hand, in SAP releases that do not yet support catching this particular runtime error (i.e., prior to Release 4.0B), trying to prevent it is a good alternative strategy.

We should add one final remark about the option INTO CORRESPONDING FIELDS. Because the number of ABAP developers who are using field lists instead of a SELECT * is steadily increasing, the option INTO CORRESPONDING FIELDS is also applied more frequently, as displayed in the following code:

```
SELECT (ta_fieldlist)
       FROM (pa_tabnm) INTO CORRESPONDING FIELDS OF TABLE <1_table>
       WHERE (ta_where).
```

Because this option is more or less neutral in that field, it won't disturb stability either. Fields that are selected (in ta_fieldlist) but not defined in the result set (<1_table>) will, in any case, be skipped. The advantage is that this can also help to prevent runtime errors. Note, however, that the selected fields that don't correspond with the fields defined in the result set won't be available. So, although you avoid runtime errors, you may not get the relevant data.

If an end user needs to determine the name of a database table at runtime, for example, preventing unknown table names from being the cause of a runtime error is relatively simple. You can do this by checking whether the table name exists in transparent table DD02L. When doing so, ensure that you don't forget to verify whether this table has the status "Active", since only active tables are recognized by the underlying database system.

Despite being able to prevent a runtime error in most cases, you still run a small risk that the definitions in the ABAP Dictionary won't match those of the underlying database. This would lead to the same error as shown in Figure 4.20. Therefore, we recommend catching runtime errors whenever possible.

---

3 This hardly ever happens. You can even argue that a system dump is actually supposed to be generated in such circumstances. However, we prefer to keep as much as possible in our own hands. For additional recommendations on exception handling, see Chapter 5.

When you determine the name of the database table and the selected fields at runtime, a direct result is that the structure of the result set can also only be defined dynamically. A *result set* is the work area or internal table into which the selected data is going to be copied. It must contain the same field names as those displayed in the field list. In addition, the types of these fields should be identical to those of the corresponding field list.

Since Release SAP R/3 4.6, you can dynamically create internal tables using the data reference technique mentioned in the previous subsection. For now, let's just say that the associated runtime error is the same as the one mentioned previously in Figure 4.20.

In a dynamic WHERE clause, you can define the rows to be selected at runtime. Here's an example of how to do this:

```
* Fill an internal table with a selection of field LIFNR
ta_where-line = 'LIFNR = ''1234567890'''.
APPEND ta_where.

Tp_tabnm = 'T001'.
* Field LIFNR does not exist in table T001.
* This will lead to a runtime error
SELECT (ta_fieldlist)
       FROM (tp_tabnm) INTO TABLE <1_table>
       WHERE (ta_where).
```

The runtime error caused by this code is identical to those errors that we've seen in the previous sections on dynamic Open SQL. Similarly, this runtime error can be caught in the same way.

Another type of runtime error can occur when the WHERE clause itself is not constructed correctly. The exception CX_SY_DYNAMIC_OSQL_SYNTAX is, for example, raised if a WHERE clause looks like this:

```
ta_where-line = 'BUKRS = ''0010'''.
APPEND ta_where.
ta_where-line = 'BUKRS = ''0021'''.
APPEND ta_where.
SELECT *
    FROM t001 INTO TABLE ta_t001
    WHERE (ta_where).
```

To understand why this is wrong, check the interpretation of the code made at runtime below. The translated code is as follows:

```
SELECT *
    FROM t001 INTO TABLE ta_t001
    WHERE bukrs = '0010'
          bukrs = '0021'.
```

As you can see, something is missing between the two conditions of the WHERE clause. It should have looked like this:

```
SELECT *
    FROM t001 INTO TABLE ta_t001
    WHERE bukrs = '0010'
      OR bukrs = '0021'.
```

This exception can be caught in the same way as the other exceptions.

We'll end this section by mentioning that there are more possible runtime errors than we can address here. Therefore, be prepared for everything. For more details on exception handling, see Chapter 5.

4.3.2   Dynamic Calls

This section discusses the error situations that may arise when programs or procedures are called dynamically. A *dynamic call* is required when the exact name of the procedure to be called cannot be determined before the actual execution of the ABAP code. Therefore, both the procedure's name and its interface parameters need to be established at runtime. You'll find a good example of the dynamic call principle in the way in which message-handling has been implemented in SAP R/3: the exact program and subroutine names are selected at runtime from the customizing table TNAPR; subsequently, the subroutine to be used is called using the command PERFORM (routine_name) IN PROGRAM (program_name).

We'll show you the stability errors to be addressed by referring, in turn, to the standard options for making dynamic calls: external program calls, external subroutine calls, function calls, object instances, and method calls. We'll distinguish two basic error situations for each type of dynamic call: either the procedure, or program, or object that is referred to does not exist; or, if it does exist, something is wrong with the parameters used.

Dynamic Program Calls

A program can be called dynamically using the SUBMIT ⟨report⟩ or the CALL ⟨transaction⟩ statement. A dynamic SUBMIT statement looks like this:

```
SUBMIT (tp_programname) AND RETURN.
```

Variable tp_programname contains the name of the program to be executed. If the program does not exist, a runtime error will occur. Because this error is not catchable, it is important to prevent it. You can do this by first checking whether the program exists, for example, by reading table TRDIR or by using functions or methods that were specifically created for this purpose.

The same holds true for executing transactions dynamically. Consider the following statement:

```
CALL TRANSACTION tp_transaction.
```

In this statement, the variable `tp_transaction` is supposed to contain the name of the transaction that must be executed. If this is not the case, a program dump will occur with the error CALL_TRANSACTION_NOT_FOUND. This runtime error is not catchable either. However, you can easily prevent this error from occurring by determining whether the transaction actually exists in the table TSTC.

If the program does exist, but the parameters and select-options that need to be passed on to the program are not correct, a dump will occur only when a type-conflict arises. If a parameter that doesn't exist in the called ABAP program is nevertheless passed on by the calling program, no error is generated. However, if a mandatory parameter is not passed on to the called program, the program will stop. How exactly this error situation is made visible depends on whether the program is executed in the background or in dialog mode. In the case of background processing, an error message is generated, whereas in dialog mode, the control over the called program is handed over to its selection-screen, in order to give the end user the opportunity to change the selection parameters.

Dynamic Subroutine Calls

Calling an external subroutine dynamically requires that you use variables that contain the names of both the program and the subroutine to be used. To make the call successful, these variables must be filled with valid values at runtime. Below, you'll find the ABAP code that is required for a dynamic call of an external subroutine:

```
PERFORM (pa_rname) IN PROGRAM (pa_pname)
       USING    pa_kunnr
       CHANGING tp_knal.
```

Again, two basic types of problems can be distinguished: the program or the subroutine contained within does not exist; or, the parameters used don't correspond with the formal parameters of the subroutine that is called. This second type of error occurs in three situations: when a parameter is missing; when the sequence in which the parameters are provided doesn't correspond with the sequence that the subroutine expects; or, when the program's parameters aren't identical with the subroutine's parameters.

If the program doesn't exist, a catchable error occurs: CX_SY_PROGRAM_NOT_FOUND. Therefore, adding a check beforehand to verify whether the program actually exists in table TRDIR is not really required. However, the check to determine whether the subroutine within the program actually exists requires special attention, since a program dump is otherwise generated (see Figure 4.21):

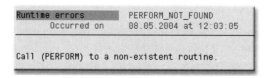

Figure 4.21 Non-Existing Routine Called

The reason why you need to pay attention to the question of whether or not the subroutine exists is because the related runtime error is not catchable. There is a way that you can verify whether a subroutine exists in a program. Consider the following ABAP code:

```
TABLES: dwtree.
DATA: BEGIN OF lst_namtr,
        typ(2)                TYPE c VALUE ' ',
        lin                   TYPE c VALUE '_',
        rest(30)              TYPE c,
      END  OF lst_namtr.

DATA: lta_tree        TYPE STANDARD TABLE OF snode,
      ltp_error       TYPE c.

e_tp_ok = abap_false.

lst_namtr-typ = 'PG'.
lst_namtr-rest = i_tp_pname.

IMPORT tree TO lta_tree
       FROM DATABASE dwtree(tr) ID lst_namtr.
* No entry is found, so the tree must be updated
IF sy-subrc NE 0.
  CALL FUNCTION 'WB_TREE_ACTUALIZE'
    EXPORTING
      tree_name         = lst_namtr
      with_tcode_index  = abap_true
    IMPORTING
      syntax_error      = ltp_error
    EXCEPTIONS
      OTHERS            = 1.

  IF sy-subrc = 0 AND ltp_error = abap_false.

    IMPORT tree TO lta_tree
           FROM DATABASE dwtree(tr) ID lst_namtr.
```

```
  ELSE.
* Error handling
  ENDIF.
ENDIF.

IF NOT lta_tree[] IS INITIAL.

  READ TABLE lta_tree TRANSPORTING NO FIELDS
       WITH KEY type = 'OPU'
                name = i_tp_rname.
  IF sy-subrc = 0.
    e_tp_ok = abap_true.
  ENDIF.
ENDIF.
```

In this code, we use what is known as the *tree-information*. The tree-information is generated by the Workbench Organizer in order to check whether a program contains a specific routine. Note that you need to consider—as we did above—that the tree-information may not yet be available. In that case, function wb_tree_actualize must be called to update it. The database table DWTREE contains an internal table with all kinds of information on a program. Routines can be found by reading the internal table using type OPU and the routine name.

There is a way to prevent a program dump from occurring—by calling the routine with the addition of the IF FOUND option:

```
PERFORM (pa_rname) IN PROGRAM (pa_pname)
        IF FOUND
        USING    pa_kunnr
        CHANGING tp_kna1.
```

A specific drawback of the IF FOUND option, however, is that it doesn't set a returncode, nor does it raise a catchable exception. For this reason, you must find a way to check whether the routine has been called in the first place. One way to do this is by determining if the data in the interface has changed after the subroutine has been called. This works only if the purpose of using the subroutine is to change the interface parameters. Another way to determine whether a subroutine has been called is by introducing your own kind of returncode: this switch must be defined as a CHANGING parameter of the subroutine. To make it act as a replacement for the returncode, you must reset the switch before the subroutine is called, and then, set the switch inside the subroutine:

```
CLEAR sw_called.
PERFORM (pa_rname) IN PROGRAM (pa_pname)
        IF FOUND
        USING    pa_kunnr
        CHANGING tp_kna1
```

```
              sw_called.
IF sw_called = abap_true.
   " Some kind of action
ENDIF.
```

We should add that this option is feasible only if you made the called subroutine yourself. We strongly advise you not to change already existing or standard SAP routines. In fact, having to take such precautions is hardly a welcome thought. You're far better off *not* using external subroutines at all (see also Section 3.4.2).

Dynamically calling external subroutines will result in even bigger problems in the event that there are inconsistencies between the used parameters of the program and the formally required parameters of the subroutine. The IF FOUND option offers no relief, and no catchable exception is generated either. The fact that checking the formal parameters is not feasible makes it only worse. Therefore, using parameters incorrectly in external subroutine calls will always generate a dump such as the one in Figure 4.22 below:

Figure 4.22 Missing Parameter

This is another reason why we recommend that you avoid using external subroutines in your own software. Dynamic function and method calls can also lead to runtime errors, however, those errors can be controlled more easily.

Dynamic Function Module Calls

As you might expect, functions can be called dynamically in much the same way as subroutines. However, one of the specific advantages of using function modules instead of subroutines is that a function's interface parameters and exceptions are specified more explicitly and clearly, that is, on the basis of internal tables with a predefined structure. A dynamic function call looks like this:

```
PERFORM fill_parameters CHANGING para_tab[]
                                 excp_tab[].
CALL FUNCTION name
  PARAMETER-TABLE
    para_tab
  EXCEPTION-TABLE
    excp_tab.
CASE sy-subrc.
  WHEN 0.
```

```
  WHEN 1.
    MESSAGE ID sy-msgid TYPE sy-msgty NUMBER sy-msgno.
  WHEN others.
ENDCASE.
```

Similar to what can happen with a subroutine, the first exception that may arise is that a function module being called does not exist. This will generate the following runtime error (see Figure 4.23):

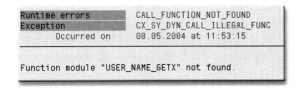

Runtime errors	CALL_FUNCTION_NOT_FOUND
Exception	CX_SY_DYN_CALL_ILLEGAL_FUNC
Occurred on	08.05.2004 at 11:53:15

Function module "USER_NAME_GETX" not found.

Figure 4.23 Non-Existing Function Module Called

There are two ways to prevent this exception. You can check table TFDIR to verify whether a function module actually exists before employing it. But, there's an even simpler way to prevent the exception—you can also anticipate the error by using the TRY...ENDTRY mechanism:

```
PERFORM fill_parameters CHANGING para_tab[]
                                 excp_tab[].
TRY.
    CALL FUNCTION name
      PARAMETER-TABLE
        para_tab
      EXCEPTION-TABLE
        excp_tab.
    CASE sy-subrc.
      WHEN 1.
        MESSAGE ID sy-msgid TYPE sy-msgty NUMBER sy-msgno.
      WHEN 2.
        MESSAGE e888(sABAPdocu) WITH 'Error in  funcion module'.
    ENDCASE.
  CATCH cx_sy_dyn_call_illegal_func INTO gl_oref.
    gl_text = gl_oref->get_text( ).
  CATCH cx_root INTO gl_oref.
    gl_text = gl_oref->get_text( ).
ENDTRY.
IF NOT gl_text IS INITIAL.
  WRITE: / gl_text. "or something else to handle this error!
ENDIF.
```

In the same way as occurs with a dynamic subroutine call, the parameters used in a dynamic function call can also contain inconsistencies compared with the formally required parameters. However, the contrast with runtime errors caused by the wrong parameter use in subroutines is significant. Because all corresponding runtime errors for function modules are catchable exceptions, function modules don't require the same complicated checks that subroutines do.

Dynamic Object Instances

Although the concept of an object is quite different from that of a function module or a subroutine, the mere action of instantiating an object can, to a certain extent, be compared with calling a function module, for example. At least the consequences of doing this correctly can be similar: the object may not exist; or, it may be handled in the wrong way. An object can be instantiated dynamically by providing the name of the reference class at runtime. You'll find an example of this in the following code:

```
CLASS c3 DEFINITION.
  PUBLIC  SECTION.
    METHODS create_object IMPORTING itp_class_name TYPE c
                          EXPORTING erf_pointer TYPE REF TO object.
ENDCLASS.
                            "C3 DEFINITION
CLASS c3 IMPLEMENTATION.
  METHOD create_object.
    CREATE OBJECT erf_pointer TYPE (itp_class_name).
  ENDMETHOD.              "CREATE_OBJECT
ENDCLASS.                 "C3 IMPLEMENTATION

DATA: rf_r3        TYPE REF TO c3,
      rf_pointer   TYPE REF TO object,
      tp_class     TYPE class_name value 'R3'.

  CREATE OBJECT rf_r3.
  rf_r3->create_object( EXPORTING itp_class_name = tp_class
                        IMPORTING erf_pointer    = rf_pointer ).
```

In method CREATE_OBJECT, an object called erf_pointer is created with reference to the class contained in the importing parameter itp_class_name. Now, perhaps, the class that is dynamically referred to doesn't exist; or, the class exists, but the object reference does not; or, the type of the class doesn't match the type of erf_pointer. We'll discuss these three types of problems below.

Instantiating an object dynamically by referencing a non-existing class generates a catchable runtime error (see Figure 4.24). One way to prevent such an error is to check whether the global class exists in table SEOCLASS. You can also implement a check in more or less the same way as we did for a subroutine. However, both checks aren't really necessary.

```
Runtime errors      CREATE_OBJECT_CLASS_NOT_FOUND
Exception           CX_SY_CREATE_OBJECT_ERROR
        Occurred on 08.05.2004 at 11:39:31

CREATE OBJECT: Class " " could not be found.
```

Figure 4.24 Reference to a Non-Existing Class

The reason why such checks aren't required is that this dump can also be avoided by adopting the simplest alternative: positioning the CREATE OBJECT within a TRY...ENDTRY block.

```
CREATE OBJECT rf_r3.

CLEAR gl_text.
TRY.
  rf_r3->create_object( EXPORTING itp_class_name = tp_class
                        IMPORTING erf_pointer    = rf_pointer ).
  CATCH cx_sy_create_object_error INTO gl_oref.
    gl_text = gl_oref->get_text( ).
  CATCH cx_root INTO gl_oref.
    gl_text = gl_oref->get_text( ).
ENDTRY.
IF NOT gl_text IS INITIAL.
*                    ---> some kind of error-handling
ENDIF.
```

A second kind of problem is specifically related to the use of objects. In particular, it is the result of an object needing to be instantiated. Of course, this could go wrong. An associated problem may be that the object reference either doesn't refer to an object instance yet, or, it doesn't refer to an object instance any longer. You can use the addition IS BOUND to verify whether an object has actually been instantiated. Note that here, also, the exception is catchable. The code below shows an example in which a method is called for an object that was, in fact, created but has also been removed before the method call was actually triggered:

```
IF rf_obj1 IS INITIAL.
  CREATE OBJECT rf_obj1.
ENDIF.

CLEAR rf_obj1.   " <--- instance removed

CALL METHOD rf_obj1->find_subcl
  EXPORTING
    itp_class    = pa_cl
  CHANGING
    cta_classes  = ta_classes
```

```
EXCEPTIONS
   no_data      = 1
   OTHERS       = 2.
```

First, the object rf_obj1 is created. At some point during its processing, a CLEAR statement removes the object again. Then, a method is called for the same object. Executing this code will result in the following dump (in Figure 4.25):

Figure 4.25 Reference Lost

Because this is also a *catchable* system-exception (from Release Web AS 6.10 and later), you can prevent this dump using a TRY...ENDTRY block:

```
IF rf_obj1 IS INITIAL.
  CREATE OBJECT rf_obj1.
ENDIF.

CLEAR rf_obj1.     " <--- instance removed

CLEAR gl_text.
TRY.
              CALL METHOD rf_obj1->find_subcl
                EXPORTING
                  itp_class   = pa_cl
                CHANGING
                  cta_classes = ta_classes
                EXCEPTIONS
              no_data      = 1
              OTHERS       = 2.
      CATCH cx_sy_ref_is_initial INTO gl_oref.
      gl_text = gl_oref->get_text( ).
ENDTRY.
IF NOT gl_text IS INITIAL.
  WRITE: / 'Method not called, object unknown'.
ENDIF.
```

A type-conflict can occur if the object reference field is defined with a type other than the corresponding class.

```
DATA: rf_vari      type ref to cl_class,
      tp_classname type class_name value 'cl_class_2'.

CREATE OBJECT rf_vari TYPE (tp_classname).
```

This piece of ABAP code will lead to a runtime error if `cl_class` and `cl_class_2` are not type-compatible. Nevertheless, in some specific situations, this code is feasible.

Dynamic Method Calls

The name of a method can be transferred at runtime using the following source code:

```
Call method rf_object->(tp_methodname).
```

Similar to the previous situation, the basic two problems are that a non-existing method is called, or the method call is conducted incorrectly. Because all of these errors are catchable exceptions, trying to prevent these problems isn't worth the effort. Therefore, we will not go into more detail at this time.

4.4   Changes in an ABAP Program's Environment

This section deals with various errors caused by changes in an ABAP program's environment. Almost every ABAP program will, at least to some extent, interact with functionality that is both inside and outside the SAP system.

It will, for example, usually refer to some ABAP Dictionary definitions, whose changes can have a substantial impact.

However, we won't concentrate on changes in ABAP Dictionary objects in this section because these changes can be addressed by using the Repository Information System (directly via Transaction SE84, or indirectly via Transaction SE80). But there are other less obvious elements in the program's outer environment that may also be liable to change. As an ABAP developer, you need to know which elements these are, and what strategies you should apply to minimize the changes in environment that can have undesirable effects. In this section, we'll discuss the dependencies that an ABAP program can have on user authorizations (in Section 4.4.1); native operating-system (OS) commands (in Section 4.4.2); filenames (in Section 4.4.3); code-page definitions (in Section 4.4.4); and client applications (in Section 4.4.5).

4.4.1   User Authorizations

Some readers may be familiar with the following problem: suddenly, several background jobs generate errors when one of the employees starts working for another department. If this occurs, you should verify whether this employee's SAP logon user is also used for running background jobs. Sometimes, the reason for such unexpected failures lies with the new authorization settings that the new department has provided to this user.

In order to avoid this situation, it is preferable to reserve one specific user for starting background jobs. By doing this, the associated user settings will be less likely to change once they've been established. The same holds true for a logon user that is applied for establishing a Remote Function Call (RFC) connection: if the dialog user ID of a regular end user is applied for this purpose, the same kind of problem can occur.

4.4.2 Native OS commands

Sometimes, external operating-system commands are executed directly in ABAP code. In the following example, you will find references to two external commands, stored in file sapactab.h. The first call fetches the directory path of a certain type of file (the runtime analysis file). The second call fetches the name of the system instance used:

```
REPORT  /ctac/r_stab_ext_command_err.

TYPES: ty_buf(70)       TYPE c,
       BEGIN OF ty_at_name,
         at(2)          TYPE c,
         syst(2)        TYPE c,
         nr(4)          TYPE n,
       END OF ty_at_name.

DATA: tp_path(60)       TYPE c,
      tp_at_fname       TYPE ty_at_name,
      tp_fname_slash(1) TYPE c. " '/' or '\'

CALL 'C_SAPGPARAM' ID 'NAME'  FIELD 'ABAP/atrapath'
                   ID 'VALUE' FIELD tp_path.

CALL 'C_SAPGPARAM' ID 'NAME'  FIELD 'SAPSYSTEM'
                   ID 'VALUE' FIELD tp_at_fname-syst.
WRITE: / 'ABAP ATRA Path :'(001), tp_path.
WRITE: / 'System Instance:'(002), tp_at_fname-syst.
```

Besides the lack of transparency of such functions, just the use of these functions makes your programs dependent on the operating system on which these commands are executed. Therefore, you shouldn't be surprised if a migration to another OS causes problems with programs using native OS commands.

They can, for example, be part of an FTP (File Transfer Protocol) script on the application server that sends a datafile to another server. This type of FTP script is often part of an interface procedure. Because of the side-effects that the use of the CALL cfunc option has, we don't recommend that you use it. You can rely on native OS commands only if no other alternative is available. To make your ABAP programs OS-independent, we recommend that you use the function module `sxpg_command_execute` instead:

```
DATA: ta_prot          TYPE TABLE OF btcxpm.
DATA: tp_opsys         TYPE syopsys.

PARAMETERS: pa_cmd     TYPE sxpglogcmd.
* PARAMETERS: pa_parm    TYPE btcxpgpar.

tp_opsys = sy-opsys.

CALL FUNCTION 'SXPG_COMMAND_EXECUTE'
  EXPORTING
    commandname                    = pa_cmd
*    additional_parameters         = pa_parm
    operatingsystem                = tp_opsys
  TABLES
    exec_protocol                  = ta_prot
  EXCEPTIONS
    no_permission                  = 1
    command_not_found              = 2
    parameters_too_long            = 3
    security_risk                  = 4
    wrong_check_call_interface     = 5
    program_start_error            = 6
    program_termination_error      = 7
    x_error                        = 8
    parameter_expected             = 9
    too_many_parameters            = 10
    illegal_command                = 11
    wrong_asynchronous_parameters  = 12
    cant_enq_tbtco_entry           = 13
    jobcount_generation_error      = 14
    others                         = 15.
IF sy-subrc <> 0.
  MESSAGE ID sy-msgid TYPE sy-msgty NUMBER sy-msgno
          WITH sy-msgv1 sy-msgv2 sy-msgv3 sy-msgv4.
ENDIF.
```

You can access and maintain the commands that can be executed by this function module with Transaction SM69. You can also test the OS system commands, which are available via Transaction SM49.

4.4.3 Filenames

Another way to make your ABAP software independent of its technical environment is by avoiding the use of physical filenames in programs that either read or create datasets on the application server. When the application server or the OS underlying the SAP system is changed, all physical filenames mentioned directly in your ABAP code can become unrecognizable.

The exact makeup of a physical filename often depends on the OS used. A good example is the use of the backslash (/) in pathnames in a Unix environment, whereas in a Windows environment both a backslash (/) and a forward slash (\) are allowed. Migrating to another OS will therefore directly introduce the problem with unrecognizable filenames. You should note that this kind of problem can also arise by simply renaming an application server, if the application server is explicitly mentioned in your programs.

Physical filenames can be determined at runtime using system parameters. SAP offers the functionality to define logical filenames (with Transaction FILE). These filenames are linked to logical paths that can be changed, depending on the OS underlying the SAP system. By calling function modules like `file_get_name` or `file_get_name_using_path`, you can directly determine a physical filename (system parameter `sy-opsys`) in your code on the basis of the associated logical filename. Obviously, the advantage is that pathnames and filenames can be maintained centrally. Therefore, not only maintenance activities but also the chances of incurring stability issues are reduced to a minimum. So, instead of using a constant in your program such as the following:

```
CONSTANTS: co_file         TYPE localfile
                           VALUE 'F:\usr\sap\CID\SYS\global\netscape'.
```

You're far better off determining the physical filename dynamically. The corresponding code of your programs should resemble the following sample piece of code:

```
REPORT  /ctac/r_stab_log_file_sol2              .
*
DATA: tp_physical_filename  TYPE string.

PARAMETERS: pa_logpa TYPE pathintern OBLIGATORY
                     DEFAULT 'HOME',
            pa_filnm TYPE localfile  OBLIGATORY.
*------------------------------------------------------------------------------*
START-OF-SELECTION.
*------------------------------------------------------------------------------*
*
   CALL FUNCTION 'FILE_GET_NAME_USING_PATH'
     EXPORTING
       logical_path               = pa_logpa
       operating_system           = sy-opsys
       file_name                  = pa_filnm
*      USE_PRESENTATION_SERVER    = ' '
     IMPORTING
```

```
    file_name_with_path           = tp_physical_filename
  EXCEPTIONS
    path_not_found                = 1
    missing_parameter             = 2
    operating_system_not_found    = 3
    file_system_not_found         = 4
    OTHERS                        = 5
            .
  IF sy-subrc <> 0.
* Error handling here
  ENDIF.
  WRITE: / tp_physical_filename.
```

If, for whatever reason, the physical filename or pathname is changed, you don't have to change the program; rather, only the definition of the link from the logical to the physical filename using Transaction FILE needs to be changed.

4.4.4 Code-Page Use

In Chapter 1, we introduced the terms *coding system* and *code-page*. Nowadays, the EBCDIC and the ASCII coding systems are the best-known coding systems worldwide; however, the Unicode coding system is destined to be their successor.

In this section, we present a stability problem that is specifically associated with the use of varying code-pages on different systems. Because each system is usually based on one particular code-page, in a heterogeneous system landscape, it is not unusual to find software components that process their data on the basis of varying code-pages.

Most systems will apply code-pages by default, that is, the code-page is set on system level, and all actions requiring the code-page definition use this default. However, this habit entails a risk that reveals itself particularly in scenarios where data is exchanged between systems, and to a lesser extent in hardware and operating-system migrations. In Figure 4.26, one such scenario is depicted—a file is transferred from an EBCDIC-based system to an ASCII-based system.

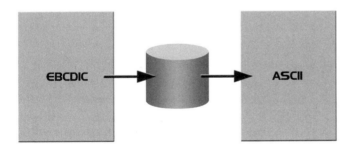

Figure 4.26 Code-Page Dependency

You incur the risk that we referred to if the default code-page of one of the systems in the landscape is changed. Consequently, the format of all the interface files produced on the basis of this default setting will change as well. In addition, all incoming interface files will be interpreted differently. Therefore, there's sufficient reason to avoid this dependency.

As such, this is not a problem. Since an SAP system will frequently be one of many components in a heterogeneous landscape, it must have the flexibility necessary to convert code-pages when reading data from, or writing data to, a file, or when directly communicating with other systems via an RFC. The appropriate ABAP language elements for this purpose are available. Explicit handling of code-pages can be achieved by using the command TRANSLATE FROM CODE-PAGE or TRANSLATE TO CODE-PAGE. As of Web AS Release 6.10, there are other options as well:

▶ Instead of using one of the variants of the TRANSLATE command, you can also use methods of a conversion class such as CL_ABAP_CONV_X2X_CE.

▶ Some additions to the command OPEN DATASET are available to indicate the code-page to be used.

In addition, SAP has added a new program attribute to define whether a program is *Unicode-enabled*. An advantage of setting the Unicode-enabled flag in the ABAP program's attributes is that you're obligated to explicitly indicate the code-page to be used in commands such as OPEN DATASET. Thus, you will still be using the correct code-page for all interface files regardless of changes in the default code-page of your own SAP system. Of course, this still isn't 100% foolproof: if the default code-page on another system in the landscape is changed, processing an inbound interface in your SAP system may still lead to incorrectly processed data. Secondly, Unicode-enabling won't prevent problems in RFC communication either.

In short, you can—to a certain extent—make at least your own SAP system behave as a stable component in the communication and file exchange with other systems in the landscape. To achieve this, we recommend that you use the appropriate ABAP elements and make your programs Unicode-enabled for an enhanced syntax check. Note, however, that Unicode-enabling won't make your ABAP programs completely immune to a code-page change in an interface file coming from another system.

4.4.5 Client Applications

In this section, we discuss the implications of using an external application on the client, which is immediately linked to an SAP system. In addition to the SAP GUI, many other user interfaces for a SAP system can be applied: applications made in office products or in programming languages such as Java and Visual Basic can serve as alternative frontends.

Note that introducing such alternative front-end functionality may introduce extra dependencies for your ABAP code on specific clients. You may not be able to afford this, particularly in cases where a large number of different desktops are used.

For example, consider a spreadsheet application that reads data from the SAP database using an RFC, which is implemented in a macro. Some of the immediate risks inherent in trying to call this RFC from another client (i.e., another desktop) would be:

▶ The macro may not available on another client.

▶ Execution of the macro may not be allowed due to security settings on the new client.

▶ The decimal notation and date format may cause interpretation problems due to country settings on the client or in the operating system.

▶ The macro may not work because the new client uses another OS version.

▶ The macro may not work because it uses a different SAP GUI version (with different DLL files).

▶ The macro may not work because the `saplogon.ini` file contains other names of SAP servers.

In other words, making ABAP functionality dependent on the available software and hardware of the client might not be such a good idea if some minimal degree of standardization is not ensured. You may, to a certain extent, be able to ensure standardization of all clients within the company. However, if clients outside the company can also directly access an SAP system, such a guarantee is virtually impossible. In that case, you'd have to ensure that the ABAP application also works with older versions of the client application, different browsers, different operating systems, and so forth. This requires a lot of testing when making such an application and a lot of extra maintenance later. Therefore, our message to you is this: Don't go too far in creating client dependencies.

4.5   Using an ABAP Program Incorrectly

This section deals with the inadvertent, wrong use of ABAP programs. In order to make optimal use of an application server's resources, a SAP system distinguishes between several tasks, such as the *dialog task*, the *background task*, and the *update task*, and two basic processing modes—*synchronous* or *asynchronous* processing.

Each of these tasks and processing modes has its own purpose and limitations, and each ABAP program must be designed to consider these constraints. As an ABAP developer, you must be aware of these limitations. Otherwise, you could make design decisions that you'll later regret. The same warning applies to a technique like SAP's *Batch Data Communication* (BDC) technique, perhaps better known as the *CALL TRANSACTION* or the *Batch Input* technique. Although more modern techniques such as BAPI and IDoc processing are intended to make BDC processing obsolete, the technique is still used in many ABAP programs. We'll discuss several design choices that can lead to stability problems and present some ways in which you can anticipate these problems.

Fortunately, most disturbances due to the wrong use of a program are usually noticed at a relatively early stage, that is, during testing or immediately after taking a program into production. But there are also those situations where a problem may arise only after a program has been in use for some time, for example, when a time-consuming dialog program is executed in the background for the first time.

First, Section 4.5.1 addresses some pitfalls inherent in dialog processing. Then, Section 4.5.2 deals with some fundamental restrictions related to the distribution of tasks. In Section 4.5.3, we discuss some specific limitations of BDC processing. Lastly, Section 4.5.4 highlights the main questions worth considering when you need to choose a process type.

4.5.1 Restrictions of Dialog Processing

When designing an ABAP program, the most fundamental choice you'll need to make is whether the program is to be used in the *foreground*, that is, under the immediate supervision of the end user, or in the *background*, without the end user playing any role in the program's actions. If a program is intended to be used in the foreground, most of the program's actions will be executed in the *dialog task* of the application server and in the SAP GUI on the client (see Figure 4.27). For heavy-duty processing that doesn't require user interaction, a program will use only the *background task* on the application server. The *update task* serves as a kind of secondary task, in the sense that both the dialog task and the background task can shift part of their workload to the update task. As the name suggests, this task is usually, although not always, done for performing updates. In this section, we'll discuss how you can prevent misuse of the dialog task and why you should be careful when using dialog functionality in the background.

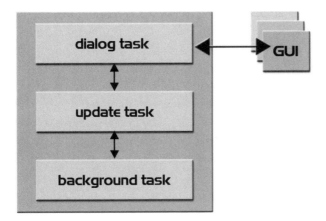

Figure 4.27 Different Kinds of Tasks Within the SAP Environment

How to Prevent Misuse of the Dialog Task

The first fundamental difference between a foreground program and a background program is the amount of data to be processed. While the background task is best suited for processing large amounts of data, a program designed to run in the dialog task is supposed to handle relatively small amounts of data. Therefore, a maximum runtime of 300 seconds is usually set for each single dialog process in most SAP systems. A dialog step exceeding this limit will generate a program dump with a *time-out exception*.

Strictly speaking, the immediate cause of a time-out exception is usually poor performance. However, a more fundamental cause of a time-out error is making the wrong design decision. A dialog program that requires more than the aforementioned 300 seconds simply shouldn't have been designed for online use. Therefore, if you intend to design a program to run in the foreground, you should build in some guarantees to prevent time-out errors.

There are two ways in which you can replace a program dump with more elegant exception handling: either by limiting the amount of data to be processed; or, by limiting the runtime allowed for the program. We have provided two code examples to show how this can be done. The first example tracks the amount of data processed:

```
* 1 Keep track of amount of data that must be processed
IF lines( th_suppliers ) > co_supplier_limit.
  MESSAGE i000(38) WITH
        'Number of suppliers to be processed is more than'(001)
        co_supplier_limit
        'Run this selection in background'(002).
  LEAVE PROGRAM.
ENDIF.
```

The second example tracks the amount of time consumed, instead of monitoring the amount of data processed:

```
REPORT /ctac/runtime_test.
* To keep track of runtime during processing
* Maximum time 200 seconds in Microseconds format
CONSTANTS: co_time_limit  TYPE i VALUE 200000000,
           co_answer_yes  TYPE c VALUE '1',
           co_answer_no   TYPE c VALUE '2'.

DATA:      tp_answer       TYPE c.

DATA:      tp_time_new     TYPE i,
           tp_time_old     TYPE i,
           tp_runtime      TYPE i.

START-OF-SELECTION.
* Initializing the time measurement field at beginning of program
  GET RUN TIME FIELD tp_time_old.
* Call the routine to measure runtime
  PERFORM select_data_1.

  PERFORM measure_runtime.

  PERFORM select_data_2.

  PERFORM measure_runtime.

FORM measure_runtime.
* Measure the runtime since last time
  GET RUN TIME FIELD tp_time_new.
* Calculate the run time
  tp_runtime = tp_time_new - tp_time_old.
* Does runtime exceed the timelimit?
  IF tp_runtime > co_time_limit.
    CALL FUNCTION 'POPUP_TO_DECIDE'
      EXPORTING
        defaultoption    = '2'
        textline1        = 'Continue?'(p01)
        text_option1     = 'Yes'(p02)
        text_option2     = 'No'(p03)
        titel            = 'Time Limit Reached'(p04)
        cancel_display   = ' '
      IMPORTING
        answer           = tp_answer
                   .
* Implement the handling of TP_ANSWER here.
    CASE tp_answer.
      WHEN co_answer_yes.
* If user wants to continu, start measuring again
```

```
        tp_time_old = tp_time_new.
      WHEN co_answer_no.
        LEAVE PROGRAM.
      WHEN OTHERS.
*  ...
    ENDCASE.
  ENDIF.

ENDFORM.                        "measure_runtime
```

Why Avoid the Use of Interactive Functionality in the Background?

The second fundamental difference between a foreground program and a background program is the presence or absence of interaction with the end user. This difference is very clearly defined: the interaction is either present (in the foreground) or absent (in the background). Because of this strict separation, there aren't many situations where a typical foreground program, containing user interaction, is transferred to the background task deliberately (as is depicted in Figure 4.28). Nevertheless, sometimes it does happen.

To demonstrate why transferring online functionality to the background task is usually contradictory with its purpose, we will briefly discuss how three typical features of interactive programs would behave in the background. These features are screen handling on the basis of dynpros and pop-ups, interactive reporting, and Control Technology.

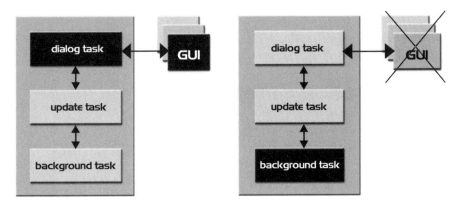

Figure 4.28 Kinds of Tasks and the Connection with the GUI

The first way to create interaction with the end user is by using screens in all sizes and types. Screen types such as dynpros and pop-ups are, technically speaking, executed on the application server. Therefore, you can also process a program containing such interactive features in the background task. However, the main reason why this usually isn't feasible is because of the very nature of an interactive program. We'll demonstrate this with a code example that uses the standard pop-up function POPUP_TO_DECIDE:

```
CALL FUNCTION 'POPUP_TO_DECIDE'
  EXPORTING
    defaultoption            = '2'
    textline1                = 'Do you want to save this data?'(001)
*   TEXTLINE2                = ' '
*   TEXTLINE3                = ' '
    text_option1             = 'Yes'(002)
    text_option2             = 'No'(003)
*   ICON_TEXT_OPTION1        = ' '
*   ICON_TEXT_OPTION2        = ' '
    titel                    = 'Ask user for answer'(004)
*   START_COLUMN             = 25
*   START_ROW                = 6
    cancel_display           = abap_true
  IMPORTING
    answer                   = tp_answer
      .
CASE tp_answer.
  WHEN co_answer_yes.
* The data can be saved
  WHEN co_answer_no.
* The data should not be saved
  WHEN co_answer_cancel.
* The action is cancelled
ENDCASE.
```

Executing this function module results in the presentation of a pop-up-screen (Figure 4.29).

Figure 4.29 Pop-up Screen to Confirm a Situation

In this example, the interaction is supported by the use of variables like tp_answer. Suppose that this piece of code is executed in the background. In that case, the content of variable tp_answer would be equal to the default value 2. Consequently, the data is not saved.

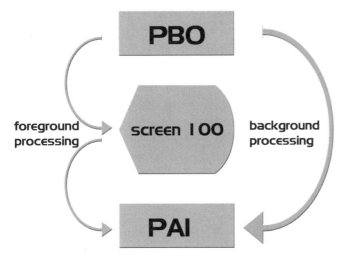

Figure 4.30 Difference in Flow Logic Processing Between Foreground and Background

Program logic such as this can be used in a report program to call a dynpro with the statement CALL SCREEN. However, in the background, both the associated screen events Process Before Output (PBO) and Process After Input (PAI) are subsequently processed without any screen interaction (see Figure 4.30). Most likely, this will lead to an endless loop because no condition to exit the screen is ever found to be true. Although these examples appear to be somewhat unlikely, please note that they are extracted from real-life situations.

The use of ABAP commands that are specifically intended for use in only interactive reporting will also cause your programs to behave strangely in background processing. The sample code includes some of these commands. When executing this code in dialog mode, that is, as intended, the pick or double-click function is simulated and the event AT LINE-SELECTION is processed immediately. Were the same code to be processed in the background, however, then both the SET CURSOR and SET USER-COMMAND would no longer work, and the normal flow of the program would be disturbed.

```
REPORT /ctac/r_stab_process_err2.

START-OF-SELECTION.

  WRITE: / 'List Index          '(001), sy-lsind.
  WRITE: / 'An interactive report line'(002).

  SET CURSOR LINE 4.
  SET USER-COMMAND 'PICK'.

AT LINE-SELECTION.
```

```
WRITE: / 'List Index            '(003), sy-lsind,
       / 'Selected line contents'(004), sy-lisel,
       / 'Selected line number  '(005), sy-lilli.
```

This example is not likely to exist in real-life ABAP programs, however, you could use it to test the effect of the SET USER-COMMAND statement in both dialog and background processing. Other possibilities to misuse interactive statements are less academic. Here is an example of how the MODIFY LINE statement is used to write the total number of pages on every page of an output list:

```
DATA: tp_page_total      LIKE sy-pagno,
      tp_page_current    LIKE sy-pagno,
      tp_text(1)         TYPE c.

START-OF-SELECTION.

* Data collection and write statements

END-OF-SELECTION.
* The fields, written at event TOP-OF-PAGE are
* modified here
  DO sy-pagno TIMES.
    MODIFY LINE 1 OF PAGE sy-index
           FIELD VALUE
           tp_text            FROM '/'
           tp_page_current    FROM sy-index
           tp_page_total      FROM sy-pagno.
  ENDDO.

TOP-OF-PAGE.

  WRITE : tp_page_current,
          tp_text ,
          tp_page_total.
```

Running this code in dialog mode for three subsequent pages would result in the three subsequent headings containing the following information:

▶ Page 1: "1 / 3" (to indicate the first of three pages)

▶ Page 2: "2 / 3"

▶ Page 3: "3 / 3"

As you might suspect, the MODIFY LINE statement, marked bold in the code, is ignored when the program is executed in the background. Consequently, the header line produced by the same ABAP code, when executed in the background, will look like this:

- ► Page 1: "0 / 0"
- ► Page 2: "0 / 0"
- ► Page 3: "1 / 3"

Therefore, based on those examples, you can infer that all statements that are directly related to interactive list reporting should be used only in dialog processing.

A relatively recent addition to the ABAP language (from Release 4.6 on) is SAP's Control Technology. On the basis of this technology, the SAP GUI has been extended with features such as tree controls, ABAP List Viewer (ALV) grid controls, editor controls, and so forth (see Figure 4.31).

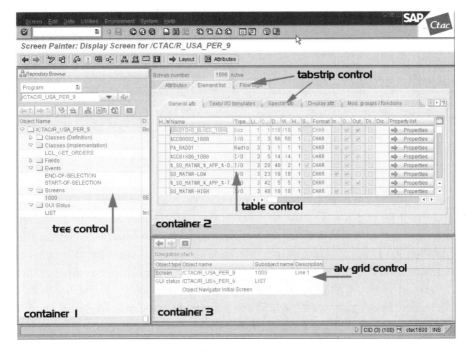

Figure 4.31 Several Kinds of GUI Controls

These *Enjoy Controls* require a so-called *object container* on the client, which is the basis for communication with the application server. What distinguishes Enjoy Control features from traditional SAP GUI functionality is that they are, by definition, executed entirely on the client. Note that this has some far-reaching consequences. A traditional pop-up screen is still processed on the application server, whereas an Enjoy Control is not. Therefore, attempting to use Enjoy Controls, such as those in Transaction MIGO (goods movement processing) or MIRO (incoming invoices) in the background is technically impossible. This will cause a program dump.

You should note that the limitations of Control Technology will not always be this apparent. Some functions that contain Control Technology can be called in any type of program, which would easily make you forget that an object container is required. To see what happens if it is forgotten, we'll refer to the example of the developer who wanted to create a flat interface file destined for an external system. This developer used the `gui_download` function module to put the file on a network directory, where the other system could pick up the file for further processing. After some tests, the program *seemed* to work fine: the file was created correctly, and the other system could process it. However, when the program was executed for the first time— after having been transported to the productive system and scheduled for execution in the background—it caused a dump. Look at the message that was generated: "Unable to initialize ABAP Control Framework ..." (see Figure 4.32):

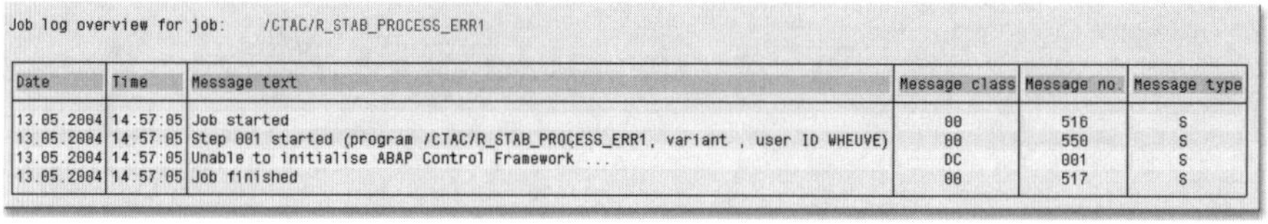

Job log overview for job:		/CTAC/R_STAB_PROCESS_ERR1			
Date	Time	Message text	Message class	Message no.	Message type
13.05.2004	14:57:05	Job started	00	516	S
13.05.2004	14:57:05	Step 001 started (program /CTAC/R_STAB_PROCESS_ERR1, variant , user ID WHEUVE)	00	550	S
13.05.2004	14:57:05	Unable to initialise ABAP Control Framework ...	DC	001	S
13.05.2004	14:57:05	Job finished	00	517	S

Figure 4.32 Job Log Overview

As the error message indicates, the reason for this failure was that the `gui_download` function actually requires an object container. Still, this doesn't mean that all Control functions will refuse to work in the background. Some functions are smart enough to discover whether a client is actually available. If a client is not available, they simply skip the program code referring to the Control functions and switch back to traditional processing instead. This is executed as usual on the application server. A good example is the function for displaying data in ALV format called `reuse_alv_grid_display`. It switches to another type of output when executed in the background. Under those circumstances, the output produced looks almost like the output produced by function `reuse_alv_list_display`, however, it is produced without the aforementioned object container having to be present. Therefore, when using a new Enjoy Control function, check where its limitations lie. You may be lucky enough to have such an intelligent function at your disposal.

A last pitfall that you should avoid is to call interactive functionality from an alternative frontend via an RFC. We've already summarized all the restrictions that are applicable in this case: no dynpro interaction, no interactive reporting, and no use of Control Technology—not even a list dynpro can be called. Therefore, it is imperative that you separate presentation logic (to be executed on the frontend) from processing logic (to be executed on the application server). This way, you can reuse the remaining logic more easily, that is, it can be called by any alternative frontend. For more information, see Chapter 8.

4.5.2 Restrictions for the Distribution of Tasks

In order to optimize the application server's resources, a program can be designed to split up its processing into several subprocesses. A program running in the dialog task or the background task can shift part of its workload to either a process in the update task, or another process within the dialog task. There are two main ways to do this: *synchronously* or *asynchronously*. Stability problems will occur if this fundamental difference between synchronous and asynchronous processing is not interpreted correctly during the design of an ABAP program.

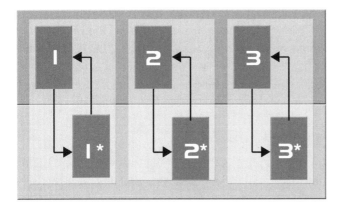

Figure 4.33 Synchronous Execution of Tasks

In Figure 4.33, a synchronous call of another process is depicted. The process that is started in the task below is supposed to respond to the calling process in the task on top. This is advantageous because other subsequent processes in the dialog or background task can immediately use the end result of the current process. For example, this can be the data that was just updated in the database. However, the price to be paid for this advantage is that the calling process has to wait until it receives a response from the process that was triggered in the other task.

In contrast, a process that is started in asynchronous mode can—but usually doesn't—return control to the calling process. Figure 4.34 shows the effect of this principle. The advantage here is that the next process in the task on top (Process 2) can immediately be started while the current process in the task below (Process 1) is still running. However, this also means that the calling process will lose control over the process called. An asynchronously created process is supposed to be self-sufficient.

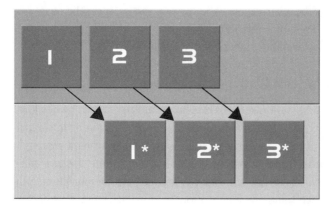

Figure 4.34 Asynchronous Execution of Tasks

To summarize, when forcing your programs to divide into several processes, you need to know exactly what kind of dependency is required: the efficient but loosely coupled asynchronous mode, or the tightly controlled, but less efficient synchronous mode. Now, we'll discuss two ways of triggering a new process: starting a new dialog process; and starting a new process in the update task. We'll also add some examples regarding specific asynchronous function calls.

Starting a New Dialog Process

A procedure or a function that is called with the STARTING NEW TASK option starts its processing in a new dialog task. The first cause of stability problems here is an unsuccessful start of the new process. There are three possible reasons why this can occur:

▶ A lack of system resources inhibits the start of the new process (all tasks are occupied). This will cause a RESOURCE_FAILURE.

▶ The new process is started in an unknown external system. Such an error situation will result in a SYSTEM_FAILURE.

▶ The communication with the external system fails, ending in a COMMUNICATION_FAILURE.

The second cause of stability problems here occurs at the end of the new process. Usually, the STARTING NEW TASK option is applied for asynchronous processing. In other words, the calling program will—in most cases—let the called process continue on its own. However, you can also use this option for a *semi-synchronous* call because you can return control to the calling program. To do this, you need a subroutine that can RECEIVE exporting parameters and exceptions. We applied this principle in the parallel processing example shown in Section 7.4.6.

If the STARTING NEW TASK option is used for a semi-synchronous scenario, the associated stability risk is that a bottleneck in the calling process may arise, because it expects a response. When, in a productive environment, an asynchronously-called function needs more time than expected, it will keep the calling program waiting. Consequently, the calling program is kept inert while occupying a dialog or background task. Moreover, if you don't force your program to track the number of tasks available, it may continue to create new processes and, eventually, block the entire system.

To summarize, in order to afford the STARTING NEW TASK option with stability, you first need to ensure that all the exceptions that might be raised during processing are caught; secondly, you need to establish a way of tracking those resources that are actually available.

Starting a New Update Process

The second way of calling a procedure or function asynchronously is by using the option IN UPDATE TASK. Unlike the STARTING NEW TASK option, the IN UPDATE TASK option is explicitly used to execute database updates in the update task. Functions that are called using this option are not executed immediately, but put on hold instead. Their parameters are stored in an intermediate table. When the COMMIT WORK statement is encountered—which may be after several function calls—all function calls previously put on hold will be released sequentially in the order in which they were called.

You need to understand the following characteristics of update functions:

▶ Update functions will not be executed unless they are explicitly triggered by a COMMIT WORK command.

▶ An explicit ROLLBACK WORK statement in your code will delete the update functions, which means that they can no longer be executed.

▶ The calling program does not have any control over the update functions unless the COMMIT WORK AND WAIT statement is used. In that case, the calling program will wait until all update functions have been finalized.

▶ The following statements aren't allowed in an update task:

  ▷ CALL SCREEN

  ▷ CALL DIALOG

  ▷ CALL TRANSACTION

  ▷ SUBMIT

You need to consider these characteristics carefully when designing or maintaining a program that performs asynchronous updates. In the example below, the effect of the indirect use of a CALL TRANSACTION statement in the update task is described. The scenario is this: a goods issue on an outbound delivery in one plant must trigger the creation of an inbound delivery in another plant.

The first step in this process, that is, the posting of a goods issue for an outbound delivery, is done in the usual way with online Transaction VL02 (change outbound delivery). Therefore, the update of the goods issue associated with this transaction should trigger the creation of an inbound delivery. Because no BAPI function is available to create inbound deliveries, this was done instead by using the CALL TRANSACTION command for Transaction VL31N (create inbound delivery):

```
CALL TRANSACTION 'VL31N' USING ta_bdcdata.
```

In addition, the standard message handling logic that handles printing SAPscript or Smart Forms output was used as the triggering mechanism: during the update of the goods issue, a "create inbound delivery" message was inserted in table NAST in the update task. Standard program RSNAST00 was used to interpret this message as the trigger to create the inbound delivery. In the productive environment, program RSNAST00 was scheduled to run a couple of times daily to process the outstanding messages and create the corresponding inbound deliveries. In terms of the tasks that were consecutively used on the application server, this made the flow of the program look like the workflow depicted in Figure 4.35:

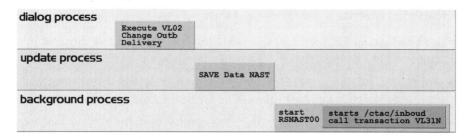

Figure 4.35 Starting Tasks (1): Call Transaction in Background Process

Some time later, the customizing settings of this message type were changed. In order to make the database more current, the creation of each inbound delivery was now triggered immediately after posting the goods issued instead of via a batch job every couple of hours. This was done by changing the processing type of the message type from "1" (send with periodically scheduled job) to "4" (send immediately when saving the application). In terms of the tasks used, the intended program flow looked like the one shown in Figure 4.36:

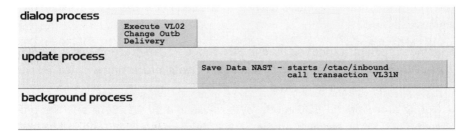

Figure 4.36 Starting Tasks (2): Call Transaction in Update Process

However, testing this change resulted in a program dump with system-exception `POSTING_ILLEGAL_STATEMENT`. As we mentioned prior to this example, you cannot execute the `CALL TRANSACTION` command in the update task.

4.5.3 Restrictions of Batch Data Communication

Most of you will be familiar with *Batch Data Communication* (BDC) techniques. Many ABAP programmers still rely on them. Basically, these techniques imply that standard SAP database tables are maintained in tailored ABAP programs by reusing existing online functionality via the `CALL TRANSACTION`, the `CALL DIALOG`, or the Batch Input technique. Although there are numerous reasons why these techniques should no longer be used, their use is too widespread to omit them from our discussion of the most common problems encountered. We'll discuss some basic limitations; the effect of date format and decimal notation of the user; and screen size settings of the user.

Basic Limitations

On very rare occasions, online functions that you tailor yourself are reused in BDC scenarios (if this does not apply to you, please feel free to skip this topic). In general, we don't recommend reusing your own tailored functions in BDC scenarios. Instead you should create BAPI and IDoc functions to make your own functionality as reusable as possible (see also Chapter 8).

The reason why we start with this remark is that `CALL TRANSACTION`, `CALL DIALOG`, or Batch Input programs tend to work somewhat differently from their online counterparts. Some commands cannot be used, and some commands must be used differently. Ignoring these limitations will result in a technical error message referring to the wrongly interpreted statement. You can overcome some of these problems by simply using the correct option when calling the transaction.[4]

---

4 Refer to the online statement documentation: `CALL TRANSACTION <tcode>`
   `USING <bdcdata> OPTIONS FROM <opt>`.

The most important differences between real online use and BDC use of a program are:

▶ Some statements cannot be used in BDC mode. If a transaction that is running in BDC mode encounters one of these statements, processing is cancelled and a return code <> 0 is generated.

▶ During processing in BDC mode, system-variable sy-binpt is set. The program flow can be changed on the basis of this variable. BDC option NOBINPT refers to this system variable when a transaction is called.

▶ As soon as the called transaction encounters a COMMIT WORK statement, transaction processing is stopped. The ABAP code following the COMMIT WORK statement is not executed. By using the option RACOMMIT, subsequent processing will be finished.

▶ The number of lines in a table control must be completely predictable when a CALL TRANSACTON statement is executed.

▶ Transactions containing Enjoy Controls will be less effective in BDC processing. None of the controls may be used.

▶ There are limitations to the use of transactions that contain interactive list reporting. The report list dynpro cannot be used directly in BDC processing; nor can the cursor be set; nor are field names and their values available. Only the function codes of a list screen can be used.

The User's Decimal Notation and Date Format

Standards for date formats and decimal notations can vary slightly from country to country. For most SAP users who use the system interactively, this variation is not a significant problem. SAP users are often allowed to set such formats themselves. Changing a date format, for example, from U.S. notation ('mm/dd/yyyy') to European notation ('dd/mm/yyyy'), is a simple action.

Things are different when a tailored ABAP program is in some way made dependent on user settings. This is the case for programs that use the CALL TRANSACTION (Batch Input) technique.

A program that uses the CALL TRANSACTION technique makes itself dependent on the default settings of the user who runs the program. CALL TRANSACTION functionality uses existing screen fields to input data, as if an actual user would be manually inputting the data. Consequently, the date format (for dates) and the decimal notation (for quantities and amounts) are first checked against the user settings, and then translated into an SAP internal format. In other words, the CALL TRANSACTION functionality simply uses the date format and decimal notation of the user who starts the program. If you simply assume that the dates, amounts, and quantities—as prepared in your own CALL TRANSACTION functionality—will be in accordance with the settings of the users employing your program, you're very much mistaken. Consider, for instance, the following sample code:

```
*----------------------------------------------------------------*
* METHOD SINGLE_POSTING
*----------------------------------------------------------------*
  METHOD single_posting.

* Fields for call transaction/batch input in character format
    DATA: ltp_date_c   TYPE ty_char10,
          ltp_amount_c TYPE ty_char16.

* Fill data
  ltp_date(2)   = sy-datum+4(2).   "Day
  ltp_date+2(1) = '.'.
  ltp_date+3(2) = sy-datum+2(2).   "Month
  ltp_date+5(1) = '.'.
  ltp_date+6(4) = sy-datum(4).     "Year
* itp_amount is a type p field
  ltp_amount_c = itp_amount.

* Fill bdcdata table
    CALL METHOD fill_bdcdata
      EXPORTING
        itp_date   = ltp_date_c
        itp_amount = ltp_amount_c.

* Make FI posting
    CALL TRANSACTION 'FB01' USING ta_bdcdata mode 'E'.

  ENDMETHOD.                         "single_posting
```

If a user processes code like this, an error message such as the one depicted in Figure 4.37 could be generated ("Enter date in the format __.__.____ ").

Errors caused by using the wrong *date format* will not be accepted and the processing of the input data will simply be stopped. Errors caused by using the wrong *decimal notation* could also result in erroneous data. According to U.S. decimal notation (___ , ___ , ___ . __), a figure such as "1,000" would be interpreted as an amount of "one thousand."

According to European notation (___ . ___ . ___ , __), the same figure would be interpreted as an amount of "one." Because both interpretations of the same figure can be considered as valid per the logic of the screen field that is used, an erroneous amount may not lead to an error message but instead result in the wrong data being updated. Strictly speaking, you should note that such an error is not a typical violation of stability, but a violation of correctness as defined in Chapter 3.

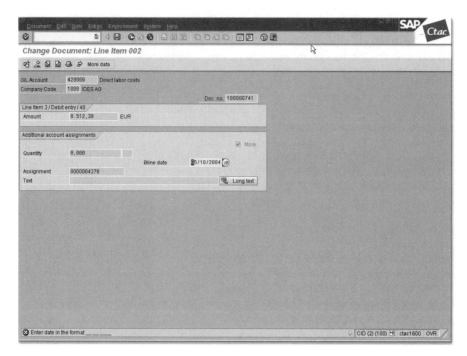

Figure 4.37 Error in Processing a Batch Input Map Because of Wrong Date Format

There is a way, however, to ensure that a program uses the settings of the current user, namely, by using the WRITE TO statement for date and amount fields, as shown in the following sample code:

```
*----------------------------------------------------------------------*
* METHOD SINGLE_POSTING
*----------------------------------------------------------------------*
  METHOD single_posting.

* Fields for call transaction/batch input in character format
    DATA: ltp_date_c   TYPE ty_char10,
          ltp_amount_c TYPE ty_char16.

* Convert data to character format
    WRITE: sy-datum  TO ltp_date_c,
           tp_amount TO ltp_amount_c.

* Fill bdcdata table
    CALL METHOD fill_bdcdata
      EXPORTING
        itp_date   = ltp_date_c
        itp_amount = ltp_amount_c.

* Make FI posting
```

```
CALL TRANSACTION 'FB01' USING ta_bdcdata MODE 'E'.

ENDMETHOD.                      "single_posting
```

There is another pitfall that you must avoid. The well-known *Batch Input* technique is a variant of the CALL TRANSACTION technique. It is still used, for example, in many situations where interface data from other systems must be processed into an SAP system. By using Batch Input, you separate the creation of the input file containing data in screen format and sequence on the one hand, and the subsequent processing of the Batch Input, on the other (see Figure 4.38). First, a file known as a *Batch Input Map* (BIM) is created. This file contains the data in the expected screen format and sequence. In a second step, this BIM is actually processed.

The advantage of this two-step approach is that it enables end users to check erroneous data on the same screens that they use to make their own postings. However, the drawback is that the same problem can occur for the CALL TRANS-ACTION function, as we already mentioned. It is possible that the default settings of the user who *creates* a particular BIM (for example, a background user) and those of the user who *processes* that BIM are different. So, if the data of a BIM is recorded according to the first user's settings, and this BIM is processed with other user settings by the second user, the wrong interpretation of date and amount fields will still occur.

There is no way to resolve this discrepancy other than by using procedural measures. A practical measure might be to always choose the same user for both creating and processing batch input. Preferably, the new user-id should be created for this purpose only.

Note that the problem that we just described is one of the reasons why BAPIs and IDocs are preferred over the use of CALL TRANSACTION functionality. Most BAPI and IDoc functions are user-independent, because they use internal data formats instead of user-specific external formats. Note, however, that some of the older functions still use the CALL TRANSACTION technique.

Screen Size Settings

Another user setting that can influence CALL TRANSACTION or batch input processing is the setting of the user's screen size. Consider batch input processing for posting FI documents with multiple lines. It is particularly those documents with many lines that can pose a problem if processed by specific users. Consequently, when processing the batch input, you would get an error message indicating, for example, that a specific screen field is not available for input.

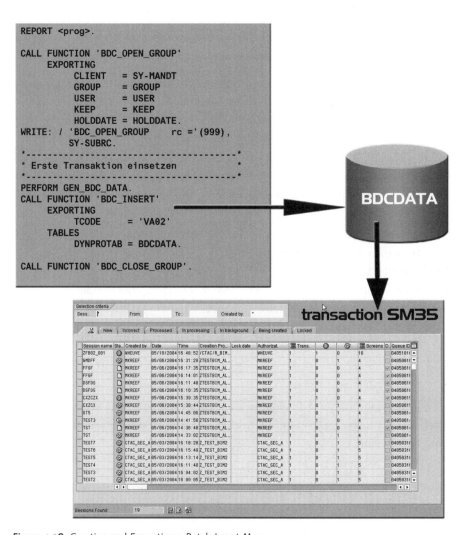

```
REPORT <prog>.

CALL FUNCTION 'BDC_OPEN_GROUP'
     EXPORTING
          CLIENT   = SY-MANDT
          GROUP    = GROUP
          USER     = USER
          KEEP     = KEEP
          HOLDDATE = HOLDDATE.
WRITE: / 'BDC_OPEN_GROUP    rc ='(999),
       SY-SUBRC.
*-----------------------------------------*
* Erste Transaktion einsetzen            *
*-----------------------------------------*
PERFORM GEN_BDC_DATA.
CALL FUNCTION 'BDC_INSERT'
     EXPORTING
          TCODE     = 'VA02'
     TABLES
          DYNPROTAB = BDCDATA.

CALL FUNCTION 'BDC_CLOSE_GROUP'.
```

Figure 4.38 Creating and Executing a Batch Input Map

This kind of error message is primarily the result of not considering variable screen size settings when screen data is prepared for CALL TRANSACTION functionality, in a screen format containing a table control.

The tricky thing about table controls is that the number of lines available on a screen in one table control depends on the screen resolution and the size of the window. For example, both screens in Figure 4.39 show the same transaction data. The first items—those items up to and including item 60—are visible on both the top and bottom screens. However, starting with item 70, many more items are available in the top screen. If this table with various items must be processed by a CALL TRANS-ACTION function, the function must know what screen size to take into account, in

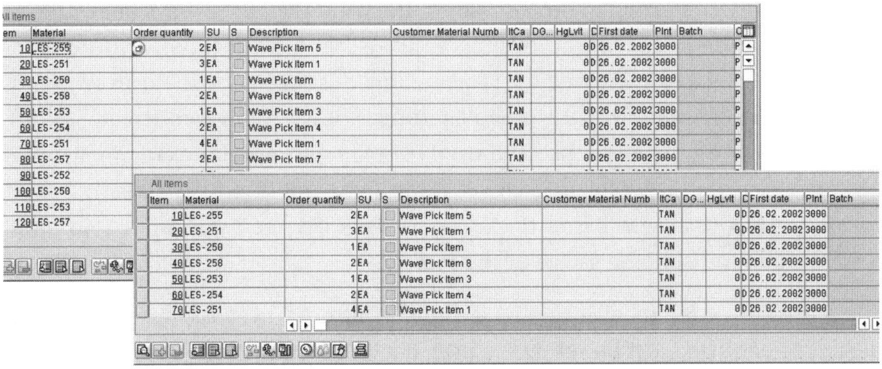

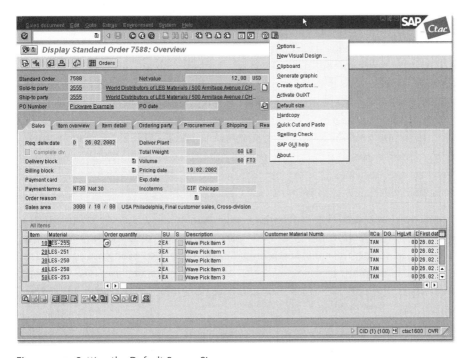

Figure 4.39 Different Sizes for the Same Screen

order to know exactly when the next screen must be prepared. Therefore, you can well imagine that a CALL TRANSACTION function, which is made dependent on fixed screen settings, will eventually fail if other screen settings are used.

You can prevent this problem if you ensure that both a CALL TRANSACTION function to be made and the user who will apply this function use exactly the same default screen size. This is the only way that this function will work. Figure 4.40 shows where you can find the Default size setting.

Figure 4.40 Setting the Default Screen Size

Therefore, before starting to process a BIM, the window must always be resized to the default screen size. You do this by ensuring that the checkbox Dynpro Standard Size is activated (switched on). This option must be set by the user who processes the batch input. It is the default setting. If it is deactivated (switched off), processing will be dependent on the user's display settings. For example, if a user has set a low resolution for the screen, fewer lines will fit on the screen. Consequently, a BIM that was based on a (larger) default screen size will try to input fields that are outside the scope of the screen.

Therefore, in order to ensure that a table control is processed correctly, the default screen size must be set by the user. If a CALL TRANSACTION is executed in the background, the same default size will be used. If a CALL TRANSACTION is executed in the foreground, the current screen settings are used. This last option can be overwritten by using the correct processing option as is shown in this code:

```
DATA: st_options TYPE ctu_params.

st_options-defsize = 'X'.

CALL TRANSACTION 'VA03' USING ta_bdcdata
OPTIONS FROM st_options.
```

There are two other ways to make a program more independent of the screen settings of the user who triggers its processing. First, you should, if possible, avoid the inclusion of screens in a CALL TRANSACTION function that contain a table (table control or steploop) for making new entries. Instead, always look for a single-entry screen first. If there is no such screen, a fall-back option is to use the table screen as if it were a single-entry screen, that is, by always filling only the table's first line (or two lines if you need to accelerate the process). In order to do this, try to find a menu option that enables you to reposition the table. If such a menu option exists, it can also be used by the CALL TRANSACTION function. In this way, the first lines that are open for input on the screen will always be the ones into which new data is input (see Figure 4.41).

A final word about testing batch input applications: make sure to do this testing with different screen resolutions. End users might have different monitors, resolutions, and so forth. Finally, the screen size problem discussed should be reason enough to avoid BDC techniques if other alternatives are available. As we already mentioned when discussing decimal and date notation, in most cases, you're better off using BAPI or IDoc functions.

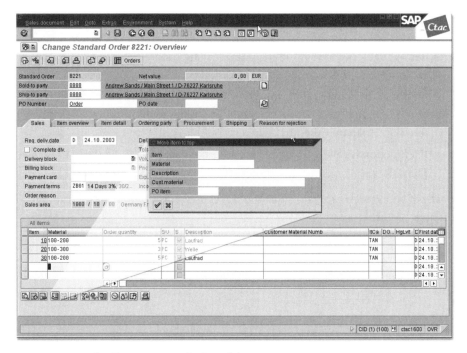

Figure 4.41 Put the Chosen Item at the Top of the Overview

4.5.4 Questions to Ask in Order to Avoid Wrong Program Use

We'll end this section by summarizing some general guidelines on the use of the different tasks that a SAP system distinguishes. Consider the following questions:

▶ Will the program need to interact with the end user?

▶ Should it be possible to run the program in another process mode?

▶ Could running the program in asynchronous mode be required?

▶ Do you plan to reuse the program in BDC processing?

If you're using ABAP constructs that are prohibited in specific process modes, you need to check the actual mode at runtime. At present, the SAP Web Application Server (Web AS) allows the following check options:

▶ System-variable `sy-batch` tells you whether a program runs in the background.

▶ System-variable `sy-binpt` shows whether the program runs in batch input mode.

▶ Function `gui_is_available` can be used to verify whether the SAP GUI is available.

- Function `rfc_logon_info` can be used to verify whether the user is a 'dialog' user.

- System-variable `sy-cprog` (literally the "calling program") is available, among other things, for the following purposes:

  - If a function is called with the `STARTING NEW TASK` option, this field contains value `SAPMSSY1`. You can verify this value in all routines, methods, or functions that are called by such a main function.

  - If a function is called `IN UPDATE TASK`, the value of this field will always be `RSM13000`.

Finally, if you want a program to be multipurpose, don't forget to test it under all possible circumstances.

5   Exceptions and Error Handling

One of the best ways to make a program behave more predictably, and thereby, enhance a program's technical quality, is by implementing proper exception handling. Simply put, good exception handling will result in fewer errors. And, because one of the goals of exception handling is to make it easier for the user to respond to any outstanding errors, it will have a positive effect on user acceptance as well.

We broadly define an *exception* to mean "any deviation from the normal program flow."[1] Consider, for example, an implicitly generated returncode not equal to zero that is returned by a `SELECT` statement, or an unexpected value of a variable that is used in an IF condition. You should note that an exception is not the same thing as a coding error. *An exception is an unanticipated situation or event encountered during the execution of program logic.*

Exception handling is the way in which deviations are detected, caught, and handled. Dealing with exceptions is directly related to the two previously discussed main topics—correctness and stability—because both of these software requirements are directly affected by the following results of sloppy exception handling: runtime errors (program dumps), obscure error messages, incorrect data on lists or screens, and even inconsistent database tables. To a certain extent, you could view adding elegant exception handling as adding the finishing touch to a program in order to support its correctness and stability. You could even argue that exception handling is actually integral to ensuring technical quality.

5.1   The Importance of Exception Handling

It's hard to predict and anticipate all the possible circumstances in which a program will be used. Which exceptions are actually considered often depends directly on the context in which a program is used. It's quite difficult to predict all the exceptional situations that may arise. To a certain extent, a program's context will be clear, and so will the logic that is applied and the data that is processed. However, there's always a point at which the developer's (and other people's) knowledge about the context ends, and particular exceptions need to be taken into account. Ignoring these types of situations is not an option. Therefore, usually, a developer must deal with the typical details of programming techniques in general and the ABAP programming language in particular. And most often, these details aren't explicitly included; for example, in the functional specifications for a new program.

---

1 Note that an exception is defined more strictly in the second volume of Horst Keller, Joachim Jacobitz, *ABAP Objects: The Official Reference*, SAP PRESS 2003.

On the other hand, even without knowing the context in which a program is used, it's not really that difficult to address each imaginable deviation from the normal program flow. All that is required is a proper and unbiased look at the program code (which makes exception handling an excellent topic to be checked during a peer review (see Section 9.1). Moreover, the ABAP language provides all the necessary means to conduct this kind of check—to raise exceptions, intercept them, and take the appropriate action when necessary, in current releases and those prior to Web AS 6.20.

And yet, it's well known that exception handling in most customized ABAP developments is incomplete. We can think of various reasons for this:

1. **Because the programmer doesn't know how to implement exception handling.**
   Imagine, for example, that a piece of program code deep down the *Call Stack* of a program causes an error: a subroutine calls a function module; this function module, in turn, calls another function module; and this last function module generates an exception. The question then is: Where should the exception be handled? If it's better to wait to give an error message until the main line of the program is reached again, all the context information about the error must also be returned through the Call Stack.

2. **Because the assumptions of initial development aren't expected to become invalid.**
   Customized developments are often made to rely on assumptions that, according to the developer, make additional exception handling superfluous. As such, this may be true. However, this ignores the fact that maintenance may have to be applied later. At the time of initial development, the assumptions that are made usually cannot be questioned ("This simply can't go wrong. We have only two material types."). However, this will make the program more fragile. Unfortunately, this usually doesn't become obvious until a small change is implemented (for example, related to the introduction of a new material type). Particularly if the change itself comprises only a few lines of code, no one will consider it justifiable to reinvestigate all the assumptions made during the initial development—this would take much more time than applying the actual change. Nevertheless, even a small change can introduce exceptions that didn't exist. Therefore, it isn't that the assumptions are invalid when they're first made; the problem is that they can *become* invalid once the program is changed.

3. **Because it takes too much time.**
   Like testing and documenting developments, implementing exception handling is hardly the most exciting of all development activities; however, it can

require a large amount of the total development time of a program. And, if there are many exceptions to consider, it's easy to predict the following all too common scenario: every exception that doesn't appear to be essential or critical, or whose exception handling seems difficult to implement, will be ignored. For programmers, who may look for ways to avoid this activity and get away with it, skipping exception handling is a way to deliver a program according to plan and budget.

In this chapter, we'll address these basic dilemmas. We'll discuss which exceptions can be used. We'll explain the types of exception handling that are less frequently applied but that can nevertheless be useful for customized ABAP programs. And finally, we'll show you how to avoid the Call Stack dilemma by using the so-called *class-based exception handling* (that is, exception handling using ABAP Objects).

In Section 5.2, we'll first provide you with an overview of the basics of exception handling in an ABAP environment. Next, in Section 5.3, we'll present the main characteristics of class-based exception handling, and show you how to combine class-based with existing exception handling. In Section 5.4, we summarize the most important conclusions.

5.2 Implementation of Exception Handling

Exception handling distinguishes among three different elements (see Figure 5.1):

▶ Generating or raising the exception event
▶ Noticing or intercepting the exception
▶ Acting on the exception

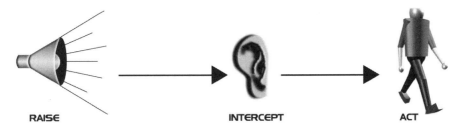

RAISE **INTERCEPT** **ACT**

Figure 5.1 Raise—Intercept—Act

The first step in exception handling is raising the exception, that is, giving a signal that something has gone wrong. On the one hand, there are *implicit exceptions*; for example, a returncode that is not equal to zero when using an ABAP command such as SELECT, or a runtime exception such as divide-by-zero. On the other hand, *explicit exceptions* are the ones caused deliberately by the program logic itself; for example, by setting a specific flag, or by using the `RAISE EXCEPTION TYPE <exception class>` command.

Independently of how an exception is raised, it must then be explicitly *recognized* (or detected, caught, intercepted) by the program code before anything can be done with it. Lastly, of course, the appropriate *action* must be taken. For example, consider sending a message to the end user. To summarize these steps, think of them as *Raise, Intercept,* and *Act*.

This section discusses the standard possibilities for implementing exception handling in an ABAP environment. In Section 5.2.1, we'll review the available options for generating and intercepting the exception *signal*. Next, in Section 5.2.2, we'll discuss the most important ways of implementing the exception handling.

5.2.1 Generating and Intercepting an Exception Signal

In this section, we'll give you an overview of how to intercept the following types of exceptions: a returncode; unexpected data in `IF` and `CASE` statements; an interface parameter of a subroutine; an exception generated by a function module; a class-based exception; and a runtime error. For the explicit types of exceptions, we'll also show you how each of them is generated.

Returncode

The first exception signal that each ABAP developer is likely to think of is a returncode that is not equal to zero (`sy-subrc <> 0`). The system field *sy-subrc* is used by many ABAP commands to indicate whether the execution of the command has been successful: all SQL commands; internal table commands such as `READ` and `LOOP AT <itab>`; and file-handling commands such as `OPEN DATASET`. However, even if programmers know this, they often don't explicitly check the returned value, especially if they expect that nothing will go wrong.

Note that not every returncode indicates an exception. In most situations, such as when reading database tables or internal tables, a returncode not equal to zero represents an exception, even if the result is not immediately disastrous. But, sometimes, a returncode is checked as part of the program logic. To see the difference, consider the following two pieces of ABAP code. The first piece of code is an example of the use of a returncode that represents a genuine exception:

```
OPEN DATASET tp_filename FOR INPUT IN TEXT MODE ENCODING DEFAULT.
IF sy-subrc <> 0.
* Exception Handling here--
ENDIF.
```

The second piece of code is an example of a returncode that does not point at an exceptional situation:

```
DO.
   READ DATASET tp_filename INTO tp_string.
   IF sy-subrc <> 0.
* This is no exception but a check whether an end-of-file has been reached
      EXIT.
   ENDIF.
ENDDO.

CLOSE DATASET tp_filename.
```

The way in which the returncode is used in the first example represents an exception because the file is expected to be available. Even if the exception was foreseen, not handling it will lead to a dump as soon as the subsequent READ DATASET statement is executed. The second returncode does not represent an exception: it's just a way of establishing an exit-condition for the DO loop for processing the file in order to determine if the end of the file has been reached.

Unexpected Data in Conditions

ABAP programs are often based on assumptions about values of data. The statements IF and CASE are examples of statements that determine the flow of a program on the basis of expected values. For example, consider a program whose flow is determined by the value of a material type, and that only two material types are expected: *RAW* (for raw materials) and *SEMI* (for semi-finished products). In terms of its exception handling, an incomplete CASE statement would look like this:

```
CASE tp_materialtype.
   WHEN co_materialtype_raw.
* Handling of material type RAW starts here
   WHEN co_materialtype_semi.
* Handling of material type SEMI starts here
ENDCASE.
```

Consider what would happen if variable *tp_materialtype* contained a value other than RAW or SEMI. (The assumption that only these two values would be processed by the program was valid during initial development, but it is no longer valid.) This situation is not anticipated in the code. Without knowing more about the context of the code, it's nevertheless fairly easy to discern that the result of the ABAP program could become unpredictable. Perhaps, the rest of the ABAP code will proceed with incorrect data, or a runtime error will occur. We recommend ensuring that the exception is always caught, in this particular case, by adding a WHEN OTHERS condition, as follows:

```
CASE tp_materialtype.
  WHEN co_materialtype_raw.
* Handling of material type RAW starts here
  WHEN co_materialtype_semi.
* Handling of material type SEMI starts here
  WHEN OTHERS.
* The exception is caught here.
ENDCASE.
```

By inserting a WHEN OTHERS condition in a CASE statement, unforeseen situations are always recognized and exceptions can be handled accordingly (the same is true for IF statements).

Interface Parameters of a Procedure

Explicit interface parameters of procedures (that is, functions, methods, or sub-routines) are often used to indicate to the calling ABAP code that an exception has occurred within the procedure. There are two possibilities: using EXCEPTIONS for functions and methods, and using EXPORTING, CHANGING, and even TABLES parameters to return results. An example of the second option is the RETURN parameter of BAPI function modules. This parameter, which has the structure BAPIRETURN, contains the result of the BAPI. The same technique is sometimes used in the interface parameters of routines. The following code is for a subroutine call:

```
PERFORM routine1 USING tp_input
             CHANGING tp_result_ok.
IF tp_result_ok = abap_true.
*
ELSE.
* Exception handling
ENDIF.

FORM routine1 USING  utp_input    TYPE c
          CHANGING  ctp_result_ok TYPE boolean.
* The specific function logic is executed here. As a result a
* corresponding returncode is set.
*  ...
  IF sy-subrc NE 0.
    ctp_result_ok = cofalse.
  ELSE.
    ctp_result_ok = co_true.
  ENDIF.
ENDFORM.
```

If an exception occurs during the execution of FORM routine1, it isn't handled there immediately. Instead, it's reported back to the calling piece of code via the interface parameter `ctp_result_ok`. So, immediately after executing the PER-FORM statement, the value of the interface parameter will indicate whether an exception has occurred.

Passing on exceptions to a higher level in the Call Stack allows you to separate the code that takes action on an exception from the code that merely checks whether an exception has occurred.

Traditional Exceptions of a Function Module

For function modules, a separate part of their interface (the EXCEPTIONS parameters) is reserved for passing on information about exception situations. The associated kind of exception is deliberately raised in the function module (or method) by executing the RAISE ⟨exception⟩ command. The following code shows an example of a corresponding function call:

```
CALL FUNCTION '/CTAC/FM_WITH_TRAD_EXCEPTIONS'
  EXPORTING
    itp_input        = tp_input_fm
  IMPORTING
    etp_export       = tp_output_fm
  EXCEPTIONS
    not_found        = 1
    OTHERS           = 9.

CASE sy-subrc.
  WHEN 0.
* Everything is OK...
  WHEN 1.
* Action needed here...
  WHEN 9.
* Action needed here...
ENDCASE.
```

If a NOT_FOUND exception is raised by function /ctac/fm_with_trad_exceptions, system field sy-subrc is automatically made to contain value 1. This returncode must be checked by the calling ABAP code directly after the CALL FUNCTION statement.

Class-Based Exceptions

The second type of exception that is raised deliberately is the exception that is raised via using the RAISE EXCEPTION TYPE ⟨exception class⟩ command. This is part of the implementation of the class-based exception handling concept available as of Release 6.20 of the SAP Web Application Server (Web AS). After the exception has been generated, it is intercepted within a TRY-ENDTRY block with the command CATCH. The exception itself is an instance of a global exception class. We have added a basic code example:

```
TRY.
    SELECT SINGLE * FROM mara INTO wa_mara
        WHERE matnr = pa_matnr.
*   ...
    IF sy-subrc NE 0.
      RAISE EXCEPTION TYPE  cx_sql_exception.
    ENDIF.
*   ...
  CATCH cx_sql_exception.
* Include exception handling here
  CLEANUP.
* This is always executed whenever an exception occurs
    CLEAR wa_mara.
ENDTRY.
```

Runtime Errors

Runtime errors such as divide-by-zero errors or type-conflicts are clear signals of exception situations that are implicitly generated by the runtime environment. For example, let's look at the following code:

```
TRY.
    tp_average = tp_total / tp_count.

  CATCH cx_sy_zerodivide.
* Include exception handling here
ENDTRY.
```

If this code is processed and variable tp_count somehow contains a value of zero, a runtime error will raise an exception CX_SY_ZERODIVIDE. The exception can then be intercepted by using the CATCH statement before it can do any harm.

Note that some runtime errors can be intercepted (or caught) using either the CATCH command (up to Release 4.6C) or the combination of a TRY and CATCH command (as of Web AS Release 6.20). However, it is not possible to catch all runtime exceptions (for more information, see Chapter 4).

5.2.2   Implementing the Actual Exception Handling

After an exception signal has been raised and intercepted, you must act on it. You cannot simply intercept a runtime exception to prevent a dump, and then take no further action. The same is true for a returncode or any other exception signal. For example, the following ABAP code and added comment lines make little sense, but are nevertheless sometimes found in customized ABAP programs:

```
READ ta_itab INTO wa_itab WITH KEY keyfield1 = tp_value BINARY SEARCH.
IF sy-subrc NE 0.
* Now I don't know what to do. I presume this will never happen
* so this explains why no more actions were taken.
ENDIF.
```

So, doing nothing is not an option. On the other hand, you may need general guidelines for situations where you don't expect an exception to happen, but nevertheless must consider the possibility. In such cases, we recommend that you stop the program immediately: this at least clearly indicates that something went wrong. Letting the program go its own unpredictable way is always worse.

In this section, we address the proper implementation of the steps to be taken after an exception has been recognized. The main criteria that determine these steps are:

▶ Should the program send a message?
▶ Should the program execute cleanup actions?
▶ Should the program ask for a correction of data?
▶ Should the program continue after the exception has been handled?

These criteria are shown in Figure 5.2:

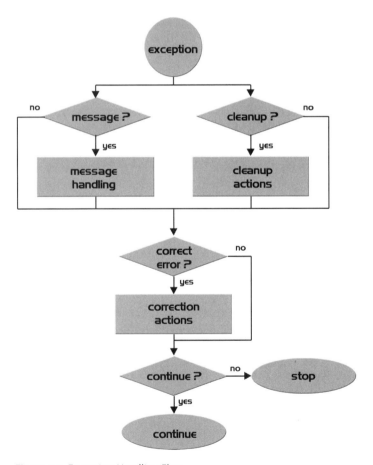

Figure 5.2 Exception Handling Flow

Let's first discuss some more details of the general exception handling logic: message handling and other important actions, mainly consisting of cleanup actions.

Message Handling

The most common part of exception handling consists of *message handling*. If a message needs to be sent, there are three things to be done: compose the content of the message (what); choose the destination of the message (to whom); and, choose the medium (how). Figure 5.3 shows these three steps:

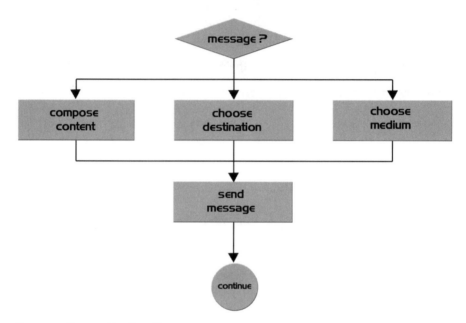

Figure 5.3 Message Handling Elements

Because most ABAP developers are already familiar with implementing regular message handling in ABAP (using the MESSAGE command), we won't elaborate further on that subject. However, we do want to emphasize an attractive ABAP feature—application logging—which is used less frequently than it warrants. This way of collecting and reporting exceptions is particularly useful in situations where the end user cannot directly be involved in the exception handling process. Therefore, programs running in the background will benefit most from this feature.

In principle, the same basic topics (what, to whom, and how) are as relevant for application logging as they are for message handling. With application logging, the destination of a message is defined in *objects* and *sub-objects* with Transaction SLG0 (see Figure 5.4).

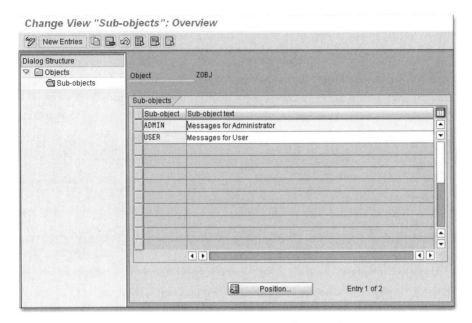

Figure 5.4 Customizing Application Log Objects and Sub-objects with Transaction SLG0

The first advantage of application logging is that its sub-objects enable you to send different types of exception information to the different people involved. For example, an administrator may benefit most from knowing the program name and the exact line number where an exception has occurred, whereas an end user may be interested primarily in knowing which data was actually skipped during the processing of a background job.

The second advantage of application logging is that it permits you to add both help information and free text to a message. Furthermore, messages can either be stored or displayed immediately. This means that the use of the Application Log is not limited to only background processing.

The third advantage of application logging is that existing functionality can be reused. Various standard function modules are available. Up to Release 4.6, this pertains to function modules whose names start with "appl...". Since Release 4.6, however, new function modules whose names start with "bal..." are also provided, but the aforementioned function modules are still supported.

Now, we'll briefly mention the latest versions of these function modules and their associated functionality. To create an exception object, use function module `bal_log_create`. The interface parameters to be supplied are identifying parameter values such as object, sub-object, and, possibly, your own extra identifying information (e.g., a document number). To add a message to the Application Log, you use function module `bal_log_msg_cumulate`. To store the Application Log with all the messages contained in it in the database, use function module `bal_db_save`.

Finally, if the Application Log cannot be viewed immediately in your program, standard Transaction SLG1 is available for displaying it (see Figure 5.5).

Figure 5.5 Display Application Log Information Using Transaction SLG1

Cleanup Actions

In addition to message-handling activities, the other important thing to consider is whether the program can continue, and if so, how. You may, for example, be able to skip an erroneous record in a file and continue as before with the rest of the data. But, even if you think you can continue, you first need to clean up the mess. In the first place, this means that you need to ensure that all the intermediate variables used still contain the correct values—this could require either initializing data (with a `CLEAR` or `REFRESH` command), or resetting data to the value it contained just before the exception occurred, for example, resetting counter information. See the following simple example of a `CLEAR` action:

```
SELECT SINGLE * FROM mara INTO wa_mara
            WHERE matnr = pa_matnr.
IF sy-subrc NE 0.
   CLEAR wa_matnr.
ENDIF.
```

If an update has failed, you should probably execute a `ROLLBACK WORK` command in order to restore the proper state of the database. Note that a database rollback is required regardless of whether the program can continue. Inconsistent database updates must always be reversed.

5.3 Class-Based Exception Handling

One of the basic dilemmas, already mentioned briefly in Section 5.1, is that adding appropriate exception handling to ABAP code can be a laborious task. This is
one of the main reasons why adding exception handling code to customized
ABAP programs is frequently avoided if it isn't absolutely necessary. In particular,
there is one basic contradiction that complicates exception handling. On the one
hand, actually executing the *handling* part of exception handling is not always
appropriate in the exact place where the exception is raised. On the other hand,
you want to have as much detailed context information available about an exception as possible. For example, a function module itself may notice an exception,
but nevertheless have to let the calling program do the associated exception handling.

Letting the calling piece of code (or the piece of code calling that piece of code)
do the exception handling means that it must also have all the available detailed
exception information. Passing all this data along the Call Stack can be particularly
cumbersome, especially if it contains several levels. This is where the advantages
of class-based exception handling come into play. We'll discuss these advantages
in the next sections. In Sections 5.3.1 and 5.3.2, we'll show you a basic implementation of class-based exception handling and discuss the most important
characteristics of an exception class. In Section 5.3.3, we'll discuss the benefits of
class-based exception handling. Next, in Section 5.3.4, we'll show you where to
start if you want to add class-based exception handling on top of your current
exception handling. Finally, in 5.3.5, we'll briefly explain how you can create your
own exception classes.

5.3.1 Basic Implementation

We'll start with a basic implementation of (ABAP Objects) class-based exception
handling in the next piece of sample code. The RAISE EXCEPTION TYPE
<exception class> command is used to generate (raise) an exception. The
TRY-ENDTRY block represents the area in which intercepting an exception is possible. The CATCH statement is used to actually intercept an exception and trigger
exception handling. In this particular piece of code, two exceptions are taken into
account: a divide-by-zero exception, and a SQL error:

```
REPORT /ctac/bk12exchandling_5a.
DATA: tp_average TYPE i,
      tp_total   TYPE i.

START-OF-SELECTION.
*
  TRY.
* This will raise cx_sy_sqlerror
```

```
      tp_average = tp_total / 0.          "SIGNAL implicit

      RAISE EXCEPTION TYPE cx_sy_sql_error."SIGNAL Explicit

    CATCH cx_sy_zerodivide.                "Intercept
* Handle exception here                    "ACT
    CATCH cx_sy_sql_error .                "Intercept
* Handle exception here                    "ACT
  ENDTRY.
```

5.3.2 Exception Classes

The fact that an exception is implemented as a class in ABAP Objects implies that it also has some of the main characteristics of a class: an exception class will always have one superclass and may have various subclasses. In fact, every exception class that is created must refer to one of three standard superclasses: CX_STATIC_CHECK, CX_DYNAMIC_CHECK, or CX_NO_CHECK. These standards all have class CX_ROOT as their superclass. Other exception classes, including those that you create yourself, must have a direct or indirect relation with one of the aforementioned three superclasses. An exception class tree may look like the one shown in Figure 5.6:

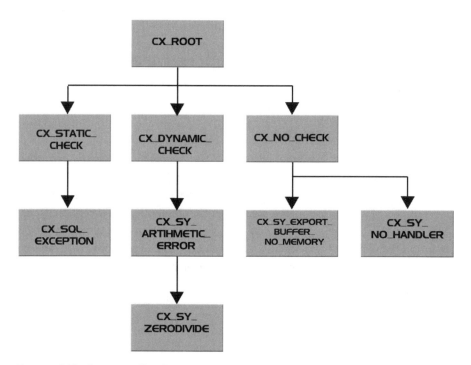

Figure 5.6 The Exception Class Tree

For example, according to Figure 5.6, class CX_SY_ZERODIVIDE inherits some of its attributes from CX_SY_ARITHMETIC_ERROR, which in turn inherits some of its attributes from CX_DYNAMIC_CHECK. It is not possible to inherit attributes directly from class CX_ROOT. In the next section, we'll describe the benefits of class-based exception handling.

5.3.3 Details of Class-Based Exception Handling

The use of class-based exception handling has two basic advantages:

▶ Passing on information about exceptions through the Call Stack is done by providing a reference to the exception object raised using a RAISING parameter. Note that (in contrast to traditional exception handling) the details of an exception don't have to be passed on because they're already contained in the exception object.

▶ Exception information can be made as context-specific as you want. If required, you can add your own context-information.

This means that you can *pack* all possible detailed information about an error into the exception object immediately at the moment when the exception occurs. You don't have to decide exactly what specific information needs to be passed on to a previous level in the Call Stack. Instead, you need only indicate in which exception object this information is stored.

How this works in real-time is explained most easily by showing various examples. We'll discuss the following: the timing of catching exceptions; the level at which interception takes place; where to intercept which type of exception; an implementation of context-specific exception information; and finally, an implementation of cleanup actions.

Timing the Interception of a Class-Based Exception

The basic advantages of class-based exception handling imply that intercepting an exception and executing the associated exception handling can be two independent actions. Hence, you can determine the best moment for actually intercepting an exception yourself. The following code example illustrates this principle:

```
REPORT /ctac/bk12exchandling_5.
*  ...
START-OF-SELECTION.
*
  TRY.
      CALL FUNCTION '/CTAC/FM_WITH_CLASS_BASED_EXC2'
        EXPORTING
          itp_input  = tp_input_fm
```

```
        IMPORTING
          etp_export = tp_output_fm.

    CATCH cx_sy_zerodivide.       "Intercept
* Handle exception here          "Act
    CATCH /ctac/cx_dynamic_check. "Intercept
* Handle exception here          "Act
  ENDTRY.

FUNCTION /ctac/fm_with_class_based_exc2.
*"--------------------------------------------------------------------
*"*"Local interface:
*"  IMPORTING
*"     REFERENCE(ITP_INPUT) TYPE  CHAR10
*"  EXPORTING
*"     REFERENCE(ETP_EXPORT) TYPE  CHAR10
*"  RAISING
*"     CX_SY_ZERODIVIDE
*"     /CTAC/CX_DYNAMIC_CHECK
*"--------------------------------------------------------------------
  DATA: ltp_total   TYPE i VALUE 10,
        ltp_average TYPE i.
  TRY.
* This will lead to a zero divide error
    ltp_average = ltp_total / 0.              "Signal implicit
*
    RAISE EXCEPTION TYPE /ctac/cx_static_check.   "Signal explicit
*
    RAISE EXCEPTION TYPE /ctac/cx_dynamic_check.  "Signal explicit

    CATCH /ctac/cx_static_check.                  "INTERCEPT
* Exception handling here                         "ACT
  ENDTRY.
ENDFUNCTION
```

The function module /ctac/fm_with_class_based_exc2 that is called in the code considers (raises) three possible exceptions. The first exception is an implicitly raised runtime error (CX_SY_ZERODIVIDE). The other two exceptions (/CTAC/CX_STATIC_CHECK and /CTAC/CX_DYNAMIC_CHECK) are explicitly raised by a RAISE EXCEPTION TYPE ⟨exception⟩ command. Only one of the three exceptions mentioned (CX_STATIC_CHECK) is actually intercepted within the function module itself. The other two (CX_DYNAMIC_CHECK and CX_SY_ZERODIVIDE are intercepted one level up in the Call Stack by using the CATCH command. To enable the calling code to do this, the function module passes on reference information about the last two exceptions in RAISING parameters. Note that the function module loses its influence on the exception handling by passing on this information. If the calling code doesn't do anything with the provided reference information, a program dump is generated.

The Class Level of the Intercepted Exception

In the sample code above, where we discussed the timing of catching exceptions, each single exception passed along the Call Stack is also intercepted separately. However, class-based exception handling allows you to intercept exceptions in a more general way. Consider the following code:

```
REPORT /ctac/bk12exchandling_5a.
DATA: tp_average TYPE i,
      tp_total   TYPE i.

START-OF-SELECTION.
*
  TRY.
* This will raise cx_sy_sql_error
      tp_average = tp_total / 0.          "Signal (implicit)

      RAISE EXCEPTION TYPE cx_sy_sql_error."Signal (explicit)


    CATCH cx_sy_sql_error.               "Intercept
* Handle exception here                  "Act
    CATCH cx_root.                       "Intercept (cx_sy_zerodivide)
* Handle exception here                  "Act
  ENDTRY.
```

In this code, two exception signals are possible: an implicit exception (divide-by-zero), and an explicitly raised exception (of class CX_SY_SQL_ERROR). Only the latter exception is intercepted with an explicit reference to the exception class in the corresponding CATCH statement (CATCH cx_sy_sql_error). The implicit exception (divide-by-zero), on the other hand, is not referred to; however, it will be intercepted by the CATCH statement that refers to exception class CX_ROOT (CATCH cx_root). Recall that CX_ROOT is the superclass for all class-based exceptions. Therefore, intercepting a CX_ROOT exception implies that all exceptions of subordinate types that are not considered elsewhere will also be caught. This means that you can use the interception of CX_ROOT exceptions as a kind of extra safety net (similar to using a WHEN OTHERS condition in a CASE statement).

However, there is one particular disadvantage to intercepting exceptions on the level of CX_ROOT, namely, you lose the context-specific attributes that would be available in more specialized exception objects. Therefore, this kind of exception handling is not appropriate for every kind of exception. In general, it is best suited for intercepting runtime errors because not all possible runtime errors can be anticipated in your program.

Where to Intercept Which Type of Exception

Each type of exception has its own appropriate place where it can best be intercepted and handled. The three most important subclasses (CX_STATIC_CHECK, CX_DYNAMIC_CHECK, and CX_NO_CHECK) represent the basic exception types. The specific type of exception determines what happens when an exception is raised within a procedure and *not* directly intercepted or passed in the RAISING part of the procedures interface parameters:

▶ CX_STATIC_CHECK
  Exceptions of this type must either be caught directly in the procedure where they are raised, or passed (propagated) along the Call Stack using the RAISING option. A syntax error will occur if your code doesn't do one of these two things. Exception classes of this type are most appropriate for relatively predictable exceptions, since they should be explicitly raised in a procedure; for example, the static exception CX_SQL_EXCEPTION can be raised after a SELECT statement.

▶ CX_DYNAMIC_CHECK
  Exceptions of this type don't necessarily have to be intercepted immediately or passed (propagated) along the Call Stack. The syntax check doesn't verify this, only the runtime environment does. If an (implicitly raised) exception of this type occurs in a procedure and is not caught there or propagated along the Call Stack, a new exception of class CX_SY_NO_HANDLER is raised by the system. Runtime errors, in particular, have this dynamic type. Because neither handling such exceptions directly in the procedure where they occur, nor propagating them, is practical, the best option is to catch these exceptions in one central place in your code. This repository is preferably located somewhere in the main program.

▶ CX_NO_CHECK
  Exceptions of this type cannot be passed along the Call Stack with the RAISING option. If an exception of this type occurs, the system will jump directly to the first relevant CATCH statement up the Call Stack and skip all other statements. Exceptions of this type are severe but highly unpredictable and are often related to system-wide problems, such as a problem with resources. Note that the aforementioned exception class CX_SY_NO_HANDLER is based on this type.

In SAP releases prior to 6.20, the propagating technique is not yet available. You can simulate it using regular interface parameters, however, the programming required is quite cumbersome. Therefore, we don't recommend applying this alternative in older releases.

Context-Specific Information About an Exception

The minimal information about a particular class-based exception that is always available is the name of the program causing the exception; the line where the exception occurred; the name of the exception; and the exception message that was generated. However, note that all kinds of additional attributes can be added on top. Consider the following piece of sample code to see how this works:

```
REPORT /ctac/bk12exchandling_5b.

DATA: rf_static    TYPE REF TO /ctac/cx_static_check,
      rf_root      TYPE REF TO cx_root.

DATA: tp_text      TYPE string,
      tp_extra_att TYPE char10,
      tp_program   TYPE syrepid,
      tp_linnr     TYPE i.

START-OF-SELECTION.

*
  TRY.
      PERFORM do_something.

    CATCH /ctac/cx_static_check INTO rf_static. "Intercept

      tp_text     = rf_static->get_text( ).    "Act
      tp_extra_att = rf_static->extra_attribute. "Act

      CALL METHOD rf_static->get_source_position "Act
        IMPORTING
          program_name = tp_program
          source_line  = tp_linnr.

  ENDTRY.
*
FORM do_something RAISING /ctac/cx_static_check.

  RAISE EXCEPTION TYPE /ctac/cx_static_check
            EXPORTING extra_attribute = 'Extra Info'(001). "Signal

ENDFORM.                   "Do_something
```

When an exception of class /CTAC/CX_STATIC_CHECK is raised (marked bold at the end of the code) in FORM do_something, an extra attribute is also passed on in terms of an EXPORTING parameter (called extra_attribute). When the exception is intercepted, this extra parameter will automatically become available in the exception object that is instantiated (or created) by using the INTO addition (see the CATCH statement marked bold). In this case, the exception handling triggered by the CATCH statement consists of, among other things, getting this extra attribute.

Let's also include a more extensive example. In the following code, class-based exception handling is combined with the use of application logging discussed earlier:

```
REPORT  /ctac/bk12exchandling_4a    .
* This local class contains the actual functions for the appl. log
INCLUDE /ctac/exchandling_new.²

CONSTANTS  : co_log_object TYPE balobj_d  VALUE 'ZOBJ',
             co_log_subobj TYPE balsubobj VALUE 'USER',
             co_error      TYPE symsgty   VALUE 'E'.
* Reference variable for the exception handler class
DATA:        rf_appl_log   TYPE REF TO lcl_exception_handler.
* Reference variables for exception classes
DATA:        rf_sql_error  TYPE REF TO /ctac/cx_sql_error,
             rf_log_error  TYPE REF TO /ctac/cx_log_error,
             rf_root       TYPE REF TO cx_root.
* Variables for the application log
DATA:        tp_nrext      TYPE balnrext.
* Context information
DATA:        tp_subrc      TYPE i,
             tp_text       TYPE string,
             tp_program    TYPE syrepid,
             tp_linno      TYPE i.

DATA:        wa_mara       TYPE mara.

PARAMETERS:  pa_matnr      TYPE matnr OBLIGATORY.

START-OF-SELECTION.

   TRY.

       SELECT SINGLE * FROM mara INTO wa_mara
                 WHERE matnr = pa_matnr.

       IF sy-subrc NE 0.
          tp_subrc = sy-subrc.
          RAISE EXCEPTION TYPE /ctac/cx_sql_error          "Signal
                      EXPORTING sqlcode = tp_subrc
                                tablename = 'MARA'.
       ENDIF.
* Intercept this SQL error
       CATCH /ctac/cx_sql_error INTO rf_sql_error.          "Intercept
```

---

2 See the appendices for this include.

```
      TRY.
* Get the information out of the exception object
         tp_text      = rf_sql_error->get_text( ).      "Act

* Create the exception handling object
         tp_nrext = pa_matnr.
         CREATE OBJECT rf_appl_log
               EXPORTING itp_object    = co_log_object
                         itp_subobject = co_log_subobj
                         itp_extnumber = tp_nrext.
* Add 1 message to the application log
         CALL METHOD rf_appl_log->free_message_to_appl_log
            EXPORTING
              itp_msgty = co_error
              itp_text  = tp_text.
* Store the messages in the database
         CALL METHOD lcl_exception_handler=>write_to_db.
* Intercepting errors during processing of the logfile
        CATCH /ctac/cx_log_error INTO rf_log_error.
* Error handling here
        CATCH cx_root            INTO rf_root.
* Error handling here
      ENDTRY.
    CATCH cx_root            INTO rf_root.
* Error handling here
  ENDTRY.
```

In this code, when selecting data from database table MARA, a SQL error is detected by checking the associated returncode (sy-subrc). An explicit exception is then raised, intercepted, and retrieved from the exception object, and finally stored in the Application Log. If exceptions occur, they will become visible in the Application Log (by using Transaction SLG1).

Executing Cleanup Actions

As discussed earlier, the actual exception handling consists of more than just collecting messages: all kinds of *cleanup actions* must also be performed such as initializing variables and performing a rollback in the event of erroneous updates. In class-based exception handling, the cleanup actions that are also part of this process are explicitly separated from the rest of exception handling. The following code shows how this is implemented:

```
DATA: ltp_subrc type i.
TRY.
    wa_luw_1-key1 = itp_key1.
    wa_luw_1-notkey = itp_notkey.
    INSERT /ctac/tbk_luw_1 FROM wa_luw_1.
```

```
    IF sy-subrc NE 0.
      ltp_subrc = sy-subrc.
      RAISE EXCEPTION TYPE cx_sy_sql_error        "Signal
                      EXPORTING sqlcode = ltp_subrc.
    ENDIF.

    wa_luw_2-key1 = itp_key1.
    wa_luw_2-posnr = itp_posnr.
    wa_luw_2-somedata = itp_somedata.
    INSERT /ctac/tbk_luw_2 FROM wa_luw_2.

    IF sy-subrc NE 0.
      ltp_subrc = sy-subrc.
      RAISE EXCEPTION TYPE cx_sy_sql_error        "Signal
                      EXPORTING sqlcode = ltp_subrc.
    ENDIF.

  CLEANUP.
* The exception is not intercepted, but a rollback is really necessary
    ROLLBACK WORK.
ENDTRY.
```

The code contains INSERT actions on two different database tables. If one of the two INSERTS is not successful, the other database INSERT must be reversed as well. Note that the code does not contain any CATCH statement to intercept an error, whereas it does have a separate CLEANUP section for executing the ROLL-BACK WORK. This means that a rollback will always be executed if there is an error in one of the database inserts, even if the error is not caught immediately within the TRY-ENDTRY block.

5.3.4 Making Existing Exception Handling Class-Based

Thus far, we have emphasized how to apply class-based exception handling as such, but we haven't explicitly mentioned that it is fairly easy to make existing exception handling class-based. All you need to do is to convert a *traditional* exception signal into a class-based signal (see Figure 5.7).

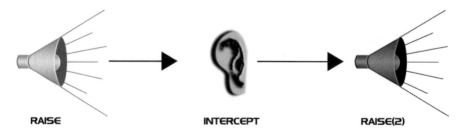

RAISE   **INTERCEPT**   **RAISE(2)**

Figure 5.7 Intercept an Exception and Raise Another One

Converting a traditional signal such as a returncode into a class-based signal is done by inserting the `RAISE EXCEPTION TYPE <exception>` command at the place where otherwise traditional exception handling would be triggered. That's all you need to do. From then on, you must do things in a class-based way. The following code shows how a traditional signal is converted into a class-based signal:

```
TRY.
  CALL FUNCTION '/CTAC/FM_WITH_TRAD_EXCEPTIONS'
    EXPORTING
      itp_input        = tp_input_fm
    IMPORTING
      etp_export       = tp_output_fm
    EXCEPTIONS
      not_found        = 1
      OTHERS           = 9.

  CASE sy-subrc.
    WHEN 0.
* Everything is OK.
    WHEN 1.
      RAISE EXCEPTION TYPE /ctac/cx_notfound.
    WHEN 9.
      RAISE EXCEPTION TYPE /ctac/cx_others.
  ENDCASE.

  CATCH /ctac/cx_notfound.
* Action needed here..
  CATCH /ctac/cx_others.
* Action needed here..
ENDTRY.
```

As you can see, instead of doing the follow-up of the exception immediately after the `WHEN` conditions are checked, you can raise another kind of exception.

5.3.5 Creating Your Own Exception Classes

In the SAP IDES system Release 6.20, which we used for all the examples of ABAP code and the screenshots, we found 1002 global exception classes.[3] So, you should be able to find a global exception class that best suits your needs. If necessary, you can always create your own exception classes. This enables you to collect your own exception attributes and documentation.

---

3 Exception classes all begin with the prefix 'CX_'. The allowed customer names are 'ZCX_', 'YCX_', or '/namespace/CX_'.

Exception classes are global classes. They must be created with the Class Builder (Transaction SE24, see Figure 5.8). They inherit the methods get_text, get_longtext, and get_source_position from the exception class CX_ROOT.

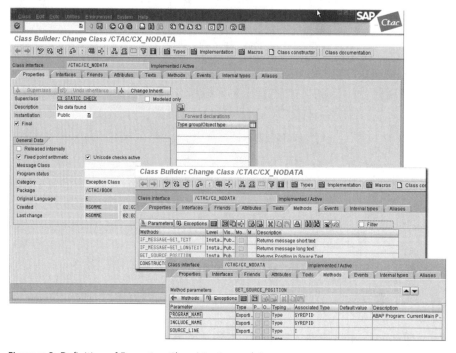

Figure 5.8 Definition of Exception Class /ctac/cx_nodata

In Figure 5.8, you can see how exception class /CTAC/CX_NODATA is defined as a subclass of CX_STATIC_CHECK, which, in turn, is a subclass of CX_ROOT. The methods if_message-get_text and if_message-get_longtext are defined in interface if_message and implemented in exception class CX_ROOT. These methods provide the error message text that is stored in the exception object. The method get_source_position is defined and implemented in CX_ROOT; it supplies information on the name of the program, the include, and the source line where an exception is raised.

Creating your own exception classes is appropriate when developing your own functionality with the ABAP Development Workbench. Exceptions that are specific for this new functionality can be raised within your ABAP code, supplying all the relevant context information.

5.4 Conclusions

In this chapter, we discussed the most important aspects of exception handling. We can summarize these aspects in the form of the following guidelines. First, we recommend that you *always* intercept every possible exception and take the appropriate action. Not knowing how to handle an exception is no excuse: if you don't expect one to occur, you can always stop the program.

Secondly, we propose that you consider application logging for message handling because of the standard features it offers.

Third, above all, we recommend implementing class-based exception handling as soon as you have access to the SAP Web Application Server Release 6.20. This offers more flexibility and reusability than traditional types of exception handling, particularly for more complicated situations in which exception information must be passed on through the Call Stack. Raising, intercepting, and actually handling exceptions are strictly separate activities. Cleanup actions are fully separated from other exception handling activities. It's relatively simple to detect exceptions in all your procedures by adding a TRY (at the beginning) and an ENDTRY command (at the end). Unforeseen exceptions can always be intercepted in the mainline of your ABAP programs for exceptions of class CX_ROOT and CX_SY_NO_HAND-LER. In short, we strongly urge you to take advantage of all these opportunities.

6 User-Friendliness

The term *user-friendliness* needs little introduction. Although, initially, you may think of what is deemed to be user-friendly as highly subjective, user-friendliness can also be looked at from a technical viewpoint. In fact, you can create fairly strict guidelines to enhance the user-friendliness of ABAP programs.

When trying to establish just how *user-friendly* an application is, you should ask yourself the following questions:

▶ How recognizable is the application for the end user in terms of its look-and-feel and behavior?

▶ How much support does it offer the end user?

The degree to which your application is recognizable depends on the extent to which its user interface (UI) has the same look-and-feel, and the same behavior, as the surrounding functionality. This comes down to the following questions:

▶ If specific details actually represent the same things as elsewhere, do they carry identical names?

▶ Are they located on the same spot?

▶ Is the same basic functionality available as elsewhere?

The term *support* shouldn't be difficult to interpret. Again, you should ask yourself:

▶ Is the user helped wherever help is needed?

▶ Can the user easily navigate between menus and screens?

▶ Is the navigation straightforward and quick, without requiring unnecessary user intervention?

6.1 The Importance of Standardization

It is important to know how things are done *elsewhere* when developing new functionality, and not just because SAP may have already created those very things others are working on. It is, of course, easier to copy things than it is to invent them yourself. However, that is not our primary focus. It is actually much more important that a *custom-made* application (i.e., an application that is developed and maintained by a company) is made user-friendly exactly *because* the way in which the user interacts with the application is similar throughout the entire system: the more standardized the interaction with the user, the more user-friendly the application.

When a single function looks and behaves identically in one place as it does elsewhere, end users can concentrate on the rest of the application's functionality because of its very predictability and consistency.

This has many advantages:

▶ Because end users can focus on the processing instead of the UI, their learning process will be faster.

▶ End users will feel safer in an environment that they recognize and understand, which will make them feel in control.

▶ Errors due to wrong input, or the wrong use of buttons, will occur less frequently.

▶ User acceptance is increased.

▶ User productivity is increased.

Not standardizing the look-and-feel and behavior of an application, on the other hand, may lead to some very nasty consequences.

Let's name just a few:

▶ End users won't know exactly or immediately what to expect, or what to do.

▶ End users will need extra support (probably from you) when trying to use new programs.

▶ End users will become frustrated and annoyed when seemingly similar functionality reacts differently throughout the application.

This chapter focuses on some basic do's and don'ts regarding the user-friendliness of your ABAP applications. For detailed guidelines on implementing GUI standards, you should refer to the SAP Style Guide. Several templates are available as well. There is even a tool that checks the layout of custom-made dynpros. So don't fall into the trap of pondering and pontificating on which standards to follow. SAP has already done most of the work for you.

In the first part of this chapter, we present some guidelines that show you how to standardize the look-and-feel and behavior of your programs. In the second part of this chapter, we show you how you can improve the navigation between screens of a custom-made ABAP program (that is, via enabling end users to skip unnecessary screens, fields, and functions) and increase the support the program offers (for example, via documentation, displaying possible entries, and providing search facilities for field values).

6.2 Guidelines for The Look-and-Feel and Behavior of Your Programs

This section shows you how to optimize the look-and-feel and behavior of your ABAP programs. The guidelines are all based on the use of the SAP GUI. Standardization is particularly important in those situations where you can perform the same task in several ways. Although the SAP GUI has documented standards, it still affords you the freedom to customize. Over the last few years, alternatives for the SAP GUI front-end—such as Web-based user interfaces—have become available. Ultimately, the current SAP GUI will be phased out and replaced by Web Dynpro. This does not mean, however, that the examples provided here will become less relevant or even obsolete, or that standardization will be less important. The Web Dynpro UI may give the developer even more freedom.

6.2.1 Things to Be Standardized in The Look-and-Feel of an ABAP Application

When standardizing the look-and-feel of an ABAP application, you should focus on the following four elements of the user interface:

▶ Selection-screens

▶ Dynpros

▶ Menus

▶ List outputs

In the following subsections, we'll list separate guidelines for each of these elements. But, before we do, here are some general tips that should prove useful.

General Rules for Standardizing Appearance

For the aforementioned reasons, the first and basic rule of thumb for the SAP GUI is to reuse all standards employed by SAP. See the SAP Ergonomics Guidelines' examples for SAP GUI's lists and screens. (Refer to SAP transactions LIBS and BIBS.) For non-SAP GUI front-ends, you might want to develop your own company standards.

Secondly, ensure that the general look-and-feel of the GUI reflects the type of functionality that you have in mind. There is usually an optimal way of communicating with a user for each type of functionality.

Generally speaking, selection-screens are best suited to start reporting. Dynpros are more appropriate for dialog and update-related functionality. Table controls are best suited when one-to-many relations must be visualized: think of overview screens that display one order with several items at the same time. Text editors are typically used for working with long texts. You should also note that an output list for an online report has its own characteristics when compared with the output of a background report.

Third, we would like to encourage you to reuse all data definitions stored in SAP's fully-integrated ABAP Dictionary. When doing so, you will find that related field attributes—such as length, data type, and labels—are automatically linked to your developments. Even Help documentation can be accessed without additional effort. If no suitable ABAP Dictionary objects are available, you can create new objects. At least, you'll have your own additional defined standards for other developments as well, which is preferable to having to define new variables locally in your programs.

Lastly, because improvements in SAP technology are an ongoing process, keep yourself informed of the latest technological options for graphical user interfaces: Enjoy controls, Business Server Pages (BSPs), and Web Dynpro are just a few examples of new techniques that were developed to meet certain requirements.

Standardizing the Look-and-Feel of a Selection-Screen

It's safe to say that the majority of ABAP developers have had to build reporting functionality before, therefore, the look of selection-screens should be familiar to most of you. We'll just quickly review the most critical elements. Look at the selection-screen in Figure 6.1. It shows some programming habits that we would rather avoid. Although these practices cannot be entirely condemned, neither will they be appreciated. This non-standard usage of screens is sometimes used by ABAP developers who haven't yet familiarized themselves with some basic standards documented in the SAP Style Guide.[1]

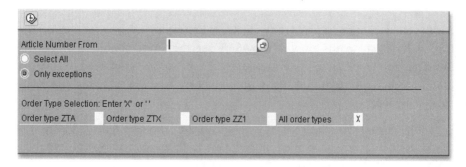

Figure 6.1 Example of a Non-Standard Selection-Screen

---

1 The SAP Style Guide can be found at *http://help.sap.com*.

So, what elements are non-standard in this screen? We'll mention four in particular:

▶ **Standard Field Labels**
The field labels used here are not the standard labels. The text "Article Number From," for example, is not a standard text for fields that refer to data element MATNR. In general, fields that refer to the same data element or table field should, if possible, use exactly the same description consistently throughout the entire system. This increases the level and ease of understanding on the part of the user.

▶ **Standards in arranging selection-screens**
The fields in this selection-screen appear to have been randomly sequenced. Consistently grouping fields that are logically interrelated, and putting the most important fields on top, are two simple yet effective measures that make screens more recognizable.

▶ **Standards in using specialized field types for specific purposes**
The selection-screen fields for the order types mentioned are character fields with a length of one character. Given the type of functionality they represent (choose one or more of these), it would have been preferable to use checkboxes instead. In this particular case, however, it is preferable to use a selection-option on Sales Order Type instead.

▶ **Standards in general look-and-feel**
The radio buttons should be grouped in a separate block with *secondary* selection-criteria instead of appearing almost on top of the screen; furthermore, the logical grouping of fields could be improved by having a descriptive header placed on top of each group or block.

The suggested improvements have been realized on the screen shown in Figure 6.2. An end user with previous SAP experience will probably be familiar with a selection dynpro that looks like the one displayed here.

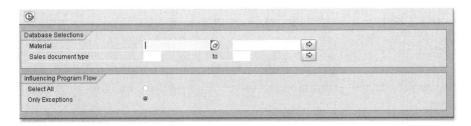

Figure 6.2 Example of a Standard Selection-Screen

Standardizing Custom-Made Dynpros

When you get the opportunity to build dialog functionality for performing database updates, you will probably have to define several dynpros (that is, screens with the associated ABAP logic attached to them) from scratch. In general, ABAP developers are offered a higher degree of freedom in doing so. This means that standardization is more important here than it would be for a selection-screen. In addition to the standards mentioned previously, you should consider several other aspects.

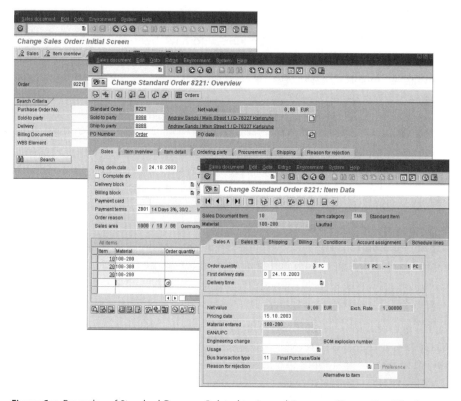

Figure 6.3 Examples of Standard Dynpros Related to Several Purposes (Transaction VA02)

Each custom-made dynpro usually has its own specific role as compared with the other dynpros used within the same dialog function or transaction. Each role can best be reflected in a corresponding screen. Figure 6.3 shows three basic screen types:

▶ **An initial screen or start dynpro**
This type of screen is for the purpose of entering identifying data, such as a document number (for **Display** and **Change** transactions), or an order type and references, to organizational elements (for **Create** transactions).

- ► **An overview dynpro**

  This type of screen typically combines basic (header) data with an overview of main items.

- ► **A detail screen**

  This type of screen typically contains detailed data for one item in particular. Two such examples are:

  - ▻ The detailed data of a sales item
  - ▻ The detailed header data of a change document

Other dynpro types are:

- ► **Enjoy Control screens, which combine different elements such as:**

  - ▻ Tree structures
  - ▻ Table controls
  - ▻ ABAP List Viewer (ALV) Controls

- ► **Modal windows:**

  - ▻ Screens that are opened on top of existing screens, often to display extra information, such as date, time, and the user who changed the object
  - ▻ Messages: information, warning or success message
  - ▻ Decision screens; for example, standard pop-up screens, generated by reusable functions, to prompt the user to confirm whether she or he wants to leave or exit without saving data

We've already mentioned this, but remember, if you want to define your own standards for screen types, you don't have to look too far. The standard SAP system offers all the examples you'll need for each specific type of screen and format. (Refer to SAP transactions BIBS and LIBS.)

Just one final remark on screen definitions: whenever you want to develop **Create**, **Change**, and **Display** dialog functionality for one business object (for example, **Create partner**, **Display partner**, **Change partner**), ensure that you define all required dynpros just once. Most screens required for each basic action on a business object can be identical. In fact, it is fairly easy to reuse one screen for all three aforementioned functions. Furthermore, you should create only one maintenance program for all basic functionality that is needed to maintain one business object.

Standardizing Menus

In an interactive program, standardizing the look-and-feel of a menu is akin to picking apples and oranges all within your reach. Within a SAP GUI context, many menu items have been made available as standard items by SAP, for example, in the form of templates that can be copied into your own menus (see Figure 6.4).

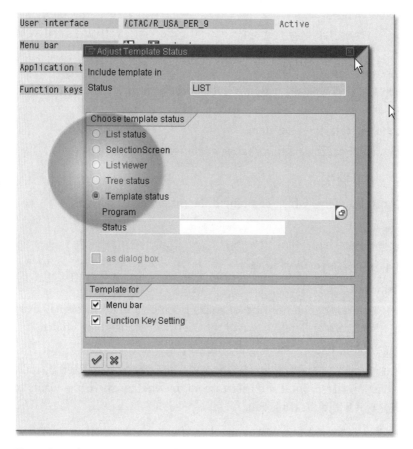

Figure 6.4 Adjust Your GUI Status by Copying a Template Status

For menus used in reports and interactive reports, predefined function codes for printing, downloading, searching, and so forth must be used (see Figure 6.5). The runtime report environment will automatically process functions like %PC (Save as local file) or %PRI (Print). Luckily, the ABAP developer doesn't need to worry about making the right choices as SAP has already done that for him/her.

In general, the following types of standards for all kinds of menus are available:

▶ Icons, names of icons, descriptions of icons; for example, ICON_PRINT

▶ Function codes; for example, SAVE, BACK

▶ Standards for menu bars; for example, **Edit**, **Goto**, **Utilities**

▶ Sequence and grouping within these menu bars

▶ Context menus

▶ Standard Function keys; for example, **F3** = back

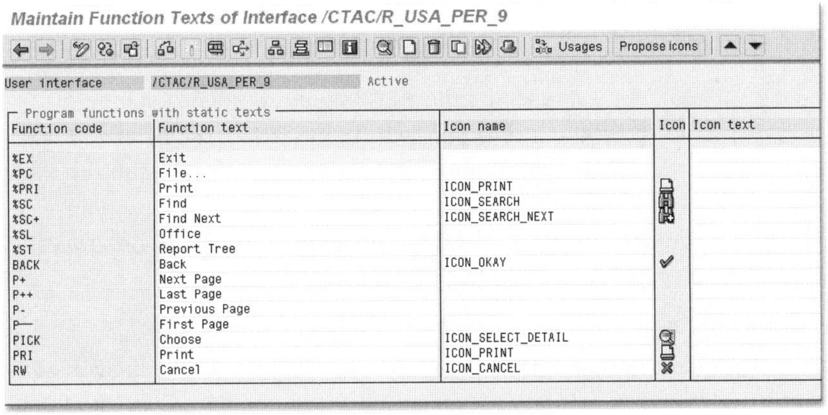

Maintain Function Texts of Interface /CTAC/R_USA_PER_9

Usages | Propose icons

User interface /CTAC/R_USA_PER_9 Active

Program functions with static texts

Function code	Function text	Icon name	Icon	Icon text
%EX	Exit			
%PC	File...			
%PRI	Print	ICON_PRINT		
%SC	Find	ICON_SEARCH		
%SC+	Find Next	ICON_SEARCH_NEXT		
%SL	Office			
%ST	Report Tree			
BACK	Back	ICON_OKAY		
P+	Next Page			
P++	Last Page			
P-	Previous Page			
P--	First Page			
PICK	Choose	ICON_SELECT_DETAIL		
PRI	Print	ICON_PRINT		
RW	Cancel	ICON_CANCEL		

Figure 6.5 Examples of Standard Function Codes, Function Texts, Icon Names, and Icons

Standardizing the Output of Reports

In keeping with our apples and oranges metaphor (see *Standardizing Menus* above), here's another type of fruit just waiting to be picked and within your reach. With the introduction of the ABAP List Viewer (ALV) technique, standardizing layouts of report outputs has become much easier. However, there are still a few things that must be managed by the developer; for example, consistently choosing colors for specialized purposes and providing correct heading texts. Fortunately, most of the output is predetermined by the ALV structure. The end user has the freedom to customize the output as well; for example, he/she can sort, sum, filter, and add or delete fields (see Figure 6.6). In fact, in most cases, this will relieve the developer from having to concentrate on the output's formatting details.

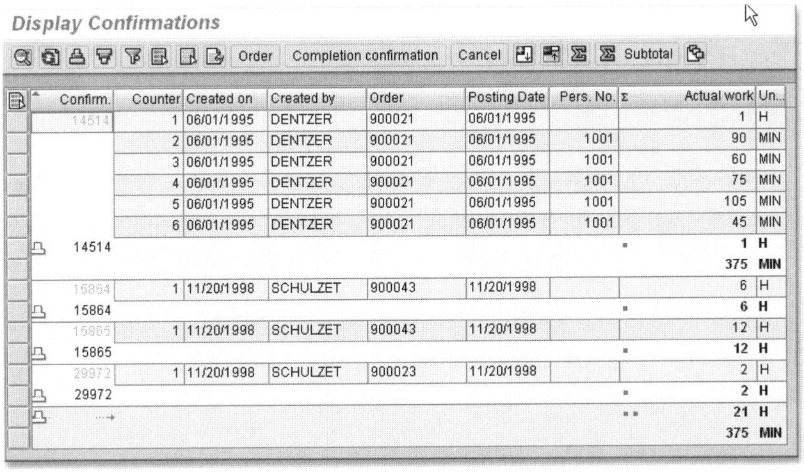

Display Confirmations

Order | Completion confirmation | Cancel | Subtotal

Confirm.	Counter	Created on	Created by	Order	Posting Date	Pers. No.	Σ	Actual work	Un...
14514	1	06/01/1995	DENTZER	900021	06/01/1995			1	H
	2	06/01/1995	DENTZER	900021	06/01/1995	1001		90	MIN
	3	06/01/1995	DENTZER	900021	06/01/1995	1001		60	MIN
	4	06/01/1995	DENTZER	900021	06/01/1995	1001		75	MIN
	5	06/01/1995	DENTZER	900021	06/01/1995	1001		105	MIN
	6	06/01/1995	DENTZER	900021	06/01/1995	1001		45	MIN
14514							▪	**1**	**H**
								375	**MIN**
15864	1	11/20/1998	SCHULZET	900043	11/20/1998			6	H
15864							▪	**6**	**H**
15865	1	11/20/1998	SCHULZET	900043	11/20/1998			12	H
15865							▪	**12**	**H**
29972	1	11/20/1998	SCHULZET	900023	11/20/1998			2	H
29972							▪	**2**	**H**
...→							▪▪	**21**	**H**
								375	**MIN**

Figure 6.6 Example of an ALV List (Transaction IW47)

6.2.2 Things to Be Standardized in The Behavior of an ABAP Application

The second way to create a recognizable ABAP application is to standardize its behavior, that is, to make the interaction with the user feel predictable, logical, and reliable. This standardized behavior will make the user feel in control of the application and reassure him/her that it is *safe* to use it. We'll show you some examples of what precautions the ABAP developer should take in order to support user-friendliness.

Predictable means that the same kind of action always leads to the same kind of result; for example, pressing the **F1**-key should always result in a display of available context-related documentation. Similarly, pressing the **F3**-key should always mean "go to the previous screen," and the **F11**-key should preferably always be associated with a **Save**.

Logical means that the result of a specific action is easily associated with the action itself. For example, pressing the **Print** button should prompt the standard window with the printing defaults—which can be changed by the user if necessary—to open. Imagine how infuriating it would be to not get this window: you want to print something and, perhaps, some printer, somewhere, is started, but you don't know which one; you don't even know whether something is actually being printed.

Reliable means that an ABAP program does what it can to safeguard the user from making mistakes; for example, by ensuring that the user cannot accidentally lose data that was just entered. This improves the ease of use and limits the possibility of errors.

Next, we provide you with some detailed examples of behavior that should be standardized. You can probably think of some more examples yourself.

Cursor Behavior

The place and behavior of the cursor on a screen should be predictable and logical. If the cursor does not appear where the user expects it to be, you can imagine how annoying this would be to the user. In Figure 6.7, the cursor appears on the least likely default button. The user is supposed to confirm that she/he does indeed intend to lose the data just inputted! Under such circumstances, however, the most likely answer to the question: "Are you sure you want to leave?" would usually be "No."

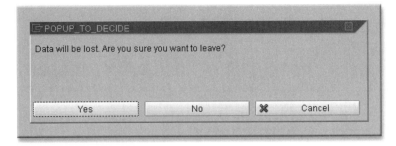

Figure 6.7 Pop-up with a Focus on the Wrong Default Button

Ambiguous Messages

Ambiguous messages reduce the reliability of the application. A user must know precisely what has occurred in order to take appropriate measures. The message shown in the following screen (see Figure 6.8) is far too vague for the user to be able to know how to respond appropriately.

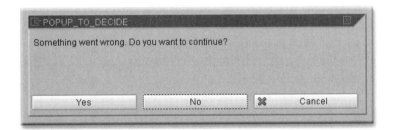

Figure 6.8 Example of a Vague or Ambiguous Message

A common problem for developers is that they often don't know what kind of message to send to the user and what the content of the message should look like. Standardizing the type and content of messages as much as possible makes life easier for programmers and users alike (see Chapter 5).

Not Sending a Message

Then, there's the situation where no message is sent, but is nevertheless required. For example, no confirmation is sent to the user after an update has been processed; or, a report *forgets* to inform the user that he/she didn't select any data (see Figure 6.9). In situations such as these, the user is left wondering what happened. Perhaps, he/she will try to start the program again. Usually, this won't help matters, because the same result will occur. Therefore, simply sending a message can do wonders to reassure and assist the user.

Figure 6.9 Example of a Useful Message

Non-Standardized Menus

We've already mentioned using the ALV technique to standardize output. Now, we'll explain it further in terms of the standardized behavior it offers. The ALV technique offers much more functionality than does traditional ABAP reporting. You cannot only create a GUI status for custom-made ALV reports based on the standard ALV template. You can also use the standard icons, function codes, and function keys on top of this template when adding your own interactive functions. This means that you no longer need to develop screens with a custom-made application toolbar such as the one displayed in Figure 6.10. It shows an ALV screen with a *traditional* application toolbar containing non-standard icons for the **Select all**, **Deselect all**, and **Save data** functions.

ID	No.	Flight Date	Airfare	Curr.	Plane type	Capacity	Occupied	Total	Capacity	Occupied	Capacity	Occupied
AA	17	06.03.2002	422,94	USD	747-400	385	339	193.457,20	31	31	21	19
AA	17	03.04.2002	422,94	USD	747-400	385	334	191.499,01	31	30	21	20
AA	17	01.05.2002	422,94	USD	747-400	385	334	192.361,84	31	29	21	21
AA	17	29.05.2002	422,94	USD	747-400	385	328	188.525,64	31	29	21	20
AA	17	26.06.2002	422,94	USD	747-400	385	328	190.602,32	31	30	21	21
AA	17	24.07.2002	422,94	USD	747-400	385	331	191.558,16	31	30	21	21
AA	17	21.08.2002	422,94	USD	747-400	385	337	195.732,73	31	31	21	21
AA	17	18.09.2002	422,94	USD	747-400	385	329	188.098,64	31	28	21	20
AA	17	16.10.2002	422,94	USD	747-400	385	331	192.771,92	31	31	21	20

Figure 6.10 An ALV List Using Non-Standard Icons

Almost all standard ALV functions are not available in this list. Now, let's look at the list output in Figure 6.11. With minimal effort, the output screen shown in Figure 6.10 could have resembled this screen.

Usage of standard icons and function keys

Selections

ID	No.	Flight Date	Airfare	Curr.	Plane type	Capacity	Occupied	Total	Capacity	Occupied	Capacity	Occupied
AA	17	06.03.2002	422,94	USD	747-400	385	339	193.457,20	31	31	21	19
AA	17	03.04.2002	422,94	USD	747-400	385	334	191.499,01	31	30	21	20
AA	17	01.05.2002	422,94	USD	747-400	385	334	192.361,84	31	29	21	21
AA	17	29.05.2002	422,94	USD	747-400	385	328	188.525,64	31	29	21	20
AA	17	26.06.2002	422,94	USD	747-400	385	328	190.602,32	31	30	21	21
AA	17	24.07.2002	422,94	USD	747-400	385	331	191.558,16	31	30	21	21
AA	17	21.08.2002	422,94	USD	747-400	385	337	195.732,73	31	31	21	21
AA	17	18.09.2002	422,94	USD	747-400	385	329	188.098,64	31	28	21	20
AA	17	16.10.2002	422,94	USD	747-400	385	331	192.771,92	31	31	21	20

Figure 6.11 An ALV List Using SAP Standard Icons

Note that the only function that was added on top of the standard template is the **Save** button! You apply the standard ALV controls, as is done in Figure 6.12.

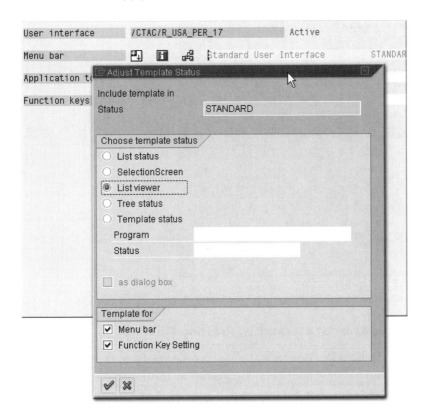

Figure 6.12 Adjust the GUI for an ALV List by Copying the List Viewer Template

Non-Standard Modal Window Functions

The **Enter** and **Esc** buttons are two keyboard functions that are often used both outside and inside the SAP GUI (see Figure 6.13). Because of their widespread use, most SAP users work more or less intuitively with these buttons. Some users will always use the keyboard buttons. Others will try to navigate with the mouse pointer to the SAP GUI symbol and click on it. Because omitting one of these options can be quite annoying, having both options is ideal. Imagine having a modal window displayed (see Figure 6.13). What sometimes happens is that it contains a standard **Enter** icon in the bottom-left corner that cannot be used by pressing the **Enter** button on the keyboard; nor can it be closed with the standard **Esc** keyboard button (which is associated with the window **Close** button in the upper-right corner). These non-standard modal window functions would most certainly not be deemed user-friendly.

Figure 6.13 A Modal Dialog Box with an Enter and Escape Icon

Triggering the Start of a Report by Pressing Enter

A typical SAP standard function for starting a report is the **F8** or **Execute** function. The list event START-OF-SELECTION is triggered by this explicit Run command. However, don't forget to use this list event. If you forget, you run the risk that the process is triggered simply by pressing **Enter**. If database updates are part of this process, such unexpected report behavior may well lead to unwanted modifications. The following sample code shows where the START-OF-SELECTION event should be inserted:

```
AT SELECTION-SCREEN.
IF pa_parm ...
ENDIF.
<- The event START-OF-SELECTION should be entered here.->
SELECT * FROM ...

UPDATE ...
```

Non-Standard Function Code Handling

It's good practice to ask a user to confirm whether she or he intends to leave the program and if this would cause a loss of data (see Figure 6.14). Leaving a transaction that is responsible for database modifications, without asking for such a confirmation, can lead to a loss of data. SAP delivers standard functions that you should use to prompt users to confirm their actions.

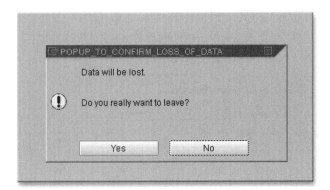

Figure 6.14 Ask a User if He/She Really Wants to Leave the Transaction

Timing of a Message

Another type of program behavior that can test an end user's patience is making him or her wait unnecessarily. Consider the following situation: data is entered, a button is pressed, and your program starts running. Then, it takes a while before a pop-up message informs you that specific data has not been entered on the screen. Typically, in these situations, the check was probably misplaced in the code. Consequently, the code is not executed in time. For the user, however, this feels like waiting in vain.

6.3 Guidelines for Navigation and Support

So far, we have focused on the first requirement of user-friendliness—making the application recognizable by standardizing both the look-and-feel and behavior. In this section, we focus on the second requirement—offering the user as much support as possible. End users might not use the same words as you, but they, too, would like a program that helps them perform their work efficiently, easily, and in a timely fashion.

An optimal ABAP program should be fun to work with, or at least, be as much fun as possible. You can achieve this by making the way that users navigate in-between screens and applications as easy as possible—by ensuring that users can avoid having to take unnecessary actions and be subjected to screen handling, and by offering help whenever needed. To some extent, you can even enable end users to adapt frequently-used functions to their own needs and level of experience.

Of course, this level of support is not only intended to meet the end user's requirements. Ultimately, it is also the productivity of the organization as a whole that counts. However, if each individual user feels comfortable in her or his working environment, there is ample reason to believe that the productivity levels of the entire organization can increase as well. If this sounds worthwhile, perhaps this section can provide you with some tips on how you can best assist users.

6.3.1 Assisting Users During Screen Input

As we mentioned in Section 6.2.1, the strength of the ABAP Dictionary is that it is a fully integrated ABAP Workbench tool. Once changes are applied, they almost instantly lead to changes in all related applications. This does not only offer advantages in terms of maintainability. It also benefits end users. Therefore, taking advantage of the strengths of the ABAP Dictionary is useful for more than just keeping your applications maintainable.

So, what are these benefits for the end user? The answer lies in the uniform look of and support for screen fields. Continuously referring to the data types and tables already defined in the ABAP Dictionary in your programs will enable the following:

▶ Possible entries values (called with the **F4** function) are inherited throughout the system. You will notice, in particular, what this inheritance means when reusing search helps, foreign key relations, and domain values.

▶ Checks are executed automatically on all input made for fields related to dictionary objects with value ranges (laid down in so-called *check tables* or in fixed domain values).

▶ Data element documentation is made available wherever needed.

Extra programming is needed only if more sophisticated help on possible entries is required; but, in that case, standard SAP functions can be reused.

We will not go into more detail here. If you want to profit from the ABAP Dictionary, note that you need much more in-depth knowledge of the objects contained in it and its integration aspects than we can present here and now. Doing so would exceed the scope of this book.

We conclude this section by affirming that every screen field should always refer to a ABAP Dictionary table or structure field. If no suitable Standard SAP field is available, you should create your own structures, data elements, and domains in order to benefit from all the aforementioned advantages.

6.3.2 Limiting Unnecessary Screen Navigation

In the past, a frequent complaint of SAP users was that they had to navigate through many screens and tab through many irrelevant input fields, regardless of the complexity of the task performed. There was some rationale for this, in particular, for releases prior to SAP R/3 4.6. Since then, however, SAP has done its homework. Now that tab strips, Enjoy controls, and alternative front-ends have become a normal part of screen handling, there is much less reason for concern. The ability to create screen variants (using Transaction SHD0) is another option that helps to improve the usability of screens and transactions.

If you need to develop a program that must contain several screens, you might benefit from the same lessons that SAP has already learned. The following could help you to increase user acceptance:

▶ Ensure that the cursor is always positioned on the correct and most logical input field on every screen.

▶ Concentrate on the most important screens and fields. In particular, ensure that it is easy to navigate to these screens and fields. Screens that aren't important for all users, or under all circumstances, should not be part of the standard navigation process. For very complex transactions, it can even be useful to create your own customizing tables to make screens and navigation user-dependent.

▶ Think of a way to navigate directly to **Detail** screens related to items. Note that in order to achieve this degree of user-friendliness, positioning functionality, as is shown in the example in Figure 6.15 below, can be helpful.

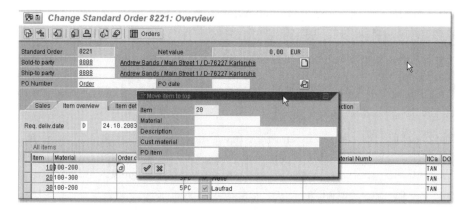

Figure 6.15 An Optimal Way to Navigate Directly to a Specific Item (Transaction VA02)

If a user wants to display details of more than one item, navigating between these items should be simple. A rather awkward way of navigating in such circumstances would be as follows:

1. From the **Overview** screen containing all the items

2. To the **Detail** screen of one item

3. Back to the **Overview** screen again with all the items

4. To the **Detail** screen of another item

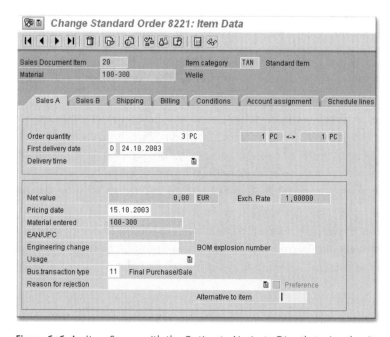

Figure 6.16 An Item Screen with the Option to Navigate Directly to Another Item

The example in Figure 6.16 shows a better way to make navigation more user-friendly. Note that the buttons for navigating directly from one selected item to the next are marked (on the top left corner of the screen).

6.3.3 Avoiding Unnecessary Repetitions of Input

When navigating from one transaction to another, end users will frequently need to use the same field values as before. Immediately after changing a material master, for example, the same material number may have to be used to create a sales order. Because it would be tiresome to repeat the same input over and over again, there are ways to keep data available, one of which is by using a type of data called a *parameter ID*. A parameter ID stays available during a user's terminal session. Using parameter IDs, the values of several fields are automatically filled when a new transaction is started. Good examples include a plant code that is repeated in consecutive transactions in logistical areas; a company code that is kept available in financial transactions; or, a material number that is *remembered* by the SAP system after you leave the material master maintenance transaction.

You can also reuse parameter IDs in your own custom-made developments. Because of their ease of use, it makes sense to reuse the available parameter IDs as much as possible. If necessary, you can also create your own. Linking a parameter ID to a screen field, for instance, can be realized via the data element defined in the dictionary. If this is not possible, you can use the statements GET PARAMETER ID and SET PARAMETER ID directly in the ABAP code.

Note that end users can maintain default values for parameter IDs using the menu option **System • User Profile • Own Data** (or Transaction SU3). These values are available as soon as the user logs on to the SAP system.

There is also another way for an end user to save data that she or he has just entered on a specific screen—by setting the HOLD DATA attribute for a dynpro. The following example (see Figure 6.17) shows how this works when Transaction VA05 is used to get a list of sales orders.

The values that are entered on this screen will be saved and remain valid during the terminal session of the user. They even overrule parameter ID values.

You can also provide this basic help for end users yourself. You do this by setting the HOLD DATA attribute as part of the screen attributes.

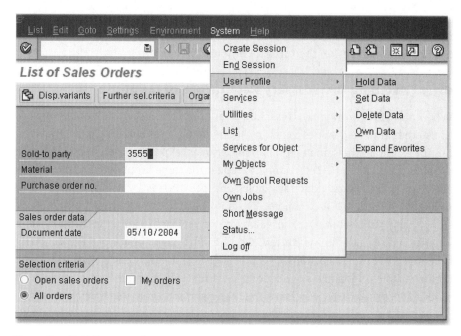

Figure 6.17 Hold Data on a Screen

6.3.4 Avoiding Unnecessary Messages

The last topic regarding the navigation between screens has to do with sending unnecessary messages, or, to be more precise, how to avoid such messages. We've already mentioned the standard procedure of asking the user whether he or she really wants to leave a transaction if the inputted data would be lost as a result. However, if nothing has actually changed, prompting the user with such a confirmation message doesn't make much sense. If you need to know how to prevent such superfluous messages, the following may be of interest to you.

The optimal way to verify whether anything has changed since the beginning of a transaction is by storing the original event at the beginning of the program. This has three advantages:

▶ If the user wants to leave the transaction without saving, the current data can be compared with the original data. If no difference is found, no confirmation has to be sent to the user.

▶ If the user presses the **Save** button, but nothing has actually changed, unnecessary **Save** actions can simply be skipped. If this is the case, you may need to notify the user that no **Save** action is needed.

▶ On the basis of the original state, Undo functionality can be developed and the user can restore the original data on the screen.

In this context, an extra detail to keep in mind is the way in which exit-type functions work. If, for example, you define the **Cancel** function as an exit-type function, you may introduce an unwanted side-effect. Since pressing the corresponding button will result in skipping the transfer of data from the screen to the program, changes made on this particular screen cannot be checked by your program—the values are simply not available. To avoid this exception, you must conduct an additional check on system field sy-datar. The corresponding ABAP code to be used should look like this:

```
IF ta_data_old[] = ta_data_new[] AND
   sy-datar       = co_false.
* No changes found and no new screen input
* Screen can be left immediately
  SET SCREEN 0.
  LEAVE SCREEN.
ELSE.
  CALL FUNCTION 'POPUP_TO_CONFIRM_LOSS_OF_DATA'
    EXPORTING
      textline1 = 'Do you really want to leave?'(001)
      titel     = 'POPUP_TO_CONFIRM_LOSS_OF_DATA'(002)
    IMPORTING
      answer    = tp_answer.
ENDIF.
```

6.4   Conclusion

As you probably noticed, this chapter on user-friendliness is relatively brief, when compared with the other chapters in this book. However, please don't think the subject of user-friendliness is less important than other more technical aspects of ensuring ABAP quality. Although we focused more on providing you with screen examples than on the technicalities, this was done for good reason. Most of the detailed guidelines on user-friendliness have been made available elsewhere.[2]

However, that's not the sole reason. We believe that user-friendliness is not primarily a technical matter. If there is one thing that you should learn from this chapter, it's this: standardization is critical to improving usability. Therefore, being a good developer is not simply a matter of honing good programming skills. You also need to be able to step into your end users' shoes and walk around awhile just to see what it feels like. The more you identify with your users and take their needs into account, the easier it will be for you to understand why seemingly irrelevant details can sometimes be so important.

---

2 See the SAP Style Guide.

7 Performance

7.1 Introduction

This chapter focuses primarily on the ABAP language elements that have the greatest impact on performance. When discussing the performance of ABAP programs, excessively slow-running ABAP programs are often cited as typical examples of poor programming. While other program deficiencies affecting robustness are often hidden or only indirectly visible, performance problems rarely go unnoticed, and often cause a lot of frustration among end users.

Usually, performance problems don't become known until database tables grow larger and the amount of data to be processed increases. To a certain extent, this makes anticipating such problems more difficult: you would need substantial amounts of test data in order to test a program specifically on its performance. However, often test data is not abundantly available. On the other hand, the absence of sufficient test data doesn't necessarily mean that performance problems can't be prevented. In fact, we'll provide you with several guidelines in this chapter that should help to prevent the most common causes of poor performance.

Note that improving performance is not only a matter of applying basic guidelines. The particular choices you make are not valid under all circumstances. Ultimately, you should always verify the choices you make. Therefore, actively monitoring the performance of custom-made programs in a SAP production environment should become a daily routine.

If you need more information on SAP tools and strategies for monitoring, testing, and checking your code, refer to Chapter 9.

To best understand the topics addressed in this chapter, you should know the fundamentals of ABAP and Open SQL. Note that more extensive descriptions of Open SQL and detailed information on all topics discussed in this chapter are also available in other sources. In addition to the SAP system's extensive online help, we also recommend that you refer to the *SAP Performance Optimization Guide* as well as several articles in the *SAP Professional Journal*.[1]

Approximately 90% of a program's runtime can usually be attributed to 10% of its code. If you know how to work with this 10%, you can solve most performance problems. The way in which this chapter is divided is best understood if you consider the three-tier client-server architecture of the SAP software: one database server, one or more application servers, and many clients (see Figure 7.1).

---

1 For a list of books and articles, see the Bibliography in Appendix D of this book.

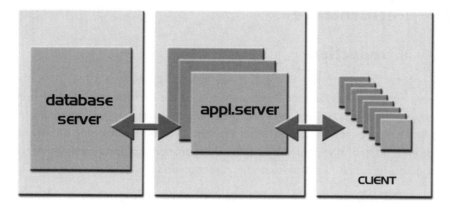

Figure 7.1 The Three-Tier Client-Server Architecture

Performance issues can arise in four places in the client-server architecture:

1. During processing on the database server
2. In the data traffic between the database server and the application server
3. During processing on the application server
4. In the data traffic between the application server and the client (and on the client itself)

The first place where processing can be delayed is on the database server itself (1), which means during the execution of SQL statements for reading and modifying database tables. SQL statements are relatively heavy operations when compared with most other program actions. Once database server performance issues arise, they typically stem from not being able to locate the data fast enough. This is usually due to poorly programmed SQL statements. Therefore, improving the performance of an ABAP program often comes down to reviewing SQL statements or changing database attributes.[2] All topics related to database access are discussed in Section 7.2.

The second place where a performance bottleneck can occur is in the data traffic between the database server and the application server (2). Although this bottleneck is primarily due to poorly programmed SQL as well, the reasons must be found in other aspects of SQL statements than the ones referred to in Section 7.1. Therefore, we will address this topic separately in Section 7.3.

The third place where you should keep an eye on performance is the application server (3). In order to limit the traffic between the application server and the database server, the ABAP language provides various ways to buffer data on the

---

2 Before you start to optimize your program, ensure that performance problems are not caused by the system as a whole.

application server. Internal table processing is the most notable of these methods. However, this ABAP feature is not always implemented properly, in which case the actual contribution to performance enhancement is rather limited, or even worse, an additional cause of performance degradation. Performance issues that are specifically related to processing on the application server are discussed in Section 7.4.

The fourth place where performance can be an issue is the data traffic between the application server and the client, and possibly on the client itself (4). Think, for instance, of uploads and downloads. The associated pitfalls and solutions are presented in Section 7.5.

7.2 Optimizing Processing on the Database Server: Using Indexes

SAP database tables are stored in one central database system that services all program sessions in all SAP system instances (see Figure 7.2). Therefore, a heavy database load will immediately have a negative impact on the entire SAP system's performance. On the other hand, there's reason to be optimistic: this also means that improving the performance of individual database operations will lead to a better overall performance.

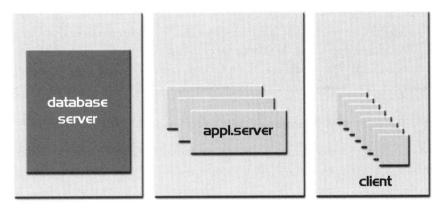

Figure 7.2 The Database Server in the Three-Tier Client-Server Architecture

To a large extent, an ABAP programmer can optimize the processing done on the database server all by herself or himself. This primarily involves maximizing the speed at which the data in the database is accessed. To better understand this, think of a SELECT statement: the WHERE clause contained within the SELECT statement is required for the speed at which data is located in the database. In other words, optimizing database access is predicated on optimizing the WHERE clause. The question as to how to achieve this objective is the main subject of this section.

Optimizing database access depends primarily on the use of the available indexes. The more that fields mentioned in the WHERE clause of a SELECT statement are inherently part of the index that you use, the better this is for the performance of the SELECT statement (i.e., the index fields used in the WHERE clause determine how quickly the required data is located in the database). While most ABAP developers are already familiar with this principle, they might struggle to apply it correctly in some circumstances. At first sight, an appropriate index (i.e., the index that offers the fastest access to the required database rows) is not always available. Worse still, when you do find an such an index, it doesn't always contain the fields that you need, or the fields aren't always in the right order.

Considering the amount of data that is usually managed in an SAP system, we cannot overstress the importance of using indexes consistently in all your ABAP programs. This doesn't apply to only those tables that contain transaction data such as financial documents, purchase orders, customer orders, and production orders. Such tables tend to grow so fast that accessing the data contained in them without using an index is simply not feasible. Moreover, the importance of using indexes consistently also applies to master data tables such as those underlying the material master, the customer master, and the bill of materials just to name a few. Although their increase in volume will be less, the central role of the master data tables makes the access frequency higher. In short, indexes are essential for managing and optimizing data access. In general, the ABAP developer is the person who is best qualified to determine the optimal way of selecting required data.

7.2.1 Primary and Secondary Indexes

As an ABAP programmer, you're probably familiar with the way Open SQL statements are processed by the SAP runtime environment. Every query you make is converted by the SAP system into a native SQL statement for the underlying database. This native SQL statement can be viewed by using the SQL trace (with Transaction ST05). Figure 7.3 shows an example of native SQL viewed using SQL trace.[3]

---

3 An *index range scan* is a range within an index that is scanned for valid entries.

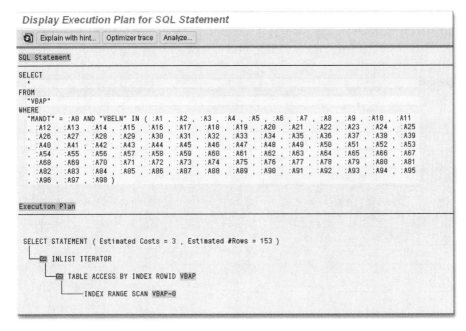

Figure 7.3 Example of a SQL trace

In the example in Figure 7.3, the index with the name vbap~0 is used for table VBAP. In other words, this is the primary index. Every database table has at least one index: the primary and unique index named 0. The primary index of a database table is formed by the combination of all its key fields (see Figure 7.4).

| Pooled table | A004 | Active |
| Short Description | Material | |

| | Attributes | Delivery and Maintenance | Fields | Entry help/check | Currency/Quantity Fields |

Field	Key	Initi...	Data element	DTyp	Length	Deci...	Short Description
MANDT	☑	☑	MANDT	CLNT	3	0	Client
KAPPL	☑	☑	KAPPL	CHAR	2	0	Application
KSCHL	☑	☑	KSCHA	CHAR	4	0	Condition type
VKORG	☑	☐	VKORG	CHAR	4	0	Sales Organization
VTWEG	☑	☐	VTWEG	CHAR	2	0	Distribution Channel
MATNR	☑	☐	MATNR	CHAR	18	0	Material Number
DATBI	☑	☑	KODATBI	DATS	8	0	Validity end date of the condition record
DATAB	☐	☑	KODATAB	DATS	8	0	Validity start date of the condition record
KNUMH	☐	☑	KNUMH	CHAR	10	0	Condition record number

Figure 7.4 An Example of the Primary Index of a Database Table

In addition to primary indexes, SAP often has defined secondary indexes (see Figure 7.5). These secondary indexes are used for tables that tend to grow fast, in order to ensure efficient access based on fields other than the primary key fields.

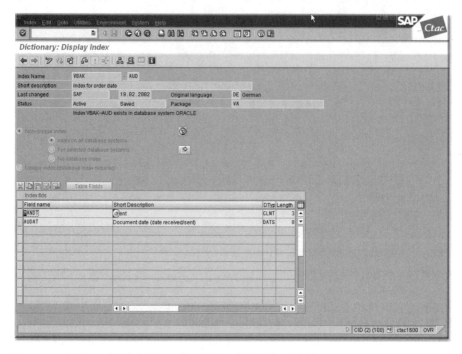

Figure 7.5 An Example of the Secondary Index of a Database Table

SAP customers can add their own secondary indexes to standard SAP tables. In fact, adding a secondary index is so easy that sometimes you may tend to underestimate the consequences of adding another index. One of the dangers for inexperienced ABAP programmers is to create a secondary index for an existing table rather carelessly. You should try to avoid this pitfall if possible because overall SAP system performance may suffer from defining too many indexes. In most cases, we recommend that you use a cautious and conservative approach.

Because an additional index can cause a degradation of the overall system performance, you should exercise caution when creating extra indexes. Every update on a database table must include an update of all its indexes. Therefore, creating a secondary index simply means that more updates are made and more database space is occupied. This will have a particularly significant impact on large tables that are subject to many INSERT, UPDATE, or DELETE statements.

Another problem that can occur when you add a secondary index is that other programs may start processing more slowly. This can be a direct result of the underlying database management system's (DBMS) decision on which index to use when executing a SQL statement. Most DBMS systems determine an index on the basis of database statistics in order to predict the most efficient index for a specific database request. In practice, however, such statistics can be outdated, or based on a relatively small part of the actual database. In exceptional situations, this can lead to choosing a wrong index. For more detailed information, see the *SAP Performance Optimization Guide*.

In summary, we strongly recommend that you limit the number of secondary indexes for any given database table. Or, to put it into the daily context of an ABAP developer, creating a new secondary index simply to make one specific report run faster in the background once a week is not worth the effort.[4]

7.2.2 What You Can Do to Prevent the Creation of Extra Indexes

As an ABAP developer, you must do more than simply find the elementary tables that contain the required data for a new program. You must also consider how to access each table as quickly as possible to ensure an acceptable performance. Finding the tables with the required data is often difficult enough. What can exacerbate this already difficult situation is whether the tables that you initially find do not, or only partly, provide the preferred access path (in the form of a primary or secondary index). As we already mentioned, in such cases, inexperienced developers may be tempted to create a secondary index.

In some circumstances, creating an additional secondary index may be unavoidable, however, experience has shown that there are other alternatives. We'll show you some examples of these alternatives in this section. First, we'll introduce several SAP R/3 database tables that actually represent a kind of index themselves. You can use one of these tables when another appropriate index is missing. Secondly, we'll provide you with some guidelines to deal with a situation whereby an index is present, but not all key fields can be filled in properly. Then, we'll discuss several issues regarding the correct implementation of SQL statements. Lastly, we'll list some practical considerations when an extra secondary index is a necessary evil.

Using Alternative Tables

Although the SAP relational data model is highly normalized,[5] in some cases, denormalizations have been applied. These denormalizations are primarily intended to enhance performance. In addition to having fully normalized elemen-

---

4 You can make an exception if a program would keep critical functionality waiting. Think, for example, of a weekly invoice run.

5 In a fully normalized database, all attributes, except the key attributes of the database tables, are defined once. In a denormalized database, non-key fields also appear in more than one database table. In other words, denormalization leads to more redundancy.

tary tables, an SAP system also contains tables that point to the data in the elementary tables through varying primary indexes. As you'll notice, the most obvious choice—selecting the elementary table that contains most of the relevant data—is not always the best choice. These so-called *alternative* tables can also be helpful for customized developments. All the examples mentioned in this section are well known and exemplify those alternative tables that enhance performance, but please note that the list could have been longer.

You can use an alternative table for one or more of the following reasons:

1. The primary index of the alternative table points directly to the required data.

2. The alternative table contains important fields of more than one elementary table. This will help you to navigate more efficiently between the elementary tables; sometimes, it will also make SELECT statements on elementary tables superfluous.

3. The alternative tables contain only data with a specific status.

Provided that an alternative table meets your needs, using it can definitely improve performance. Three types of alternative tables in SAP R/3 are worth mentioning:

▶ Tables that help to find transaction data via *related master data*

▶ Tables that help to find transaction data via *related documents*

▶ Tables that support tracing transaction data on the basis of the *status* of the data

These three examples are explained in more detail hereafter.

The need for information on sales data per material or per business partner is a straightforward example of a logical and predictable end-user requirement. ABAP developers who have struggled with this requirement will know that all required information is available in the elementary SAP R/3 tables VBAK (sales order headers) and VBAP (sales order items). Unfortunately, neither of these two tables has an index on customer number or material number. Therefore, we don't recommend that you use these tables directly, because their lack of an index will inevitably generate serious performance problems as soon as database sizes increase.

The obvious thing to do—creating an extra secondary index—is not necessary in this case. Table VAPMA (Customer Orders per Material Number) will provide the required information without performance problems. Figure 7.6 shows how this table can be used. You can first use the material number and other organizational selection criteria like the sales organization to find details such as the order number and the item number in table VAPMA. These criteria will help you to identify the data in the elementary tables. Then, the associated detail order data can be read from the appropriate elementary tables via their regular primary index containing the order number and order item.

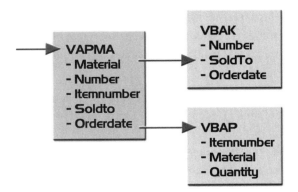

Figure 7.6 Access to Sales Data Via Table VAPMA

Besides table VAPMA, other alternative tables are available in the SAP R/3 Sales and Distribution (SD) module. All of these tables offer a logical search path, each of which is tailored to meet certain requirements and situations (see Table 7.1):

Table	Description
VLPMA	Delivery index per material number
VRPMA	Sales invoice index per material number
VAKPA	Sales order index per business partner
VAKGU	Sales index, quotation validity
VLKPA	Delivery index per business partner
VRKPA	Sales invoice index per business partner
VBKPA	Sales activities by partner function
VBKOF	Open sales activities by partner function
VKAOF	Open sales activities
VKDFS	SD index, billing initiator
VBOX	Billing document, rebate index
VEPVG	Delivery due index
VETVG	Delivery due index for stock transfer
VTRDI	Shipment planning index

Table 7.1 Alternative Tables for Sales and Distribution

A second type of requirement involves the search for documents based on their relation with other documents. The document flow functionality in Sales and Distribution is a well known example. It gives an overview of a sales order and, among other things, all the related deliveries, pick-up orders, goods issue documents, and invoice documents. This series of interrelated documents is created in a fixed and chronological order. Some tables in the SAP R/3 system, mainly in the Purchasing and Sales areas, are specifically maintained to record the required references between documents.

In most cases, reading and processing such document flow tables will not cause any difficulties. However, the search for a document must be based on a chronological predecessor in the document flow. For example, searching a goods issue document based on the preceding purchase order can be done using table EKBE (Purchase Order History). Similarly, finding sales invoices based on preceding deliveries can be done using table VBFA (Sales History). The standard function module RV_ORDER_FLOW_INFORMATION is even available to accommodate an efficient search for related Sales and Distribution documents.

We should briefly mention a specific misconception about the use of the document flow. Some programmers use it for the exact opposite purpose for which it is intended. They try to find a *predecessor* document instead of a *successor*. This concerns questions like: Which sales order item corresponds with a specific delivery item? A corresponding SELECT statement would look like this:

```
SELECT vbelv posnv FROM vbfa INTO wa_order_item
  WHERE vbeln = tp_delivery_number
  AND   posnn = tp_delivery_item
  AND   ..
```

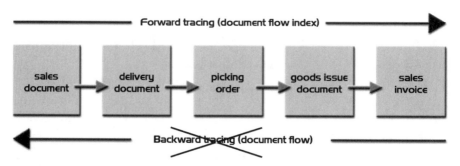

Figure 7.7 Using the Document Flow

Although you can use the document flow index as-is if you want, we don't recommend it (see Figure 7.7). In the long run, it will most likely cause performance problems. Document flow tables such as table VBFA were not created for *backward* tracing. Its primary index is not suitable and a secondary index does not exist. Developers often wonder why, and then decide that this is a flaw in SAP's design, and resolve the *problem* by creating a secondary index (on the two fields vbeln and posnn marked bold in the sample code above). Actually, the optimal solution for tracing documents backwards in a document flow is much simpler. The elementary tables contain the necessary references themselves. For sales documents, these references are available in table lips, in the following fields:

- lips-vbeln: Delivery
- lips-posnr: Delivery item
- lips-vgbel: Document number of the reference document (In this situation sales order number)
- lips-vgpos: Item number of the reference item (In this situation sales order item)

The code should therefore have looked like this:

```
SELECT vgbel vgpos FROM lips INTO wa_order_item
       WHERE vbeln = tp_delivery_number
       AND   posnr = tp_delivery_item
       AND   ..
```

This wrong usage of document flow tables is also possible for table EKBE (document flow Purchasing). If you want to trace related documents backwards in the purchasing document flow, don't do so on the basis of this table. Just use the goods movements data in table MSEG or the invoice data in table RSEG for that purpose.

The third kind of table that can help to optimize database access is a search table based on the status of transaction data. In some cases, the tables containing actual status information are the only tables that offer access to the detailed data, which makes your choice an easy one to make. Consider, for example, status tables such as table VBUK (Sales Document Header status) and table VBUP (Document Item status).

However, there are also alternative tables based on status information that indirectly point to the data in elementary tables. Sometimes, these tables are actually indispensable. Think of the selection of financial documents in SAP R/3. Financial document tables BKPF (Document Header) and BSEG (Document Item) are not only notorious for the amount of data they can contain. They also don't offer efficient ways to select document items from table BSEG, other than via their primary key.[6]

---

6 Table BSEG is a cluster table. A cluster table is created for storage optimization. There is no table on the RDBMS with the same name. Only the cluster RFBLG exists for the database system. Therefore, secondary indexes cannot be defined for fields in table BSEG. Another drawback of cluster tables is that they cannot be used in joins.

Searching financial document data is therefore usually done using status tables. These contain both header and item data from tables BKPF and BSEG. Separate tables are maintained per account type (like creditor and debtor) and clearing status (open, cleared). An overview is shown below (in Table 7.2). These tables combine all of the advantages mentioned earlier (quick access, detailed document data, and status information). All tables are almost identical in terms of their contents.

Account Type	Open (Not-cleared)	Cleared[1]
Supplier/Creditor/Vendor	BSIK	BSAK
Customer/Debitor	BSID	BSAD
General Ledger Postings	BSIS	BSAS

Table 7.2 Alternative Tables Based on Status Information

1. Tables with *cleared* data also contain document items that aren't relevant for clearing.

To demonstrate the effect of using one of these alternative tables, consider the following example. Open document items for a specific customer and company code must be processed. If that functionality is implemented, referring directly to tables BKPF and BSEG, the source code would look like this:

```
* First select data from BSEG
  SELECT bukrs belnr gjahr buzei kunnr wrbtr
         FROM bseg
         INTO TABLE ts_bseg
         WHERE bukrs IN so_bukrs
           AND kunnr IN so_kunnr
           AND koart = co_koart_deb
           AND augbl = co_augbl_ini
           AND augdt = co_augdt_ini.

* Then select data from BKPF related to data found in BSEG and posting
* data
  IF NOT lines( ts_bseg ) = 0.
    SELECT  bukrs belnr gjahr budat waers
            FROM bkpf
            INTO TABLE ts_bkpf
            FOR ALL ENTRIES IN ts_bseg
            WHERE bukrs = ts_bseg-bukrs
              AND belnr = ts_bseg-belnr
              AND gjahr = ts_bseg-gjahr
              AND budat IN so_budat.
  ENDIF.

* Merge these two tables.
  LOOP AT ts_bkpf INTO wa_bkpf.
```

```
LOOP AT ts_bseg INTO wa_bseg
                    WHERE bukrs = wa_bkpf-bukrs
                      AND belnr = wa_bkpf-belnr
                      AND gjahr = wa_bkpf-gjahr.

   wa_postings-kunnr = wa_bseg-kunnr.
   wa_postings-bukrs = wa_bkpf-bukrs.
   wa_postings-belnr = wa_bkpf-belnr.
   wa_postings-gjahr = wa_bkpf-gjahr.
   wa_postings-buzei = wa_bseg-buzei.
   wa_postings-budat = wa_bkpf-budat.
   wa_postings-wrbtr = wa_bseg-wrbtr.
   wa_postings-waers = wa_bkpf-waers.
   INSERT wa_postings INTO TABLE ts_postings.
 ENDLOOP.
ENDLOOP.
```

The following SELECT statement yields the exact same result. In addition to being much faster,[7] it is also easier to understand and maintain.

```
SELECT kunnr bukrs belnr gjahr buzei budat wrbtr waers
       INTO TABLE ts_postings
       FROM bsid
       WHERE bukrs IN so_bukrs
         AND kunnr IN so_kunnr.
```

We end our discussion of alternative tables with a general axiom—if no efficient access path for an elementary table exists, and the need for such an access path is apparent and logical, an alternative table is probably available somewhere. Therefore, if you think that's the case, try to look for such an alternative. We recommend that you use SAP tools such as SQL trace (ST05), Runtime Analysis (SE30), or the Debugger. Often, an end user can help by providing you with an example of a standard transaction that shows the same information efficiently.

Leveraging an Existing Index

Once you've established suitable tables to select the data that you need, the second trap you can fall into is to *forget* to use the available indexes properly. For various reasons, it may not always be possible to determine a value for all the required index fields. The index fields that you have to use in your SELECT statement may have unknown values, or initial values, or their contents may vary. The effect this has on performance is substantial, particularly if a value for one of the first fields in the index is missing.

---

7 On our 6.20 IDES system, the second query was about 2000 times faster than the first query for one company and one customer.

To briefly explain the effect of omitting an important index field value in the WHERE clause of your SELECT statement, consider combing through a phone book sorted by city, name, and street address. Furthermore, suppose that your first criterion *city* is the missing *index field*. This means that you would have to search the person to be contacted using only his or her name and street address. Consequently, you would have to check every single city listed in the directory. Worse still, you cannot afford to simply stop once you find the first person with the name and street address that you're looking for. Because you can't verify that this person is the only individual throughout all the cities with that name and street address (the index may not be unique), you would have to continue checking the entire phone book!

In SQL terms, this is called a *full table scan*. The general effect it has is illustrated again in Figure 7.8. A completely qualified index, supplying values for all index fields, is used on the right. The value for the first index field is "2" and the value for the second index field is "1". In this case, the number of table rows actually selected is limited to the bare minimum (this is depicted by the arrow left of the table pointing immediately to the right location). If the index used is unique, exactly one database row is actually accessed. On the left, a search is depicted with a missing value for the most important first index field. Only the second index field (with value "1") is supplied. Consequently, the database server has to scan the entire table (again represented by an arrow on the left of this table) and literally check every single row. In other words, not supplying values for the first index field is disastrous for performance.

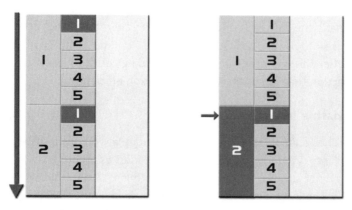

Figure 7.8 The Effect of Not Using the First Index Field (Left) Compared with Normal Use of the First Index Field

Hopefully, this example shows clearly how important it is to use at least those index fields placed first in the index. However, this still doesn't solve the problem of not knowing which value to use in the first place. Therefore, we'll now introduce some workarounds that should prove useful.

The indexes of many tables start with references to organizational elements, such as the company code (field `bukrs`), the plant (`werks`) or the sales organization (`vkorg`). If you consider the importance of using the first key fields, it should become apparent that knowing the values of every relevant organizational element is absolutely essential. Consider the sample code below. It does not fully use the index of table BKPF (financial documents header):

```
SELECT bukrs belnr gjahr FROM bkpf INTO TABLE ts_documents
    WHERE belnr IN so_belnr
      AND gjahr EQ pa_gjahr.
```

As you can see in the ABAP Dictionary, the index for table BKPF starts with the field `bukrs` (besides the key field `MANDT` for the client). Although, a SQL trace may, in this case, show that the primary index is used, it will not be very efficient, because a full table scan will be executed.

Instead, you can use the fields `bukrs` in a more practical way. You have the following options:

▶ Define a select option to enable the user to enter a value.

▶ Use a constant value for the selection in your program.

▶ Determine a range of index values at runtime that can be used for the selection.

In this case, we recommend that you use the last option. Defining an extra select-option for the end user is a good option, but it would not be full proof. Imagine introducing a select-option in which the user is allowed to enter a generic value (such as "S*"). In native SQL, such a value might be translated into `LIKE "S%"`. However, this would require a full table scan. Therefore, it still doesn't lead to an efficient the database query. Using a constant value is also an easy solution, but you might want to avoid it from the point of view of maintenance (see Chapter 8).

The following code shows a more flexible approach. Note that even if the end user hasn't provided a company code, the use of the primary index is ensured.

```
SELECT bukrs FROM t001 INTO TABLE th_companies
      WHERE bukrs IN so_bukrs.
IF lines( th_companies ) > 0.
  SELECT bukrs belnr gjahr FROM bkpf INTO TABLE ts_documents
          FOR ALL ENTRIES IN th_companies
          WHERE bukrs EQ th_companies-bukrs
            AND belnr IN so_belnr
            AND gjahr EQ pa_gjahr.
ENDIF.
```

Another alternative is also possible:

```
SELECT bukrs belnr gjahr FROM bkpf INTO TABLE ts_documents
       WHERE bukrs IN ( SELECT bukrs FROM t001
                                     WHERE bukrs IN so_bukrs )
         AND belnr IN so_belnr
         AND gjahr EQ pa_gjahr.
```

To see why this is much more efficient, consider Figure 7.9, which shows the effect of this code:

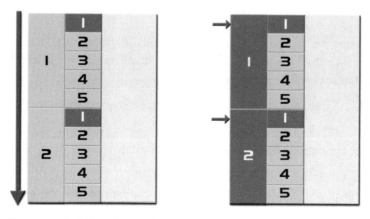

Figure 7.9 The Effect of Using the First Index Field with All Possible Values (right) Compared with a Full Table Scan

This kind of solution tends to work well for organizational fields such as company code, plant, sales organization, and so forth. If a field value can be derived from a set of possible values of a domain, you can also extract its possible values from table DD07V.

Introducing SELECT options in order to enable users to control selections is recommended as long as users can determine the values to be used. Sometimes, it means that you have to ask for values that a user understands and then translate these end-user values to values that are stored in the database. For example, when a user is asked to choose debit or credit values, these values are converted by the program to a value for field shkzg (debit would then be translated to value "S" and credit to value "H"[8]).

We've already discussed examples of controlled redundancy (denormalization) to support performance optimizations. You will recall the alternatives described ear-

---

8 SHKZG stands for **"Soll-/Haben-Kennzeichen"** where **S** stands for **Soll** and **H** stands for Haben. Because SAP is a German company, there are still many places where you will find German abbreviations. To help you remember this example, note that the alphabetical order of Debit and Credit and Soll and Haben is the same (D comes after C, and S follows H).

lier in this section, under the topic *Using Alternative Tables*. Other examples of controlled redundancy are tables containing aggregated data known as *infostructures* or *statistics tables*. At the moment of posting transaction documents such as sales orders, purchase orders, or goods movements, all figures relevant for later reporting are automatically added to the existing aggregate figures (in database tables such as S001, S011, or S034). Therefore, you don't have to calculate period-related totals on the basis of detailed transaction data in each program again. Instead, you can directly use the totals that the SAP R/3 system has prepared.

The reason that we specifically mention infostructures is because ABAP developers often don't know what values to supply for the many important index fields. This may prevent them from leveraging the optimal performance when selecting data from an infostructure, whereas performance optimization is one of the reasons why infostructures exist, that is, infostructure tables exist primarily because they are intended to enhance performance.

Understandably, it's easy to get confused when trying to reference all the key fields of an infostructure in the WHERE clause of a SELECT statement. Finding the correct value of fields like *statistics origin* (ssour) or *version number* (vrsio) is problematic enough by itself. However, we want to focus on the other key fields—those fields that determine the correct time basis for the totals (day, week, month, or posting period). Only one of the four fields will, by definition, be used (a total is either a day total, a week total, etc.). The other three fields will therefore have an initial value. The question is what to do with these fields. Look at the following SQL statement. To select the statistics source and version number, it refers to constants. The time interval that can be selected by the user (with a parameter) is *day* (field s004-sptag), which means that all totals mentioned are daily totals.

```
SELECT * FROM s004 INTO TABLE ta_s004
    WHERE ssour  = co_ssour_s004
       AND vrsio  = co_vrsio_s004
       AND sptag  = pa_sptag
       AND matnr  = pa_matnr.
```

This WHERE clause leaves room for improvement. The key fields that refer to the time intervals that are not used (week, month, and posting period) are missing. Although fields spmon (month), spwoc (week), and spbup (posting period) will have an initial value, they should nevertheless be used in the WHERE clause, because it will make the SELECT quicker. The following code is preferable:

```
CONSTANTS: co_spwoc_ini TYPE spwoc VALUE IS INITIAL,
           co_spmon_ini TYPE spmon VALUE IS INITIAL,
           co_spbup_ini TYPE spbup VALUE IS INITIAL.
```

```
SELECT * FROM s004 INTO TABLE ta_s004
       WHERE ssour  = co_ssour_s004
         AND vrsio  = co_vrsio_s004
         AND sptag  = pa_sptag
         AND spwoc  = co_spwoc_ini
         AND spmon  = co_spmon_ini
         AND spbup  = co_spbup_ini
         AND matnr  = pa_matnr.
```

To complete this topic, we should again briefly refer to the alternative search tables in Table 7.2 (the status tables for accessing financial document data). Some of these alternative tables (BSIK, BSID, and BSIS) also contain several key fields that will always be empty: augdt (reconciliation date) and augbl (reconciliation document). We recommend that these key fields should also be fully qualified in a WHERE clause as well.

Implementing Efficient SQL

We should add that there are many other practical uses regarding the proper implementation of SQL statements, most of which can best be interpreted as *tips and tricks*.

Sometimes, you can produce great results with relatively simple measures. Look at the graphical representation (Figure 7.10) of the following SELECT statement. It selects three fields: the first two of these fields (field1 and field2) are also part of the index used; the third field (field3) must be selected from the database table itself.

```
SELECT <field1> <field2> <field3> FROM <dbtab>
       INTO <workarea>
       WHERE <field1> EQ <value>
         AND <field2> EQ <value>.
...
ENDSELECT.
```

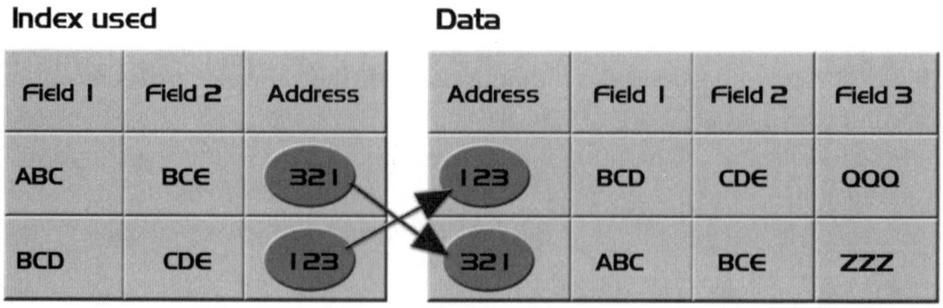

Index used

Field 1	Field 2	Address
ABC	BCE	321
BCD	CDE	123

Data

Address	Field 1	Field 2	Field 3
123	BCD	CDE	QQQ
321	ABC	BCE	ZZZ

Figure 7.10 SELECT Index and Database Table Fields

Now, suppose that `field3` is no longer required. Consequently, the `SELECT` statement no longer has to get its data from the database table itself (see Figure 7.11). Therefore, if you choose the fields that you need carefully and wisely, you may boost your performance considerably and at no cost.

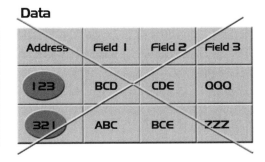

Figure 7.11 SELECT Index Only

Of course, we can also reverse the example where `field3` is required. In this case, you might consider adding this field to the secondary index.

If a `SELECT` option is absolutely essential in order to utilize an index field, we recommend that you also limit the values that the user can enter there. Simply making the `SELECT` option *obligatory* is not enough: entering an asterisk (*) would suffice (and possibly lead to a full table scan anyway). Therefore, if you face this dilemma, consider using function module `SELECT_OPTIONS_RESTRICT`. It will help you to limit the possible values of a specific `SELECT` option (e.g., prevent a user from entering generic values such as the asterisk *).

If, for one reason or another, you want to determine the index that is used in an ABAP program yourself, you can elect to use so-called *database specific hints*. Note, however, that these hints are highly database-specific, and therefore, we recommend that you avoid using them. You can read more about this topic in related OSS notes.[9]

There are situations where you might expect an unknown key field to have an initial value, but you're not certain if it does. If creating a new index is not possible, or not allowed, or simply not important enough a task to undertake, you can try the following trick. At least, in this way, you can ensure that the field is included in the `WHERE` clause:

```
CONSTANTS: co_field_ini  TYPE <type> VALUE IS INITIAL.
SELECT <field1> <field2> FROM <dbtab>
       WHERE <field> GE co_field_ini.
```

---

9 Refer to OSS note 129385.

Although it may not help much, at least you can indicate to other ABAP developers that you considered this performance issue. If, however, the key field actually contains an initial value as expected, this code guarantees a better performance. As a result, a full table scan is avoided. If, however, the key field contains a not-initial value, performance is not improved.

Sometimes, you don't have the option to choose the most efficient access method. Consider, for example, the situation in which a report should allow the user to choose between a selection of sales orders by material, or by customer (see Figure 7.12):

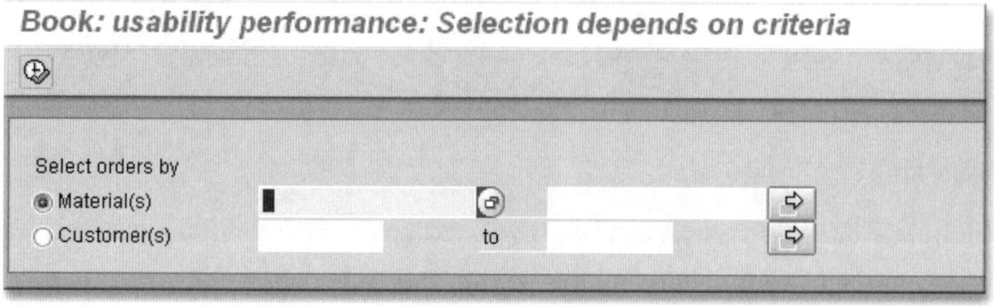

Book: usability performance: Selection depends on criteria

Select orders by
- Material(s)
- Customer(s)

Figure 7.12 Example of a Report with Two Possible Index Options

Using one of the two access paths provided by SAP (refer to Table 7.1) may not suffice. If you must enable the two-way selection (via either material number, *or* customer number), the only thing you can do is to prepare the ABAP code for both options. It requires more coding, but it also offers the required flexibility at runtime:

```
IF pa_rad01 = true.
  CALL METHOD rf_ref->get_orders_by_material
    EXPORTING
      ira_materials = ra_matnr
    IMPORTING
      ets_orders    = ts_orders.
ELSE.
  CALL METHOD rf_ref->get_orders_by_customer
    EXPORTING
      ira_customers = ra_kunnr
    IMPORTING
      ets_orders    = ts_orders.
ENDIF.
```

Practices That Disturb Index Use

In addition to ensuring that values are entered for the most important index fields, there are other practices to consider, namely, some specific programming habits that have a negative impact on performance.

From a functional point of view, applying a NOT condition can seem perfectly logical. From a technical point of view, however, it is not always advisable. For example, look at the following SELECT statement, in which such a condition is inserted in the WHERE clause:

```
SELECT bukrs belnr gjahr FROM bkpf INTO TABLE ts_documents
      WHERE NOT bukrs EQ tp_bukrs
        AND belnr IN so_belnr
        AND gjahr EQ pa_gjahr.
```

Actually, accessing a database in this way can make performance unpredictable. To use the phone book analogy again (described earlier in this section), trying to access a database via using a NOT condition in a WHERE clause is like looking for a phone number knowing the street address and the name of the person to be contacted, with only one restriction—knowing that this person does *not* live in one particular city. In order to find this person's phone number, you would have to search through all the cities listed in the phone book except this one city. Consequently, you would have to comb through almost the entire phone book. Therefore, you should avoid WHERE conditions that include a NOT or NE operator on a key field (see Figure 7.13).

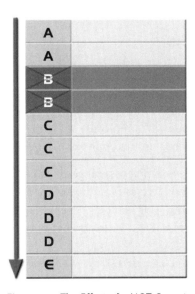

Figure 7.13 The Effect of a NOT Operator on the First Index Field

A preferable alternative is described below. In a first and quick selection (on customizing table T001 —company codes), the NOT condition is still applied. However, because customizing tables are not that large, using the NOT condition won't greatly impact performance. In a second step, when the size of the database does matter, the FOR ALL ENTRIES option is used. In this way, the selection is converted into a positively formulated selection on company code (bukrs). This helps to expedite the selection.

```
SELECT bukrs FROM t001 INTO TABLE th_companies
       WHERE NOT bukrs EQ tp_bukrs.
IF lines( th_companies ) > 0.
  SELECT bukrs belnr gjahr FROM bkpf INTO TABLE ts_documents
          FOR ALL ENTRIES IN th_companies
          WHERE bukrs EQ th_companies-bukrs
            AND belnr IN so_belnr
            AND gjahr EQ pa_gjahr.
ENDIF.
```

Frequently, only a part of the value of an index field will be known. Instinctively, many of you will be inclined to use a wildcard to represent this in the WHERE clause. Imagine, for example, the selection of all rows from database table coep (cost accounting document lines) for controlling area (kokrs) '1000' and document numbers starting with '02000.....'. Implementing the query with a wildcard would result in the following code:

```
SELECT * FROM   coep
       INTO TABLE ts_coep_recs
       WHERE  kokrs  = co_kokrs
       AND    belnr  LIKE '02000%'.
```

Although this option is not entirely erroneous, neither is it ideal. As with the NOT condition, logically, using a wildcard appears to make sense, however, technically, this option is not recommended because this code will often cause the database server to use a full table scan (although this depends on the underlying DBMS).

Instead of using a wildcard, you are far better off referring to a range of values in the WHERE clause. You can program such a range in two different ways: by using the BETWEEN option in the WHERE clause, or by using RANGES. The BETWEEN option has the same effect as when an end user specifies a BT in a select-option:

```
tp_belnr_low  = '0200000000'.
tp_belnr_high = '0200099999'.
SELECT * FROM   coep
       INTO TABLE ts_coep_rec
       WHERE  kokrs  = co_kokrs
       AND    belnr  BETWEEN tp_belnr_low AND tp_belnr_high.
```

The same effect is achieved with the following code:

```
TYPES: ty_range_belnr   TYPE RANGE OF co_belnr.
DATA: ra_range          TYPE ty_range_belnr.
DATA: wa_range          LIKE LINE OF ra_range.


START-OF-SELECTION.

  REFRESH ra_range.
  CLEAR wa_range.
  wa_range-sign   = 'I'.
  wa_range-option = 'BT'.
  wa_range-low    = '0200000000'.
  wa_range-high   = '0200099999'.
  APPEND wa_range TO ra_range.
  SELECT * FROM  coep
         INTO TABLE ts_coep_rec
         WHERE  kokrs = co_kokrs
         AND    belnr IN ra_range.
```

Hence, a wildcard is not the optimal option. Instead, try using a WHERE clause with a BETWEEN, EQ, or IN condition, if you can, for wildcard scenarios.[10]

There are still numerous other ways in which to create an ill-performing SQL statement. The next example to consider is a complex WHERE clause:

```
SELECT
        belnr gjahr blart bukrs
          FROM rbkp
            INTO TABLE ts_invoices
              WHERE  ( belnr IN so_belnr
                AND  ( ( gjahr EQ pa_gjahr OR
                        bldat BETWEEN pa_datfr AND pa_datto )
                AND    NOT blart IN so_blart )
                OR   ( gjahr IN so_gjahr
                AND     bukrs IN so_bukrs
                AND NOT bldat BETWEEN pa_datfr AND pa_datto ) ).
```

One way to create a complex SELECT statement is by introducing the OR option. For most programmers (indeed, for most people), it is difficult to understand a statement that combines AND and OR operators. If a NOT operator is included as well, most of us will become even more confused or worse, completely lost. Strictly speaking, this complexity has more to do with understanding logic than it does performance.

A complex WHERE clause, however, will make it more difficult for the DBMS to determine the best possible access path. All SELECT statements trigger a database

---

10 Using BETWEEN or BT options for character-type fields can lead to portability problems between different code-pages. See also Section 4.4.4 on code-page use.

optimizer to determine the best possible access routine. Complex SELECT statements, however, sometimes succeed in confusing the database optimizer. This can lead to the use of an inefficient index.

However, note that WHERE clauses can be complex for reasons other than those mentioned thus far. Moreover, they may also include inner and outer joins. Shortly after the introduction of inner and outer joins with Open SQL in the ABAP language, many programmers were eager to apply these techniques immediately. However, this often resulted in complex SELECT statements with a combination of several joins and FOR ALL ENTRIES options, like the one below:

```
SELECT
        rbkp~belnr
        rbkp~gjahr
        rbkp~bukrs
        rbkp~blart
        rseg~buzei
        ekpo~matnr
        ekko~ebeln
        ekpo~ebelp
        ekko~bstyp
        ekko~bsart
            INTO CORRESPONDING FIELDS OF TABLE ts_purchord
            FROM rbkp
            INNER JOIN rseg ON rseg~belnr = rbkp~belnr
                          AND rseg~gjahr = rbkp~gjahr
            INNER JOIN ekko ON ekko~ebeln = rseg~ebeln
            INNER JOIN ekpo ON ekpo~ebeln = rseg~ebeln
                          AND ekpo~ebelp = rseg~ebelp
            FOR ALL ENTRIES IN ts_link
            WHERE rbkp~belnr = ts_link-belnr
              AND rbkp~gjahr = ts_link-gjahr.
```

After subsequent performance problems, statements such as these have frequently been divided again into separate queries.

The FOR ALL ENTRIES option is often used without checking the contents of the internal table being used:

```
SELECT <field> FROM <dbtab>
        FOR ALL ENTRIES IN <itab>
        WHERE <field> = <itab>-<field>.
```

The strange effect that this code has is that—if the internal table is empty—all conditions of the WHERE clause are actually omitted. Instead, everything is selected. Note that we have previously raised this issue (see Section 3.2.4). We mention it here again, because it is also important for performance. Although the solution was mentioned in Chapter 3, we present it here again. Before you apply a SELECT statement that includes the FOR ALL ENTRIES option, you should always verify whether the internal table is filled:

```
IF NOT <itab>[]  IS INITIAL.
  SELECT <field> FROM <dbtab>
         FOR ALL ENTRIES IN <itab>
         WHERE <field> = <itab>-<field>
...
ENDIF.
```

Speaking in terms of performance, we should add that when using the FOR ALL ENTRIES option it is recommended that all database fields used are index fields. Consider the following example:

```
IF LINES( th_materials ) > 0.
  SELECT vbeln posnr FROM vbap INTO TABLE ts_orders
         FOR ALL ENTRIES IN th_materials
         WHERE matnr EQ th_materials-matnr.
ENDIF.
```

The performance of this statement will be very poor because of the way the FOR ALL ENTRIES option is translated into native SQL.

```
SQL Statement

SELECT
  "VBELN" , "POSNR"
FROM
  "VBAP"
WHERE
  "MANDT" = :A0 AND "MATNR" IN ( :A1 , :A2 , :A3 , :A4 , :A5 , :A6 , :A7 , :A8 , :A9 , :A10 , :A11
  , :A12 , :A13 , :A14 , :A15 , :A16 , :A17 , :A18 , :A19 , :A20 , :A21 , :A22 , :A23 , :A24 , :A25
  , :A26 , :A27 , :A28 , :A29 , :A30 , :A31 , :A32 , :A33 , :A34 , :A35 , :A36 , :A37 , :A38 , :A39
  , :A40 , :A41 , :A42 , :A43 , :A44 , :A45 , :A46 , :A47 , :A48 , :A49 , :A50 , :A51 , :A52 , :A53
  , :A54 , :A55 , :A56 , :A57 , :A58 , :A59 , :A60 , :A61 , :A62 , :A63 , :A64 , :A65 , :A66 , :A67
  , :A68 , :A69 , :A70 , :A71 , :A72 , :A73 , :A74 , :A75 , :A76 , :A77 , :A78 , :A79 , :A80 , :A81
  , :A82 , :A83 , :A84 , :A85 , :A86 , :A87 , :A88 , :A89 , :A90 , :A91 , :A92 , :A93 , :A94 , :A95
  , :A96 , :A97 , :A98 , :A99 , :A100 , :A101 , :A102 , :A103 , :A104 , :A105 , :A106 , :A107 ,
  :A108 , :A109 , :A110 , :A111 , :A112 , :A113 , :A114 , :A115 , :A116 , :A117 , :A118 , :A119 ,
  :A120 , :A121 , :A122 , :A123 , :A124 , :A125 , :A126 , :A127 , :A128 , :A129 , :A130 , :A131 ,
  :A132 , :A133 , :A134 , :A135 , :A136 , :A137 , :A138 , :A139 , :A140 , :A141 , :A142 , :A143 ,
  :A144 , :A145 , :A146 , :A147 )
```

Figure 7.14 SQL trace for the FOR ALL ENTRIES Option

As Figure 7.14 shows, every entry in the table th_materials is added to an IN option. If the number of entries in table th_materials is large (in this example, greater than 1,500), more than one native SQL statement will be executed. Moreover, every single SQL statement will contribute to there being a full table scan! Actually, it is probably more efficient to process one full table scan and check the materials later. In this particular case, the best solution would be to use the alternative table VAPMA as was explained earlier in this section (see *Using Alternative Tables*).

The same kind of problem can arise if a JOIN condition is programmed referring to non-key fields. The database optimizer will probably decide to read the two tables first, using the WHERE conditions. Then, it will merge the results based on the JOIN conditions. Because this can be very time-consuming for large tables, we suggest that you first try the other options that were previously mentioned.

The next practice that can disturb index use is the careless use of the ORDER BY option in a SELECT statement. In more precise terms, if the ORDER BY sequence that you specify differs from the sequence of the index used, this can significantly degrade performance. This is reason enough for not using the ORDER BY option, unless you're certain that the sequence is correct.

Things to Remember if a Secondary Index Is Inevitable

So far, we have tried to show you how to avoid creating a secondary index. However, you should know that sometimes this is not possible. For those instances when a secondary index is inevitable, you must do the following:

▶ Remember to limit the number of fields in the index.

▶ Choose a clever sequence of the index fields.

Limiting the number of fields should be fairly obvious, because it directly affects the amount of data required for storage of the index. The importance of finding the optimal sequence of the index fields, however, may need further explanation.

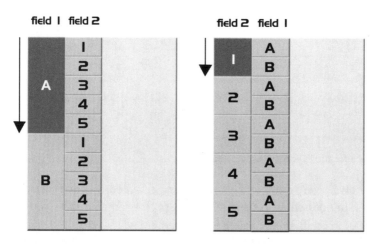

Figure 7.15 The Location of Distinctive Values Within a Secondary Index

To better appreciate these recommendations, note that, in general, an index will help to improve the performance of database accesses if fields with a high number of distinctive values are placed at the beginning. Figure 7.15 depicts an index with a low number of distinctive values in the first index field on the left. The opposite is shown on the right. By using a field with highly distinctive values as one of the first index fields, even a partial use of the index will limit the amount of data selected almost immediately. Note that this rule holds true only if you can predict what value these fields will actually have when used in the programs for which you created the index.

7.3 Minimizing Data Traffic Between the Database Server and the Application Server

As we mentioned earlier in the chapter, in addition to accessing data in the database as quickly as possible, your second goal to ensure optimal performance should be to limit the amount of data traffic between the database and your application (see Figure 7.16).

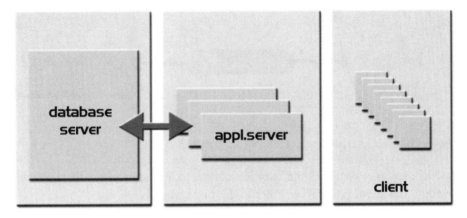

Figure 7.16 Data Traffic in the Three-Tier Client-Server Architecture

In terms of a `SELECT` statement, "limiting data traffic" literally means "asking for as little data as possible in the `SELECT` statement" (see Figure 7.17). For example, a `SELECT *` is not exactly the most fortunate of all available choices if you know that the corresponding database table contains a large amount of data and many different fields. Each database request results in data being transferred back to the application program in separate data packages. Although the connection between a database server and an application server is typically fast, the amount of data traffic between the servers can significantly reduce the overall performance.

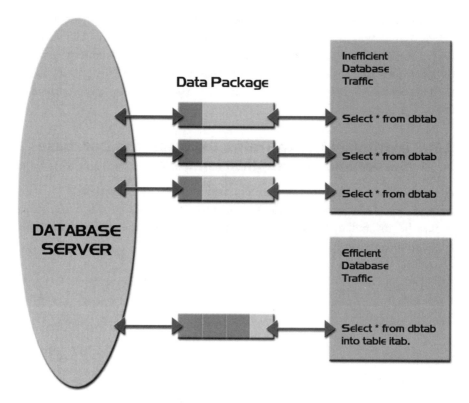

Figure 7.17 Inefficient Data Traffic Versus Efficient Data Traffic

In this section, we address the question of how to limit database traffic and shift work to the application server. You can do this in three ways:

▶ By limiting the number of *rows* selected

▶ By limiting the number of *fields* (table columns) selected

▶ By limiting the number of *times* that data is selected

To achieve this goal via a step-by-step process, we begin with an example of a simple, but inefficient, SELECT statement:

```
SELECT * FROM vbak INTO wa_vbak
      WHERE vbeln IN so_vbeln.
  CHECK wa_vbak-auart IN so_auart.
  CHECK wa_vbak-audat IN so_audat.
ENDSELECT.
```

We won't comment on the code just yet. For now, you only need to know that we intend to change this SELECT into a more efficient statement during the course of this section. We ran this query on a SAP Web Application Server (Web

AS) 6.20 IDES system for a table with 3300 entries. After each change that we applied ourselves, we measured the resulting actual and relative performance gains. Of course, in reality, these gains are mere indicators of improved performance, however, they should help you target where to look first in order to improve data traffic with the database server. You might try using the performance Tips & Tricks (Transaction SE30) to do the same.

7.3.1 Limiting the Number of Rows Selected

In addition to the effect that a WHERE clause has on the speed at which a database table is accessed, it also directly affects the number of rows returned to the calling program. Therefore, it can be very beneficial to add fields to a WHERE clause even if these fields aren't relevant for the index currently used. The intended effect can best be presented via two graphics. The first graphic (see Figure 7.18) shows what the SELECT prompts the database server to do before the extra conditions are added to the WHERE clause in the sample code. The second graphic (see Figure 7.19) shows what happens after you add the extra WHERE conditions, namely, the number of rows selected is significantly less.

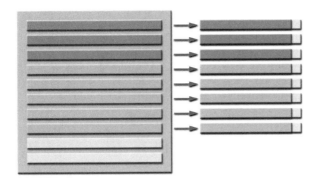

Figure 7.18 Before Adding an Extra WHERE Condition

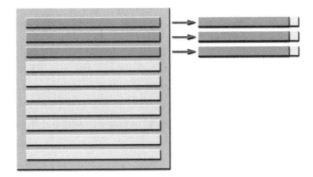

Figure 7.19 After Adding an Extra WHERE Condition

Now, let's *prove* that this works. Exactly the same fields are referenced as in the preceding code, however, this time, we'll avoid the CHECK statements. Instead, we'll extend the WHERE clause:

```
SELECT * FROM vbak INTO wa_vbak
      WHERE vbeln IN so_vbeln
      AND   auart IN so_auart
      AND   audat IN so_audat.
ENDSELECT.
```

The following graph shows the first improvements (see Figure 7.20). Series 1 shows the execution of the first code, and Series 2 shows the execution of the changed code.

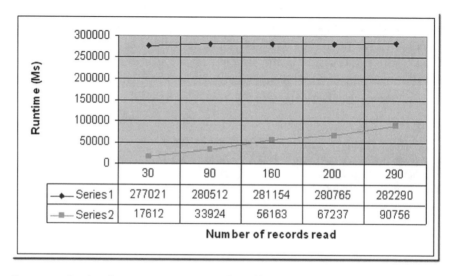

Figure 7.20 Runtime Statistics: Improvement After Adding Extra WHERE Conditions

Limiting the number of rows selected can pose a particular problem when modifications to existing source code must be made. It's often tempting to leave existing SELECT statements unchanged, without verifying whether the data selected is still required, or is already made available elsewhere.

Note that a check on identical SELECT statements is supported by the SQL trace. Although the results will be limited to completely identical statements (the comparison is based on strings), it may indicate possible improvements. Minor changes can often lead to considerable performance improvements without having to completely re-implement existing functionality.

As in the preceding example, an issue that often arises is the sequence in which tables are processed. Usually, important checks are done in ABAP code *after* most of the data has already been selected. Consequently, database traffic no longer benefits from these checks.

Optimizing the Efficiency of Database Updates

For database update statements, limiting the number of database rows to be processed is also critical. You can change database entries directly, without first having to read them into your program. Look at the following code:

```
SELECT * FROM <dbtab> INTO <workarea>
WHERE <field> EQ <value>.
       <workarea>-<field1> = 'X'.
       UPDATE <dbtab> FROM <workarea>.
ENDSELECT.
```

The same functionality can be executed more efficiently in one statement:

```
<workarea>-<field1> = 'X'.
UPDATE <dbtab> SET <field1> = 'X'
       WHERE <field> EQ <value>.
```

The Impact of Using FOR ALL ENTRIES Instead of a JOIN

The last thing that you should take into account—with regard to performance—is the way the options JOIN and FOR ALL ENTRIES work. Let's start with an example in which an INNER JOIN is used:

```
SELECT vbap~posnr    " ... (a lot of vbap fields)
       mara~mtart    " ... (a lot of mara fields)
       FROM vbap
       INNER JOIN mara ON mara~matnr EQ vbap~matnr
       INTO WA_ORDERDATA
       WHERE vbap~vbeln IN so_vbeln.
  APPEND wa_orderdata TO ta_orderdata.
ENDSELECT.
```

This code is not optimal for minimizing database traffic. The selection of rows from table MARA is repeated for every selected vbap row. If, for example, every material occurs on average in 10 order lines, 9 of the joins will contain superfluous data (see Figure 7.21).

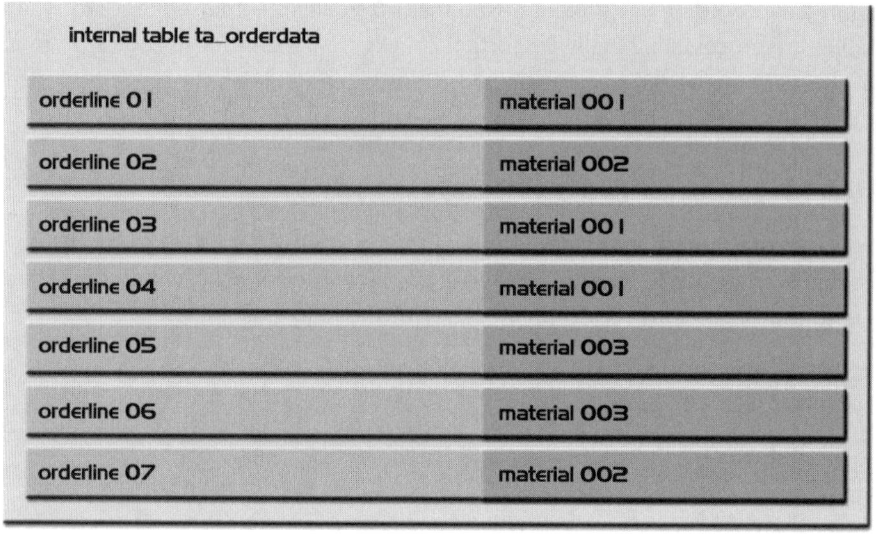

Figure 7.21 The Effect of an INNER JOIN

Consider changing the code as follows:

```
SELECT *
        FROM vbap
        INTO wa_orderdata
        WHERE vbeln IN so_vbeln.

  APPEND wa_orderdata TO ta_orderdata.

ENDSELECT.

IF lines( ta_orderdata ) > 0.
  SELECT * FROM mara
        INTO wa_mara
        FOR ALL ENTRIES IN ta_orderdata
        WHERE matnr EQ ta_orderdata-matnr.
    READ TABLE th_mara TRANSPORTING NO FIELDS
              WITH TABLE KEY matnr = wa_mara-matnr.
    IF sy-subrc NE 0.
      INSERT wa_mara INTO TABLE th_mara.  "hashed table
    ENDIF.
  ENDSELECT.

* Merging the two tables into one
  LOOP AT ta_orderdata INTO wa_orderdata.
    READ TABLE th_mara INTO wa_mara
    WITH TABLE KEY matnr = wa_orderdata-matnr.
  ENDLOOP.
ENDIF.
```

The effect this code has is depicted in Figure 7.22.

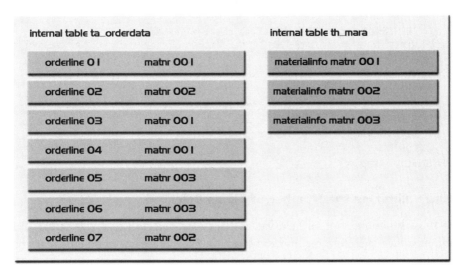

Figure 7.22 The Effect of Using the FOR ALL ENTRIES Option

After this specific improvement, some other improvements can be applied on top; table `ta_orderdata` may still contain many double entries that will all be processed in the `FOR ALL ENTRIES` clause. Ensuring that the table used for many `FOR ALL ENTRIES` contains only unique values will probably further reduce the number of rows selected, as follows:

```
SELECT *
      FROM vbap
      INTO wa_orderdata
      WHERE vbeln IN so_vbeln.

   APPEND wa_orderdata TO ta_orderdata.

ENDSELECT.

IF lines( ta_orderdata ) > 0.

   LOOP AT ta_orderdata INTO wa_orderdata.
     wa_matsel-matnr = wa_orderdata-matnr.
     COLLECT wa_matsel INTO ta_matsel.
   ENDLOOP.

   SELECT * FROM mara
         INTO wa_mara
         FOR ALL ENTRIES IN ta_matsel
         WHERE matnr EQ ta_matsel-matnr.
```

```
    READ TABLE th_mara TRANSPORTING NO FIELDS
              WITH TABLE KEY matnr = wa_mara-matnr.
    IF sy-subrc NE 0.
      INSERT wa_mara INTO TABLE th_mara.   "hashed table
    ENDIF.
  ENDSELECT.

* Merging the two tables into one
    LOOP AT ta_orderdata INTO wa_orderdata.
      READ TABLE th_mara INTO wa_mara
      WITH TABLE KEY matnr = wa_orderdata-matnr.
    ENDLOOP.
  ENDIF.
```

7.3.2 Limiting the Number of Fields Selected

In most situations, not all field values from each selected row will actually be required. We therefore recommend that you explicitly name the fields that you want to use in a program and do so routinely. If, in our example, only three fields are required, a simple improvement would look like this:

```
SELECT vbeln auart audat FROM vbak INTO wa_vbak
      WHERE vbeln IN so_vbeln
      AND    auart IN so_auart
      AND    audat IN so_audat.
ENDSELECT.
```

To see how limiting the number of fields selected will affect performance, see Figure 7.23.

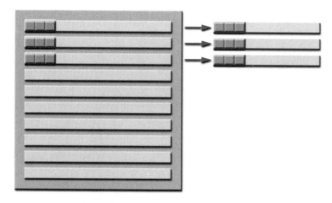

Figure 7.23 The Effect of Using a Field List

Note that the performance is gradually improving (although not spectacularly), as you can see in Figure 7.24.

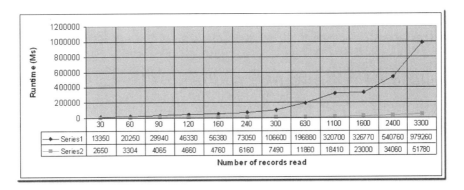

Figure 7.24 Runtime Statistics: Improvement when Using a Field List

Series 1 refers to the previous SELECT * FROM vbak example. Series 2 refers to the example with the field list above.

We will now review some other interesting possibilities.

Dynamic Field Selections at Runtime

All fields to be selected may not be known before a program is actually executed. If an end user has the option to select the fields that are relevant to him or her, for example, on a selection screen of a report, an inefficient SELECT statement that selects all fields (SELECT * FROM ⟨dbtab⟩) can be avoided. You can define the required field names at runtime, store them in an internal table, and refer to the internal table later in the SELECT statement:

```
APPEND 'AUART' TO ta_fieldnames.

SELECT (ta_fieldnames) FROM vbak
        INTO CORRESPONDING FIELDS OF wa_vbak
        WHERE vbeln IN so_vbeln
        AND   auart IN so_auart
        AND   audat IN so_audat.
```

There are, however, some drawbacks to using Dynamic SQL. First, there is the extra overhead caused by creating the native SQL statement; secondly, the possibility that runtime errors are raised when wrong field names are used. We think, however, that these drawbacks shouldn't prevent you from using Dynamic SQL if it is appropriate. This is still a preferable option to always using a SELECT * FROM.

The INTO CORRESPONDING FIELDS option

Another factor to consider is the necessity of avoiding syntax like this:

```
SELECT * FROM <dbtab>
        INTO CORRESPONDING FIELDS OF <workarea>.
```

Perhaps ABAP developers who use this construction assume that Open SQL will be intelligent enough to automatically limit the fields selected based on the <workarea>. In reality, however, something else occurs: all field values from each table row are selected and transported to the application server first. Then, the fields that are required are copied to the workarea fields with the same name. You can verify this with a SQL trace.

Try to limit this type of programming to test programs, or use it only for those tables that contain a limited number of fields. Generally, the preferred option, regarding both performance and maintenance, is to explicitly name the fields to be selected.

7.3.3 Limiting the Number of Times That Data Is Selected

The third fundamental way to optimize data traffic is by reducing the number of times that data will actually be traveling between the database server and the application server. As you may have noticed, the effect that reducing the number of selected fields has on performance is not that great. Its effect is likely to be limited because some minimum package size, defined on DBMS level, will be sent anyway. You can take a bigger step if you combine this with a reduction of the number of times that data is selected. You do this by selecting as much data as possible with one SELECT statement and store the rows found temporarily in internal tables of your program or in semi-persistent memory of an application server (see Section 7.4.5).

Consider the difference in performance between the last SELECT shown and the following:

```
SELECT vbeln auart audat
        FROM vbak
        INTO TABLE ts_vbak
        WHERE vbeln IN so_vbeln
        AND    auart IN so_auart
        AND    audat IN so_audat.
```

Instead of forcing the database server to send a separate data package to the application server for every single row selected from the database table, the INTO TABLE option will force the database server to send the entire series of rows in one package (or, at least the smallest number of packages possible). This effect is shown in Figure 7.25.

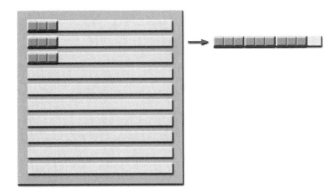

Figure 7.25 The Effect of the SELECT INTO TABLE Statement

After the addition of the `INTO TABLE` option in our sample code, the performance in the IDES system used improved, as shown in Figure 7.26. Series 1 represents the `SELECT` without `INTO TABLE` option; Series 2 represents the `SELECT` with `INTO TABLE` option:

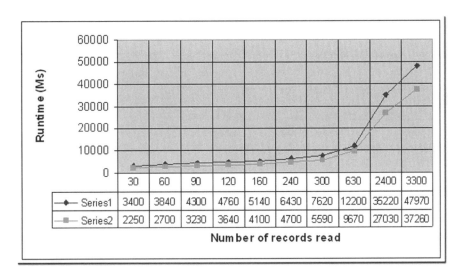

	30	60	90	120	160	240	300	630	2400	3300
Series1	3400	3840	4300	4760	5140	6430	7620	12200	35220	47970
Series2	2250	2700	3230	3640	4100	4700	5590	9670	27030	37260

Number of records read

Figure 7.26 Runtime Statistics: Improvement when Using the INTO TABLE Option

Nested SELECT Statements

The effect on performance of a `SELECT INTO TABLE` statement compared with a regular `SELECT` statement will be multiplied if we extend the example to a nested `SELECT` statement. Poorly performing ABAP programs often contain nested select statements like the one below. It contains a nested `SELECT` of three levels deep:

```
SELECT * FROM vbak INTO wa_vbak
      WHERE vbeln IN so_vbeln.
  SELECT * FROM vbap INTO wa_vbap
         WHERE vbeln = wa_vbak-vbeln.
    SELECT SINGLE * FROM mara INTO wa_mara
           WHERE matnr EQ wa_vbap-matnr.
  ENDSELECT.
ENDSELECT.
```

On our reference IDES system, this statement took approximately 8.5 seconds for 1000 orders. Each SELECT will generate its own data package traveling from database server to application server. In addition, the database also has to keep track of the individual positions in the database for every individual SELECT cycle executed during the two SELECT loops. Performance will be disastrous if the number of levels in a nested SELECT is high.

Therefore, beware of nested SELECTs! You are far better off with separate SELECT statements, combined with the introduction of internal tables. If you also specifically ask for a limited list of fields in your SELECT statements, you are apt to notice a significant reduction in response times. If, however, you do find yourself battling nested SELECTs, you have two options for improvements.

First, you can split the nested SELECT statements into two separate SELECT INTO TABLE statements. In order to do this, you should use the FOR ALL ENTRIES option in the second SELECT (or use an INNER JOIN):

```
SELECT vbeln auart FROM vbak INTO TABLE ts_vbak
      WHERE vbeln IN so_vbeln.
IF lines( ts_vbak ) > 0.
  SELECT vbeln posnr matnr kwmeng vrkme
         FROM vbap
         INTO TABLE ts_vbap
         FOR ALL ENTRIES IN ts_vbak
         WHERE vbeln = ts_vbak-vbeln.
  LOOP AT ts_vbak INTO wa_vbak.
    LOOP AT ts_vbap INTO wa_vbap
         WHERE vbeln EQ wa_vbak-vbeln.
      SELECT SINGLE * FROM mara INTO wa_mara
             WHERE matnr EQ wa_vbap-matnr.
    ENDLOOP.
  ENDLOOP.
ENDIF.
```

After this modification, the response time for 1,000 orders in our IDES system was reduced to 5.5 seconds. This is 65% of the time required by the original code (with the SELECT *).

Secondly, we also specified field lists for every SELECT. We measured an additional reduction in the response time of 1.5 seconds. The combined improvement amounts to a greatly reduced response time, that is, 47% of the time needed originally. Note that the larger the amounts of data selected, the greater the percentage of performance reductions.

A second possible improvement when dealing with nested SELECTs is to change the SELECT SINGLE * FROM mara statement executed during every cycle of the internal table loop into one SELECT INTO TABLE query. This will not only limit network traffic, it will also reduce the number of rows selected, because every material will be read just once.

```
SELECT vbeln auart FROM vbak INTO TABLE ts_vbak
      WHERE vbeln IN so_vbeln.
IF lines( ts_vbak ) > 0.
  SELECT vbeln posnr matnr kwmeng vrkme
         FROM vbap
         INTO TABLE ts_vbap
         FOR ALL ENTRIES IN ts_vbak
         WHERE vbeln = ts_vbak-vbeln.
  LOOP AT ts_vbap INTO wa_vbap.
    wa_matsel-matnr = wa_vbap-matnr.
    COLLECT wa_matsel INTO ts_matsel.
  ENDLOOP.
  IF lines( ts_matsel ) > 0 .
    SELECT matnr mtart matkl FROM mara
           INTO TABLE th_materials
           FOR ALL ENTRIES IN ts_matsel
           WHERE matnr = ts_matsel-matnr.
  ENDIF.
  LOOP AT ts_vbak INTO wa_vbak.
    LOOP AT ts_vbap INTO wa_vbap
         WHERE vbeln EQ wa_vbak-vbeln.
      READ TABLE th_materials INTO wa_materials
         WITH TABLE KEY matnr = wa_vbap-matnr.
    ENDLOOP.
  ENDLOOP.
ENDIF.
```

When compared with the code we started with, this last piece of ABAP code had a response time of 0.2 seconds. The improvement has now gone up by a factor of 50!

Risks When Introducing the INTO TABLE Option

If you plan to change your own code this way, be prepared for two potential pitfalls. The first possible pitfall is that the introduction of internal tables can lead to new performance problems if you choose the wrong type of internal table. The internal tables used here are SORTED and HASHED in order to ensure the best possible performance. For more details, see Section 7.4.

The second pitfall arises in those instances where the number of rows to be processed is extremely large, for example, hundreds of thousands of rows or possibly more. Under such circumstances, memory problems are likely to be incurred due to the limits on the roll area as part of the system settings. You can resolve this problem by introducing the PACKAGE SIZE option to the SELECT statement:

```
SELECT vbeln auart
       FROM vbak
       INTO TABLE ts_vbak
       PACKAGE SIZE 10000
       WHERE vbeln IN so_vbeln.

    SELECT vbeln posnr matnr kwmeng vrkme
           FROM vbap
           INTO TABLE ts_vbap
           FOR ALL ENTRIES IN ts_vbak
           WHERE vbeln = ts_vbak-vbeln.
    ...

ENDSELECT.
```

When adopting the performance-enhancing changes that we just recommended, you may have observed that the readability of the resulting ABAP code is not always improved by these changes. There is definitely some truth in that. On the other hand, note that having nested SELECT statements scattered throughout ABAP source files is probably far worse for the maintainability of your code.

Furthermore, note that the improvements discussed so far are not only possible for SELECT statements. Other SQL statements such as INSERT, UPDATE, MODIFY, and DELETE all have their own array-supported variant. Be aware, however, that choosing such variants should not endanger the Logical Unit of Work (LUW) principle discussed in Chapter 3.

Directly Selecting Aggregate Data

Another way of limiting the data traffic between the database server and the application server is by introducing aggregate functions like SUM and MAX and combining these functions with the GROUP BY option. If you combine these options with the use of internal tables, most of the processing that would otherwise be done in your ABAP code is taken over by the database server. Implementing this, however, will not, by definition, make a program run faster. Therefore, don't forget to conduct a performance test with a large amount of test data before making your final decision on how best to achieve optimal performance.

Table Buffering

Relatively small tables that aren't changed often, but are frequently used simultaneously by several users, should preferably be buffered on the application server. This option can be activated in the technical attributes of a database table definition in the ABAP Dictionary (see Figure 7.27).

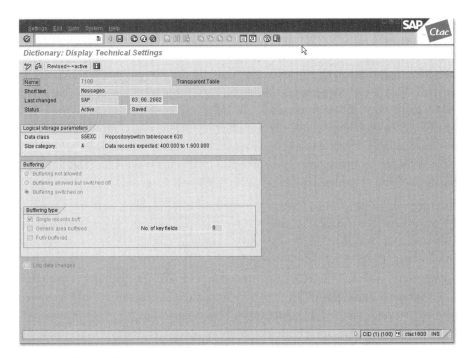

Figure 7.27 Table Buffering

Table T100 is a good example of such a table. It contains the messages that can be sent with the MESSAGE statement. It is used in almost every program or function. Moreover, the table's contents are not changed very often. If they are, the system can automatically manage buffer synchronization among all application servers of the same SAP system.

The fact that a table is buffered is transparent to Open SQL. A SELECT statement first verifies whether a table is buffered. If it is, and the data is available on the application server buffer, the data is fetched there directly. A programmer does not have to worry if an ABAP program uses invalid or old values when buffered transparent tables are used.[11]

The impact that table buffering has on performance is significant. Therefore, note that several documented options for Open SQL statements exist that will obstruct the use of buffers. One of these options is the BYPASSING BUFFER addition to the SELECT statement. You'll find a complete list of these SQL options in SAP's online help.

7.4   Optimizing Processing on the Application Server

Now we'll shift our attention to the third possible performance bottleneck: the processing of your application on the application server (see Figure 7.28). Most performance problems in this area are caused by the wrong implementation of internal tables in ABAP programs. Internal table processing has been a powerful ABAP feature since the introduction of SAP's R/2 system. The performance of internal table handling has greatly improved in recent years. Internal tables are not only suitable for containing large amounts of data.[12] The data in an internal table can also be processed very efficiently in various ways—via table indexes, binary search techniques, collecting techniques, and AT events.

During the period of initial development, how the implementation of internal tables affects performance is often underrated because as long as the internal tables remain relatively small, associated problems will not occur. However, as soon as the database tables start to grow, the internal tables used in your ABAP applications will also increase in size. Sometimes, the initial performance improvements that were achieved via the introduction of internal tables are even eclipsed by new performance problems. This occurs because you can inadvertently choose a wrong type of internal table, or use it incorrectly.

---

11 Programmers are sometimes confronted with synchronization problems, i.e., the data in the table buffer of an application server is not the same as the data in the database itself. These problems can be avoided by the correct setup of the synchronization techniques in overall system settings. We will not delve into this further as this lies outside the scope of this book.

12 Limitations on the size of internal tables are a result of available memory, and the value of the related SAP system profile parameter. Most SAP systems will have no technical problems when processing very large internal tables.

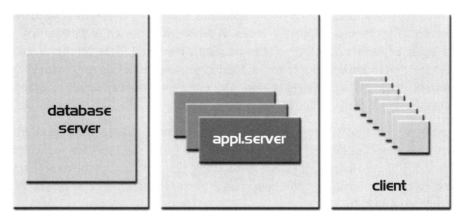

Figure 7.28 The Application Server in the Three-Tier Client-Server Architecture

7.4.1 Performance Issues Related to Internal Table Processing

The first question that you may ask yourself is how to recognize a performance problem due to poor internal table processing. The answer is straightforward. If a program suffers from poor performance and the larger part of the response time is caused by non-SQL statements, nine times out of ten this poor performance is caused by using internal tables incorrectly. Check out the following performance data[13] in Figure 7.29 (this example is based on an actual ABAP program).

```
Analysis of time in work process

CPU time              2867049 ms    Number    Roll ins          2
RFC+CPIC time               0 ms              Roll outs         0
                                              Enqueues          0

 Response time       98845622ms      Load time  Program       6  ms
                                                Screen        0  ms
Wait for work process       0 ms               CUA interf.   1  ms
Processing time      97589184ms
Load time                   7 ms    Roll time  Out           0  ms
Generating time             0 ms               In            3  ms
Roll (in+wait) time         3 ms               Wait          0  ms
Database request time 1256428 ms
Enqueue time                0 ms    Frontend   No.roundtrips 0
                                               GUI time      0  ms
```

Figure 7.29 Runtime Statistics When Using an Internal Table Incorrectly

The total response time for this customized ABAP program was 83,757 seconds. In other words, the total response time exceeded 23 hours! Note, however, that the database request time amounts to only 4% of the total response time. The

---

13 This data can be obtained via the Workload Analysis tools (ST03), Top-40 response times.

remaining response time is *processing time*. This poor performance was due to the inefficient processing of internal tables. A functional redesign of this particular program enabled the performance to be greatly improved. Thus far, the average runtime has improved by a factor of 10, and response times no longer show an exponential increase as they did before. This effect was achieved simply by changing the internal table processing.

In the next section, we'll introduce you to the basics of internal table types and give you some tips on how to use internal tables. Lastly, we'll provide you with a summary of specific guidelines. For more detailed information, please refer to the extensive information in ABAP help sources such as *help.sap.com*, or one of the books on ABAP.[14]

7.4.2 Basics of Internal Table Types

Starting with SAP Release 4.0B, three types of internal tables can be used: STAN-DARD, SORTED, and HASHED. We will concentrate on these three table types in the remainder of this section. Each of the three table types has its own specific advantages. Internal tables without an explicitly defined type will, by definition, be type STANDARD. Note that the internal table type must explicitly be defined in ABAP Objects. This is yet another way in which ABAP Objects can be used to help you make clear thoughtful development decisions.

On a higher level, two generic table types exist: ANY and INDEX. You can use these table types only in TYPE definitions, formal parameters, and field-symbols.

```
TYPES: ty_itab        TYPE ANY TABLE OF mara.
FIELD-SYMBOLS: <fs>    TYPE ANY TABLE.
DATA:  ta_itab        TYPE ANY TABLE OF mara. "This option is not possible
CLASS lcl_class DEFINITION.
  PUBLIC SECTION.
    METHODS: do_something IMPORTING ita_itab TYPE ANY TABLE.
ENDCLASS.
```

As the name implies, ANY refers to any type of internal table. This means that the actual table type must be determined at runtime. An internal table of the generic type INDEX can further be specified as either a STANDARD or a SORTED table. Tables of both types are called INDEX tables because they can be read using an internal table index.

You should be aware of the way in which the key is defined for each internal table type, and the consequences that this has for its processing. For SORTED tables, either a unique or a non-unique key must be defined. By definition, this key also determines the sorting order. It cannot be changed. If SORTED tables are pro-

---

14 For a list of available books and articles on several topics, see the Bibliography in Appendix D.

cessed using (part of) this key, the SAP system will automatically use a binary search technique. These characteristics make SORTED tables especially useful (and they perform well) for the loop processing of an entire internal table's contents in a fixed order.

Unlike SORTED tables, STANDARD tables are used for more varied purposes. As you might infer from the name, this table type is more flexible. You can define key fields for STANDARD tables as well. However, this has no additional impact on the performance. The flexibility occurs because the sort sequence of a STANDARD table is not fixed. You can change it several times and re-sort an internal table's contents accordingly. To do this, however, you must explicitly define the sort sequence just before actually performing a sort.

Unlike the first two table types, a HASHED table is not intended for loop processing. Instead, you always use it when you need to access one specific entry at a time of an internal table's contents. A HASHED table cannot be processed using a table index. HASHED tables always have an explicitly defined unique key. The performance of reading one entry from a HASHED table is independent of the number of entries in the internal table.

All modification statements for the three table types mentioned have limitations related to their type. Some of these limitations will be left undetected by the syntax check; others can even lead to runtime errors. An example of such an error is when data is appended to a sorted table. This disturbs the sorting order of the defined table key.

To ensure that we have covered all related issues, we should briefly mention that there are some other special types of internal tables—tables that contain references to objects using TYPE TABLE REF TO, and table definitions that create a range-like structure with TYPE RANGE OF (the latter should be used instead of the obsolete keyword RANGES). Internal tables can also contain complex types and deep structures. These complex internal tables are intended for storing more complex types of data in a flexible way. These types of tables contain other internal tables, structures and fields of type STRING or XSTRING. However, we won't delve into the performance issues of these special types of tables here.

7.4.3 How to Use Internal Tables

As we previously mentioned, the difference between the possible table types lies in their functionality and in the way they should be accessed. In the next sections, we'll go into these differences in more detail. Meanwhile, we'll provide you with some examples of possible performance improvements. The differences between the three main internal table types are further emphasized on the basis of examples of nested LOOP processing and READ actions.

The Impact of Nested Internal Table Processing

The first ABAP technique that we use to show the effects of choosing a wrong internal table type is nested loop processing, that is, the loop processing of an internal table within the loop processing of another internal table. The effect of varying the type of the internal table used is illustrated in Figure 7.30. It compares the performance related to choosing either a STANDARD, a SORTED, or a HASHED table type for the inner table ⟨itab2⟩:

```
LOOP AT ⟨itab⟩ INTO ⟨wa⟩.
  LOOP AT ⟨itab2⟩ INTO ⟨wa2⟩ WHERE ⟨field⟩ = ⟨wa-field⟩.
    ...
  ENDLOOP.
ENDLOOP.
```

The number of times that the internal table ⟨itab2⟩ is processed depends on the outer loop. In this example, internal table ⟨itab⟩ contains no more than ten entries. However, we continue to change the number of entries of internal table ⟨itab2⟩. The number of entries processed started with 10. This number was gradually increased to 1,000 entries.

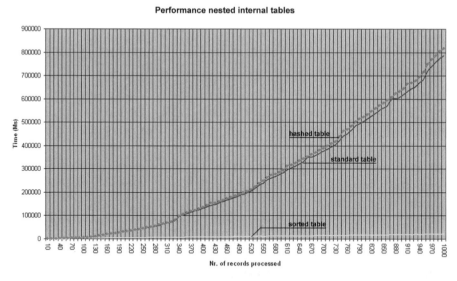

Figure 7.30 Runtime Statistics for Nested Internal Tables

As the graph in Figure 7.30 shows, the increase in runtime is more than linear, except if internal table ⟨itab2⟩ is defined as a SORTED table. Suppose that you change the table type from STANDARD to SORTED, and the table contains approximately 500 entries. In this case, you don't gain much in terms of an absolute time improvement. On the other hand, a SORTED table is already 20 times faster under these circumstances. Therefore, the relative difference is substantial. Moreover, it (the performance improvement) keeps increasing. For 1,000 entries, the relative improvement we measured was already a factor of 50, therefore, the relative improvement rate continues to grow with the number of entries.

The performance deterioration during loop processing of HASHED and STANDARD tables is caused by the fact that the ABAP processor will always process the entire internal table <itab2>. This occurs because no key exists that can be used when the WHERE option is actually processed. If you want, you can compare this result with how a WHERE clause affects a database SELECT statement if it isn't based on an underlying index. Examples of this were described in Section 7.2.

This example of improved performance shows that it makes no sense either to change <itab2> into a HASHED table using only a part of the unique key. The HASHED logic works only if the complete key is fully qualified. Therefore, the performance of a HASHED table in LOOP constructions is as poor as that of a STANDARD table.

What are the preferred internal table types for nested processing? Typically, SORTED internal tables are the preferred table type for regular loop processing, however, note that it won't always be possible to use a SORTED table. For example, we already mentioned the situation that called for repeated sorting of the same internal table. Another reason for not being able to use a SORTED table is that the exact sorting might not be determined until runtime. In the latter case, using a STANDARD table is preferable; fortunately, STANDARD tables can also be processed with a LOOP statement using the internal table index, thus achieving an equally acceptable level of performance.[15] If defining an internal table as a SORTED table is not possible, there are two options. The first option uses a combination of a single read and an index supported loop process:

```
SORT <itab2> BY <field>.
LOOP AT <itab> INTO <wa>.
* First determine the first entry that meets the condition.
  READ TABLE <itab2> WITH KEY <field> = <wa-field>
                     BINARY SEARCH.
  IF sy-subrc = 0.
    tp_tabix_from = sy-tabix.
```

---

15 This also applies to SORTED tables, however, we don't recommend using table indexes for SORTED tables. First, because using the defined key of the SORTED table is more efficient, and secondly because a table index can only be used if its value has already been determined.

```
* Start at the correct table index position
    LOOP AT <itab2> INTO <wa2> FROM tp_tabix_from.
      IF <wa2-field> GT <wa-field>.
* Now we have read one entry too much
        EXIT.
      ENDIF.
    ENDLOOP.
  ENDIF.
ENDLOOP.
```

Processing a table using its index is actually a bit slower than using SORTED keys. However, changing the STANDARD table processing from sequential processing to processing the table using its index still makes it worthwhile. At least, processing will be much faster than it was when using the original WHERE option.

If a STANDARD table cannot be sorted, or, if the sorting order cannot be ensured, there is a second option—you can simply define an extra SORTED internal table of the same line type with the correct key fields. This doesn't require much additional work. You need only one statement to fill this new table (sorting will occur automatically):

```
ts_itab[] = ta_itab[].
```

Note, however, that if the amount of memory used by an ABAP program is already an issue, this solution could lead to new problems. In that case, the only thing that you can do is to keep the code as-is.

The Impact of Internal Table Type on Read Access

Internal tables aren't always intended for loop processing. If exactly one entry must be read, the internal table type also determines the way in which the table must be accessed in order to use as little processing time as possible. Of course, one entry is just one entry. It is the number of times that a table is accessed that actually determines if associated performance problems will be noticed and reported.

Figure 7.31 is based on the following ABAP structure:

```
LOOP AT <itab> INTO <wa>.
  READ <itab2> INTO <wa2>.
ENDLOOP.
```

The average access times, related to the number of entries in <itab2>, are shown in Figure 7.31.

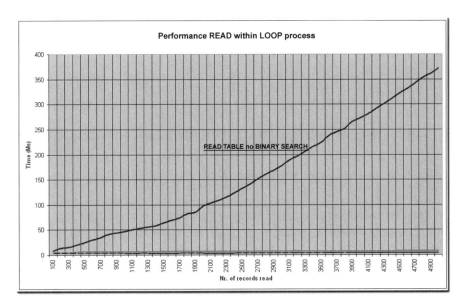

Figure 7.31 Runtime Statistics Related to the READ Statement

Four different types of internal table access are compared in this graph, based on the three internal tables types mentioned:

1. Reading a STANDARD table without using a BINARY SEARCH option

2. Reading a STANDARD table with a BINARY SEARCH option

3. Reading a SORTED table

4. Reading a HASHED table

These four alternatives are briefly discussed below.

The first and worst-performing option is reading a STANDARD table without using a BINARY SEARCH option:

```
LOOP AT <itab> INTO <wa>.
  READ <itab2> INTO <wa2> WITH KEY <field> = <value>.
ENDLOOP.
```

Consequently, every single READ statement actually leads to a full scan of <itab2>, until a row is finally found that meets the condition. Therefore, this option is not recommended.

A considerable improvement is achieved after adding the BINARY SEARCH option, as shown in the following code example:

```
LOOP AT <itab> INTO <wa>.
  READ <itab2> INTO <wa2> WITH KEY <field> = <value>
                      BINARY SEARCH.
ENDLOOP.
```

However, beware! The effectiveness of this option depends on the sorting order of <itab2>. If the table isn't sorted by <field>, the binary search logic won't work properly. In that case, the subsequent performance results will become completely unpredictable.

Because SORTED and HASHED tables are always sorted by their explicitly defined keys, adding some kind of binary search option isn't necessary. Reading a SORTED or a HASHED table looks slightly different from reading a STANDARD table:

```
LOOP AT <itab> INTO <wa>.
  READ <itab2> INTO <wa2> WITH TABLE KEY <field> = <value>.
ENDLOOP.
```

As was already depicted in Figure 7.31, from a performance perspective, there is little difference between processing a STANDARD table using a BINARY SEARCH and accessing a SORTED or HASHED table. Therefore, as long as you avoid reading a STANDARD table without a BINARY SEARCH option, performance should be fine.

You can also access STANDARD and SORTED tables with the READ statement using the table index. However, there is little point in doing this. In most cases, if you wanted to read a STANDARD or SORTED table using a table index, you simply won't be able to determine which value the index will have. Therefore, you won't be able to change a READ <itab2> WITH KEY into a READ <itab2> INDEX.

Accessing Internal Tables Without Using Workareas

A typical ABAP language construct involves the processing of internal tables using workareas. A *workarea* is a separate part of memory. Up until Release 4.5, all internal table processing could be done only via this workarea. This principle is exemplified in Figure 7.32.

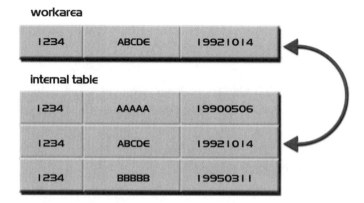

Figure 7.32 Processing an Internal Table Using the Workarea

Workareas can be defined and used implicitly and explicitly (an *implicit workarea* is called a *header line*). An *explicit workarea* uses the `INTO` addition. Because using this option can help to prevent confusion, it should be used for reasons of correctness. Therefore, it should not come as a surprise— in ABAP Objects, internal tables cannot be defined and accessed using implicit workareas.

More recently (i.e., as of Release 4.5), SAP has enabled developers to directly access, or modify, an internal table without the need for a workarea. For this purpose, `<field-symbols>` are used. Changing the internal table using a `MODIFY` statement is not necessary when using this option:

```
LOOP AT ta_itab ASSIGNING <field-symbol>.
  <field-symbol>-value =  tp_value. "changes the ta_itab line directly!
ENDLOOP.

READ TABLE ta_itab ASSIGNING <field-symbol>.
<field-symbol>-value =  tp_value. "changes the ta_itab line directly!
```

Although reading and modifying internal tables is much faster using the `<field-symbol>` than it is using workareas, don't overstate the time difference. It is far too negligible to assume that you should immediately start changing all your existing ABAP code accordingly.

Improving the Performance of Internal Table Modifications

The way in which table entries are added to an internal table and later modified is not really relevant to performance. However, because adding entries to tables and making table modifications are options that are easy to understand and use, we will address them here.

Adding New Entries to an Internal Table

There are several options for adding data to internal tables. Some of them are intended for adding more than one entry at once. Others are intended for entering one entry at a time. Table 7.3 shows an overview of both traditional, average or low-performing options, and new and slightly better performing ones. Note that the table is by no means complete; therefore, check each new SAP release for new options.

Append and Insert Options	That Can Be Replaced By
| ```
LOOP AT ta_itab INTO wa_itab.
  APPEND wa_itab TO ta_itab_copy.
ENDLOOP.
``` | ```
ta_itab_copy[] = ta_itab[].
``` |
| ```
LOOP AT ta_itab INTO wa_itab
  FROM <index>.
  APPEND wa_itab TO ta_itab_copy.
ENDLOOP.
``` | ```
APPEND LINES OF ta_itab TO ta_
itab_copy FROM <index> TO <index>.
``` |
| ```
SELECT * FROM <dbtab> INTO <wa>.
  APPEND <wa> TO <itab>.
ENDSELECT.
``` | ```
SELECT * FROM <dbtab> INTO TABLE
<itab>.
``` |
| ```
* Build a standard table in a
* sorted way
READ TABLE <itab> INTO <wa>
    WITH KEY <field> = <value>
      BINARY SEARCH.
IF sy-subrc NE 0.
  <wa>-<field> = <value>.
  <wa>-<field2> = <value2>.
  APPEND <wa> TO <itab>.
  SORT <itab>.
ENDIF.
``` | ```
* The returncode can be used

READ TABLE <itab> INTO <wa>
    WITH KEY <field> = <value>
      BINARY SEARCH.
tp_tabix = sy-tabix.
CASE sy-subrc.
  WHEN 0.
* Entry already available
  WHEN 4.
    <wa>-<field> = <value>.
    <wa>-<field2> = <value2>.
    INSERT <wa> TO <itab>
            INDEX tp_tabix.
``` |
| | ```
  WHEN 8.
    <wa>-<field> = <value>.
    <wa>-<field2> = <value2>.
    APPEND <wa> TO <itab>.
ENDCASE.
``` |
| ```
* Build a standard table with
* summed amounts
READ TABLE <itab> INTO <wa>
    WITH KEY <field> = <value>.
IF sy-subrc EQ 0.
  <wa>-<field> = <value>.
  <wa>-<field2> =
      <wa>-<field2> + <value2>.
  MODIFY <itab> FROM <wa>.
ELSE.
  <wa>-<field> = <value>.
  <wa>-<field2> = <value2>.
  APPEND <wa> TO <itab>.
ENDIF.
``` | ```
* Build a standard table in a
* sorted way and sum amounts

<wa>-<field> = <value>.
<wa>-<field2> = <value2>.
COLLECT <wa> to <itab>.
``` |

Table 7.3 APPEND and INSERT options
```

Changing Existing Entries in Internal Tables

There are also several options for changing data in internal tables. We already discussed the use of `ASSIGNING` as an alternative for working with header lines. If header lines are used, there is still a difference between statements that change one line at a time and statements that change more than one line. For alternatives to more traditional internal table processing, see Table 7.4.

Modify and Delete Options	That Can Be Replaced By

`LOOP AT ta_itab INTO wa_itab`
    `WHERE checkfield = false.`
  `wa_itab-checkfield = true.`
  `MODIFY ta_itab  FROM wa_itab.`
`ENDLOOP.`
	`wa_itab-checkfield = true.`
	`MODIFY ta_itab FROM wa_itab`
	      `TRANSPORTING checkfield`
	      `WHERE checkfield = false.`

`LOOP AT ta_itab INTO wa_itab.`
  `DELETE ta_itab.`
`ENDLOOP.`
	`CLEAR ta_itab[].`

`LOOP AT ta_itab INTO wa_itab`
     `FROM tp_tabix_from.`
  `DELETE ta_itab.`
`ENDLOOP.`
	`DELETE ta_itab FROM tp_tabix_from.`

`LOOP AT ta_itab INTO wa_itab.`
`* Check something here`
    `CALL METHOD lcl_class=>check`
    `EXPORTING`
      `itp_field = wa_itab-field`
    `IMPORTING`
      `etp_field = ltp_result.`
`* only if result is ok change`
`* table`
    `IF wa_itab-field = ltp_result.`
      `wa_itab-value`
        `= wa_itab-value + 1.`
     `MODIFY ta_itab FROM wa_itab.`
   `ENDIF.`
  `ENDLOOP.`
	`* Use of a static method with one`
	`* returning parameter`
	  `LOOP AT ta_itab INTO wa_itab`
	  `WHERE field = lcl_class2=>check`
	        `( wa_itab-field ).`
	
	    `wa_itab-value = wa_itab-value +`
	`1.`
	     `MODIFY ta_itab FROM wa_itab.`
	  `ENDLOOP.`

Table 7.4 MODIFY and DELETE options

7.4.4 When to Choose Which Internal Table Type

So far, we've discussed internal table processing to optimize processing on the application server. Now, we will briefly summarize some requirements that pertain to internal table use only. You'll find an overview of some general guidelines for choosing the best internal table type in Table 7.5.

Requirement	Standard	Sorted	Hashed
Data is not sorted and may not be sorted, for example, an internal table containing IDoc data.	X		
Sorting order is not relevant.	X		
Use in a table control.	X		
Use in a formal parameter in subroutines and functions with `TABLES` keyword.	X		
Use as an internal buffer for data from a database table. Every item can be identified uniquely.			X
Fixed sorting order is used in complete LOOP, processed with AT events.		X	
Fixed sorting order is used in a partial `LOOP AT WHERE`.		X	
Table is used for an ALV-function.	X		
Different sorts are required for one, relatively small table.	X		

Table 7.5 When to Choose Which Internal Table Type

Now, we'll repeat some key issues. First, keep in mind that SORTED tables will usually work for loop processing. The most important exception to this rule occurs when the sorting order cannot be explicitly defined beforehand.

Secondly, you cannot review guidelines for internal table processing based solely on performance. Other functional and technical requirements are equally important when choosing a suitable table type. However, for every situation where internal table processing is involved, you will always find one optimal way of adding, changing, deleting, or accessing data.

Lastly, remember that different sorts can be required for one relatively small table (see Table 7.5.). This situation deserves your special attention. Question: What if you need to sort the same table in various ways? Answer: It depends.

Sorted tables require their own index space to store the sorting keys. If you need a relatively small table that must be sorted in various ways, it is better to use one internal table and sort it again whenever needed. There are, however, two particular reasons for not being too dogmatic about this last point.

First, it is not always possible to distinguish whether you're better off using a STANDARD table that is sorted several times, or whether using various and separate SORTED tables is preferable.

Secondly, you might not have the opportunity to choose one of the two options mentioned. If the amount of data to be processed grows significantly, but memory use is already a restriction for your ABAP program, neither of the two options is likely to work properly. In both cases, the amount of memory required will simply be missing. Therefore, whether you need this memory for executing different SORT statements, or for allocating space for various SORTED tables, both options lead ultimately to the same problem. Therefore, choosing one of these options is no longer an issue.

If you need to do several sorts and want to squeeze out every drop of inefficiency, we recommend the following approach: combine one big STANDARD table with separate SORTED tables; then, fill these SORTED tables with the sorting keys, plus a reference to the index of the STANDARD table. That may reduce the likelihood of runtime errors being raised due to missing memory.

7.4.5 Semi-Persistent Memory

Up to this point, we've discussed internal table processing to enhance the performance of your ABAP applications. Note, however, that internal table processing is limited to one program session at a time. There are more ways to buffer data from the database server on the application server. Imagine, for example, situations where you prefer to buffer data for more than one program session. Several programs—each running in their own independent program session—may need the same buffered data. A good example is a product catalog that serves several sales applications, which can be accessed over the internet.

The term *semi-persistent memory* is used for this purpose. A program can make data remain available for other program sessions on the application server, even after it ends itself. The data in semi-persistent memory is kept available until the application server is shut down. The advantage should be apparent—you don't need to fetch the data again in the database. You might not even be able to; some calculations may have been applied on the data. Other programs may have to process the intermediate data further. As long as the application server is active, semi-persistent data will remain available.

Using the Database Server to Store Intermediate Data

As a first option, which is often used to keep intermediate data available, you can store the data to be reused later in a cluster such as table INDX. This is not really the semi-persistent data that we alluded to earlier, however, we refer to it here in order to show you all the possible solutions.

In a cluster, you can store single fields, flat structures, and internal tables of any kind of type and structure. They are stored using the statement:

```
EXPORT <field> <struct> <itab> TO DATABASE dbtab(ar) ID key.
```

Reading this data can be achieved by using the IMPORT FROM DATABASE statement.

The primary advantage of storing intermediate data on the database server is that the data is stored even after an application server has shut down. Because INDX is a database table, it will be part of a database backup. In addition, the technique is, in itself, fairly straightforward.

However, you don't always need to store intermediate data in such a permanent manner. If the information can be recreated again by simply running a program, you don't have to put this added burden on the database. Furthermore, reading a database is more time-consuming than reading data directly from memory on the application server. This is why using techniques to store data in the global memory of an application server is the preferred alternative in these situations.

Using the Application Server to Store Intermediate Data

Since Release 4.0B, SAP has introduced several ways to keep intermediate data available on the application server itself. We won't overemphasize this point, because ongoing developments at SAP make it difficult to provide actual and lasting guidelines just yet. We will, however, briefly discuss the main possibilities in this subsection: Shared Buffer, Shared Memory, and Shared Objects.

Shared Buffer and Shared Memory

In releases 4.0B and 4.5B, SAP introduced the statements EXPORT TO SHARED MEMORY and EXPORT TO SHARED BUFFER. These statements make it possible to store data in application server memory, however, each has associated pitfalls that might make them less attractive.

The shared buffer and the shared memory mechanism store data in the shared application buffer of the application server. All programs on this application server have access to this data using the IMPORT FROM SHARED BUFFER or IMPORT FROM SHARED MEMORY statement.

The difference between the shared buffer and the shared memory mechanism lies in the way each handles the situation where space is missing. How much space is actually available is indicated in profile parameters of the application server.

If you store data in the shared buffer, and the buffer is full, the data that is used the least is automatically purged. Therefore, you cannot be sure that all the data is available. This, of course, is not a reliable principle for important data.

Shared memory, on the other hand, might not trigger your enthusiasm either. If you want to store data in shared memory and no available space is left, a runtime error will be raised. To prevent this from happening, you alone must manage all data explicitly in shared memory. You will need to verify whether enough memory space is left each time you want to use it. You will also need to have your own customized procedures in order to create available space if necessary.

If you really need one of these techniques anyway, you may need some additional advice. We have included an example below in which a product catalog is used. This is a collection of articles whose availability is period-related. What was available last month may not be sold anymore. Reading the entire catalog every time you need information on the current month does not boost performance ratings. Therefore, in order to prevent unnecessary database traffic, you must extract the data once every day (from the database server) and store it in SHARED MEMORY (on the application server). All programs that need this information can then use the IMPORT FROM SHARED MEMORY to fetch it.

The ABAP code for storing data in shared memory looks like this:

```
REPORT /CTAC/PROVIDE_DATA.

TABLES indx.

DATA: st_indx_key LIKE indx-srtfd.

    st_indx_key = <unique_identifier>
* Export data.
    EXPORT <itab>
            TO  SHARED MEMORY indx(z1) ID st_indx_key.
```

The structure of data that is stored in memory is based on the structure of table indx. The data is not actually stored in the database table indx. The data in shared memory is uniquely identified by the area z1 and the ID st_indx_key.

Shared Objects

The most recent SAP development for buffering data on the application server may be much more promising than the preceding solution. It is called *Shared Objects*. It is available from SAP Web Application Server (Web AS) Release 6.40 onwards. Using shared objects, you can store objects in application server memory and manage them with a specially designed Transaction SHMP and related methods. We'll only mention it here, so that you at least know it exists. More information on this subject can be found on the Internet.[16]

---

16 At this moment, the most up-to-date information is provided by *sdn.sap.com*, the SAP Developer Network.

7.4.6 Parallel Processing[17]

The last topic regarding optimizing the performance of an ABAP application on the application server deals with the parallel execution of updates. Most updates done by ABAP programs will use single processing mode. This means that each task is in charge of only one process. This places a restriction on the program, which can therefore handle only one performance-intensive database change at a time. Only when this change is ready can the next change be started (see Figure 7.33):

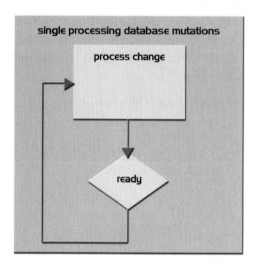

Figure 7.33 Single Processing

One way of handling database changes in parallel is simply by starting several programs at the same time. This option is often implemented by using several background jobs, all starting the same program but with different selection variants. A drawback of this option is that variants and jobs are static: if the amount of data increases, extra jobs and variants need to be defined. You can, however, achieve the same result via using parallel processing techniques directly in your ABAP program. To do this, use the STARTING NEW TASK option of the CALL FUNCTION statement (see Figure 7.34).

---

17 Read more on this subject in the article by Susanne Janssen and Werner Schwarz, "How to Build Optional Parallel Processing into Your Applications for Increased Throughput and Reduced Processing Time," *SAP Professional Journal* March/April 2002.

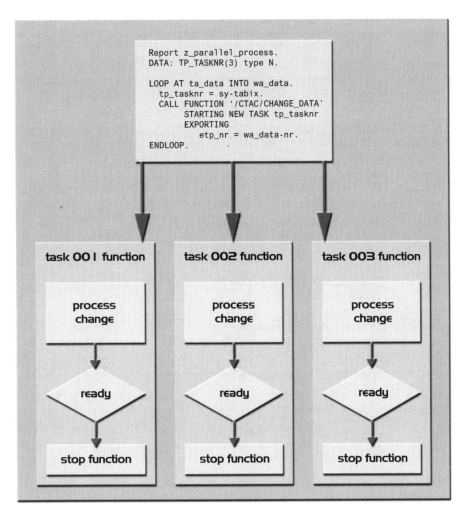

```
Report z_parallel_process.
DATA: TP_TASKNR(3) type N.

LOOP AT ta_data INTO wa_data.
  tp_tasknr = sy-tabix.
  CALL FUNCTION '/CTAC/CHANGE_DATA'
       STARTING NEW TASK tp_tasknr
       EXPORTING
            etp_nr = wa_data-nr.
ENDLOOP.
```

| task 001 function | task 002 function | task 003 function |

process change — ready — stop function (for each task)

Figure 7.34 Parallel Processing

We also added the following sample code in order to demonstrate what to do to make parallel processing work. The function is started for every group of documents in the internal table ta_data. Implementing the code this way will probably lead to problems, because too many tasks are being allocated. Therefore, an explicitly specified maximum number of tasks should be taken into account. You can calculate the number of active processes using the RECEIVE option of the CALL FUNCTION. Therefore, you can determine (at each moment) whether there is room to start a next task.

```
* Maximum number of active tasks
PARAMETERS: pa_tasks TYPE i DEFAULT 5 OBLIGATORY. "Maximum tasks

START-OF-SELECTION.

  LOOP AT ta_data    INTO wa_data   .

    APPEND wa_data TO ta_data_in.
* Bundle into one packet for one supplier
    AT END OF lifnr.
* new task number
      tp_count    = tp_count + 1.
      tp_task_new = tp_count.
* keep track of active tasks
      tp_task_act = tp_task_act + 1.
* wait with starting following task until number active tasks
* not above limit
      WAIT UNTIL tp_task_act LE pa_tasks.
* Start new task
      CALL FUNCTION '/CTAC/CHANGE_DATA'
        STARTING NEW TASK tp_task_new
        PERFORMING catch_end_of_task ON END OF TASK
        TABLES
          tta_incoming          = ta_data_in
        EXCEPTIONS
          Resource_failure      = 1
          communication_failure = 2  MESSAGE tp_msg
          system_failure        = 3  MESSAGE tp_msg
          others                = 4.
      IF sy-subrc NE 0.
* Error handling here
      ENDIF.
      REFRESH ta_data_in.

    ENDAT.

  ENDLOOP.

FORM catch_end_of_task USING utp_tasknumber type c.

  tp_task_act = tp_task_act - 1.

  RECEIVE RESULTS FROM FUNCTION '/CTAC/CHANGE_DATA'
          TABLES
                tta_changed    = ta_data_out
          EXCEPTIONS
                nothing_changed = 5
                OTHERS          = 9.
```

```
  IF sy-subrc NE 0.
* Error handling here
  ENDIF.

ENDFORM.                      "CATCH_END_OF_TASK
```

The number of tasks that are actually running is increased for every function called. Once the function is finished, the routine CATCH_END_OF_TASK is automatically performed. The number of parallel tasks is decreased by this routine. If the number of running tasks reaches its maximum value (in variable pa_tasks[18]), the program will wait until a task becomes available.

If a new task is not available, the exception RESOURCE_FAILURE is returned to the calling program, so that it can take appropriate action.

7.5 Minimizing Data Traffic Between the Application Server and a Client

Our last topic regarding performance deals with the network traffic between a client and the application server (see Figure 7.35). Two particular issues should be, at least briefly, addressed: the data transfer between client and application server, and control flushing.

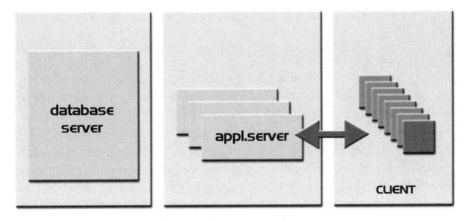

Figure 7.35 Data Traffic in the Three-Tier Client-Server Architecture

7.5.1 Uploads and Downloads

Data transfer between a client and the application server is executed using the GUI_UPLOAD and GUI_DOWNLOAD functions (or the methods that they use). Uploading or downloading large amounts of data can be very time-consuming.

---

18 The number of possible tasks can be derived using the standard function SPBT_INITIALIZE. This implies the use of server groups. We will not go into more detail here.

The reason for this is that the data to be uploaded or downloaded is sent from or to the client itself, and not to the application server. This results in an increase in network traffic and a dependency on the processor capacity of the client (see Figure 7.36). Consequently, the network or client processor capacity can become a bottleneck during the upload or download of data.

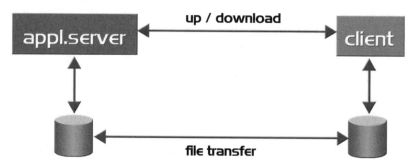

Figure 7.36 Upload and Download Versus File Transfer

Sometimes, however, uploads and downloads are inevitable. The transfer of data may need to be fully interactive: the ABAP application may start processing, and the data processed may be downloaded to a spreadsheet application on the desktop, and be further processed there; the results may have to be uploaded again and processed in the ABAP application; then, a second download may follow, and so on.

Clearly, most upload and download scenarios are not like this; typically, the exchange of data is a one-time action. If this is the case, and you need to accelerate this data exchange, consider handling the transfer of data in a more batchlike manner: with a regular file transfer. This would mean that instead of performing a download, your ABAP program sends a file to the application server first, using the transfer dataset statement. From there, a regular file copy is made to the desktop and picked up by the desktop application. Similarly, instead of performing an upload, the data is copied from the desktop to the application server first and stored there as a file. Then, an ABAP application reads the file with a READ DATA-SET and processes it. Such procedures are much faster for very large amounts of data. The speed at which the application server can read a file that is already stored there will far exceed the speed of a regular upload.

7.5.2 Control Flushing

Control technology works by flushing the control commands to the desktop at a specific point in time. Remember to ensure that you select the right moment, since this is also a relatively time-consuming process.

7.6 Summary

In this chapter, we have described and provided examples for the most important methods of enhancing the performance of ABAP software. We have done this by first distinguishing the four potential bottlenecks for performance in descending order of importance: processing on the database server; data traffic between the database server and the application server; processing on the application server; and finally, data traffic between the application server and the client. Then, we introduced guidelines to minimize the impact of ABAP programs on each potential bottleneck and therefore, increase performance.

First, in Section 7.2 we saw that processing on the database server is optimized primarily by carefully designing SQL statements. In this section, we stressed the importance of finding an existing index or alternative database table before creating an extra secondary index. We also presented various solutions to help you learn how to get the most out of your index.

In Section 7.3, we shifted our focus to the data traffic between the database server and the application server. We cited three ways of minimizing this data traffic: by limiting the number of rows selected; by limiting the number of fields selected; and by limiting the number of times that data is selected.

In Section 7.4, we addressed the performance of processing on the application server. We stressed the importance of choosing the right kind of internal table type depending on the circumstances. We also showed you various ways in which to process an internal table's contents faster.

Finally, in Section 7.5, we briefly discussed several ways in which to limit performance problems regarding data traffic between the application server and the client.

Despite the many guidelines we provided, it is still imperative that you continuously monitor the performance of ABAP developments in your SAP production system. Moreover, we should point out that we didn't address any other performance-enhancing measures, such as the archiving of data or other system optimizations.

8 Maintainability

Maintainability indicates how easy it is to change existing software. This is a quality that the software may or may not possess. Typically, if you make a small change to the functionality of a well maintained program, it usually involves just a few lines of code, and takes several minutes. Conversely, if you attempt to perform this same task for a poorly maintained program, you may have to change many lines of code and require several hours to do so. Standard causes of poor maintainability are unreadable and poorly structured code, and an unnecessary repetition of the same functionality in various places.

Making customized ABAP software as maintainable as possible is critical because it saves time for both the individual ABAP developer and IT management. Maintenance activities often consume a considerable amount of the overall IT budget. Note that the majority of programs will need to be maintained at some point after the initial development, simply because requirements change over time. What further complicates matters is that maintenance will most likely be applied by a developer other than the author of the code. For IT organizations, applying strict guidelines to enhance the maintainability of the software that is developed will help you to limit the total amount of time and money spent on maintenance activities.

Implementing standard ERP software, such as SAP R/3, adds another dimension to the aspect of maintainability. An ERP implementation usually consists of both standard and customized software. If the standard software is well maintained (i.e., by applying OSS Notes, or implementing hotpackages or new releases), the customized software should interfere as little as possible with these processes. SAP customers should use the tools provided by SAP to apply changes to standard SAP software. Applying changes to standard SAP software without using these tools is not beneficial for later maintenance of this standard SAP software.

This chapter presents guidelines for enhancing the maintainability of ABAP software. In Section 8.1, we discuss how to safeguard the maintainability of the SAP software when applying changes to it. In Section 8.2, we deal with the maintainability of your own customized software. Finally, in Section 8.3, we provide examples that show how using ABAP Objects can improve the maintainability of ABAP software.

8.1 Maintainability of Standard SAP Software

This section deals with the various ways in which standard SAP software can be changed and the consequences this has for its maintenance. In Section 8.1.1, we briefly explain how to process OSS Notes of SAP into a customer implementation. In Section 8.1.2, we then detail how the possibilities that SAP customers have for changing the standard SAP software affect the maintenance of the standard software.

8.1.1 OSS Notes

Most changes applied by SAP to its own software are corrections that can be selected and applied by the customer in the form of OSS Notes. The way in which these Notes are added affects the degree of maintainability, especially when a new release of the SAP software or a hotpackage is implemented.

Note Assistant: Note Browser

Note	Short text	Appl. component	Proc. Status	Implementation Stat.	User Name
531424	FS BP:Incorrect Modify of the address uses for DI	FS-BP	Not Relevant	Cannot be implemented	
532246	FS BP:Missing address number for the EDT address uses	FS-BP	Not Relevant	Cannot be implemented	
535175	Profit center changeable in spite of subsequent documents	SD-SLS-GF-CO	Not Relevant	Cannot be implemented	
535497	CJ2B/CN22/CNS41: Critical path in network/Gantt chart	PS-ST-OPR-PPB	Finished	Completely implemented	SHEARMAN
536636	FS BP: EDT:Error FSBP519 with Modify/Delete of address usage	FS-BP	Not Relevant	Cannot be implementod	
538302	Continuous loop in link work center - HRMS	PP-BD-WKC	In Processing	Cannot be implemented	BIRNLEY
538524	ProMan: Termination an overview is called	PS-MAT-PRO	Finished	Can be implemented	SHEARMAN
539070	ProMan: No goods issue for requirements grouping	PS-MAT-PRO	Finished	Can be implemented	SHEARMAN
539173	CDESK: Error when changing the work directory	CA-CAD	In Processing	Cannot be implemented	BIRNLEY
539772	ProMan: Termination with F3 or F12 on the selection screen	PS-MAT-PRO	Finished	Cannot be implemented	SHEARMAN
540537	No display of costing for WINGUI620	PS-CLM	Finished	Cannot be implemented	SHEARMAN
540944	FS BP: Termination during EDT of alias names for BP	FS-BP	In Processing	Completely implemented	GENTNERB
544393	CRM-RW Integr.:Fehler beim Anlegen der Abrechnungsvorschrift	CRM-BTX-COI	Finished	Cannot be implemented	BRANDTM
544558	Rechnungswesenüberleitung CRM -> FI, Unicode-System	FI-AR-AR-C	In Processing	Cannot be implemented	OLBERT
544759	SAP BP: Conversion/maintenance of address uses (XXDEFAULT)	FS-BP	In Processing	Completely implemented	GENTNERB
547299	SAP BP: Address usages (conversion, parallel maint., dialog)	FS-BP	In Processing	Completely implemented	GENTNERB
549947	Error 'No user assignment found' E000(ALM_ME)	PM-WOC-MB	Finished	Completely implemented	POPLAWSKI
550547	FS BP:EDT:Termination if internal address number not filled	FS-BP	Not Relevant	Cannot be implemented	
550842	Mobile Asset Management does not synchronize against WEB AS	PM-WOC-MB	Finished	Completely implemented	POPLAWSKI
550843	Dump NOT_FOUND bei aktivierten BADI ALM_ME_PARTNER	PM-WOC-MB	Finished	Completely implemented	POPLAWSKI
550854	SAP BP: Address usages (miscellaneous)	FS-BP	In Processing	Completely implemented	GENTNERB
550881	Button "Differences POD" grayed out in item detail	LE-SHP-DL-POD	Finished	Completely implemented	TOMB
551364	Fields in the sales order not ready for input	SD-SLS-GF-ST	Finished	Completely implemented	DERN
552206	RPTIME00: UC_OBJECTS_NOT_CONVERTIBLE	PT-EV	In Processing	Completely implemented	HEATWOLE
554480	CJ2B: short dump when calling maintenance order overview	PS-ST-OPR-PPB	Finished	Completely implemented	SHEARMAN
555558	SAP BP address uses:Various corrections	FS-BP	In Processing	Completely implemented	GENTNERB
556174	MSC: Short dump GETWA_NOT_ASSIGNED in case of tax refund	PY-US	In Processing	Cannot be implemented	HEATWOLE
559617	SAP BP address uses:Various corrections	FS-BP	In Processing	Can be implemented	MKREEF

Figure 8.1 The Note Browser in Transaction SNOTE

Using the *Note Assistant* (Transaction SNOTE, see Figure 8.1) for one particular Note has the following benefits:

▶ You don't have to request a Change Key via OSS for applying the Note.

▶ Changes to source code are automatically applied. This means that only other changes, such as those made to the interface parameters of a function module, or to ABAP Dictionary definitions, still have to be made manually (which is a good reason why only ABAP developers should be responsible for using the Note Assistant).

▶ The Note Assistant checks whether the Note that is added is relevant for the current release and hotpackage level of the customer's SAP installation.

▶ The Note Assistant checks whether the Note to be added requires other Notes to be implemented first. If so, it verifies whether these Notes have actually been added. If they haven't, it automatically imports the missing Notes and implements these first.

The general advantage of using the Note Assistant is that it makes the processing of release upgrades (and the implementation of hotpackages) of standard SAP software run more smoothly. During the associated activities (processing the SPAU and SPDD list: see also Section 2.5.1), the SAP system automatically determines which Notes are still relevant for the new version and implements these automatically. This is applicable for only those Notes that have been implemented with the Note Assistant.

8.1.2 Changes Made by the Customer

There are various ways to apply your own changes to standard SAP software. Most changes have been anticipated by SAP in the form of user exits, enhancements, and BADIs, however, unforeseen changes can also, if necessary, be implemented. We'll discuss these two main categories, anticipated and unanticipated changes, in turn. Note that we emphasize how to make such changes in a way that ensures the best possible maintainability for the standard SAP software, especially during upgrades and the implementation of hotpackages.

Anticipated Changes

An *anticipated change* is represented in the standard SAP software by a reference—on a predefined location in the standard software to a subroutine in an include, a function module, or a method—in order to indicate that customized functionality can be added there.[1] SAP guarantees that the anticipated change will remain available with the same interface in future releases. This enables SAP customers to add their own ABAP code (in the referenced include, function module, or method) and ensure that this code remains available as long as needed. Currently, there are three types of anticipated changes (in chronological order of appearance): user exits, enhancements, and BADIs.

---

1 In addition, there are options to change standard screens, menus, and database tables.

The original way to make additions to standard functionality was supplied by SAP in the form of *User Exits*. They already existed in the SAP R/2 product. On pre-defined places in the software, a reference to a subroutine in an include has been made by SAP. In the include, the actual customer change can be implemented. A well known example is include MV45AFZZ (in Sales Order functionality). In order to apply a user exit, you must first obtain a change key from SAP.

Enhancements were introduced in SAP R/3 Release 3.1. Compared with user exits, they offer some particular advantages. First, searching for available Enhancements and implementing them can be done using transactions SMOD (to display definitions) and CMOD (to implement projects). In addition, you no longer need to use includes, just function modules, with all their associated advantages (such as separate testing and documenting possibilities, a separate function library, etc.). In the standard software, a statement containing the CALL CUSTOMER-FUNCTION command supplies the reference. Finally, because enhancements are part of an Enhancement Project, you can activate and deactivate customized changes of one project collectively. This can be beneficial when, for example, a new release level of the standard SAP software is implemented (upgrades, hotpackages), and you need to temporarily switch off the enhancements to determine whether the standard software works as expected.

BADIs are the (object-oriented) successor of enhancements. While enhancements were only provided by SAP, BADIs can also be created by those outside SAP, such as suppliers of third-party solutions. The new Transaction SE18 can create such opportunities for changes in your own ABAP software. Transaction SE19 has the same function for BADIs that Transaction CMOD has for enhancements (support for the implementation). An extra advantage of BADIs, when compared with enhancements, is that more than one implementation can be active, provided that the BADI is classified as suited for *multiple use*.

Furthermore, various implementations of the same BADI can be active, one of which is actually selected depending on a *filter* value, which means that you can make a BADI dependent on the value of fields such as country or line of industry.

The general advantage of the aforementioned kinds of anticipated changes is that the associated references to customized ABAP code (i.e., the references to subroutines in includes, function modules, and methods) will remain intact in future releases of the SAP software. Therefore, the customized ABAP code can be implemented in each new release. For example, more than ten years after SAP replaced its R/2 software with the R/3 product, user exits that were already available in the R/2 software still exist in R/3.

Because of the higher flexibility of BADIs and enhancements when compared with the original user exits, we recommend that you always look for the latest (most current) type of an anticipated change: first a BADI, then an enhancement, and finally a user exit.

Unanticipated Changes

An unanticipated change is a change to standard SAP ABAP code for which SAP has not provided a user exit, enhancement, or BADI. If no change has been anticipated in SAP's software in the exact place where you need to implement one, you can still directly modify the standard SAP programs yourself. However, this way of changing SAP software isn't recommended because its effect may be only temporary: in the next release, the modification may no longer work due to changes made to the standard SAP code.

If modifications are inevitable, you have good and bad ways of implementing them. First, we recommend that you apply a modification using the Modification Assistant. You can switch the Modification Assistant on or off in the ABAP editor (see Figure 8.2). We advise you to leave it switched on at all times.

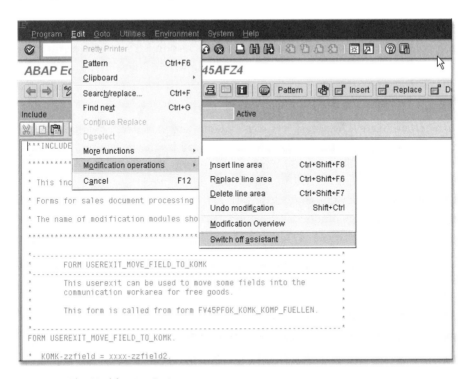

Figure 8.2 The Modification Assistant

The benefits of the Modification Assistant become apparent when implementing a new release or hotpackage. Then, a modification that was implemented using the Modification Assistant will automatically be recognized as such by the SAP software (in the list produced by Transaction SPAU). *If* the new version of the SAP software allows this modification to be implemented, this can be done automatically. Without the Modification Assistant, you would have to type in the associated source code manually all over again. (You can use the Modification Browser—Transaction SE95—to display an overview of all changes.)

A second piece of advice is to always isolate the ABAP code of the modification from the standard code by inserting only a reference to an include in the standard source code, and implementing the actual change in the include.

8.2 Maintainability of Customized ABAP Software

Enhancing the maintainability of customized software has three important aspects. In Section 8.2.1, we first discuss the general requirement of creating as much structure as possible in even the simplest program. This has more to do with general programming standards than it does with ABAP programming. Then, in Section 8.2.2, we introduce some guidelines to improve the readability of customized software. In Section 8.2.3, we focus on various ways to reuse standard SAP software components in customized software. Finally, in Section 8.2.4, we give you some practical tips for enhancing the reusability of your own ABAP software.

8.2.1 Separating Different Actions

To a certain degree, how easy it is to maintain a program depends purely on the extent to which the program has been structured by the developer. An experienced developer will always separate the statements that deal with the selection of data, the processing of data, the creation of output, and the update of database tables. These groups of program actions should be established into corresponding subroutines, function modules, or methods. Such a subdivision makes both a program's details more recognizable and the different parts of the program more reusable.

An important detail is the naming of the subroutines that are created. A good way of making the name of a subroutine self-explanatory is by starting with a verb and adding the object of the action. Straightforward names might include `read_data`, `process_data`, `display_output`, or `update_data`.

When dealing with a report, you can also make the distinctive parts of the report genuinely reusable, even for non-SAP programs. You can't do this simply by using subroutines or local methods; you can do this only by creating remote callable function modules (RFC functions). Note that, in particular, logic for displaying report output should not be mixed with selection, processing, and updating data because this makes it impossible to reuse the report, for example, for Web-enabling purposes. At present, most Web-enabling of reporting functionality done so far by SAP is based on the use of RFCs, although methods have also been used.

To reuse different parts of module pool programs, the same principle applies, that is, separating the reading, processing, outputting, and updating of data. However, it's difficult to apply this principle to module pool programs because of the way they're constructed. Each screen in a module pool is processed on the basis of standard PBO (Process Before Output) and PAI (Process After Input) events. Since the ABAP code linked to the PAI event of a screen is usually split up in accordance with the screen fields of the screen, there will usually be many isolated pieces of code for each screen. Attempting to prepare Web-enabling for a module pool program is not really worth the effort.[2] The only thing you can do is to create separate RFC functions for the parts of the code that *can* be completely separated from the rest; for example, the code that performs a database update. With Java-based Web Dynpros, SAP will introduce a stricter separation between screen handling and application logic. Eventually, the SAP GUI will be replaced by Web Dynpros.

8.2.2 Improving Recognizability

The implementation of any change to existing ABAP source can be accelerated if the developer, who is implementing the change, can immediately grasp what the existing code actually does. Although SAP's ABAP development environment provides numerous ways for making source code more readable, part of this task still depends on the discipline of the ABAP developer and the use of standards. In this section, we address the most important guidelines for doing this—by adhering to naming conventions; and by properly using the basic possibilities that the ABAP language offers for structuring code in reports and module pool programs.

Naming Conventions

The first practical measure to make customized ABAP software more recognizable and readable for all developers (and others) involved is the introduction of naming standards or *naming conventions* for all kinds of objects created during development. Naming conventions are particularly useful for program internal data definitions, and to a lesser extent, for other types of objects.

---

2 Actually, the Internet Transaction Server enables the reuse of specially adapted module pool programs. We won't go further detail here because this technique is rather outdated.

We need to emphasize that naming conventions are not guidelines for making better or faster programs. You should primarily view them as standards for making *more recognizable* programs. The most important property of a standard is that there is just one standard to which everybody adheres. However, don't fall into the trap of trying to find the best naming standard—there is no such thing as one best standard. What is more important is that the developers working for a development organization accept its standards, consistently use them, and continue to use them. If you need to establish naming conventions, we recommend that you look carefully at the standards that are available from other sources; for example, standards used by SAP, other companies that use SAP, and even outside the SAP world.

Let's briefly discuss the considerations that we've gone through when creating our own standards. We distinguish the following types of objects:

1. Program internal data such as types, variables, constants, select-options, and parameters
2. ABAP Dictionary elements such as database tables, database views, and lock objects
3. Procedures such as subroutines, methods, and function modules
4. Function groups and classes
5. Programs and transaction codes

For each of these objects, we'll now mention the most important naming conventions that we apply, and the reasons for doing this. We added a list of naming conventions in Appendix 1, which you can use as a reference.[3]

Naming Conventions: Program Internal Data

In general, we considered various aspects of program internal data definitions that we would use as a basis for naming conventions:

▶ Type and Basic Function
Not every type of data should be immediately recognized by its name, but some general distinction can be helpful. Such a distinction is particularly relevant if the kinds of operations on the data that are allowed by the ABAP language are restricted to one type of data. For this reason, we recommend that you make a clear distinction between variables and internal tables. For the same reason, you should also explicitly distinguish between the existing types of internal tables (STANDARD, SORTED, and HASHED). Because each of these

---

3 In addition, note that SAP has published naming standards in OSS Note 16466.

internal table types requires its own way of processing, a distinctive naming convention can help to quickly establish whether a specific internal table is correctly used.

We use prefixes in our own naming standards to identify different types of data, such as: co (for constants), tp (for most variables), rf (for reference variables, used in dynamic programming), ta (for internal tables of type STANDARD), th (for internal tables of type HASHED), and ts (for internal tables of type SORTED).

Because it would be excessive to also give different names to different types of variables such as integers (type i) and packed fields (type p), we don't consider variable names such as tp_count_i (for an integer field) and tp_total_p (for a packed field) really necessary.

▶ **Interface Parameters of Procedures**
We recommend that you pay special attention to the naming conventions of interface parameters: it's helpful in many situations to know whether a specific interface parameter serves only as an ingoing (input, import) parameter, as an export (outgoing) parameter, or both (in and out). Besides, it may be useful to see if a formal interface parameter is used. To reflect this in the naming convention, we use the additional prefixes i (for import parameters), e (for export parameters), c (for CHANGING parameters), u (for USING parameters), t (for TABLES parameters). So, we'd create names such as itp_langu (inputted data), tta_orders (table data), and ctp_sales_su (data that is inputted, changed, and exported again) in interface parameters of subroutines, function modules, and methods.

▶ **The Visibility of Data**
Data is either local or global, and should be easily recognized as such. We use the extra prefix / only for names of local variables, as in /tp_matnr. In our naming conventions, global variables don't have a specific prefix.

▶ **The Meaning of Data**
Source code is more readable if the names of all types of data used clearly indicate which data is exactly used. An intuitive name should reveal more than simply the technical function of data. Therefore, you should use names such as ta_orders in stead of, for example, ta_itab. Note that standard SAP names are often reused to avoid having to think about inventing new names all the time. For example, think of the name tp_matnr for a variable that reuses standard data element matnr (material number), and avoid names such as tp_artnr.

The same principle can be applied to the names of internal tables. For example, most ABAP developers will understand that the name th_kna1 refers to an internal table with the same structure as standard database table KNA1. However, there are situations where general names such as `th_customers` may be more appropriate. Interface data must usually be recognizable for developers other than just ABAP programmers. Consider the data definitions in interface programs, and the interface parameters of function modules that are used in RFCs. Note that, probably, also for reasons of recognizability, SAP uses general names for interface parameters of BAPI functions.

In order to further specify the meaning of a variable, you can consider adding a suffix to its name. Think, for instance, of names such as:

- `tp_lifnr_cnt` (for a variable containing a supplier *count*)
- `tp_menge_max` (for a variable containing a *maximum* quantity)
- `ta_orders_old` (for an internal table containing order data before they are changed)
- `ta_orders_new` (for the changed order data)

However, giving meaningful names should not lead to giving *long* names. A name must also be practical. Therefore, avoid names such as `tp_sum_of_sales_in_preceding_month`, and use a name such as `tp_sales_lastmonth`.

Regarding constants, developers sometimes tend to use neutral names such as `co_waers` (currency), where a more meaningful name could be used. One reason for using a neutral name is that this makes it easier to change the value of the constant later without having to change the name of the constant (i.e., creating a new constant). However, we think it's better to assign a more meaningful name to the constant, such as `co_waers_local` (local currency).

Sometimes you'll need constants whose names refer to a status, such as `co_lfsta_b` (meaning that a delivery line has been partially delivered). In such cases, you may prefer to give the constant a more useful name like `co_partial_deliv`. Finally, note that standard SAP type-groups are available that contain the names of general types of constants such as `abap_true` and `abap_false` (in type-group `abap`).

▶ **Consistency**
The form of the name of one particular type of data must be similar to the form of other types of data. So, if you use prefixes in names, we recommend doing this consistently for all kinds of names: instead of using the name `tp_matnr` for a variable and `itab_orders` for an internal table, we prefer to use `tp_matnr` and `ta_orders`.

▶ **Ensure That You Can Add Naming Conventions When Needed**
You should consider the probability that there will eventually be new objects to be named, and therefore, ensure that you can accommodate more naming conventions when needed. In Release 4.6, for example, data references have

been introduced as new types of data. You need to avoid the situation whereby the name of a new object doesn't correspond with the existing naming conventions.

Naming Conventions: ABAP Dictionary Objects

For *ABAP Dictionary objects*, the first character of each name is determined by the namespace used. If you stay within the SAP standard naming range, you can use Y or Z as the first character of the name of, for example, a database table. You can also request your own namespace at SAP (as we did for namespace /ctac/, which is used in various code examples).

In addition, you may want to explicitly distinguish between the names given to database tables, structures, and database views, since it is not always clear in ABAP code to which of these the code is actually referring. So, in that case, you may prefer using names starting with zt (customized database tables), zs (customized structures), and zv (customized database views).

Naming Conventions: Procedures

For *procedures* (subroutines, function modules, and methods), assigning a meaningful name is sufficient. We recommend always starting the corresponding name with a verb. Consider, for example, get_sales_order, calculate_total_invoices, and so forth. If you don't use your own name range for function modules, you must add the Y or Z as a prefix for each function module name.

Naming Conventions: Function Groups and Classes

Except for the use of a prefix (Y or Z, or your own name range), function groups don't really require a specific naming convention, since they are not referred to in ABAP programs. The names of classes, however, are explicitly referred to, so they do require some minimal naming convention. We recommend at least using a prefix to distinguish local classes (/c/) and local interfaces (/if). This is also important in order to avoid confusion with existing global classes. Because no check exists on naming conflicts, SAP recommends this naming standard.

As classes are implemented in accordance with a model of the real world, it is particularly important to carefully choose the names used. Above all, remember to avoid technical names. Think, for example, of class names such as /cl_mortgage. It may be helpful to reuse existing standard SAP terms as in /cl_rushorder.

Naming Conventions: Programs and Transactions

There is always considerable debate about naming standards for ABAP programs and transaction codes. Some developers prefer using actual names (i.e., names that describe the function of a program), while others use names containing sequence numbers such as Z001. Sometimes, the name of the SAP application component, or the type of program, is explicitly made part of the name as well. However, the general problem with naming a program in this way is that a clear distinction between application components and different types of programs cannot always be made. Also consider that end users don't really mind that this type of distinction cannot be made, since most programs are accessed via user menus instead of directly via their name. For these reasons, we don't have a preference for any specific recommendations (except, of course, the recommendation to adhere to one naming standard).

Structuring Reports and Module Pool Programs

The second way to make your ABAP programs easier to read is via choosing and maintaining a proper structure, which comes down to subdividing programs into logical units. To achieve the optimal readability, it is critical that other programmers don't have to step through the details of a unit in order to understand what it does. In the case of ABAP programs and reports, the highest levels of modularization are enforced by the type of program.

▶ Reports

For reports, the first level at which modularization is enforced is the level at which the predefined *reporting events* are available, such as INITIALIZATION, START-OF-SELECTION, TOP-OF-PAGE, and AT LINE-SELECTION. As such, the order of appearance of reporting events in the source code doesn't matter, since the runtime environment will always go through these events in the same fixed order. However, for the readability of a report, we recommend placing the events in that predefined order, which is best achieved by defining them in a template report. Sometimes, there's discussion about the correct place for the TOP-OF-PAGE and END-OF-PAGE events. The question then is whether the two events should be placed before all the other events, or after. We have no preference for either of the two choices. What is more important is that the two events are consistently located at the same place. In addition, we recommend placing interactive reporting events such as AT LINE-SELECTION and AT USER-COMMAND at the end of the report. This results in the following sequence:

```
REPORT /ctac/reporting_events.

* Events in the sequence of processing
LOAD-OF-PROGRAM.
*...
INITIALIZATION.
*...
AT SELECTION-SCREEN OUTPUT.
*...
AT SELECTION-SCREEN.
*...
START-OF-SELECTION.
*
PERFORM read_data.
PERFORM process_data.
*
END-OF-SELECTION.
*
PERFORM display_output.
*
* Events that occur more than once during processing
TOP-OF-PAGE.
*...
TOP-OF-PAGE DURING LINE-SELECTION.
*...
END-OF-PAGE.
*...
* Interactive events
AT LINE-SELECTION.
*...
AT USER-COMMAND.
```

▶ **Module Pool Programs**

For module pool programs, there can also be little doubt about the main structure, since this is automatically proposed in the form of the main includes when creating the program. The main structure is also enforced by the use of the standard screen events: Process Before Output (PBO), Process After Input (PAI), Process On Help request (POH), and Process On Value request (POV).

Most of the actual functionality will be part of the PAI event. In this event, we prefer to combine the selection and processing of data with the corresponding error handling. We don't do this primarily for reasons of readability, but just because it's more practical: especially if error handling cannot be started before some processing has been done, you are better-off having all the required logic in one place. Besides, it's only in the PAI event that you can execute a check when a field value has actually changed (via using the addition ON REQUEST).

A good habit to adopt to improve the readability of the code is to do the following:

- ▷ Place `EXIT` modules (for leaving a screen).
- ▷ Add the modules performing checks on screen input (in the same sequence that the fields have in the screen).
- ▷ Add the modules in which the other functionality is located last; for example, for reading and processing extra data, and processing the OK code.

Depending on the size of the functionality, it might be beneficial to further subdivide your code into procedures such as subroutines, methods or function modules, as we mentioned in Section 8.2.1.

SAP sometimes also uses includes to subdivide code into separate units, for example, one include containing global data, another include containing all subroutines. We consider this to be primarily a matter of personal taste. Perhaps, it offers better navigation through large amounts of source code. In most cases, however, this way of adding more structure to your code is not necessary.

8.2.3 Reusing Standard SAP Software

Besides making your own software more readable and recognizable, the second way to improve its maintainability is via reusing as many software components as possible. In this respect, you can follow two complementary approaches: you can try to reuse as many standard SAP components as possible, and you can make your own software as reusable as possible. For SAP customers, improving the reusability of customized ABAP software primarily comes down to reusing as much standard functionality as possible. Various standard SAP developments can be reused. Consider the following objects:

- ▶ External subroutines
- ▶ Function modules (including BAPIs)
- ▶ Methods
- ▶ Reports
- ▶ Transactions (with the `CALL TRANSACTION` technique)
- ▶ Forms (SAPscript and Smart Forms)

However, you cannot completely reuse existing functionality in its original form in all cases. A frequent dilemma for ABAP developers is whether to copy an existing SAP development. A strategy that is sometimes used is to copy an existing object from the SAP system, and then, to change the copy. This is done most frequently with forms (both SAPscript forms and Smart Forms), and to a lesser extent, with function modules or sometimes reports and programs. However, we're not in favor of such *reuse* strategies. Although during initial development, copying a program or form and implementing your changes in this copy version appears to be the fastest and easiest option, from a maintenance point of view, this is not recommended. Performing maintenance on a copied development object is always more difficult. Usually, much of a copied object is not used but, since it still remains visible to the developer who performs maintenance, this only disturbs the maintenance process. Moreover, the art of copying actions tends to disturb the management of customized software (cleanup actions before release upgrades, hundreds of development objects to be removed).

When attempting to reuse standard SAP functionality, some specific points should be emphasized in order to achieve the best maintainability possible. First, we do this for function modules. Second, we specifically compare the use of BAPI function modules with the more traditional CALL TRANSACTION technique. Third, we present a way to reuse an entire report. Fourth, we discuss the benefits of the ABAP List Viewer (ALV) technique. And fifth, we present the best ways to reuse standard SAP forms.

Reusing SAP Function Modules and Methods

Much of the standard SAP functionality has been established in function modules. Almost 200,000 function modules currently exist in the SAP R/3 system. About 6000 of these function modules have been released for customer use. BAPI functions represent a specific type of function: they're available for interfacing with non-SAP systems, but they can also be called from within your own customized screen-handling functionality as update functions. Now, we'll address the most frequently asked questions when a developer is trying to reuse function modules and methods:

▶ **How Can an Existing Function Module Be Found?**

An ABAP developer will often know, or at least suspect, that standard functionality is already available when needed. This could be the case, for instance, when a new report must be developed that needs to include part of the functionality of an existing standard transaction, say, a material availability check. The first question to be answered then is how to determine whether a standard function is actually available.

The first way to check this is via the standard transaction for maintaining function modules (SE37) and the Repository Information System that is integrated in its search help. In doing so, we recommend that you familiarize yourself with SAP's Application Hierarchy. In addition, when searching a function module (or method) by using a part of its name, you may benefit from the fact that, in some cases, SAP uses rather strict naming conventions for function modules. The names of BAPI functions, for example, always start with `bapi_...` and include a reference to a business object, such as `salesorder` (strict naming conventions are also used for function modules in enhancements). Furthermore, update functions have names including terms such as `create` or `confirm`. So, you can use this knowledge by entering a search string such as `bapi*create*`. Often, an indication of the application component is also part of the name, such as `V` (*Vertrieb*) for Sales, or `L` (*Lagerverwaltung*) for Warehouse Management.

Since SAP's naming conventions have changed over time, you may also need other search methods. A practical search procedure is to apply the Runtime Analysis (Transaction SE30) on a standard program that you expect to contain the function module that you need. A third option is to use the Debugger, although it can be rather time-consuming. Finally, don't forget that you can also find a great deal of information on the Internet (for example, go to *ifr.sap.com* for all information about standard interfaces).

▶ **How Can You Verify Whether a Function Module Is Reusable?**
When you think you've found an appropriate function module, the second question is whether this function module can immediately be applied. First, you'll have to verify whether the function has been released by SAP (in the attributes of the function module) and whether documentation is available (if not in English, then, perhaps in German). Then, the function may not do exactly what you want it to do. To some extent, you can overcome this barrier by wrapping the standard function module into a function module of your own. This strategy tends to work well in a limited number of situations:

▷ If just an extra input or output parameter is required

▷ If an extra check on the input of the function module is required, as a kind of filter to narrow down the input values, for example, you may want to use the function module for only certain
order types

▷ If extra processing is required before the output can be used in the way you want

More questionable is reusing a function for a purpose other than the one for which the function was originally designed. Just using the information of a function module that also makes an update is not a good example of reuse. As a reference, remember the distinction made in Section 8.2.1 between subroutines that read data, process data, update data, and write output. Our advice is this: Don't reuse a function module for one of these purposes if it also serves another purpose.

Another strategy that we don't recommend is copying a function module, and then, changing the copy. Note that you usually need to copy much more than is actually required: the remainder of the function group that contains the function module that you need must also be copied. This doesn't only complicate maintenance. In fact, you may find that, in the next release, part of the function group has been changed by SAP—perhaps, some includes have been removed or replaced. This means that you have to start your work all over again.

If no suitable standard function module is available, but the exact standard functionality that you need is nevertheless available in a certain program, you might consider copying the corresponding part of the code into your own customized function module. However, this strategy may well be the most difficult one, so you should use it only as a last resort.

We conclude this topic by listing some examples of reusable function modules and methods:

▶ ALV functions: look, for example, at `reuse_alv_grid_display` (or other ALV function modules – with the search term `*alv*`)

▶ Interactive functions: `pop-up_to_decide`

▶ Unit conversions: `unit_conversion_simple`

▶ Currency conversions: `convert_to_foreign_currency`

▶ Date functions: `day_names_get`

In addition, we'll also mention various reusable classes and methods:

▶ Treecontrols and other Enjoy Control classes; for example, `cl_gui_alv_grid` and `cl_gui_html_viewer`

▶ Various classes used for the connection with the GUI; for example, class `cl_gui_frontend_services`, including, e.g., methods `gui_upload`, `gui_download`, `file_open_dialog`

▶ Exception classes; for example, `cx_sy_no_handler` (see Chapter 5, Section 5.3)

▶ Runtime Type Identification classes (RTTI), to be used for determining characteristics of a variable at runtime such as type, length; for example, `cl_abap_classdescr`. As dynamic programming is increasingly used in standard SAP, these classes may become very useful.

Reuse BAPI or CALL TRANSACTION Functionality?

BAPI functions and other function modules that perform the same updates as standard transactions can often be combined with your own screen handling or background programs, in much the same way as is still often done by using the CALL TRANSACTION technique. However, reusing BAPI functions offers considerable advantages over reusing existing standard transactions:

▶ Since BAPI functions don't include screen processing, their performance is much better than the performance of corresponding standard transactions.

▶ The interface and functionality of a BAPI don't change in newer releases, whereas the user interface of standard transactions (which must be reused in CALL TRANSACTION functionality) continuously changes.

There's only one relatively small disadvantage to using BAPI functions compared with CALL TRANSACTION functionality: when using a BAPI function for online processing, you have to build your own exception handling (on the basis of the contents of the RETURN parameter of the BAPI). Conversely, if an error occurs in CALL TRANSACTION functionality that is processed in mode *E*, processing will stop on the standard screen where the error occurs. This enables the end user to correct the input immediately, and then continue to process the transaction.

If a BAPI function is used for processing large amounts of data in the background, a good fall-back mechanism for error handling is the generation of an IDoc message instead. The IDoc message can then be processed using the associated standard tools for finding and processing erroneous IDoc messages. The required IDoc definition can be generated automatically on the basis of the existing BAPI function, using Transaction BDBG.

We're strongly in favor of reusing BAPI functions whenever possible. Creating CALL TRANSACTION functionality on the basis of standard transactions should be done only when no BAPI function is available.

Reusing Entire SAP Reports

Reusing complete standard SAP reports is something that isn't done very often. In most cases, you're better-off developing your own reports from scratch. What sometimes also happens is that reports are copied, and customized logic is added to the copy. Although this isn't our favorite strategy, typically, there will be fewer complications with this approach than when copying a SAPscript form or a function module. As when copying a function module, you run the same risk of adding your own logic on top of something that may no longer exist in the next release; for example, consider the situation where a report consists of several includes. If you decide to copy these includes, you run the risk of extra maintenance. If you don't copy them, the includes may have disappeared in the next release.

There is, however, a quick and relatively easy way to reuse the output of an existing standard report without having to make a copy of the report. Provided that you adhere to some strict conditions, this option may be worth exploring. Imagine that you find a report that delivers exactly the output that you need for your own report. If the output of the standard report is produced by using WRITE statements in the code, you might be able to reuse the entire report. Scenarios in which you could do this are:

▶ When the outputs of several standard reports have to be combined in one report

▶ When the output of an existing standard report contains calculated values that you need as input for your own report

▶ When the output of the standard report should not be displayed in a SAP GUI format but in another format; for example, in HTML format

▶ When a demo scenario is prepared in order to get some results very quickly

Changing a standard report is not a good option, and copying the report and changing a copy may be too laborious. On the other hand, the functionality that you need may be available only in this standard report, and not in a function module or method. In this case, you can catch the output of the standard report in your own report, and then further process it. You do this by using a SUBMIT <report> AND RETURN EXPORTING LIST TO MEMORY statement. Then, the WRITE output of the standard report is not displayed but, instead, it remains available in memory. You can read the data in memory by using the standard function module list_from_memory, and convert the data into character format by using the function module list_to_asci.

The advantages are obvious. You can achieve results quickly, and you don't need to modify any code in the existing report, however, you should be aware of some pitfalls:

▶ You don't receive the output in the form of any structure. Instead, you receive only one large character string. Therefore, you must separate this character string into separate fields again (parsing). For that purpose, you need information from the original report about the offset and length of each output field in the list.

▶ Because the output of the standard report will contain only characters, you'll also have to check fields that have specific formats, such as date, amount, and quantity fields. Note that the exact layout of such fields depends on the user settings of the user who is running the report, in the same way as for Batch Data Communication (see Section 4.5.3).

▶ If the output of the original report changes, then, of course, you'll have to change your own program as well.

For these reasons, it's practical to use the option of catching the output of a standard report only if very little additional processing is required.[4] The following sample code shows how this would work (the relevant statements are marked bold):

```
REPORT  /ctac/bk_submit_to_memory           .
DATA : tp_matnr     TYPE matnr.
DATA : ta_list      TYPE STANDARD TABLE OF abaplist,
       wa_list      TYPE abaplist,
       ta_list_txt  TYPE STANDARD TABLE OF char255,
       wa_list_txt  TYPE char255.

SELECT-OPTIONS: so_matnr FOR tp_matnr.

START-OF-SELECTION.
* submitting a report, but output remains in memory
  SUBMIT /ctac/overview_orders   AND RETURN
           EXPORTING LIST TO MEMORY
           WITH so_matnr IN so_matnr.

* read the output from memory
  CALL FUNCTION 'LIST_FROM_MEMORY'
    TABLES
      listobject = ta_list
    EXCEPTIONS
      not_found  = 1
      OTHERS     = 2.

  IF sy-subrc = 0.
* Convert to character format
    CALL FUNCTION 'LIST_TO_ASCI'
* EXPORTING
*    LIST_INDEX               = -1
*    WITH_LINE_BREAK          = ' '
      TABLES
         listasci              = ta_list_txt
         listobject            = ta_list
      EXCEPTIONS
         empty_list            = 1
         list_index_invalid    = 2
         OTHERS                = 3.

    IF sy-subrc = 0.
* Here, your own logic can be added
      LOOP AT ta_list_txt INTO wa_list_txt.
        WRITE: / wa_list_txt.
      ENDLOOP.
    ENDIF.
  ENDIF.
```

---

4 We use this technique only for one-time programs, or programs to automatically compare output of two near-identical reports.

Reusing ABAP List Viewer Functionality

As of Release 4.0, SAP has started to include ABAP List Viewer (ALV) functionality. This enables you to extend the possibilities of your own reports. Apart from the benefits discussed elsewhere in terms of correctness (see Section 3.3.1), stability (see Section 4.2.1), and user-friendliness (see Section 6.2.1), you can also enhance the maintainability of your own reports by using ALV functionality.

You can reuse ALV functionality for both regular and interactive reports. It removes several disadvantages inherent in traditional reporting. Apart from the less attractive look-and-feel that a traditional report has when compared with an ALV report, it also requires more development and maintenance time for details such as sorting, totalizing, creating headings, and so forth.

In contrast, a report that's developed on the basis of ALV functionality for displaying its output offers the following benefits:

▶ It offers a standard for all kinds of output.

▶ It takes very little effort to include functions for changing the format of a list: selecting the columns to be displayed, changing the display sequence, adding (sub)totals, sorting the output, applying filters, etc.

▶ In dialog mode (that is, when the SAP GUI is available), the end user can determine the layout format, which can be saved and reused for each individual user.

▶ All ABAP Dictionary definitions are automatically reused: standard heading texts, standard formatting, documentation, the option to display possible entries, etc.

▶ Additional functions are included such as integration with word processing, spreadsheets, scrolling, and printing.

▶ You can easily add your own additional interactive functions.

▶ It's easy to convert existing reports to ALV format.

▶ Various help functions are available.

To be able to implement ALV output functionality, the only precaution you need to take is to separate the logic for creating the actual output from the rest of the logic. Furthermore, the only real restriction of ALV functionality is that you need the SAP GUI to look at an ALV list.

The oldest form of ALV functionality was implemented by SAP in Release 4.0. This is function module `reuse_alv_list_display`. It still uses `WRITE` statements for the output of data, and it doesn't presuppose the availability of Enjoy Controls on the client. As of Release 4.6, Enjoy Controls were added, so that part of the functionality is actually executed on the client instead of the application server. The class `cl_gui_alv_grid` contains the associated methods, which are reused by function modules `reuse_alv_grid_display` and `reuse_alv_grid_display_lvc` (note, however, that this last function module has not been released for customer use). In most cases, just reusing the function modules in your own reports will suffice.

Actually, there are very few situations for which ALV functionality is not appropriate. You cannot generate multiple-line output with the *grid* versions, and, in the case of varying output formats in one list, only the first output format is shown on screen; only when you leave the list in the first output format is the next output format displayed. For hierarchical and tree-like lists, other functions and Enjoy Controls are available.

The most important thing to remember about the ALV functionality is when to reuse which of the available functions or methods. We offer the following advice:

▶ As mentioned, the *grid* versions can be used only when a SAP GUI is available (in background processing, this is of course not the case). You can use function `gui_is_available` in your code to check for availability. Furthermore, the grid functionality performs somewhat less well than the list version.

▶ The *list* version is more appropriate for processing large volumes of data, when the performance of a report is important. It can also be used without restrictions in background processing. Furthermore, only this version supports multiple-line output (i.e., more than one line of output per processed item).

▶ If you want to combine various controls, for example, a Tree Control and an ALV Control, in one screen, you must program the ALV Control yourself. You do this by including one custom container for each Control in the screen definition.

Using an ALV function works as follows:

▶ The ALV function requires input in the form of an internal table of type STANDARD (interface parameter `t_outtab`).

▶ Besides the data, you also need to explicitly provide the structure of the data to the ALV function, in one of the two following ways:
  ▶ In terms of a fixed DDIC structure (interface parameter `i_structure_name`)
  ▶ In an internal table that contains metadata (interface parameter `it_fieldcat`). You can build up this field catalog in your own program by using function module `reuse_alv_fieldcatalog_merge`.

▶ When using interface parameter `it_fieldcat`, you can change field attributes such as the column headings.

- Standard ALV functionality uses its own GUI toolbar. You can overrule this by defining your own customized GUI status (in interface parameter i_callback_pf_status_set). Creating a customized PF status is done most easily by copying the standard PF status from function group SALV. Then, you can add your own function to the copied PF status and, if necessary, deactivate the standard functions that you don't need (see also Section 6.2.1, Figure 6.4).

- To enable end users to create and store their own output variants, you must specify the input parameters i_save, is_variant, and i_callback_program.

- You can change a number of layout settings by specifying the input parameter is_layout. For detailed information, look at the online help of function module reuse_alv_grid_display.

The following code example shows how an ALV function[5] is reused. An extensive example of a report template that reuses ALV functionality is available in Appendix 3.

```
REPORT  /ctac/r_alv_simple_example        .
* This example can be compared to what you get when you execute
* transaction SE16 (Data Browser).
DATA  : tp_structure_name  LIKE dd021-tabname,
        tp_save(1)         TYPE c,
        tp_callback_progr  type syrepid.

DATA  : ta_kna1    TYPE STANDARD TABLE OF kna1,
        wa_kna1    TYPE kna1.

SELECT-OPTIONS:
        so_kunnr   FOR  wa_kna1-kunnr.

START-OF-SELECTION.

  SELECT * FROM kna1 INTO TABLE ta_kna1
        WHERE kunnr IN so_kunnr.

  tp_callback_progr  = sy-repid.
  tp_structure_name  = 'KNA1'.
  tp_save            = 'A'.        "Layout can be saved for user and for
                                   "system

  CALL FUNCTION 'REUSE_ALV_GRID_DISPLAY'
    EXPORTING
      i_callback_program            = tp_callback_progr
      i_structure_name              = tp_structure_name
```

---

5 The function reuse_alv_grid_display has many more interface parameters than mentioned in this example. For more information, see the corresponding documentation for this function.

```
    i_save                      = tp_save
      TABLES
        t_outtab                  = ta_knal
      EXCEPTIONS
        program_error             = 1
        OTHERS                    = 2

  IF sy-subrc <> 0.
* Error handling here
  ENDIF.
```

Reusing SAPscript and Smart Forms

When developing output forms, such as sales order confirmations, purchase order confirmations, or invoices, two questions must be answered:

▶ Why use a SAPscript form if you can use the Smart Forms technique?

▶ When would you reuse an existing standard form? Do you make a copy of the program or the form and modify the copy, or start from scratch?

To help you answer these questions, we'll first discuss the most important benefits of the more modern Smart Forms technique over the SAPscript technique. To understand these benefits, you first need to know the basic differences between the two techniques.

In the SAPscript technique (see Figure 8.3), the program that collects the data to be printed (on the left) also contains the processing logic that controls the content of each form element and the order in which the form elements are established. However, some logic in the form of pseudo-code can also be included in the form itself (in the middle), and some logic in external subroutines (on the right) can be called from within the form. Note that a SAPscript form definition must be made per client and language.

In contrast to the SAPscript technique, the Smart Forms technique (see Figure 8.4) has been defined on the basis of a strict separation between the collection of data and the control over establishing the actual form. All the logic to be processed for a form is defined in the form itself. Based on this logic, a function module is generated that controls how a form is established at runtime. Note that, unlike the SAPscript technique, the Smart Forms technique requires only one version of each form to be managed. Each Smart Form is a client-independent development object identified only by its name, whereas a SAPscript form is, apart from its name, also identified by client and language (compare Figure 8.3 and Figure 8.4).

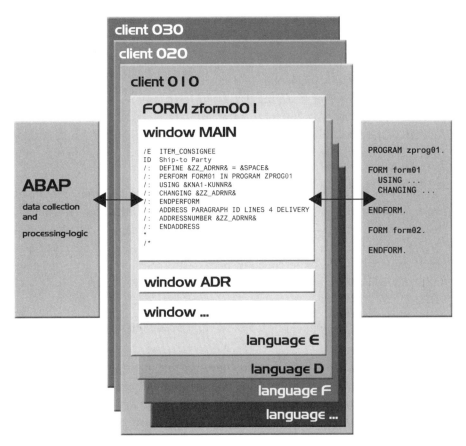

Figure 8.3 The SAPscript Technique

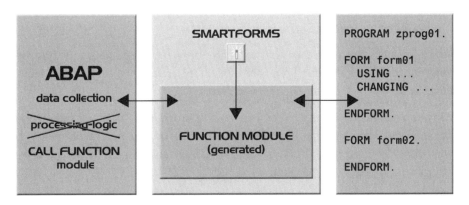

Figure 8.4 The Smart Forms Technique

The Smart Forms technique offers the following benefits over the SAPscript technique:

- ▶ Less maintenance is required for a Smart Form. Both in the SAPscript technique and the Smart Forms technique, one calling program can be combined with several forms. However, since the processing logic for a SAPscript form is contained in the calling program, this program must be changed for each new form added. In the Smart Forms technique, the calling program merely supplies the data. Therefore, it doesn't necessarily have to be changed when a new form is added.

- ▶ Troubleshooting activities will usually be less difficult to perform on a Smart Form than on a SAPscript form. When exactly each single form element is established is not really clear with SAPscript forms, whereas this cannot be misinterpreted with Smart Forms. Only errors in the definition of a Smart Form itself could still cause some difficulty, because troubleshooting activities have to be done in generated, and therefore less-readable, ABAP code.

- ▶ The Smart Forms tool (Transaction SMARTFORMS) is easier to use.

- ▶ The Smart Forms technique offers more output possibilities, such as HTML and XML.

- ▶ In a Smart Form, there is no pseudo-code available as there is in a SAPscript, but real ABAP code can be used. First, this means that there is less to learn for an ABAP developer. Secondly, it enables you to perform a regular syntax check, whereas there is no syntax check for pseudo-code in a SAPscript form.

- ▶ Because each Smart Form is defined as an object that is independent of both client and language, there are many more different versions of a SAPscript form than there are for a Smart Form. Therefore, the management of different versions is much easier for Smart Forms.

Not surprisingly, the advantages of the Smart Forms technique far outweighs the SAPscript technique, leaving little room for doubt as to which of the two techniques is better for the maintainability of forms.

Many companies still choose to copy an existing program or form and then modify the copy. Although this is understandable, it's usually not recommended, when considered from the point of view of maintainability, particularly if a SAPscript form (or program) is copied.

The consequences of copying a SAPscript form (and sometimes also the program) are usually underestimated. Even a seemingly small change in an existing SAPscript form may be difficult to realize. To explain this, imagine the following change request example for a SAPscript form. Someone who doesn't know how a

SAPscript form is technically processed will show the developer a printout of the existing form, and ask him/her to shift one field value just a little. While the field can be pointed out on paper, doing the same in the form may be more complicated for various reasons:

▶ In a SAPscript form, the same field can be filled several times within the same window of a form (see Figure 8.5). Finding out exactly which part of the logic must be changed may therefore not be immediately apparent.

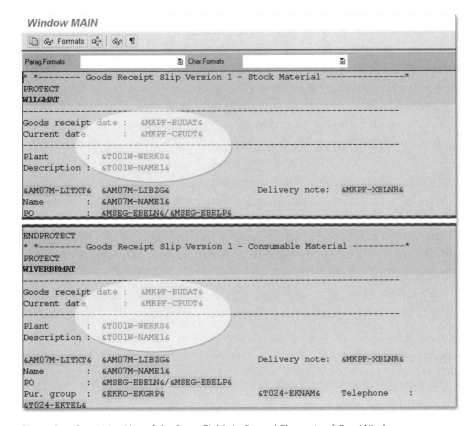

Figure 8.5 Repetitive Use of the Same Fields in Several Elements of One Window

▶ Determining the content of a SAPscript element is done in the calling program. Beause the same field and SAPscript element can be found in several places in the ABAP code, it's often difficult to change only one field. Sometimes, developers react to this by also changing logic that is not relevant.

▶ Small changes to one field, such as shifting a field one millimeter to the left or right, can immediately affect the positioning of other fields. Therefore, repositioning one field may force you to reposition various other fields.

Because of the iterative way in which a SAPscript form is typically developed, we even doubt whether developing a form from a copy is faster than creating a form from scratch.

So, although making a copy of a SAPscript program and form is possible—and tempting—we urge you to discriminate carefully when choosing the situations in which you can do this. To a lesser extent, the same is true for Smart Forms, for example:

1. Only certain types of changes are relatively easy to implement. Think, for instance, of fetching a descriptive text for a material number, changing the print sequence of existing fields, or adding a company logo on a form. Most other kinds of changes may be more difficult to realize.

2. Making a copy means that much of the copy is not going to be used. Both program and form may be designed initially for many more purposes than those that are relevant. This means that much of the copied source code in the calling program may be *dead* code, which already makes initial development more difficult, as well as all further maintenance activities.

3. If a form is sent to suppliers and customers (such as a sales order or purchase order confirmation, or a sales invoice), most companies will want the form to look perfect. Developing such a form on the basis of a copy often means that much of the copied form must initially be changed. Besides, the frequency of maintenance will usually be higher than it is for an internally-used form.

4. *Dead* code can also indicate that many superfluous and time-consuming program actions (such as unnecessary SELECT statements) are executed. If many forms have to be printed daily, this will harm performance.

Because of these circumstances, we recommend that you avoid making a copy of a SAPscript form if:

▶ The type of changes to be made are not straightforward.

▶ It's likely that maintenance will be necessary.

▶ In particular, externally used forms need to be changed.

▶ Performance is important.

For the Smart Forms technique, such restrictions are less important. Experience proves that standard Smart Form programs (for data collection) can often be left completely unchanged, and only new forms are required. However, we've already noticed that using the copy strategy for a Smart Form can lead ultimately to similar maintenance problems as those that would occur for a SAPscript form. Imagine, for example, copying a relatively complex Smart Form such as the standard form for a Sales invoice (*VB_BIL_INVOICE*). After a year, you'll probably regret having made the copy because of the maintenance efforts involved. Hence, even with the Smart Forms technique, copying may offer only some short-term benefits.

If you consider converting a current SAPscript form to a Smart Form you can start by copying the existing SAPscript form layout into the Smart Form layout (menu **Utilities • Migrate SAPscript** form in Transaction SMARTFORMS). However, since the SAPscript technique allows the logic to be defined in various places, you cannot convert any of the current logic from a SAPscript form to a Smart Form. Therefore, all the logic for a Smart Form must be created from scratch again.

8.2.4 Practical Tips

In this section, we'll provide you with some other tips that can help you to further enhance the maintainability of your ABAP software. But first, we'll remind you of some straightforward ways in which to make your code more maintainable:

▶ Make your code independent of the logon language.

▶ Add inline documentation and comment blocks.

▶ Use one ABAP statement per line.

▶ Use the Pretty Printer option.

▶ Use template programs and reports.

▶ Clean up the existing source code periodically.

Now, we'll elaborate on some other tips for enhancing maintainability. We'll discuss the reuse of customizing settings to avoid constants; the reuse of patterns to make ABAP code more readable; and the Reuse Library in which you can build up a collection of the most valuable reusable components. We end this section by mentioning some valuable standard programs that you can use to import data into a SAP R/3 system.

Avoiding Constants for Organizational Units

In customized ABAP software, *constants* are often defined as organizational units (i.e., plant code, company code, sales organization, and so on). However, if you understand the relations between organizational units, you can avoid using constants for organizational units by determining them dynamically in your program. You can almost always start by selecting a specific organization unit and derive the corresponding *higher* organizational unit in the organizational hierarchy via the associated customizing table.

Suppose that a plant code is known, but you actually need the corresponding company code. In the following sample code, a constant value is used to select the company code (field bukrs):

```
SELECT SINGLE * FROM  bkpf
       WHERE  bukrs  = 'NL01'
       AND    belnr  = tp_belnr
       AND    gjahr  = tp_gjahr.
```

In this particular example, a preferable option would be to derive the company code via using the relation between the plant code and the company code as it's recorded in the database table T001K. This would require only a small addition to the code:

```
SELECT SINGLE bukrs
       INTO tp_bukrs
       FROM  t001k
       WHERE  bwkey  = tp_plant.

IF sy-subrc EQ 0.

  SELECT SINGLE * FROM  bkpf
         WHERE  bukrs  = tp_bukrs
         AND    belnr  = tp_belnr
         AND    gjahr  = tp_gjahr.

ENDIF.
```

Similar logic could be useful to reuse, for example, the customizing settings that connect a sales organization with a company code (via table TVKO); a valuation area with a company code (table T001K); a company code with a controlling area (table TKA01); or, a purchase organization with a company code (table T024E). It would be beyond the scope of this book to enumerate all the possible relations between the organizational units in an R/3 system here; however, if you need more information, see the customizing settings in the Customizing Implementation Guide (IMG, Transaction SPRO): branch to menu **Enterprise Structure • Assignments**.

Patterns

A particularly nice feature to improve the uniformity of ABAP programs is the tool to import so-called *Patterns*, which are pieces of template code. Two forms of patterns exist—static and dynamic. *Static patterns* are fixed code templates for certain statements (such as CASE, DO, SORT, SUBMIT). *Dynamic patterns* are used to generate code. Figure 8.6 shows how to choose a pattern. Figure 8.7 shows what the result looks like if a Dynamic Pattern is applied for a method.

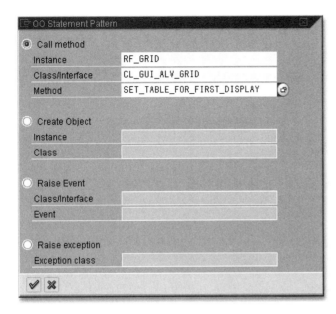

Figure 8.6 Calling a Dynamic Pattern for a Method Call

```
CALL METHOD rf_grid->set_table_for_first_display
*   EXPORTING
*     I_BUFFER_ACTIVE              =
*     I_BYPASSING_BUFFER           =
*     I_CONSISTENCY_CHECK          =
*     I_STRUCTURE_NAME             =
*     IS_VARIANT                   =
*     I_SAVE                       =
*     I_DEFAULT                    = 'X'
*     IS_LAYOUT                    =
*     IS_PRINT                     =
*     IT_SPECIAL_GROUPS            =
*     IT_TOOLBAR_EXCLUDING         =
*     IT_HYPERLINK                 =
*     IT_ALV_GRAPHICS              = I
*     IT_EXCEPT_QINFO              =
    CHANGING
      it_outtab                  =
*     IT_FIELDCATALOG              =
*     IT_SORT                      =
*     IT_FILTER                    =
*   EXCEPTIONS
*     INVALID_PARAMETER_COMBINATION = 1
*     PROGRAM_ERROR                = 2
*     TOO_MANY_LINES               = 3
*     others                       = 4

IF sy-subrc <> 0.
* MESSAGE ID SY-MSGID TYPE SY-MSGTY NUMBER SY-MSGNO
*          WITH SY-MSGV1 SY-MSGV2 SY-MSGV3 SY-MSGV4.
ENDIF.
```

Figure 8.7 The Result of the Dynamic Pattern Call

It's important to know how to make your own patterns. Since not every programmer knows how to create dynamic patterns, we'll briefly discuss this option here. Creating a dynamic pattern requires you to take the following steps:

1. From within the ABAP editor, you create a pattern (via menu **Utilities • Patterns**).

2. Enter the code `*$&$MUSTER` in the pattern in order to make it dynamic.

3. Make a function module with the name `<pattern>_editor_exit` as in the following example, for pattern `zdynamic`:

```
function zdynamic_editor_exit.
*"----------------------------------------------------------------------
*"*"Global interface:
*"  TABLES
*"      BUFFER TYPE  RSWSOURCET
*"  EXCEPTIONS
*"      CANCELLED
*"----------------------------------------------------------------------

* Add your own code here that fills the interface table BUFFER.

endfunction.
```

The contents of the function module should fill its interface table BUFFER. When applying the dynamic pattern, the code from the function module will then be copied into the source code at the position of the cursor.

Dynamic patterns can be used, for example, to import code templates for function calls, method calls, and `SELECT` statements. In Figure 8.8 and Figure 8.9, we've included screenshots of a customized Dynamic Pattern that helps to create the definition of a sorted table.

The Reuse Library

If you're serious about making your customized software as reusable as possible, you can set up a library of your own development objects with SAP's *Reuse Library*. You can view the objects in the Reuse Library using Transaction SE83 (see Figure 8.10).

This tool is particularly useful for large development organizations. The biggest benefit of the tool is that it enables you to create categories for development objects. You can define more than one index of categories (that is, more than one library). For example, you can categorize technical types of development objects (i.e., reports, function modules, etc.), and create another category for application components. This means that you can look for the same development object through various search methods. Furthermore, you can do a full text search.

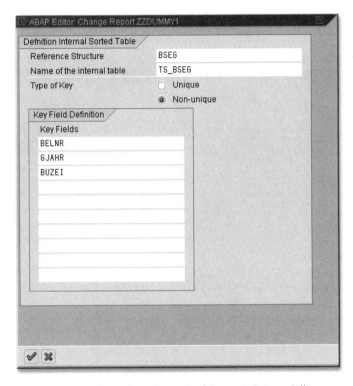

Figure 8.8 One of Our Own Customized Dynamic Pattern Calls

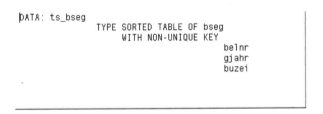

Figure 8.9 The Result of the Customized Dynamic Pattern Call

The libraries containing your index can be maintained using Transaction SLIBN. On the lowest level of a library, you include so-called *Reusable Products*. A Reusable Product is a set or group of development objects, which is maintained using Transaction SLIBP. Then, a set of objects can be assigned to one or more nodes in a library using Transaction SLIBN. If necessary, you can transport an entire library from one SAP system to another. You can access the Reuse Library directly from the ABAP editor to look for an object and then return with it to the ABAP editor. Note that a library doesn't distinguish between your own customized development objects and standard objects. This allows you to build up your own mix of the most valuable components, regardless of their origin.

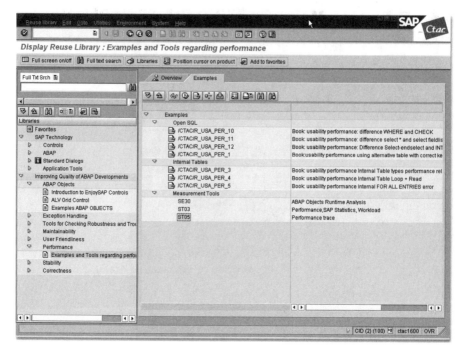

Figure 8.10 The Reuse Library

Reusable Standard Programs for Importing Large Volumes of Data

Specifically for importing large volumes of master and transaction data into an SAP system, a number of standard programs have been made available that may make using your own batch input or BAPI interfaces superfluous. Therefore, you might want to add the following programs to your own Reuse Library:

▶ RFBIBL00
   Import Accounting Documents

▶ RFBIDE00
   Import Customer Master

▶ RPULKT00
   Import Payroll Account

▶ RMDATIND
   Import Material Master

▶ RM06BBI0
   Import Purchase Requisitions

▶ RCSBI010
   Create Bill of Materials

▶ RVINVB00
   Import Open Sales Orders

8.3   Enhancing Maintainability with ABAP Objects

So far, we've referred to all kinds of measures that can enhance the maintainability of customized ABAP software, however, we haven't explained why using ABAP Objects is beneficial for this aspect of technical quality. Furthermore, we haven't stressed why—from the point of view of maintainability—code written in ABAP Objects is superior to code written in procedural ABAP. In this section, we do. Because we want to avoid a theoretical approach, we use two practical cases that should be easily recognized by most ABAP developers, even if the implementation in ABAP Objects is not immediately clear. Then, on the basis of the two cases, we show which drawbacks of procedural ABAP disappear when the functionality is implemented in ABAP Objects.

Note that both cases describe the kind of functionality that makes procedural ABAP programs rely rather heavily on IF and CASE statements, such as this:

```
IF <condition1>.
    PERFORM function1
ELSE.
    PERFORM function2
ENDIF.
```

Much of the main logic of procedural ABAP programs depends on conditional logic such as this in order to cope with the various situations that need to be addressed. This dependency on conditional logic persists even if you make well-structured code and use subroutines or function modules wherever possible.

The first example pertains to subclasses (in Section 8.3.1). The second example pertains to interfaces (in Section 8.3.2).

8.3.1   Using Subclasses

Imagine that you have to develop an interface logic to import sales document data into an SAP system. Five different types of sales documents must be distinguished (see Figure 8.11). Each document type varies only slightly from the others. Most of the data in these document types is common to all, however, each type of document also has some data that is unique. In addition, let's assume that three specific actions need to be executed for each sales document that is received: first, a corresponding document must be created in the SAP system; second, some output must be written on a list; and third, an e-mail confirmation must be sent to the person who requested the order. Although most of the logic inherent in these three specific actions is identical for all the document types involved, each document type requires its own variation of the main functionality (i.e., extra options, attributes, etc.).

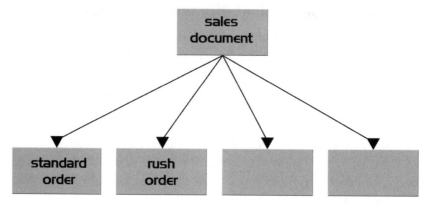

Figure 8.11 Types of Sales Documents

You can probably imagine that handling such slight variations of data and functionality would require many IF and CASE statements when using procedural ABAP. Since three different actions have to be performed for five different types of documents, a total of fifteen specific situations need to be distinguished in the associated ABAP code.

By properly structuring the code, you can limit later maintenance activities. Suppose that this is done in one of the three following ways:

1. By creating three different function modules: one for each action to be performed, for example, z_create_salesorder, z_write_output, and z_send_mail. The variation in document types is addressed in the logic of each of these function modules.

2. By creating a different function module for each situation: this would amount to fifteen different function modules, with similar names to the aforementioned three examples, but with an additional indication of the document type, such as z_create_std_salesorder, z_create_rushorder, and so on.

3. By creating one general class for all sales documents, and five subclasses, one for each document type. Further detailed functionality is defined in terms of three methods at each level: first, on the level of the (general) sales documents class; and secondly, in each subclass for the underlying document types. The methods in the subclasses are redefinitions of the methods defined for the general class. They carry exactly the same names. This can result in as much as eighteen different method implementations. However, only the difference in functionality needs to be reimplemented. In ABAP Objects terms, this is called *polymorphism* through *inheritance*.

Now, what are the differences between these three implementations of the same functionality in terms of their maintainability? When looking at these differences, you should bear in mind that a new document type may, at some point, have to be considered:

1. **One function module for each of the three main actions to be performed**
   In fact, this option represents the way in which BAPI functions are constructed. Each function module deals with all possible types of documents. Only three function modules are required. But each function module has to contain conditional logic to check the document type. Such logic may be located throughout the code of a function module, which makes the code complex. Moreover, all the imaginable interface parameters for all kinds of document types must be defined for each function. When a new document type must be considered, this option has the following consequences:

   ▶ The three existing function modules need to be maintained.

   ▶ The program code that calls the function modules doesn't have to be maintained (unless new interface parameters are required).

   ▶ All the code of the function module must carefully be checked for conditional logic, and new conditions (extra ELSE IF or WHEN conditions) must be added.

   The main advantage of this option will become apparent when the functionality that is valid for all document types changes; in that case, changes will have to be applied just once, which makes the corresponding maintenance activities relatively easy to perform. However, this option is still not ideal: the complexity of the code can hinder maintenance activities considerably.

2. **One function module per kind of action and document type**
   In this alternative, a maximum of fifteen function modules need to be created: one function module for each of the three main actions combined with each of the five document types. The code of every single function module will be relatively straightforward. The interface parameters of individual function modules must correspond to only one specific situation. However, there is a risk that the code can be easily duplicated when new function modules need to be created. Only careful design can prevent this inadvertent duplication of code. Another drawback of this alternative is that the code of all the calling programs must contain the conditional logic necessary to select the correct function module. When a new document type must be considered:

   ▶ Three new function modules need to be created (for each new document type that is introduced), although this incurs the risk of duplicating code.

   ▶ All existing programs that call the existing function modules must contain IF or CASE statements to select the correct function module to be executed. Therefore, all the calling programs need to be traced and maintained.

This alternative has the advantage that maintenance to a single function module will be relatively simple. But that is not enough. Maintenance may be much more difficult because only a careful overall design can prevent the duplication of code in the fifteen function modules. Maintenance to general functionality may even be disastrous if all the individual function modules also contain code for the general functionality.

3. **A superclass with three methods and five subclasses**

The ABAP Objects alternative is to create a sales order class containing three methods for the basic actions (create order, write output, send mail), and a subclass for each of the five document types. Only the *differences* with the implementation of the methods in the sales order class need to be reimplemented in the methods of each subclass (that is, they and the methods of the superclass are named identically). The only restriction is that the interface parameters of the methods on all class levels must be equal. Therefore, as in the first alternative, all interface parameters required for all document types must be included in one definition.

The consequences of introducing a new document type are limited:

▶ The bare minimum of extra functionality is added in the form of a new subclass with (if necessary) a redefinition of the three methods.

▶ The program code that calls the existing methods doesn't have to be changed.

Moreover, changing general functionality isn't problematic. Because all the general functionality is encoded in just the superclass, maintenance will only have to be applied there.

Actually, the ABAP Objects alternative enables you to combine the advantages of the first two alternatives. Adding new functionality is not complex, and neither is overseeing the maintenance of existing general functionality, because of the *CASE-less* code. If class definitions have been defined properly, there is always just one place where code must be added or changed. You don't have to know exactly how the existing code works in order to add new code; and, you don't need to change the calling programs.

In the following simplified pieces of sample code, we show how the principle of inheritance works. First, a (local) superclass for sales documents is defined. It contains the `determine_subclass` static method (to determine the correct subclass on the basis of the document type of a sales document), and the `display_data` method (to present some information about a sales document).

```
*----------------------------------------------------------------------*
*       CLASS lcl_sales_document DEFINITION
*----------------------------------------------------------------------*
* General functionality Sales Documents
*----------------------------------------------------------------------*
```

```abap
CLASS lcl_sales_document DEFINITION.
  PUBLIC SECTION.
* Static method to determine the correct class
    CLASS-METHODS: determine_subclass IMPORTING itp_docty
                                                 TYPE auart
                                       EXPORTING etp_classname
                                                 TYPE string.

    METHODS      : constructor        IMPORTING ist_vbak
                                                 TYPE vbak,
                   display_data       .

  PROTECTED SECTION.
    CONSTANTS:
          co_docty_standard   TYPE auart VALUE 'TA', "Standard order
          co_docty_rush       TYPE auart VALUE 'RO'. "Rush order
  PRIVATE SECTION.
* Attributes for the super class
    DATA: tp_vbeln           TYPE vbeln,
          tp_auart           TYPE auart.

ENDCLASS.                    "lcl_sales_document DEFINITION
*----------------------------------------------------------------------*
*       CLASS lcl_sales_document IMPLEMENTATION
*----------------------------------------------------------------------*
CLASS lcl_sales_document IMPLEMENTATION.
  METHOD determine_subclass.
    CASE itp_docty.
      WHEN co_docty_standard.
        etp_classname = 'LCL_SALES_DOCUMENT_TA'.
      WHEN co_docty_rush.
        etp_classname = 'LCL_SALES_DOCUMENT_RO'.
      WHEN OTHERS.
* The default document type is used
        etp_classname = 'LCL_SALES_DOCUMENT'.
    ENDCASE.
  ENDMETHOD.                 "determine_subclass
  METHOD constructor.
    tp_vbeln = ist_vbak-vbeln.
    tp_auart = ist_vbak-auart.
  ENDMETHOD.                 "constructor
  METHOD display_data.
    WRITE: / 'MAIN DATA',
             tp_vbeln,
             tp_auart.

  ENDMETHOD.                 "display_data

ENDCLASS.                    "lcl_sales_document IMPLEMENTATION
```

Then, we defined a second class for two types of sales documents: standard orders and rush orders. We show only the code that is related to the standard order here. This subclass inherits its methods from the superclass. The `constructor` method is called to make the data, which has already been defined in the superclass, available for the subclass. Note that the functionality of the `display_data` method is slightly changed. First the method of the superclass is called. Then, an attribute is added to the displayed data:

```
*--------------------------------------------------------------*
*        CLASS lcl_sales_document_ta DEFINITION
*--------------------------------------------------------------*
* Specific functionality for standard orders
*--------------------------------------------------------------*
CLASS lcl_sales_document_ta DEFINITION
                           INHERITING FROM lcl_sales_document.
   PUBLIC SECTION.
     METHODS: constructor  IMPORTING ist_vbak TYPE vbak,
            display_data  REDEFINITION.
   PROTECTED SECTION.

   PRIVATE SECTION.
* Attributes for this subclass
     DATA:
           tp_kunnr              TYPE kunnr.

ENDCLASS.                      "lcl_sales_document_ta DEFINITION
*--------------------------------------------------------------*
*        CLASS lcl_sales_document_ta IMPLEMENTATION
*--------------------------------------------------------------*
*
*--------------------------------------------------------------*
CLASS lcl_sales_document_ta IMPLEMENTATION.
   METHOD constructor.
     CALL METHOD super->constructor
       EXPORTING
         ist_vbak = ist_vbak.
* Set the other attributes
     tp_kunnr = ist_vbak-kunnr.

   ENDMETHOD.                     "constructor
   METHOD display_data.
     CALL METHOD super->display_data.
     WRITE: / 'Type TA: Extra attribute KUNNR', tp_kunnr.
   ENDMETHOD.                     "display_data
ENDCLASS.                      "lcl_sales_document_ta IMPLEMENTATION
```

Finally, the following report uses the functionality defined in the two related classes to process sales data. Note that the call of the `display_data` method (marked bold) doesn't need information about the specific sales document type, which is processed in order to be able to find the implementation on the correct class level.

```
REPORT /CTAC/EXAMPLE_INHERITANCE_1.

DATA: ta_vbak TYPE STANDARD TABLE OF vbak,
      wa_vbak TYPE vbak.

TYPES: ty_document TYPE REF TO lcl_sales_document.

DATA: rf_document  TYPE ty_document,
      ta_docrefs   TYPE STANDARD TABLE OF ty_document.

DATA: tp_classname TYPE string.

SELECT-OPTIONS: so_auart FOR wa_vbak-auart,
                so_vbeln FOR wa_vbak-vbeln OBLIGATORY.

START-OF-SELECTION.

  SELECT * FROM vbak INTO TABLE ta_vbak
  WHERE auart IN so_auart
    AND vbeln IN so_vbeln.

  LOOP AT ta_vbak INTO wa_vbak.
* Determine the name of the class, based on sales document type
    CALL METHOD lcl_sales_document=>determine_subclass
      EXPORTING
        itp_docty     = wa_vbak-auart
      IMPORTING
        etp_classname = tp_classname.
* Dynamic assignment of the correct subclass
    CREATE OBJECT rf_document TYPE (tp_classname) EXPORTING ist_vbak
                                                   = wa_vbak.
* Append the object reference to an internal table with
* object references
    APPEND rf_document TO ta_docrefs.

  ENDLOOP.
* The correct implementation of method DISPLAY_DATA
* is chosen automatically
  LOOP AT ta_docrefs INTO rf_document.
    CALL METHOD rf_document->display_data.
  ENDLOOP.
```

8.3.2 Using Interfaces

The second example of enhancing the maintainability of your code is based on reusing an `interface` definition in a class. This is another way of applying polymorphism in ABAP Objects. Don't confuse an interface with, for example, the interface parameters of a function module. In ABAP Objects, an *interface* is a kind of template definition for functionality. It cannot be used directly. However, its outer behavior, that is, the method names that are used, can be inherited by various classes. Unlike a subclass that can directly inherit the entire implementation of methods from its superclass (i.e., including all their associated functionality), a class that inherits an interface definition merely inherits the *right* to use the method names defined in the interface. The actual implementation of the method still needs to be done in the class. To summarize, two classes that use the same interface will inherit the method names defined in that interface, but all the associated code must be implemented twice.

What good this brings may not be apparent at first. Therefore, to demonstrate the practical advantages in terms of the maintainability of ABAP software, here's an example that should appeal to most ABAP developers. Imagine that you want to equip all the reports that you develop with the same capabilities for reusing ALV functionality. However, there are various versions of ALV functionality: a list version and a grid version (see Figure 8.12). But, you'd probably just want to include one general way of handling the output in all your reports, without having to maintain each individual report when the output functionality itself changes.

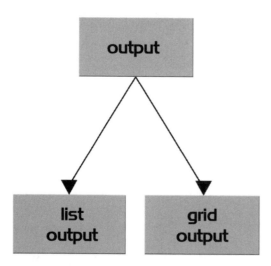

Figure 8.12 Different Output Types

We suppose that you'd like the end user to choose the output formatting version that is actually required. However, then, you would also have to prevent the ALV grid version from being used in the wrong circumstances, that is, when a SAP GUI is not available (see also Section 4.5.1).

The following pieces of code show a class-based way of dealing with these requirements. A class is created for each of the two output versions. Both classes inherit the way their functionality is called from one common interface definition. For practical reasons, we've used a local interface definition and local classes. In reality, you would use global interfaces and classes.

The interface that is reused by the two classes doesn't do much more than refer to the display_output method:

```
INTERFACE lif_output.
  METHODS: display_output IMPORTING idr_output TYPE REF TO data
                                    itp_tabnm   TYPE tabname.
  TYPE-POOLS: abap.

ENDINTERFACE.                     "lif_output
```

First, this interface is implemented in class lcl_output_alvlist. This class just represents a way of reusing the standard SAP function module reuse_alv_list_ display:

```
CLASS lcl_output_alvlist DEFINITION.
  PUBLIC SECTION.
    INTERFACES lif_output.

ENDCLASS.                     "lcl_output_alvlist DEFINITION

CLASS lcl_output_alvlist IMPLEMENTATION.
  METHOD lif_output~display_output.
    FIELD-SYMBOLS: <output>     TYPE STANDARD TABLE.
* Create a local handle for the data reference
    ASSIGN idr_output->* TO <output>.

    CALL FUNCTION 'REUSE_ALV_LIST_DISPLAY'
      EXPORTING
        i_structure_name = itp_tabnm
      TABLES
        t_outtab         = <output>
      EXCEPTIONS
        program_error    = 1
        OTHERS           = 2.
    IF sy-subrc <> 0.
* Exception handling here
    ENDIF.

  ENDMETHOD.                     "lif_output~display output
ENDCLASS.                      "lcl_output_alvlist IMPLEMENTATION
```

Then, the INTERFACES lif_output is also implemented in a second class representing functionality for displaying output with the *ALV grid* functionality. This class is wrapped around standard SAP function module reuse_alv_grid_display. In addition to creating a class-based solution, another check has been added to verify whether the grid functionality can be used. If the SAP GUI isn't available, you can't use the ALV grid function. In that case, use the ALV list instead.

In particular, note that by also wrapping the standard function for ALV grid functionality into a class that uses the same interface as the class for the ALV list, we have introduced one way of calling the functionality of both classes:

```
CLASS lcl_output_alvgrid DEFINITION.
  PUBLIC SECTION.
    INTERFACES lif_output.

ENDCLASS.                     "lcl_output_alvgrid DEFINITION

CLASS lcl_output_alvgrid IMPLEMENTATION.
  METHOD lif_output~display_output.
    FIELD-SYMBOLS: <output>    TYPE STANDARD TABLE.
    DATA: lrf_output TYPE REF TO lif_output.
    DATA: ltp_active TYPE boolean.

* Check if SAPGUI is ACTIVE
    CALL FUNCTION 'GUI_IS_AVAILABLE'
      IMPORTING
        return = ltp_active.

    IF ltp_active = abap_true.
* Create a local handle for the data reference
      ASSIGN idr_output->* TO <output>.

      CALL FUNCTION 'REUSE_ALV_GRID_DISPLAY'
        EXPORTING
          i_structure_name = itp_tabnm
        TABLES
          t_outtab         = <output>
        EXCEPTIONS
          program_error    = 1
          OTHERS           = 2.

      IF sy-subrc <> 0.
* Exception handling here
      ENDIF.
    ELSE.
* No SAP GUI Available: start the LIST version of the report
      CREATE OBJECT lrf_output TYPE lcl_output_alvlist.
* The correct method implementation is automatically chosen here.
```

```
      CALL METHOD lrf_output->display_output
        EXPORTING
          idr_output = idr_output
          itp_tabnm  = itp_tabnm.
    ENDIF.
  ENDMETHOD.                        "lif_output~display_output
ENDCLASS.                      "lcl_output_alvgrid IMPLEMENTATION
```

Finally, the following code represents an ABAP report whose output must be formatted. To do this, it calls the `display_output` general method that has been redefined in both the aforementioned classes. This ABAP report allows the end user to choose either the list or the grid version of the ALV functionality to format its output:

```
REPORT /ctac/example_polymorphism_1.


* Type-groups
TYPE-POOLS : abap.
* Data
DATA       : rf_output  TYPE REF TO lif_output.

DATA       : dr_output_tab  TYPE REF TO data.
FIELD-SYMBOLS
           : <output>   TYPE STANDARD TABLE.
* SELECTION-SCREEN
PARAMETERS : pa_tabnm   LIKE dd031-tabname  OBLIGATORY VALUE CHECK,
             pa_rowcn   TYPE i              OBLIGATORY DEFAULT 10 .

* Parameters that determine the type of output
PARAMETERS : pa_alvli   RADIOBUTTON GROUP rad1 DEFAULT 'X', "ALV LIST
             pa_alvgr   RADIOBUTTON GROUP rad1           . "ALV GRID

START-OF-SELECTION.
  TRY.
* Dynamic creation of internal table with same linetype as the used DB
* table
      CREATE DATA dr_output_tab TYPE TABLE OF (pa_tabnm).
* Fieldsymbol <output> will be the handle to manage the data reference
      ASSIGN dr_output_tab->* TO <output>.
* Dynamic * Dynamic SQL
      SELECT * FROM (pa_tabnm) INTO TABLE <output>
                              UP TO pa_rowcn ROWS.
*

      IF pa_alvli = abap_true.
        CREATE OBJECT rf_output TYPE lcl_output_alvlist.
      ELSEIF pa_alvgr = abap_true.
        CREATE OBJECT rf_output TYPE lcl_output_alvgrid.
      ELSE.
* Raise class-based exception here
```

```
      ENDIF.

      CATCH cx_sy_create_data_error.
*   Exception handling here
      CATCH cx_sy_no_handler.
*   Exception handling here
      CATCH cx_root.
*   Exception handling here
    ENDTRY.

END-OF-SELECTION.

    TRY.
*   The correct method implementation is automatically chosen here.
      CALL METHOD rf_output->display_output
        EXPORTING
          idr_output = dr_output_tab
          itp_tabnm  = pa_tabnm.

      CATCH cx_sy_no_handler.
*   Exception handling here
      CATCH cx_root.
*   Exception handling here
    ENDTRY.
```

Now, what are the advantages for maintainability of doing things class-based in this particular case? The same questions are valid here as in the previous section (8.3.1): What would the consequences be of adding new functionality, that is, a new way of formatting output? What would happen after a change in the existing functionality?

▶ New functionality for formatting output (for example, in spreadsheet format) can be implemented in a new class that uses the same interface. This means that new functionality can be introduced without having to adjust the way in which the associated functionality is *called* by ABAP reports. Again, you need to add only the new functionality in one place. So, if you had 100 different reports using the general method call display_output, nothing would change except, perhaps, things such as the parameters used on the selection-screen (because parameters are implementations of traditional reporting).[6]

▶ All the maintenance to existing output formatting functionality needs to be done in just one place. This means that you can change the actual implementation of each of the two output classes, but without having to change every single report that requires the new output format. If, for example, function

---

6 Note that our sample code should be slightly changed to facilitate this; the determination of the actual class should take place outside of the program, for example, in a function module or global method.

`reuse_alv_grid_display` was replaced by `reuse_alv_grid_display_lvc`, this only has to be changed in class `lcl_output_alvgrid`. That's all that needs to be done.

We conclude that, as in the previous example with one main class and various subclasses, the smart use of interface definitions also makes it possible to limit maintenance to the bare minimum. Of course, these are only examples. To further explore the possibilities of ABAP Objects, you should refer to the ABAP Objects reference book.[7]

8.4 Summary

In this chapter, we discussed three aspects of the maintainability of ABAP software. First, we showed you how to implement changes to standard SAP software in a way that makes the implementation of new versions of the standard software as easy as possible. Secondly, we suggested a number of ways to make your own ABAP software easily recognizable and reusable. We also presented several ways of reusing available standard ABAP software components such as function modules, existing reports, ALV functionality, SAPscript forms, and Smart Forms. In doing so, we emphasized the restrictions of copying standard development objects and changing such copies. We then gave you some practical tips and introduced tools that can help you to optimize the maintainability of your ABAP software.

Finally, we provided two examples of ABAP Objects implementations that should help you to further enhance the maintainability of ABAP software.

---

7 Horst Keller, Joachim Jacobitz, *ABAP Objects: The Official Reference*, SAP PRESS 2003.

9   Checking Robustness and Troubleshooting

In the previous chapters, we discussed the different kinds of criteria to use in order to evaluate the technical quality of customized ABAP software. In this chapter, we'll show you which tools and techniques you can use to evaluate the technical quality of your ABAP code. SAP provides numerous tools that can help you check the technical quality of ABAP code, and analyze and solve the problems that can occur. When checking the quality of the code, and troubleshooting potential and existing problems, developers often need to know which are the optimal tools necessary in order to meet each particular situation. We will address these issues in this chapter.

There are two occasions when you may need to verify the technical quality of your ABAP code—during development and problem-solving. Knowing how to problem-solve and knowing which tools to apply and when to apply them are both very useful skills, and can come in very handy, especially when a problem occurs in a production system; for example, program dumps, error messages, incorrect data, and missing updates. You should note that these skills are also required for situations other than emergencies, that is, when a program is created or changed.

The two main sections in this chapter deal with the two aforementioned circumstances (i.e., development and problem-solving) in which the technical quality of ABAP programs may have to be evaluated. Section 9.1 shows you how to use SAP tools during the regular development process. Whenever appropriate, we'll refer to the following chapters: Chapter 3 (Correctness), Chapter 4 (Stability), Chapter 5 (Exception Handling), Chapter 6 (User Friendliness), Chapter 7 (Performance), and Chapter 8 (Maintainability). Section 9.2 shows you how to use SAP tools to troubleshoot problems that can occur in a production system. Our primary goal here is to show you how to find the causes of problems as quickly as possible. Most of the tools mentioned are already well known to most programmers. Nevertheless, we'll discuss some of these tools in more detail in order to present those less familiar test options.

9.1   Changes and New Developments

This section discusses which tools and techniques are best suited for a developer who needs to check aspects of robustness during development and maintenance. Because it's impossible to foresee every problem that can arise during the initial development, you need tools to support you during each stage of development. The same holds true when updating an exisiting program.

In this section, we'll address four main topics. In Section 9.1.1, we'll give you some practical guidelines for finding, creating, and reusing test data, in addition to providing you with several standard test scenarios in detail. Next, in Section 9.1.2, we'll define *colleague checks*. In Section 9.1.3, we'll present several long checklists for testing robustness that can be used in a colleague check. Finally, in Section 9.1.4, we'll discuss various standard SAP tools and show you the kinds of quality checks for which these tools can best be applied.

9.1.1 General Guidelines for Testing

This Section is devoted to general guidelines that are intended for the ABAP developer. First, we discuss a practical approach for finding test data. Then, we indicate which test cases to look for: both predictable standard test situations and unpredictable test situations. Lastly, we present which SAP tools are available to support you when testing smaller units of code.

Finding Test Data

ABAP developers must know how to create, use, and reuse test data. Often, they're expected to do this completely by themselves, which is not an easy task. Composing proper test data presupposes considerable knowledge of both business processes and SAP logic. However, most developers won't have this in-depth knowledge. Nevertheless, they may even be expected to create their own test data in situations where both the business process and the corresponding SAP implementation are new to them. Therefore, as an all-around ABAP developer, you must know more than just how to use the development tools and the ABAP programming language. Quickly familiarizing yourself with the main functionality of a new SAP application component is also part of your job. Even if help is scarce, you have little choice: either you can invest a significant amount of your time to understand the business logic, the SAP application, and the composition of test data; or, you can do very limited testing, or no testing at all. Therefore, let's begin by providing some general tips on how to navigate through a specific SAP environment as quickly as possible, how to find proper test data, and how to create reusable test situations:

▶ **Getting Acquainted with an Application**
  The first thing to do when a development must be made on top of an existing SAP application component is to familiarize yourself with this application and the most important database tables that it uses. One way to get an overview is by using the available Data Model (Transaction SD11). However, the best approach is to ask an experienced functional specialist (i.e., a consultant or a key user) to show you the most important programs and transactions of the

component, and explain the associated business logic. For example, if you're new to plant maintenance, you should become familiar with Transaction IW31—its most predominantly used transaction.

▶ **Finding Test Data**

However, finding the most important database tables of an application component is usually something you must be prepared to do yourself. The people who know all about the functionality of an application component won't always be able to explain the more technical details as well.

You can find database tables by carefully examining which data an important transaction uses. We recommend using the Debugger or SQL Trace (Transaction ST05) during the execution of such a transaction. Both tools can help to determine the tables that contain relevant test data, and the underlying relations between table rows. Once you've established these tables and relations, you can use standard ABAP Dictionary tools such as Transaction SE11 to provide additional information on the structure of the data and the relations between the data (on the basis of the value tables). Finally, by using the Data Browser (Transaction SE16) or the QuickViewer (Transaction SQVI), you can look at the existing data.

▶ **Creating Reusable Test Data**

Because testing usually isn't as much fun as developing code, we recommend that you make creating test data as easy as possible. Since a considerable number of customized programs added on top of standard SAP functionality pertain to reports, we must stress the importance of creating selection variants as a way to make your test data more reusable. In addition, consider giving each selection variant that you use a name that is intuitive so you and others can easily remember the original purpose of this variant. Therefore, please avoid names such as "Test 1," "Test 2," and so forth. Instead, use names that refer to the test case itself, such as "Test U.S. date settings." The same holds true when using the standard SAP test tool CATT (or its successor eCATT) to test update (Screen) functionality, which primarily concerns database updates.

Looking for Standard Test Situations

Apart from being able to establish proper test data, a developer must be able to create the most important (or critical) situations to be tested. This is particularly true for exceptional and extreme situations that should trigger a program's error-handling logic. Most exceptional situations usually won't be tested by people who have no development knowledge, such as consultants and key users. They simply can't be expected to look into the code and recognize the most critical errors. As we discussed in Chapter 3 and Chapter 4, a lack of error handling can lead to incorrect data or unstable program behavior.

In general, establishing exceptional test situations is a fairly straightforward process. Since the benefits—in terms of quality assurance—can also be relatively high, we recommend that you do this for every unit of ABAP code.

Here are some examples of standard test cases:

▶ Zero-values and amounts: verify whether divide-by-zero dumps can occur; if they can occur, check whether they can be prevented; and if they cannot be prevented, check whether such runtime errors are caught correctly (see Section 4.2.1).

▶ Maximum-values and amounts: verify whether field-overflow dumps can occur, and whether large values are displayed correctly.

▶ Negative values and amounts: verify whether the sign is taken into account; in calculations, in IF and CASE statements, and in screen or list displays.

▶ Database data not found: verify whether appropriate error handling is present and whether the variables that are involved are cleared correctly (see Section 3.4.1).

▶ Database updates not successful: verify whether the error handling is correct and whether the rollback mechanism has been implemented correctly in order to prevent database inconsistencies (see Section 3.5.2).

▶ Exceptions for function modules and methods: verify whether the program anticipates these exceptions, sends a message, and initializes the variables involved (see Section 5.2).

▶ Errors in internal table processing: verify whether the program anticipates these exceptions, sends a message, and initializes the variables involved (see Section 3.4).

▶ Changed user properties: verify whether your program reacts properly to another date or decimal format, another time zone, or another language setting (see Section 4.5.3).

▶ Changed process type: verify whether the behavior of an *all-around* program is equally stable both in the dialog task and in the background task (see Section 4.5.1).

While the test cases themselves are straightforward, creating the corresponding test data may sometimes be rather time-consuming. In order to gain time, you can use the Debugger to change values with the *Replace* option, thereby simulating the input. See the section on the Debugger (9.4.1) for more details.

The 'Fool-Proof' Test

In addition to testing standard situations that can be derived from the program logic, you can also take the complete opposite approach: just ignore the logic and see how a program reacts to unpredictable and seemingly meaningless input (i.e., input that makes no sense, which could be entered due to an inadvertent error on the part of the user). This might help you find errors in your program that wouldn't otherwise be detected via testing with normal input.

Note that input for this kind of test can be provided either manually or by other programs.

If data is supplied via screen input, you must anticipate that a user can be anyone from an absolute beginner to an experienced expert. Fortunately, most front-ends already contain automatic checks. For example, the SAP GUI will verify whether the value entered in a date field on a screen is actually a valid date. However, this implies that everything that is *not* checked automatically by the user interface should be checked by your program. You simply can't rely on the assumption that meaningless data won't be entered.

If a program is dependent on other programs for its input, the situation is not entirely comparable. Consider, for example, an IDoc interface. In this case, no automatic checks on input are performed, therefore, all such checks must be included in your own code; for example, a check on invalid date values in interface data provided by another program.

Testing Code Units

Not all testing has to cover complete programs. You can also test separate modularization units. Checking a method or function module separately should be done preferably prior to testing the applications that call this unit. Here, we'll describe the three different options that SAP offers for testing ABAP code on a unit level: testing function modules, testing global class methods, and ABAP Unit testing.

▶ **Testing Function Modules**

The oldest way to test a separate unit of ABAP code as a *black box* (i.e., checking only the input and output of the unit, and not the separate unit of ABAP code) was created for function modules. A function module can be debugged (with Transaction SE37) like a regular program. The fact that you need to enter all the input data yourself can sometimes be a problem. Fortunately, however, SAP enables you to store test input data together with each function module for later reuse.

It is not only possible to store test input data for a function module: the same holds true for test results. This is relevant for doing so-called *regression tests:* the values that the function returns are stored and compared later with the output of prior tests (see Figure 9.1). This kind of test is suitable when the technical implementation of a function module is changed; for example, to improve performance. Consequently, you can quickly test whether the output of the function is still the same.

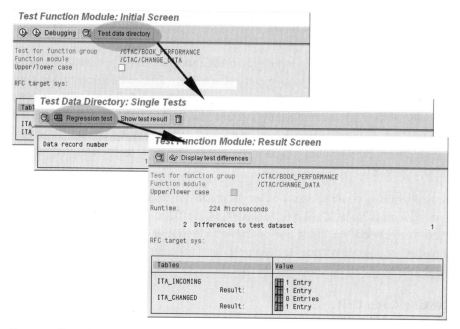

Figure 9.1 Executing a Regression Test for a Function Module

▶ **Testing Global Classes**

With the introduction of global classes, maintained with the Class Builder (SE24), it was also logical to expect SAP to provide separate class-testing facilities. If an instance method is tested, the test environment automatically creates the object. The separate methods can then be tested in the same way as function modules (see Figure 9.2). However, no possibilities yet exist for saving test input and executing regression tests with global classes.

▶ **Testing with ABAP Unit**

As of Web AS Release 6.40, new unit testing functionality is available under the name "ABAP Unit." The associated functionality allows for testing specific modularization units that are called within a program, such as form routines or methods. This functionality provides ways to separate the input data for a test run, to execute an isolated unit test, and to display the corresponding test results. The functionality is based on the extension of a local class and at least one method with the variant FOR TESTING. The code to be tested must be placed inside the test method. There is a special global class CL_AUNIT_ ASSERT that provides methods that help to verify the test results. This tool looks very promising.

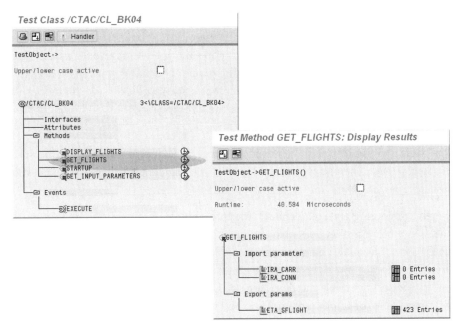

Figure 9.2 Testing a Global Class

9.1.2 Colleague Checks

So far, we have discussed some practical tips for testing that were particularly oriented towards individual ABAP programmers. Obviously, there is much more to be said about this subject; for example, there are many test methodologies that can be used to further improve the quality of software development. Here, however, we have chosen to focus on some practical measures that can help individual developers assume less responsibility for having to check their own work.

There are various reasons why code checks made by the author of a piece of code are insufficient means to achieve an increase of the quality of developments. Apart from the fact that no developer is infallible, not every programmer has the same amount of experience and knowledge. Furthermore, even experienced programmers may, over time, have developed blind spots for their own routine mistakes. Other circumstances can also influence the quality of individually performed tests; for example, sometimes, due to the pressure of meeting certain milestones, developers focus solely on delivering the asked-for functionality, and inadvertently neglect other issues.

Therefore, lasting quality improvements cannot depend just on the initiative of individual developers. Additional measures must be implemented by the surrounding development organization in order to achieve these improvements.

The *colleague check* or *peer review* is such an addition. A peer review or colleague check is a review of a piece of program code by one or more colleagues.[1] The principle of consistently having another developer check the work of a colleague has the advantage that it can be implemented relatively quickly, and yet it doesn't require investments in non-SAP test tools, new testing methods, and training programs.

The tools and the test approach used during a colleague check need not be special: a colleague check can be done by using the standard SAP test tools, but also just by reviewing the code itself.

When considering colleague checks, the first solution that might come to mind is to set in motion a strict and far-reaching implementation process orchestrated by an independent quality assurance team, which can be made up of employees who are both internal and external to the company. This team maintains quality standards, checks how these standards are used, organizes feedback to individual programmers and development groups, and reports findings to IT management. However, we don't expect you to adopt these ambitious measures in order to be effective. There is always the possibility that programmers of one team can agree to check each other's work (small companies with only one ABAP developer could consider hiring an external expert from time to time). Not only can this be a significant step towards quality improvement; it also has the added advantage that it can be started immediately.

Therefore, let's now consider the benefits of peer reviews, as well as some practical questions, and common pitfalls.

Benefits

The main direct benefits of colleague checks are:

▶ Most errors in the program logic that are directly linked to the required functionality are detected at a relatively early stage. This will lead to less problems in the delivered functionality and less rework.

---

[1] For an extensive article on code reviews, see the *SAP Professional Journal*, Volume 5, Issue 4 (July/August 2003).

▶ Errors in the technical quality of software are also detected earlier, especially if checklists (see Section 9.1.3) and checking tools (see Section 9.1.4) are used.

Other more indirect benefits can also be expected:

▶ The knowledge about newly developed programs is more easily spread among developers.

▶ Both the general level of ABAP knowledge and the knowledge of technical quality standards increase. Note that knowledge won't necessarily be transferred only from the experienced to the less experienced; a new developer can also teach new ABAP features to an old developer. Often, experienced developers continue to use obsolete ABAP commands rather than explore newer and better ones. In short, old habits die hard.

Various studies[2] have been conducted to determine the effects of code reviews done by colleagues. All of these studies report impressive improvements in terms of quality, time spent on solving production problems, and cost savings. To understand why (refers to the cost savings), note in particular that the amount of time spent on testing and rework can be a significant percentage of the total development effort in development projects (e.g., up to 60% of the total development time).

It is precisely this amount of rework that can be drastically reduced via a proper implementation of peer reviews; for example, in the aforementioned studies, a ten-fold reduction of error-solving costs is cited.

A particular misconception about peer reviews is that they're time-consuming. To the contrary, these same studies (as referenced above) show that each hour spent on code reviews is offset many times by tangible reductions in testing efforts and rework.

Although these studies were oriented towards programming languages other than ABAP, we have no reason to believe that the results would differ substantially with ABAP developments.

Implementation

If you're convinced that peer reviews can work, some practical questions naturally arise, when proposing the implementation of colleague checks. Consider questions such as: What to check? How to perform the check? And what to do with the results?

---

2 David F. Jenkins, "Put Better Programs into Production in Less Time with Code Reviews: What They Are, How to Conduct Them, and Why," *SAP Professional Journal,* Volume 5, Issue 4 (July/August 2003).

We have the following suggestions:

▶ **What to Check**
The scope of a peer review of SAP software involves the ABAP code and related objects such as ABAP Dictionary objects and documentation. The check is targeted first at robustness issues, such as correct error handling, acceptable performance, and correct use of standards, clear program structure, and understandable inline documentation. The reviewer should be able to understand the code fairly quickly. In addition, the reviewer may sometimes be able to offer alternative solutions for specific programming problems; for example, by pointing at available standard functions or methods.

▶ **How to Perform the Check**
As the name suggests, a code review basically means getting a detailed look at the code. You cannot rely completely on automated tools. Nevertheless, automated tools are a valuable addition because they can make part of the testing activities much more efficient. In order to accelerate manual checks, we recommend that you use checklists of criteria and apply these checks in your testing. You can use the checklists in Section 9.1.3 as a prototype from which to create your own. You could even consider developing your own tools to perform specific checks, however, don't underestimate how time-consuming this development would be.

▶ **What to Do with the Results**
Executing a colleague check is useless if you don't know beforehand what to do with the results. Therefore, you must first determine what to do with the several types of results, that is, what type of checking result should lead to must-changes, what type to nice-to-have, and so on. A practical way of doing this is by classifying the findings into categories such as *must-change*, *change recommended*, and *nice-to-have*. Then, you need to decide what measures should be taken if there are findings related to one of these categories. At least every finding classified as a *must-change* should be sufficient reason to actually apply changes to the checked code and test it again.

Pitfalls

Before you can start applying colleague checks, we should warn you against being overly optimistic—you will undoubtedly encounter obstacles that you will need to overcome. Here is where we should emphasize the two critical success factors: the need for management involvement and a mutual trust among the developers. Perseverance is another critical requirement for all involved.

▶ **Commitment**

Both IT management and the developers must be fully convinced of the added value of peer reviews; without their full support, these reviews will inevitably fail. This requires a full commitment to the required changes. Change is never easy. Various arguments against the introduction of peer reviews will be used: they cost extra time and money; the project planning is already tight; the organization is not ready for it; the quality of the developers is already high enough. The easiest conclusion is always that there is no real need for peer reviews. The only answer that we can give is that the improvement figures as summarized by David F. Jenkins should speak for themselves.

IT management needs to actively support the implementation of code reviews by ensuring that time is allocated for such reviews, even if deadlines are looming. Developers need to support the implementation of code reviews by actively participating in them. This requires a mutual trust. Without it, remarks from other team members aren't accepted. It's also helpful to have a developer in the group whose expertise is widely respected.

Above all, we should emphasize that peer reviews should be regarded as a means of improving the quality of the programs, not the overall quality of the programmer's skills. If the IT management attempts to use the results of colleague checks to review its developers, the very purpose of the checks is no longer about ensuring quality, and consequently, failure is the most likely outcome.

▶ **Expectations**

The second obstacle to overcome is that the expectations may initially be inflated. Immediately following the start of colleague checks, many quality issues are often revealed. Although this is proof that code reviews work, this will often contribute to an increase in development time. However, at some point, what the developers have learned from these peer reviews will be implemented at an earlier stage in the code development, and quality will be integrated from the beginning, that is, while the ABAP code is being written. Then, the amount of rework will decrease; programmers will deliver higher quality code; and, the additional amount of time built into the process will be offset entirely by the increase in development productivity.

▶ **Embedding Peer Reviews in Routine Activities in Development**

The embedding of the actual peer review in routine activites in development may initially cause some difficulties. A peer review is preferably set in motion before people other than ABAP developers, such as *functional specialists* (consultants), start testing the new functionality. In real-time, this means the moment before the related transport request is released to an acceptance test environment. In addition to the time reserved for the code review, time must be allotted to implement at least the *must-change* remarks. Peer reviews cannot be conducted at this point because there has to be ample time to properly review the code before any peer reviews can take place.

During the planning of activities, the programmer's personal experience and the complexity of the proposed work should also be considered. If a relatively large program is written by an inexperienced programmer, it is preferable to organize several reviews during the course of development, particulary in its early stages.

9.1.3 Checklists for Testing Robustness

Checklists are particularly useful during colleague checks (discussed in Section 9.1.2). These checklists can be embedded in the development process in order to verify whether a particular development object should be released for transport to another environment; for example, these checklists could be used by the person responsible for releasing and transporting development objects.

Another reason for using checklists is to ensure the minimum quality level of all ABAP development objects that can be accepted, regardless of the developer who created them. Over time, the checklists can be expanded and the level of quality required can be steadily increased. In this way, quality assurance becomes an ongoing process.

In this section, we have included sample checklists that were composed separately for each main aspect of robustness, as discussed in most of the other chapters. You may want to use these checklists as a prototype when first creating your own checklists. The order of the checklists is the same as the order of the individual topics in each corresponding chapter. For each single topic, we provided a reference to the place where it was discussed in detail.

Correctness

Are database selections executed correctly?

▶ Is the full table key used if exactly one row needs to be selected from a database table?
(See Section 3.2.1.)

▶ Are complex WHERE clauses avoided? (See Section 3.2.2.)

▶ Is the selected data checked on their validity date or delete flag? (See Section 3.2.3.)

▶ If a database view is used, are the consequences of inner join processing clear? (See Section 3.2.4.)

- ▶ If the `FOR ALL ENTRIES` option is used, is it used properly? (See Section 3.2.4.)
  - ▶ Is a check included to see whether the internal table has been filled?
  - ▶ Is it ensured that the resulting table contains unique combinations of values?
- ▶ If authorization functionality is included, have the consequences of not having an authorization been checked? (See Section 3.2.5.)

Is processing executed correctly?

- ▶ Is the correct reference field used when processing amount or quantity fields? (See Section 3.3.1.)
- ▶ Are rounding problems avoided? (See Section 3.3.2.)
  - ▶ Are computations placed in the right sequence?
  - ▶ Is the use of intermediate values avoided if these values aren't really necessary?
  - ▶ If intermediate values are required, do they have the right type and number of decimal places?
- ▶ Is the `ON CHANGE OF` command avoided? (See Section 3.3.3.)
- ▶ Is the combination of the `LOOP AT <itab> WHERE` command with the use of an `AT` event avoided? (See Section 3.3.3.)
- ▶ If interactive reporting statements are used, has the `CLEAR` command been used?
  (See Section 3.3.4.)
- ▶ Is interactive reporting functionality used where dialog functionality would have been more appropriate? (See Section 3.3.4.)
- ▶ Are all global data cleared correctly? (See Section 3.4.1.)
  - ▶ During internal table processing?
  - ▶ In the workarea for selecting data from database tables?
  - ▶ During function module processing (the global data of the function group)? (See Section 3.4.5)
- ▶ Is global data handled properly in module pools? (See Section 3.4.4.)
- ▶ Is the `TABLES` statement avoided? (See Section 3.4.3.)
- ▶ Is the use of external subroutines avoided if preferable alternatives (function module or class methods) are available? (See Section 3.4.2.)

Note: Several of these guidelines don't need to be emphasized if you used ABAP Objects instead of traditional ABAP. (See Section 3.4.7.)

Are updates handled correctly?

▶ If unique numbering for a customized database table is required, is standard SAP number range functionality used for inserting data? (See Section 3.5.1.)

▶ Are standard SAP lock objects used well? (See Section 3.5.1.)

  ▷ Is locking also applied in background functionality?

  ▷ Are locks set as soon as possible, and released as late as possible?

  ▷ Are exclusive locks used for update functionality?

  ▷ Has it been decided whether a lock is required for display functionality?

▶ Is SAP's Logical Unit of Work (LUW) concept used properly? (See Section 3.5.2.)

Are interfaces processed correctly?

▶ Has the proper interfacing principle been applied: either *best effort*, *exactly once*, or *exactly once in order*? (See Section 3.6.2.)

▶ If an *exactly once* scenario is required:

  ▷ Does all the interface data carry its own identifier?

  ▷ Is each identifier explicitly checked on both ends of the interface? (See Section 3.6.2.)

▶ Is some kind of locking principle applied for interface files (particularly for interface files waiting to be processed)? (See Section 3.6.3.)

  ▷ Was everything that was necessary done to prevent the same file from being processed twice?

  ▷ Are you sure that the receiving end of the interface cannot start processing until the sending end has finished its job?

Stability

Are programming errors due to wrong type use avoided?
(See Section 4.2.1)

▶ Are program dumps avoided (with `CATCH...ENDCATCH` or `TRY...CATCH...ENDTRY`)?

▶ Is a division by zero avoided?

▶ Are large enough variables defined (especially in arithmetic)?

▶ Are type-conflicts avoided?

▶ If function modules are called:

  ▷ Are all mandatory interface parameters filled?

  ▷ Do the actual interface parameters have the correct type definition?

- ▶ If data is transferred from one structure to another using an offset and length specification, is the transferred data defined with identical types?
- ▶ If data is transferred by copying the contents of an entire structure to another, are the structures defined identically?
- ▶ In the case of executing a repetitive statement such as:
  - ▷ `ADD f1 THEN f2 UNTIL fz`
  - ▷ `DO VARYING f FROM f1 NEXT f2`
  - ▷ `WHILE ... VARY f FROM f1 NEXT f2`

  Are all fields from `f1` to `f2` to `fz` defined with the same type and length?

Are endless loops avoided?
(See Section 4.2.2)

- ▶ In the case of `DO...ENDDO` or `WHILE...ENDWHILE` loops:
  - ▷ Has an exit-condition been defined?
- ▶ In the case of recursive programming:
  - ▷ Has an exit-condition been defined?

Is the wrong use of dynamic data avoided?
(See Section 4.3.1)

- ▶ Are program dumps avoided (with `CATCH...ENDCATCH` or `TRY...CATCH...ENDTRY`)?
- ▶ Is a check included to verify whether field symbols are actually assigned (using `IS ASSIGNED`)?
- ▶ Is a check included to verify whether data has been created (using `IS BOUND`)?
- ▶ Are type-conflicts avoided?
  - ▷ When assigning variables to field symbols?
  - ▷ When creating data using the `CREATE DATA` statement (data references)?
- ▶ If an instance is created with a dynamic reference to a class:
  - ▷ Is a check included to verify whether the class exists?
  - ▷ Is the reference type compatible with the original class?
- ▶ If a method is being called for a specific instance:
  - ▷ Is a check included to verify whether the instance is still available (using `NOT IS INITIAL`)?

Is the wrong use of dynamic SQL avoided?
(See Section 4.3.1)

- ▶ In the case of a dynamic database table name:
  - ▷ Is a check included to verify whether the database table exists?

- In the case of a dynamic field list:
  - Is a check included to verify whether the fields exist in the database table?
  - Will the result set have the same type definition as the field list in the `SELECT` statement?
- In the case of a dynamic `WHERE` clause, will the syntax be valid at runtime?

Are wrong dynamic calls avoided?
(See Section 4.3.2)

- In the case of a `SUBMIT`, is a check included to verify whether the called program exists
  (Database table TRDIR)?
- In the case of a `CALL TRANSACTION`, is a check included to verify whether the called transaction exists (Database table TSTC)?
- Are dynamic subroutine calls avoided?
- In the case of a function module:
  - Is a check included to verify whether the function module exists (Database table TFDIR)?
  - Will all the formally required parameters be passed to the function module in the right format?
- In the case of a class method:
  - Is a check included to verify whether the method exists (Database table SEOCOMPO)?
  - Will all the formally required parameters be passed to the method in the right format?

Is a program protected against changes in its outer environment?

- In the case of background jobs or Remote Function Calls (RFCs), are specific SAP user IDs applied? (See Section 4.4.1.)
- Are direct native OS commands avoided (by using function module `SXPG_COMMAND_EXECUTE`)? (See Section 4.4.2.)
- Are "hard-coded" pathnames or filenames avoided (by using Transaction FILE)? (See Section 4.4.3)
- In the case of file transfer from or to another system: (See Section 4.4.4.)
  - Is the code page specified?
  - If the externally and internally used code pages don't match, are conversion techniques used?

- If an ABAP program calls functionality of an application running on a client: (See Section 4.4.5.)

  - Does your program react properly if this functionality is not available on the client?

Is the use of a program in the wrong circumstances avoided?

- In the case of interaction on the basis of dynpros: (See Section 4.5.1.)

  - Is a check included to verify whether a SAP GUI is available (by using function module 'gui_is_available)?

- In the case of using control technology: (See Section 4.5.1.)

  - Is a check included to verify whether a SAP GUI is available (by using function module `gui_is_available`)?

- In the case of using the dialog task: (See Section 4.5.1.)

  - Is a time-out prevented?

- In the case of interactive reporting: (See Section 4.5.1.)

  - Is a check included to verify whether a SAP GUI is available (by using function module (`gui_is_available`)?

- In the case of custom-update functionality: (See Section 4.5.2.)

  - Has the use of update task functionality been considered?

- In the case of parallel processing using `STARTING NEW TASK`: (See Section 4.5.2.)

  - Is a check included to verify whether sufficient resources (tasks) are available?

  - If a new task is started in an external system:

  * Is a check included to verify whether this external system exists?

  * Is a check included to verify whether communication with the external system is possible
  (e.g., in case of authorization errors)?

- If a customized transaction is reused in BDC processing: (See Section 4.5.3.)

  - Have the limitations of BDC processing been considered?

- If a customized program calls one or more standard SAP transactions with BDC processing (`CALL TRANSACTION`, `CALL DIALOG`, `Batch Input`): (See Section 4.5.3.)

  - Are date, quantity, and amount fields used according to the user settings?

  - If the called transaction uses table controls, is the default screen size used for both creating and processing the screen data?

Exception Handling

Is Exception Handling implemented?

▶ Does the ABAP code comply with company standards regarding exception handling if available?

▶ Are explicit exceptions raised when needed? (See Section 5.2.1.)

  ▶ Are remote callable functions passing their results using a formal interface parameter?

  ▶ Are not-remote callable functions passing their results raising EXCEPTIONS or using a formal interface parameter?

  ▶ Are subroutines passing their results to calling programs using a formal interface parameter?

▶ Are implicit and explicit signals of exceptions intercepted by the program? (See Section 5.2.1.)

  ▶ Are all possible returncodes intercepted?

  ▶ Are unexpected data values intercepted with WHEN OTHERS or ELSE options?

  ▶ Are interface parameters containing results of a procedures validated?

  ▶ Are all EXCEPTIONS of functions or methods linked to a returncode?

  ▶ In case of a SAP release up to 4.6, are catchable runtime errors caught using CATCH ... ENDCATCH?

  ▶ In case of the SAP Web Application Server, are catchable runtime errors caught using TRY. ... ENDTRY?

  ▶ In case of the Web Application Server, are all explicitly raised Class-Based exceptions caught using TRY ... ENDTRY?

▶ Are proper exception messages sent? (See Section 5.2.2.)

  ▶ Does the content of a message take the experience of the receiver into account?

  ▶ Does the message help the receiver with regard to what steps to take next?

  ▶ Has the use of Application Logging been considered and implemented?

  ▶ In case of no user interactivity, will messages be send to the correct person or persons?

▶ Are the correct cleanup actions executed? (See Section 5.2.2.)

  ▶ Are variables initialized using CLEAR or REFRESH statements?

  ▶ Are variables reset to values they had prior to the procedure?

  ▶ Are database updates rolled back using the ROLLBACK WORK statement?

In case of developing on a SAP Web Application Server, is Class-Based Exception-Handling implemented?

▶ Is the timing of catching class-based exceptions correct? (See Section 5.3.3.)

  ▶ Are all explicitly raised exceptions caught or propagated up the Call Stack using the RAISING option?

  ▶ Are all implicitly raised exceptions of the dynamic or no-check type at least caught in the mainline of the program by catching exception class CX_SY_NO_HANDLER?

  ▶ Are all types of class-based exceptions that can occur in the mainline of the program caught by catching exception class CX_ROOT in every TRY... ENDTRY block?

▶ Is all relevant context information gathered from the exception object? (See Section 5.3.3.)

▶ Are all types of exception signals converted into class-based exceptions? (See Section 5.3.4.)

▶ Does the raised class-based exception match the actual problem? (See Section 5.3.5.)

▶ In case of custom exception classes, do they inherit from the correct type of superclass?
(See Section 5.3.3.)

User-Friendliness

Is the look-and-feel of the application standardized?
(See Section 6.2.1.)

▶ Are the ABAP Dictionary definitions reused for all fields (to include the same help information and standard field labels as elsewhere)?

▶ In the case of a selection-screen:

  ▶ Are the selection criteria placed in their logical sequence (the most important fields on top)?

  ▶ Are related selection criteria logically grouped in a separate frame?

  ▶ Are the right types of input fields used for all selection criteria, for example radiobuttons, checkboxes, pushbuttons?

▶ In the case of report output:

  ▶ Have the ergonomic standards available in Transaction LIBS been used?

  ▶ Has the use of *ABAP List Viewer* (ALV) been considered?

- ▶ In case of customized dynpros:
  - ▶ Have the ergonomic standards available in Transaction BIBS been used?
- ▶ In case of customized menus:
  - ▶ Are standard functions defined on the basis of the available templates?

**Is the behavior of the ABAP program standardized?
(See Section 6.2.2.)**

- ▶ Are the ABAP Dictionary definitions reused for all fields (to include the same conversion exits, possible entries, and value checks as elsewhere)?
- ▶ Is the cursor placed on the most logical place (usually on the first input field, or on the most logical pushbutton in a pop-up screen)?
- ▶ Are messages sent when needed, for example:
  - ▶ If a report has not selected any data?
  - ▶ If an update has been executed?
  - ▶ If no data has been changed in a transaction?
- ▶ Are all checks that may result in a message timed to be executed as soon as possible?
- ▶ If a message is sent:
  - ▶ Will the message make sense to the end user?
  - ▶ Will the end user know how to react?
- ▶ In the case of modal windows:
  - ▶ If an **ENTER** icon is used, is it actually linked to the **ENTER** key?
  - ▶ Is the **ESC** symbol linked to the **ESC** key?
- ▶ In the case of a report:
  - ▶ Does the report contain a START-OF-SELECTION event (to prevent it from being started by pressing **ENTER**)?
- ▶ In the case of updates:
  - ▶ If the user leaves the transaction without saving changed data, is the correct pop-up screen shown ("Are you sure?" and with the cursor placed on the answer "No")
  - ▶ If the user leaves the transaction without saving unchanged data, is a pop-up screen to confirm this avoided?

Navigation and Support

- ▶ Is it easy to navigate directly to the most important screens and fields? (See Section 6.3.2.)
- ▶ Are screens that are not important for all users skipped where possible? (See Section 6.3.2.)

- Is there a way to navigate directly to a detail screen for one specific item? (See Section 6.3.2.)
- Are parameter IDs used to provide the user with field-values that the user already has entered previously: (See Section 6.3.3.)
  - Activated in dynpro screens (GPA/SPA)?
  - Programmed in selection-screens (memory ID)?
- Are unnecessary messages avoided? (See Section 6.3.4.)

Performance

Is processing on the database server optimized?

- Is an efficient index available for every database table? (See Section 7.2.1.)
  - If an index does not seem available, are alternative database tables available (e.g., selection of documents via the document flow, selection of financial documents, and sales documents by status, selection of sales data via master data)?
- Is each index used properly? (See Section 7.2.1.)
  - Are all relevant index fields used?
  - Are the first index fields used?
  - Are index fields with initial values also used?
  - Can extensive use of select-options disturb index usage?
  - Are NOT or NE conditions avoided in the WHERE clause?
  - Are wildcards avoided in the WHERE clause?
  - Are complex WHERE clauses avoided? (Refer also to the checklist for Correctness)
  - Is the FOR ALL ENTRIES option applied on only index fields?
  - If an ORDER BY clause is used, does it have the same sorting order as the index used?
- If the creation of a secondary index is unavoidable: (See Section 7.2.1.)
  - Is the number of fields in the index reduced to the minimum?
  - Is a clever sequence for the index fields chosen (the most distinctive fields first)?
- After implementing the SQL statement: Has the SQL Trace been used in a representative environment (acceptance) in order to verify index use? (See Section 7.2.1.)

Is the data traffic between the database server and the application server minimized?

▶ Are the database rows selected limited by a proper WHERE clause? (See Section 7.3.1.)

▶ Are the fields selected limited to the fields actually needed (in a field list)? (See Section 7.3.2.)

▶ Are SELECT...ENDSELECT statements avoided (by using the INTO TABLE option)? (See Section 7.3.3.)

▶ Are nested SELECT-statements avoided? (See Section 7.3.3.)

▶ Are multiple SELECT SINGLE statements on the same database table avoided (by using the FOR ALL ENTRIES option)? (See Section 7.3.3.)

▶ Are aggregate functions used if possible? (See Section 7.3.3.)

Is processing on the application server optimized?

▶ If nested loop processing is done on internal tables: (See Sections 7.4.3.)

  ▶ Is the nested table not defined as a HASHED table?

  ▶ If the nested internal table is a SORTED table, does the WHERE clause refer to the key of the SORTED table?

  ▶ If the nested internal table is a STANDARD table, is the FROM clause used?

▶ If direct reads must be executed on an internal table: (See Sections 7.4.3.)

  ▶ If the internal table is accessed directly, has it been defined as a HASHED table?

  ▶ If the internal table must be a SORTED table, does the WITH KEY clause refer to the key of the SORTED table?

  ▶ If the internal table must be a STANDARD table, is the BINARY SEARCH option explicitly applied?

▶ If new entries must be added to an internal table, are table rows added collectively (e.g., by using APPEND LINES)? (See Section 7.4.3.)

▶ If an internal table's contents need to be changed, are table rows changed collectively (e.g., by using MODIFY WHERE)? (See Section 7.4.3.)

▶ Have you considered processing internal tables without using workareas (ASSIGNING)? (See Section 7.4.3.)

▶ If the same data is needed by various programs, is semi-persistent memory (stored on the application server) an option? (See Section 7.4.5.)

- If very large amounts of data need to be updated by one program, have you considered parallel processing as an option (STARTING NEW TASK)? (See Section 7.4.6.)

Is data traffic between the application server and the client minimized?

- If large amounts of data need to be exchanged between the client and the application server:
  - Has a file transfer been considered instead of uploads and downloads? (See Section 7.5.1.)
  - Is flushing control commands implemented properly? (See Section 7.5.2.)

Maintainability

Maintenance of standard SAP software

- In case of implementing an OSS Note: (See Section 8.1.1)
  - Has the Note Assistant been used?
  - If the Note Assistant has been used, have other corrections than those applied to ABAP source also been implemented?
- In case of implementing changes to SAP software (See Section 8.1.2): Have changes anticipated by SAP been checked first, and in the following sequence?
  - BADIs (SE19)
  - Enhancements (CMOD)
  - User Exits
- In case no anticipated change is available:
  - Has the change been implemented using the Modification Assistant?
  - Has the customized ABAP code been isolated properly from the standard SAP source: for example, by using an include?

Maintenance of customized ABAP programs

- Have the basic program actions been separated: selection, processing, display of output, and updating? (See Section 8.2.1)
- Is this separation clearly visible in the program structure?
- Does the ABAP program comply with your company standards and templates? (See Section 8.2.2.)
  - Have the naming conventions been applied properly?
  - In case of a report: Are the reporting events used in the correct sequence?

- In case of a module pool: Are the modules called in the proper sequence, especially during the Process-After-Input (PAI) screen event?

▶ Does the source code correspond with available templates and statement patterns?

▶ Has the source code been organized using Pretty Printer?

▶ Has the use of constants for referencing organizational units been avoided?

▶ Has copying of standard SAP software been avoided (See Section 8.2.3)?

▶ If a standard SAP function module is used: (See Section 8.2.3)

- Has this function been released by SAP?

- Does the function match the required functionality?

▶ In case of reusing SAP Update functionality (See Sections 8.2.3 and 8.2.4):

- Has a BAPI function or IDoc been used, if available, instead of `CALL TRANS-ACTION` or Batch Input logic?

- In case of mass updates: Has the available standard SAP functionality for mass updates (programs or transaction MASS) been considered?

▶ In case of a report: Has the ABAP List Viewer (ALV) been used for displaying report output? (See Section 8.2.3)

▶ In case of Form processing (See Section 8.2.3)

- Has Smart Forms been used to develop a new form?

- Has copying a standard SAP form been avoided (except for minor changes)?

- Has redeveloping SAPscript forms using Smart Forms been considered?

▶ Has an ABAP Objects solution for modularization purposes been considered?

9.1.4 Tools for Testing and Quality Checks

Now, we'll look at the SAP tools that are available for assessing the quality of ABAP code. There are basically two types of ABAP checking tools: *static* tools and *runtime* tools. Static tools check only the ABAP source code for deficiencies. Runtime tools collect data about ABAP code, and interpret the behavior of the code during its execution. We'll explain how you can apply several of these types of tools to trace robustness problems.

Extended Syntax Check

The *Extended Syntax Check* (accessible via Transaction SLIN or via the ABAP editor) is a static check: it evaluates only the source code. This check can help to prevent several types of robustness errors, for example:

▶ Correctness

  ▷ `LOOP AT <itab> WHERE` combined with `AT` statements

  ▷ Amounts (of money) without a reference to a corresponding currency field

  ▷ Quantities without a reference to a corresponding unit-of-measure field

  ▷ Missing return code checks (e.g., after function calls)

▶ Stability

  ▷ Non-existing programs, functions, or external routines; for example, in a statement such as `PERFORM <routine> IN PROGRAM <programname>`

  ▷ Missing (but mandatory) or wrong (i.e., their type definition) interface parameters in called procedures

▶ Maintainability

  ▷ Wrong use of text elements

  ▷ Unused subroutines (i.e., only subroutines within one program, no external procedures) and data definitions

When starting the Extended Syntax Check, you can select the ABAP program's elements that you want to check (see Figure 9.3):

In our opinion, every programmer should execute a complete Extended Syntax Check before handing it over to anyone else for further testing. You can get the SAP system to prompt you to execute an Extended Syntax Check by setting an automatic reminder in the Transport Organizer (Transaction SE01, see Figure 9.4). This setting must be maintained for each individual developer. Consequently, a transport cannot be released until all the objects in the transport have explicitly undergone an Extended Syntax Check.

Sometimes developers wonder what they should do with the information supplied by the extended check. We recommend that a program shouldn't be transported to a SAP production system as long as it contains *extended errors*. Typically, most warnings and information messages aren't cause for alarm, nevertheless, they should be heeded. You should pay special attention to *syntax check warnings*; although they're just warnings, they can, in fact, reveal severe deficiencies in ABAP code. An example of such a warning is a `SELECT SINGLE` statement with an incompletely qualified primary key. We discussed this shortcoming as a typical correctness problem in Section 3.2.1.

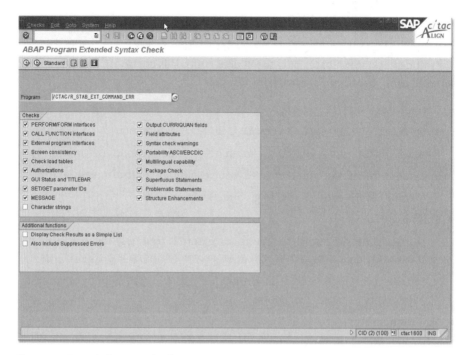

Figure 9.3 Extended Syntax Check Starting Screen

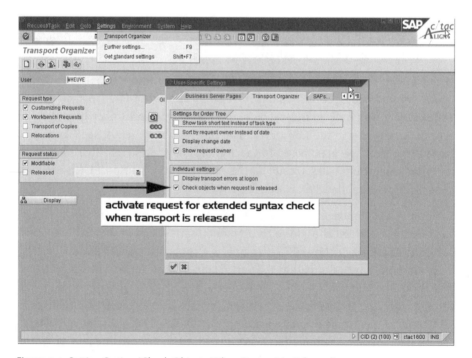

Figure 9.4 Setting Option 'Check Objects When Request Is Released'

If your code contains an *extended* error or warning, the only thing that you can do is to modify or correct the code that caused it. Executing checks makes sense only if you also take the appropriate measures. In our experience, a consistent use of the Extended Syntax Check leads not only to more robust ABAP code, but also improves the developer's understanding and coding habits. Because of what developers learn from these extended checks, the number of program errors will steadily decrease over time. Developers will become accustomed to the types of messages raised, and will therefore learn to anticipate these messages during the initial design and throughout the overall development.

In some rare cases, you may have to suppress an *extended* message. Usually, you suppress a message only for a few specific statements. A good example is the error message that is generated to indicate possible portability problems when character-like fields are compared. The following piece of code is such an example:

```
DATA: tp_veld1 TYPE c value '9',
      tp_veld2 TYPE c value 'C'.
* The results of the comparison of two character fields depends on the
* code-page used, for example an EBCDIC or ASCII code-page.
IF tp_veld1 > tp_veld2.
ENDIF.
```

In ASCII code-pages, the binary value of character '9' lies before the 'C,' whereas in an EBCDIC-system, the '9' comes after the 'C.' The Extended Syntax Check will report that this may cause portability problems. However, you may decide that this error is not important if your program is not going to be executed on the basis of different code-pages.

If you think that suppressing the Extended Syntax Error is justified, we recommend mentioning this in the inline documentation of your ABAP code, so that other programmers will understand the reasoning behind this action. There are two ways of suppressing an extended error. The first option is to insert the ABAP statement SET EXTENDED CHECK OFF/ON into your code. However, this option doesn't suppress all types of extended checks. The second option is to add a special literal as a comment behind the statement. Below, we added an example of this second option:

```
DATA: tp_veld1 TYPE c value '9',
      tp_veld2 TYPE c value 'C'.
* The result of the comparison of two character fields depends on the
* code-page used, for example an EBCDIC or ASCII code-page.
IF tp_veld1 > tp_veld2.  "#EC PORTABLE
ENDIF.
```

The literal '#EC PORTABLE' suppresses the portability message that would otherwise be generated. You can find the type of '#EC' comment that is related to a specific extended error in the long text of the error.

Don't suppress extended errors for the sole purpose of concealing your mistakes! Besides, you cannot completely conceal them. The number of suppressed checks is still part of the output of the tool, and you can even show the hidden extended messages in detail.

Now, let's look at some examples of Extended Syntax Check results. You'll find that the large number of checks and the corresponding errors, warnings, and messages are subdivided into groups (see Figure 9.5 for an overview). We'll discuss some of these groups in greater detail. If you need to know what checks are executed, refer to the online help of every check group.

Check for program /CTAC/R_STAB_EXT_COMMAND_ER	Error	Warnings	Messages
Test Environment	0	0	0
PERFORM/FORM interfaces	0	0	0
CALL FUNCTION interfaces	1	0	0
External program interfaces	1	0	0
Screen consistency	0	0	0
Authorizations	0	0	0
GUI Status and TITLEBAR	0	0	0
SET/GET parameter IDs	0	0	0
MESSAGE	0	0	0
Character strings	1	0	0
Output CURR/QUAN fields	0	0	0
Field Attributes	0	2	0
Superfluous Statements	0	0	0
Syntax check warnings	0	1	0
Portability ASCII/EBCDIC	1	0	0
Check load sizes	0	0	0
Multilingual capability	0	0	0
Problematic Statements	0	0	0
Structure Enhancements	0	0	0
Package Check	0	0	0
Hidden errors and warnings	0	0	0

Figure 9.5 Example of the Result of an Extended Syntax Check

▶ PERFORM/FORM **Interfaces**
This group of checks verifies the correctness of subroutine calls. These checks help you to prevent runtime errors as a result of type conflicts between actual and formal parameters (see Sections 4.2.1 and 4.3.2).

▶ CALL FUNCTION **Interfaces**
This group of checks pertains to function module calls. These are the same kinds of checks as the aforementioned checks for subroutine calls. This group also includes a check that verifies whether the return codes that result from function exceptions are handled immediately after the function call.

- **External Program Interfaces**
  This group of checks verifies the existence of transactions that are called and programs that are submitted. These checks can prevent the stability problems described in Section 4.3.2.

- **Screen Consistency**
  This group of checks deals with the correct definition of (individual parts of) the screens in a program. An error is raised, for example, whenever a dynpro or module is called that doesn't exist. A warning is raised if a module is not called. Most of the messages in this group don't point to deficiencies that will lead directly to program dumps or error messages. However, they can be relevant, because they sometimes indicate situations that can cause strange program behavior.

- **Character Strings**
  Although this group of checks isn't executed by default in Transaction SLIN, the information they provide is nevertheless useful in order to determine whether a program has enough flexibility for the introduction of new languages. Several types of tests are executed on text elements and text literals. The most frequently occurring error in this group is the use of a text literal that doesn't refer to a text element. Because such a literal cannot be translated into other languages, it limits the maintainability of the source.

- **Output** CURR/QUAN **Fields**
  In Section 3.3.1, we stressed the importance of using the correct reference fields for amounts and quantities. The Extended Syntax Check verifies whether fields of type CUKY or UNIT are used when amounts or quantities are being written. In traditional ABAP reports, this has always been one of the most common extended errors. When ABAP List Viewer (ALV) techniques are used, this error is less likely to occur: every amount or quantity field in an ALV must refer to a currency or unit-of-measure (unit) field. However, remember that the Extended Syntax Check won't trace the use of a wrong reference field.

- **Field Attributes**
  In the course of developing or maintaining a program, several variables that were initially defined in it may ultimately appear to be extraneous. Using this check option, you can trace such variables so that you can remove unused data definitions.

- **Syntax Check Warnings**
  This group of checks contains all warnings raised also by the normal (standard) Syntax Check. Be sure to take these syntax warnings seriously!

► **Portability Check ASCII/EBCDIC**

This group of checks ensures the validity of character string comparisons. Such comparisons can lead to errors when a particular program is used on different hardware platforms and with different code-pages.

► **Superfluous Statements**

If this group of checks is active, a program is checked for specific commands (such as BREAK-POINT) or combinations of commands that will never be relevant at runtime. For example, if a procedure contains a jump statement such as EXIT, it doesn't make sense to add ABAP code to this procedure, as we did in the following piece of sample code:

```
FORM routine.
  EXIT.
  WRITE: 'HELLO'. "Will never be executed.
ENDFORM.
```

► **Problematic Statements**

This group contains checks on many potentially problematic statements that can lead to correctness or stability problems. An example of a problematic statement is checking on the occurrence of the LOOP AT ⟨itab⟩ WHERE statement in combination with AT events (see Section 3.3.3 for an example).

Code Inspector

In the SAP Web Application Server (Web AS) Release 6.10, SAP introduced an extra tool to inspect ABAP code—the Code Inspector[3] (Transaction SCI or SCII). Because this tool is a valuable extension to the standard check tools, we recommend it to every developer. The Extended Syntax Check is an integral part of the Code Inspector. Unlike the Extended Syntax check, the Code Inspector points to ABAP code that is expected to perform poorly. The Code Inspector is a relatively new and unknown tool, and its use isn't really straightforward. Therefore, we'll explain some basic features of the tool. You can skip this discussion if you already know how to use the tool. Next, we'll show you some examples of the results of our checks, and explain how they can best be used.

---

3 The Code Inspector is also available for Release 4.6C (Refer to OSS Note 543359).

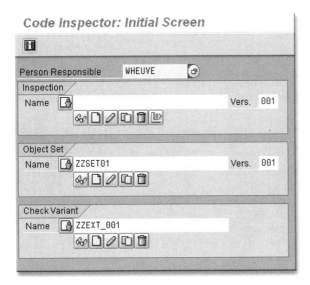

Figure 9.6 Starting the Code Inspector Using Transaction SCI

If you want to execute a Code Inspection, you must take the following steps (see the first screen of the Code Inspector in Figure 9.6):

▶ Define a *Check Variant*. In a variant, you can choose which checks have to be executed.

▶ Define an *Object Set*. The Object Set contains the objects that will be checked.

▶ Define a *Code Inspection* by giving it a name and assigning an Object Set and a Check Variant. The results of an inspection are saved.

▶ Execute the *Code Inspection*. Note that, in contrast to the Extended Syntax Check, you can save the results of the Code Inspector.

In a Check Variant (see Figure 9.7), you can indicate which checks you want to perform. You can either use an existing, predefined variant or define (create) your own. There are seven different groups of checks of which the following are the most interesting:

▶ *Performance Checks:* Inefficient usage of Open SQL, internal tables and other statements

▶ *Security Checks:* Return code handling, and critical statements such as SYSTEM-CALL

▶ *Syntax Checks:* This group contains the old Extended Syntax Check

▶ *Search Checks:* You can enter ABAP statements or strings that you want to search for in the ABAP code

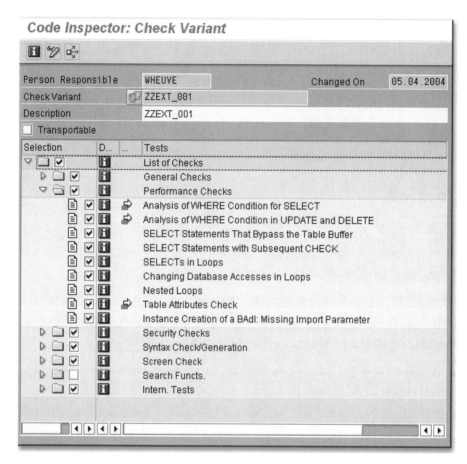

Figure 9.7 Defining a Check Variant for the Code Inspector

The next step is to define the Object Set (see Figure 9.8):

As Figure 9.8 shows, an Object Set can be created dynamically by referring to a package name (i.e., the successor of a development class), program names, and so forth.

The last step is to define the Code Inspection. In an inspection, the Check Variant and the Object Set are entered (see Figure 9.9).

You can now execute your inspection.

Using version numbers, several inspections—performed on the same set of objects and with the same Check Variant—can be saved under the same name. This can be useful, for example, to determine whether improvements have been made over time.

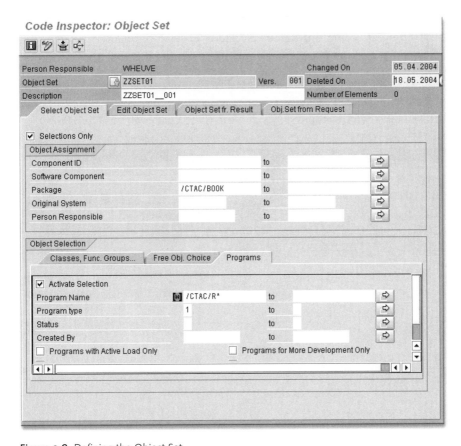

Figure 9.8 Defining the Object Set

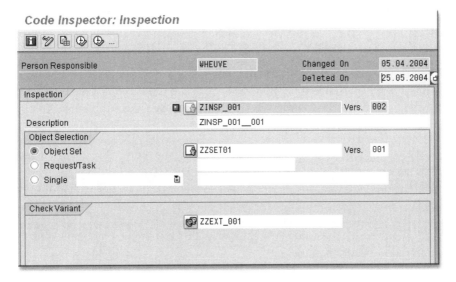

Figure 9.9 Defining the Code Inspection

Instead of using an Object Set, you can also enter a Transport Request number or a specific program name. This can be particularly useful for quality assurance purposes because it allows you to check only those objects that will be transported.

Not only can a Code Inspection be started via Transaction SCI or SCII; it can also be started directly via the ABAP Editor (Transaction SE38) (see Figure 9.10), the Function Builder (Transaction SE37), and the Class Builder (Transaction SE24).

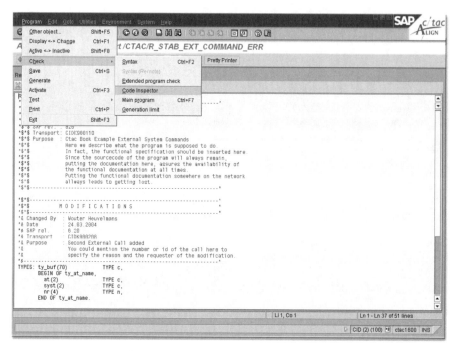

Figure 9.10 Starting a Code Inspection from the ABAP Editor

Now, let's focus on some of the results that occur when running an inspection. We'll discuss these results in relation to some of the robustness issues that were addressed in Chapters 3 , 4, and 5. This should be viewed as a supplement to our discussion of the Extended Syntax Check.

The first example concerns a correctness violation. In Section 3.3.3, we discussed why the statement ON CHANGE OF should not be used. Using the Code Inspector, you can include a search on this statement in the selected objects. Figure 9.11 shows you an example of this type of check.

We are informed by the Code Inspector that this statement has been used in function group /CTAC/BOOKSEL.

Figure 9.11 The Command ON CHANGE OF Has Been Encountered

A second example pertains to one of the issues addressed in Chapter 4. Using the option **Security Checks**, you can verify whether the statements are highly dependent on the Operating System used (see Figure 9.12).

Code Inspector: Results from CTAC_BOOK 001 BMEIJS

Person Responsible BMEIJS   Inspection CTAC_BOOK   Vers. 1

Messages

Tests	Error	Warnin...	Inform...
List of Checks	8	17	25
Performance Checks	8	15	16
Security Checks	0	2	8
Critical Statements	0	2	5
Warnings	0	2	0
Message Code 0001	0	2	0
Program /CTAC/R_STAB_EXT_COMMAND_ERR Include /CTAC/R_STAB_EXT_COMMAN... Call System Function: 'C_SAPGPARAM'	0	1	0
Program /CTAC/R_STAB_EXT_COMMAND_ERR Include /CTAC/R_STAB_EXT_COMMAN... Call System Function: 'C_SAPGPARAM' Call System Function: 'C_SAPGPARAM'	0	1	0
Information	0	0	5
Dynamic and Client-Specific Accesses in SELECT	0	0	3
Dynamic and Client-Specific Accesses with INSERT, UPDATE, MODIFY, DELETE	0	0	0
Check of SY-SUBRC Handling	0	0	0
Changing Database Accesses not in Update Modules	0	0	0
Screen Check	0	0	0
Search Functs.	0	0	1

Figure 9.12 A Call of a System Function Has Been Encountered

The warning message is prompted because of the following ABAP code:

```
CALL 'C_SAPGPARAM' id 'NAME'    field 'abap/atrapath'
                   id 'VALUE'   field tp_path
```

In Section 4.4.2, we argued that the use of this CALL statement makes a program dependent on the OS used.

The third example pertains to a correctness error. In Section 3.4 and Section 5.2, we described why checking the return code after an Open SQL statement is important. Among other things, the Code Inspector contains a powerful option to verify whether return codes are consistently checked immediately after commands such as SELECT or CALL FUNCTION. The following inspection contains many related warnings that point in this direction (see Figure 9.13).

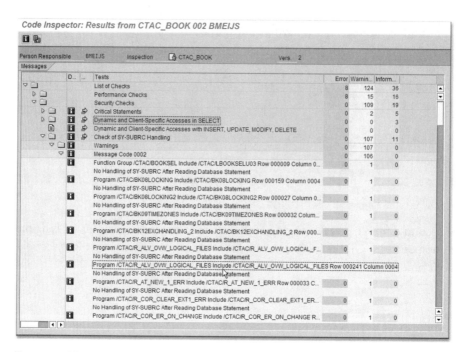

Figure 9.13 Warnings Because SY-SUBRC Has Not Been Checked Directly After SELECT statements

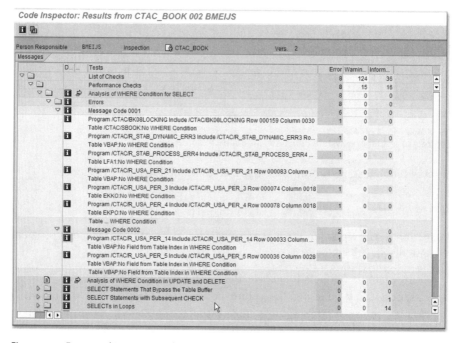

Figure 9.14 Errors and Warnings Related to Inefficient Open SQL statements

The fourth and last example where the Code Inspector can help is to pinpoint statements that may cause performance to deteriorate. Figure 9.14 displays some errors and warnings caused by ABAP code, which contains both a SELECT statement with a WHERE clause that doesn't use index fields, and a SELECT statement without a WHERE clause.

Note that it can be useful to select the contents of a relatively small table without using a WHERE clause. If this is the case, you can skip the check on this SELECT statement by adding the pseudo-comment #EC CI_NOWHERE immediately after the SELECT statement. Such comments are available for most Inspection Checks, however, they should be used only if you explicitly choose to apply a statement in a specific way. If such a choice is not apparent, we recommend adding inline documentation to explain your choice.

Investing time in getting to know the ins and outs of the Code Inspector, and applying changes based on its messages will lead to programs that can be considered more robust in many ways.

Unicode Check

In Chapter 1, and particularly in Chapter 4, we saw that Unicode Enabling improves the technical quality of your ABAP software; for example, because stability problems regarding type conflicts and mixed up code-pages are less likely to occur. From SAP Web AS Release 6.10 onward, we recommend that every new ABAP program developed is marked as Unicode-enabled.

Transaction UCCHECK, available as of SAP Web AS Release 6.10, checks whether your ABAP programs are Unicode-compliant. The use of this transaction is particularly worthwhile for programs that don't have the **Unicode checks active** attribute set (see Figure 9.24). This makes the transaction an excellent tool to help you plan the effort required to make your software Unicode-compliant.[4] Figure 9.15 shows the results of the Unicode check program.

Then, you can jump immediately from the result list to the programs with Unicode errors and correct them. Furthermore, you can set the **Unicode checks active** flag automatically for every program that meets the Unicode demands by using the Set Unicode Attribute button.

You should also note that using this tool isn't limited to just the one-time support that's required during a Unicode-Enabling project. At any point in time, you may want to verify whether the **Unicode checks active** flag has actually been set for new ABAP programs. This characteristic makes the UCCHECK worth using to ensure quality assurance.

---

4 An early version of this tool is available in SAP Release 4.6 under the program name RSUNIS-CAN. This can be used to investigate the effort required to make your ABAP programs Unicode-enabled after an upgrade. There are no checking possibilities in releases prior to 4.6.

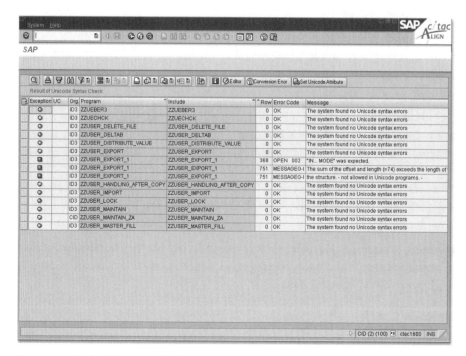

Figure 9.15 Result of the Unicode Check Transaction UCCHECK

Coverage Analyzer

In releases prior to the SAP Web Application Server (Web AS) Release 6.10, it isn't easy to monitor the actual use of ABAP programs, function modules, and global classes. Consider, for example, information such as the number of times a specific program or function module was actually used, or the number of times that a function module has ended in a runtime error.

In releases prior to SAP Web AS Release 6.10, only part of such information is available in the Workload Analysis tool (Transaction ST03). With this tool, you can investigate the number of dialog steps executed for a program and the total and average response times. However, the Workload Analysis tool has some disadvantages: the required detailed data to be collected cannot be stored for a longer period of time; in most production systems, detailed data is kept available online for only three months; furthermore, this tool offers only high-level information: the use of function modules or global methods, for example, cannot be monitored with it.

With the introduction of the Coverage Analyzer (Transaction SCOV), such drawbacks now belong to the past. This tool offers useful information on both the actual execution of ABAP programs and the so-called underlying *processing blocks*, such as function modules, subroutines, methods, and reporting events. This information can be advantageous in several ways—to assess the stability of a SAP system; to evaluate the maintainability; or, to rate possible performance measures:

► To measure the overall stability of an SAP system, you could use information such as the number of times that a function module has caused runtime errors.

► For maintenance purposes, a question that is sometimes asked is how to establish whether pieces of ABAP code are actually used. Before the introduction of the Coverage Analyzer, collecting this information for customized pieces of ABAP code was sometimes done by adding extra logic to update counter data in customized database tables. Now, Transaction SCOV directly provides this kind of information.

► To determine whether performance measures can be useful. It might be worthwhile for the overall system performance, for example, to implement only a relatively small performance improvement in a function module, because it is used (called, executed) so frequently.

The Coverage Analyzer works as follows. Data collection is started by switching on the Coverage Analyzer flag via the Administration menu of Transaction SCOV (see Figure 9.16). As soon as recording has been switched on, runtime information is automatically stored and saved in the SAP database.[5] Using the Display menu in the transaction, you can navigate to either a global or a detailed view of the Coverage Analyzer results. Figure 9.17 shows what the Details report looks like.

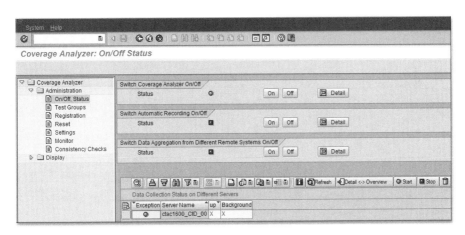

Figure 9.16 Settings for the Coverage Analyzer

---

5 This is not executed immediately, but via a data collection job that is scheduled after switching on the recording.

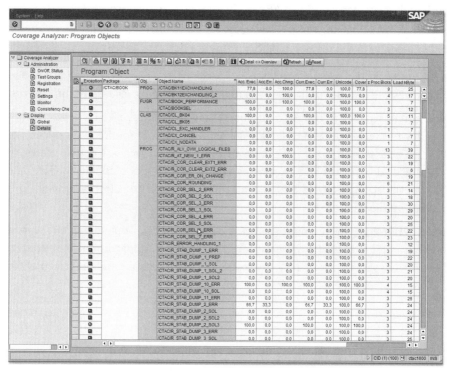

Figure 9.17 Example of Results of the Coverage Analyzer

As you can see, the overview offers information on the level of package name, object type (program, function group, class, etc.), and object name. More detailed information can be viewed by double-clicking on a specific line. Consequently, you get an overview of the counters per processing block (see Figure 9.18).

Processing Blocks

	Exception	Type	Name	Class	Acc. Exec.	Acc.Err.	Acc.Chng.	Curr.Exec.	Curr.Err.	Unicode	Tested
	○	ESEL			1	0	93	1	0	1	1
	○	METH	CONSTRUCTOR	LCL_EXCEPTION_HANDLER	1	0	93	1	0	1	1
	■		MESSAGE_TO_ADMIN		0	0	93	0	0	1	0
	○		MESSAGE_TO_APPLICATION_LOG		1	0	93	1	0	1	1
	■		MESSAGE_TO_USER		0	0	93	0	0	1	0
	○		SOME_METHOD	LCL_SOME_CLASS	1	0	93	1	0	1	1
	○		WRITE_TO_DB	LCL_EXCEPTION_HANDLER	1	0	93	1	0	1	1
	○	PROG			1	0	93	1	0	1	1
	○	SSEL			2	0	93	2	0	1	1

Figure 9.18 Detailed Information from the Coverage Analyzer on Program '/ctac/bk11exchandling'

For every processing block, the following data is collected:

▶ Number of executions since the start of the data collection

▶ Number of runtime errors since the start of the data collection

- Number of changes of the ABAP code (at each change, some of the counters are reset)
- Number of executions since the last reset (i.e., the last change of the code)
- Number of runtime errors since the last reset
- Indication if the Unicode flag is active
- Indication if the processing block has been tested. The criteria to determine whether a processing block has actually been tested can be set separately via the menu settings of Transaction SCOV.

On the level of a specific object name, the counter information is also translated into percentages. On the basis of such percentages you could, for instance, evaluate what percentage of the procedures in a program has actually been triggered.

Other important information on this general level is:

- Number of processing blocks with a main object (e.g., a program)
- Number of calls of the main object

We recommend that you keep the Coverage Analyzer switched on permanently in a production SAP environment. There is an entire range of quality checks that can be performed using the Coverage Analyzer; for example:

- A measure for the stability of the production system: What percentage of the programs has raised runtime errors? And which processing blocks caused these errors?
- A Unicode check: Were any programs executed that aren't Unicode-enabled?
- The level of modularization: Which functions and methods are executed often? Imagine, for exmaple, that a function module is called from just one program and is executed an equal number of times as the calling program: in that case, the conclusion might be that, so far, this modularization attempt hasn't been successful.
- *Dead* code: Which programs, subroutines, functions, methods, and so forth were not called since the last reset?
- The impact of changes: For example, what is the impact of changing a certain global class method? How many programs will be affected and must therefore be tested?
- The impact of changes on performance: Does a small change on a processing block that is frequently executed have an advantageous effect on the entire system?

The benefits of the Coverage Analyzer also make it a good candidate for testing quality assurrance. This could, for example, enable a test manager to see what percentage of programs, and even processing blocks, have actually been tested.

Debugger

Since its introduction to the SAP environment, the Debugger has become one of the most important tools for developers. Because it enables developers to examine—and sometimes also influence—every step in a program while it is being executed, the Debugger is a very powerful feature for testing the robustness of ABAP code. It is also the primary tool that helps developers discover the cause of errors. We'll discuss this further in Section 9.2. Now, our focus will be on how you can use the Debugger during the creation and maintenance of programs.

The Debugger is especially well suited to track problems in the areas of Correctness and Stability. It enables you to proceed step-by-step through the ABAP code; verify whether the correct data is selected and updated; verify the contents of single fields, structures, and internal tables; and track the execution of statements and procedures, such as functions, methods, and subroutines. Although most developers have practical experience using the tool, not all developers are equally familiar with all of its aspects.

We'll start by mentioning the different ways in which the Debugger can be activated, since not all readers may know all the options. Then, we'll present some important debugging settings that also allow you to debug pieces of code that are normally not visible during a debugging session. Lastly, we'll discuss some powerful debugging features that the average ABAP developer may have not yet tried. We won't cover all settings and features; we'll just mention the most important ones. In addition, note that every new SAP release has introduced new options that have made the tool even more useful. We recommend that you check out these options when you start working with a new release.

We assume that you're familiar with the basic options to start a debugging session: by entering '/H' in the command field; by setting dynamic or static breakpoints in the ABAP code; and, by executing a program in debugging mode via the ABAP editor. However, there are also more options:

▶ A function module or global method can be tested (debugged) as a separate entity. To do this, simply select the test function that you want and then choose debugging.

▶ A less well known option is the ability to debug a program that is already running, that is, without having to rely on a breakpoint somewhere in the program. This option allows you to interrupt an active process, for example, to investigate why it is running so long. In order to do this, you must activate the Debugger from the process overview (Transaction SM50, see Figure 9.19). Even background tasks can be debugged in this way—a new process is started automatically to execute the debugging session.

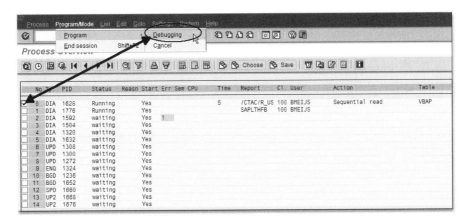

Figure 9.19 Start Debugging from the Process Overview (Transaction SM50)

▶ As of SAP Web AS Release 6.10, there's another way to start debugging a background process: you need to navigate to the Job Overview (Transaction SM37) and start function **Capture: active job** (see Figure 9.20).

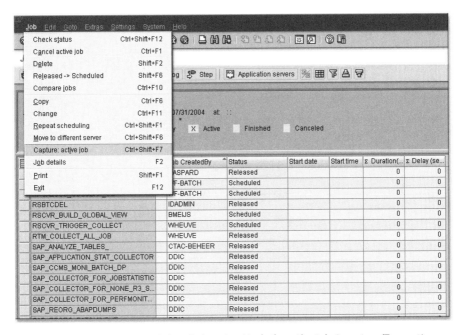

Figure 9.20 Capture an Active Job in Debugging Mode from the Job Overview (Transaction SM37)

▶ The last option is perhaps the least familiar—starting a debugging session from a SAP GUI pop-up window. This solves a problem that developers often encounter when debugging a dialog transaction: you may sometimes find yourself in a situation where you want to start debugging immediately after getting a pop-up screen. However, this isn't possible because a modal window has no command field in which the command '/H' can be entered. Setting a dynamic breakpoint is not an option either, unless you know exactly where the pop-up dynpro originates. You can overcome these obstacles, however, by using the settings shown in Figure 9.21.

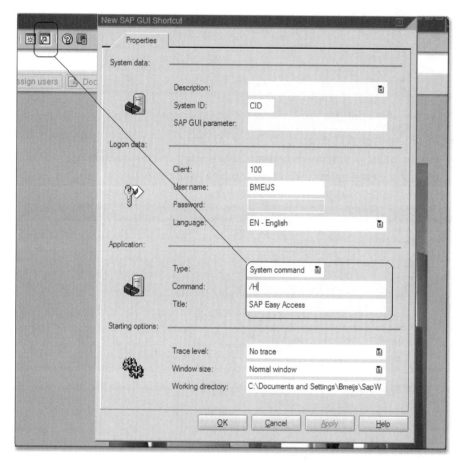

Figure 9.21 Creating a Shortcut on Your Desktop That Uses System Command '/H'

After having created the shortcut on your desktop, you can activate a debugging session by dragging it from your desktop to a modal window, and dropping it there (as is shown in Figure 9.22). This activates the debugging session.

Now that we've shown you where you can start debugging, we'll explain the most important settings to be activated in order to optimize the debugging possibilities. In Figure 9.23, the main settings are shown. Note that, by default, all of these settings are switched off.

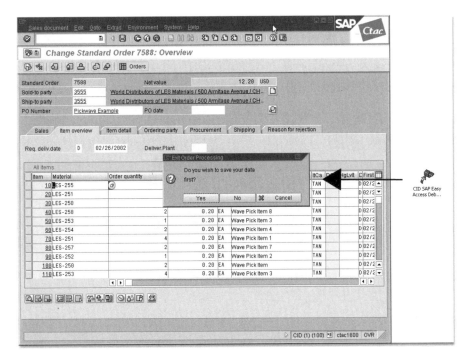

Figure 9.22 Dropping the Debugging Shortcut on a Pop-up Screen

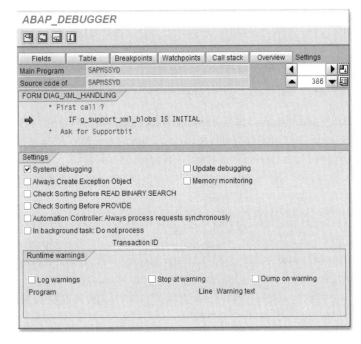

Figure 9.23 Debugging Settings

A first option that you may find helpful is to switch on the standard setting for debugging a system program (as is done in Figure 9.23).

An example of a system program is RSDBRUNT (you can see this program's attributes in Figure 9.24).

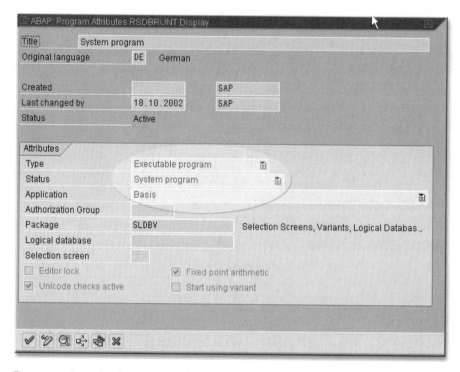

Figure 9.24 Example of a Program with Status 'System Program'

In most cases, you won't be interested in system programs, since they merely fulfil technical tasks; for example, enabling you to test a function module. Sometimes, however, you may want to see what happens in a system program, perhaps to learn if you can reuse something in your own code. You can do this by choosing the **System Debugging** option in the debugging settings screen.[6]

Another limitation of the standard debugging settings is that processes running in the update task cannot be debugged. However, if you activate the **Update Debugging** option, this limitation is removed, and update task functions become visible in the debugging mode. By activating this option, you can also test the processing of message types that are handled by the update task; for example, an order confirmation that should be printed immediately after a newly created customer order has been saved.

---

6 System Debugging can be activated directly by entering '/HS' in the command code field.

As you can see on the Settings portion of the ABAP Debugger screen (in Figure 9.23), there are various other settings that can be activated in order to increase your options for debugging. For more information, check the SAP online help using the ABAP keyword 'Debugger' and other standard help information resources.

The last aspect of debugging that we want to discuss involves the options that you can choose from when debugging a program. When you fully utilize the powerful features of the Debugger, you're not only able to check and test the technical quality of a program more efficiently; you can also make troubleshooting activities easier. For example, you can deliberately cause an error to occur, or find the origin of the error. In order to show you just how flexible a tool the Debugger is, we'll mention some of its less well known options.

An option that you may already be familiar with is the option to replace the content of a single field or an internal table with another value or values. You could call it *fooling the system*. This option allows you to force a program in the direction that you want it to go. For example, if you want to check how a program reacts to an unforeseen value of database table field material type (mara-mtart), you can change the value of the related variable, and then check the flow of the program. This is a very valuable option, particularly, if your test data doesn't provide you with the options that you need to test. During troubleshooting activities, the Debugger sometimes allows you to simulate an error that occurred in a production environment.

The debugging navigation options **Step In (F5)**, **Step Out (F7)**, **Execute (F6)**, and **Run to cursor (F8)** are all well known. But there are more ways to jump directly or more efficiently to the ABAP code that you're looking for, particularly, the options **Breakpoint at** and **Create watchpoint**.

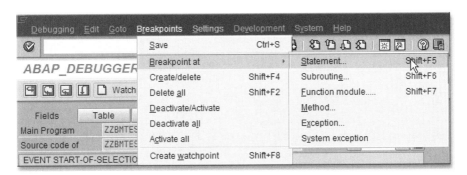

Figure 9.25 Breakpoint at Options

In Figure 9.25, all **Breakpoint at** options are displayed. These options allow you, for example, to jump directly to an error message or exception. If you're investigating the circumstances under which a program sends an error message, you can choose **Breakpoint at • Statement** to go directly to the place from where the message is sent.

Setting watchpoints is an even more flexible way to navigate through an ABAP program. A watch- point can be considered to be a conditional breakpoint: you enter one or more conditions; and if one of these conditions is true, the program will stop.

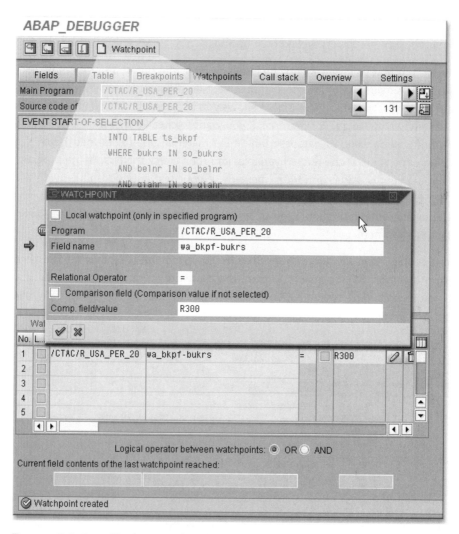

Figure 9.26 Setting a Watchpoint and Reaching It

In the example shown in Figure 9.26, the program stops as soon as the field wa_
bkpf-bukrs contains value R300. This may be useful to accelerate problem analysis, if you know that this particular value has led to an error.

A last navigation alternative worth pointing out is the **GOTO statement** option.
This option allows you to skip the execution of specific ABAP statements; for
example, the update of a database table. You can also skip the selection of data
from a database table in order to check how a program reacts to this option.

Besides changing the values of variables and navigating in an efficient and flexible
way through an ABAP program, the Debugger also offers several types of useful
information. Viewing the contents of variables and internal tables is the most basic
example. For more information, use the Goto menu option (see Figure 9.27).

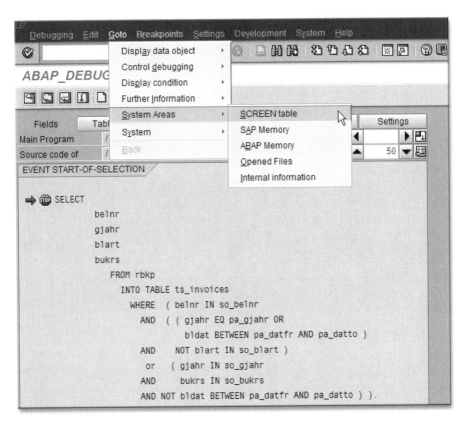

Figure 9.27 Different Types of Debugging Information

Two important types of information that we should mention are the *Call Stack* and
values of Parameter IDs. The Call Stack, which can be reached directly via the
CALLS button, is convenient for troubleshooting purposes. It shows the naviga-

tion path that a program has followed up to the current ABAP statement. See Figure 9.28 for an example: at the event START-OF-SELECTION, form routine a001_selection has been called, which hasn't yet ended; and this routine has, in its turn, called method select_orders, which is also still active.

Investigating the Call Stack may be particularly convenient when dealing with complex programs, from which many methods, routines, and functions are called. This will enable you to quickly find the path that led to a specific point in the ABAP flow; for example, an error message that you have found using the **Breakpoint at • Statement** alternative.[7]

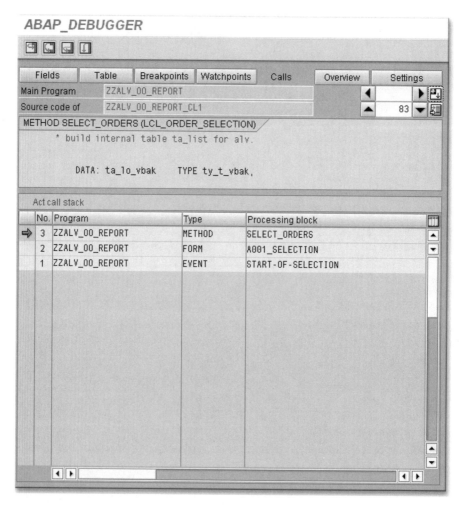

Figure 9.28 Example of an Active Call Stack: Method Select_orders Has Been Called by Form a001_selection.

---

7 A program that has been started by another ABAP program—using a SUBMIT or CALL TRANSACTION command—has its own Call Stack. Within this Call Stack, it is not possible to see from which point the program has been submitted.

To view the current values of different parameter IDs, select the **Goto • System Areas >> SAP memory** menu option (see Figure 9.29).

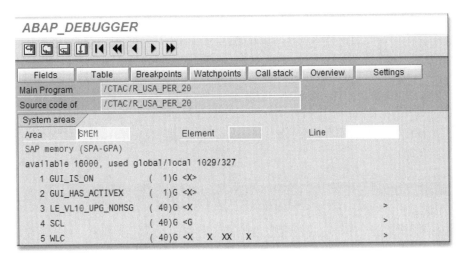

Figure 9.29 Displaying the Current Values of 5 Parameter IDs

Figure 9.29 shows that parameter ID GUI_IS _ON contains value X. This kind of information can be useful when analyzing problems in complex programs.

Note that we've discussed only a fraction of the many options offered by the Debugger. We have highlighted those options that are less well known in order to show you just how versatile and flexible a tool the Debugger can be.

Runtime Analysis

The Runtime Analysis tool (Transaction SE30) is primarily used to check the performance of ABAP code, however, it can also be used to evaluate the maintainability of ABAP programs. This tool enables you to examine the performance of any kind of ABAP program and of its composite parts, such as subroutines, function-modules, or methods. On the basis of detailed output, you can investigate exactly which procedures are called, and in what sequence. You can also use this tool to trace procedures that aren't executed. However, we've already seen that the Coverage Analyzer is a better tool to support such activities. Therefore, we'll review only those Runtime Analysis options that are used to check the performance of ABAP code.

The results of a runtime analysis are stored in a performance data file. Depending on the settings you make in the *Restriction Variant*, the following information can be made available:

- ► Total program information:
  - ► Total response time of the program
  - ► Relative response time of database handling
  - ► Relative response time of the remaining program activities such as internal table handling
- ► Data about the measured units:
  - ► Call Hierarchy: The sequence in which the units were processed (see Figure 9.30)
  - ► Hit List: The gross and net processing time of measured units (see Figure 9.31)

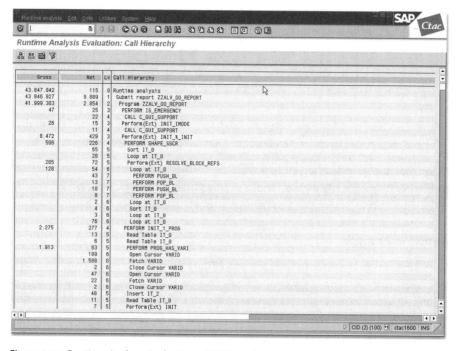

Figure 9.30 Runtime Analysis Evaluation: Call Hierarchy

The most important piece of information in the hit list is the net percentage of every measurement unit, that is, the part that this unit plays within the total response time of the program. This makes the tool very useful for the identification of program parts that cause performance problems. However, the tool itself doesn't provide any solutions to these problems. For additional help, refer to the earlier discussion of the Code Inspector, and, for information about performance-enhancing solutions, see Chapter 7.

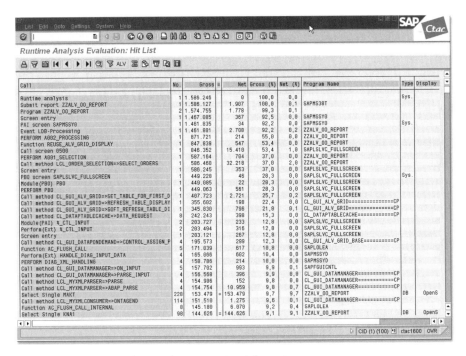

Figure 9.31 Runtime Analysis Evaluation: Hit List Information

A common observation made about the Runtime Analysis tool is that its use is limited because it cannot be applied in environments with a relatively low amount of (test) data, such as an SAP development environment. In that case, the amount of data used is regarded as insufficient to perform runtime tests effectively. While there is some truth in this generalization, you can overcome this limitation by using so called plausibility checks;[8] that is, by investigating the *growth* of the net runtime of measurement units such as subroutines, functions, methods, or SQL statements. In order to achieve this, however, you must first run a program using a small amount of data; then, you have to repeat the test with various other test sets of increasing size. After a couple of measurements, all with a small, but increasing, amount of data, you'll be able to calculate the growth of the net performance percentage. You may, for example, discover that, in an initial test run, a specific subroutine takes 0.1% of the total runtime; then, 0.3 % if double the amount of data is used; and when the associated program is tested with even more data, the increase in runtime escalates. Therefore, it is logical to assume that this specific subroutine is the reason for a degradation in performance when running the program with large amounts of data.

---

8 Axel Kurka, "How Plausibility Checks Detect Bottlenecks in ABAP Programming," *SAP Insider,* January-March 2001.

Another problem associated with the Runtime Analysis tool is that, sometimes, the ATRA-file containing the runtime details is completely full. Furthermore, it takes the analyzer some time to prepare the information it has collected for presentation. If you really feel hindered by these restrictions, you may want to use the following alternative for the Runtime Analysis tool with a more limited functionality. You can add the ABAP statement GET RUN TIME FIELD in your ABAP code in order to measure the response time of any measurement unit that you want. The following example demonstrates how to do this; it shows two GET RUN TIME FIELD statements—the first statement is placed in front of the piece of code to be measured; the second statement is placed immediately after the piece of code. To determine the response time, the time between the two measure points is calculated:

```
* Start of the measurement unit
  GET RUN TIME FIELD tp_time_begin.
  SELECT * FROM  vbak
          INTO wa_vbak
          WHERE vbeln  IN so_vbeln
          AND    auart  IN so_auart
          AND    audat  IN so_audat.
    ADD 1 TO tp_count.
  ENDSELECT.
  GET RUN TIME FIELD tp_time_end.
* End of the measurement unit

* Calculation of the runtime of this unit.
  tp_time_diff = tp_time_end - tp_time_begin.
```

SQL Trace

If a program performs poorly, the first tool that you should resort to is the Runtime Analysis tool. When examining a program with this tool, you may find that the access of one of the database tables is the primary cause of the program's poor performance. However, the Runtime Analysis won't tell you exactly what went wrong. If you also need information on how a specific database access was performed by your program, you can evaluate this by activating the SQL Trace (Transaction ST05).

In most cases, it won't be necessary to measure all database accesses. Usually you already know exactly which table access is causing the problem. If you want to concentrate only on the table in question, we recommend that you click on the **Activate Trace with Filter** button. This option should make this operation a lot easier.

After the program has been executed, you can examine the results by clicking on the **Display Trace** button. An example of the results is shown in Figure 9.32.[9]

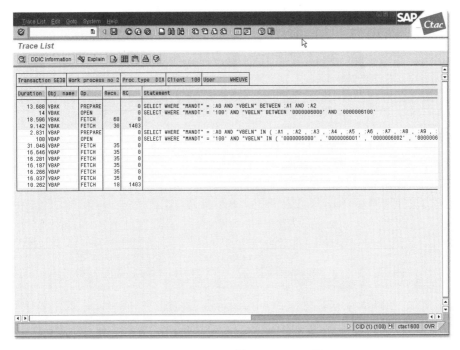

Figure 9.32 Example of a Trace List as Generated by Transaction ST05

By positioning the cursor on one of the executed database operations (PREPARE or OPEN) for the table in question, and clicking on the Explain button, an information screen similar to the one shown in Figure 9.33 will be displayed.

The example in Figure 9.33 shows how table VBAP is accessed. It shows the components of the WHERE clause. In addition, the execution plan shows which index is determined by the database management system as the most optimal index to access the table. This screen will differ in appearance for each specific database management system.

Screen Layout Check

From within the Screen Painter tool, you can verify whether the layout of a screen matches some of SAP's ergonomic guidelines (see Figure 9.34).

---

9   Note that the results of a SQL Trace are dependent on the underlying database management system. Our system runs on an Oracle Release 8.1.7.4.1. When running on other database management systems, the output will look different.

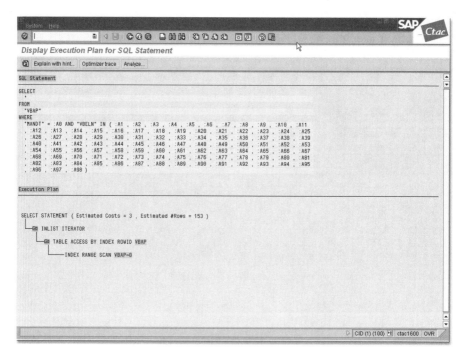

Figure 9.33 Example of an Execution Plan for a SQL Statement

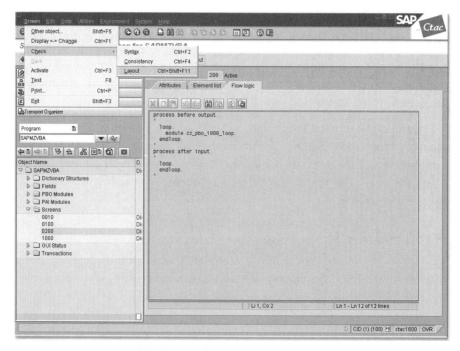

Figure 9.34 Checking Options for a Dynpro

If the system encounters any violations of the ergonomic guidelines, an error report is generated. Figure 9.35 shows an example of the output.

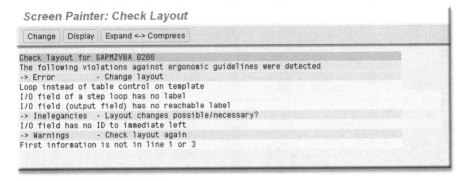

Figure 9.35 Output of a Layout Check in Screen Painter

In this example, the output shows that Dynpro 0200 of program SAPMZVBA is not completely in accordance with SAP's ergonomic guidelines; for example, because it contains an I/O field without a field label.

The screen layout check is an expedient way of verifying whether a screen complies with several basic rules for user-friendliness. Currently, this is the only standard function that is available for checking user-friendliness.

SAPscript and Smart Forms

When developing SAPscript forms, you can use two check tools: a static check of the consistency of a SAPscript form (see Figure 9.36); and a separate SAPscript Debugger to check the interaction between a SAPscript form and the calling ABAP program.

Both the definition and the text elements of the SAPscript form can be checked. Errors in text elements could, for example, be due to references to variables that don't exist in the calling program. The program name of the calling program must be provided when executing the check.

The SAPscript Debugger can be activated from within SAPscript Transaction SE71. First, a pop-up appears and prompts you to confirm whether you want to start debugging. You can enter debugging options here. As soon as the text elements are entered, the Debugger becomes active (see Figure 9.37).

Figure 9.37 shows how you can view the contents of variables that are used in a window. You can also toggle between the SAPscript Debugging screen and the ABAP Debugger.

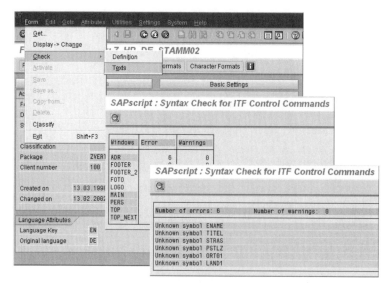

Figure 9.36 Results of Checking Text Elements of a SAPscript Form

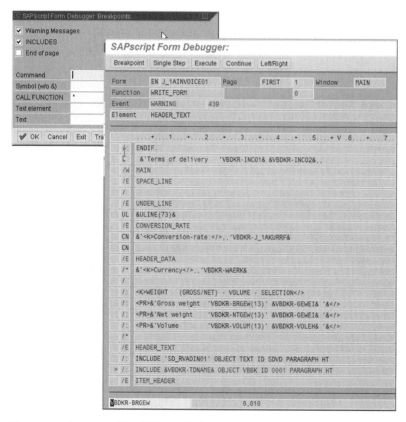

Figure 9.37 Contents of the SAPscript Debugger

Smart Forms, the SAPscript successor, doesn't require a separate debugging function. Instead, a function module that is generated by the Smart Forms transaction (Transaction SMARTFORMS) can be tested as a separate unit, and debugged like any other program.

Repository Information System

A powerful component of the ABAP Development Workbench is the *Repository Information System*. You can access this tool separately, but the way it is used most frequently is via the *Where Used List*, which is integrated in the ABAP Development Workbench. In the maintenance transactions of most Workbench Objects, this feature is available by clicking on the icon displayed in Figure 9.38.

Figure 9.38 The Where Used Button—Available Throughout All Development Tools

This feature enables you to check where a specific object is used when you need to change the object; for example, you can approximate the impact that the change will have. For this reason, the *Where Used List* is particularly important in terms of the stability of the SAP system. You may not only find out where an object is actually used; you may learn that an object is not used at all. In that case, you could decide to deactivate or remove it (which, incidentally, supports the maintainability).

Creating Your Own Check Tools

So far, we described various standard SAP tools to check your programs on robustness issues. Now, we'll show you how to create your own check tools; for example, to test the specific standards and guidelines defined within your own company. Several ABAP commands have been created that can be used for this very purpose. If you combine these specific commands with more general ABAP commands, especially character string commands like SEARCH or SPLIT, you can create your own check tools.

Specific ABAP commands are, for example, READ REPORT, READ TEXTPOOL, SYNTAX CHECK, and SCAN. All of these commands are primarily used to copy ABAP sources and text elements into internal tables and to perform checks and scans on ABAP code. Note, however, that SYNTAX CHECK and SCAN are marked by SAP "for internal use only." This means that "incompatible changes or further development may occur at any time without warning or notice" (for an example of the corresponding online help information, see also Figure 9.39). Therefore, we highly recommend that you use these types of statements in programs that are used only for quality control.

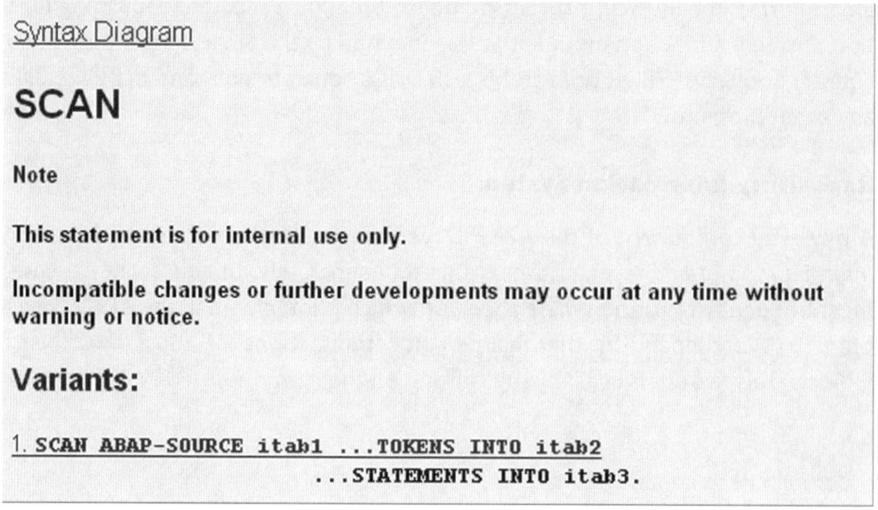

SCAN

Note

This statement is for internal use only.

Incompatible changes or further developments may occur at any time without warning or notice.

Variants:

```
1. SCAN ABAP-SOURCE itab1 ...TOKENS INTO itab2
                      ...STATEMENTS INTO itab3.
```

Figure 9.39 SAP Indicates That the SCAN Statement Is for Internal Use Only

Other, more general ABAP commands that you could apply when making your own check tools include several kinds of string-processing statements such as SEARCH, FIND, and SHIFT. Once the ABAP sources have been copied into internal tables using the READ REPORT command, you can use these string commands to search for specific patterns. Note, however, that the Code Inspector already contains an option to look for statement patterns. So, before you start investing time and effort in creating your own tools, ensure that your requirements aren't already met by standard SAP tools.

Summary of Check Tools

To summarize this discussion of check tools, we have included Table 9.1, which lists all the tools that we mentioned. We checked (X) those aspects of technical quality that can be monitored with each of these tools.

	Correct-ness	Stability	Performance	User-friend-liness	Maintain-ability
Extended Syntax Check	X	X			X
Code Inspector	X	X	X		X
Unicode Check	X	X			
Coverage Analyzer		X	X		X
Debugger	X	X			
Runtime Analysis	X		X		X

	Correct-ness	Stability	Performance	User-friend-liness	Maintain-ability
SQL Trace			X		
Screen Layout Check				X	
SAPscript Check	X				
Where Used Lists		X			X

9.2　Troubleshooting Incidents

If an incident occurs in a SAP production environment (or at any point during program development), you need to be able to find the cause of the problem as quickly as possible. This section provides you with some guidelines that are useful for troubleshooting activities. Troubleshooting doesn't require only knowledge of which tools to use; you must also be able to analyze the ABAP software as efficiently as possible.

It shouldn't surprise you that the Debugger is the most appropriate tool for troubleshooting. To a certain extent, using the Debugger in troubleshooting activities can be like balancing on a tight rope, particularly when you're forced to do debugging in the production environment. Debugging in a production environment is not preferable, particularly for programs that perform database updates or process interface data—you might accidentally create wrong updates yourself. However, sometimes, there's no alternative: you may not be able to create exactly the same circumstances as those in which a specific error was raised.

We'll start this section by providing some general tips on how to best approach incidents in a production environment (in Section 9.2.1). Then, we'll describe the typical signs of incidents that occur. In Section 9.2.2, we'll present common signs and frequent causes of correctness incidents, and the best tools to investigate these incidents. In Section 9.2.3, we'll discuss typical stability problems, and in Section 9.2.4, we'll address performance problems. The underlying assumption that we make is that particular types of incidents will usually be caused by the same type of deficiency. Therefore, they will usually also require the same kind of methods and tools to tackle them.

9.2.1　Basic Incident Analysis

Solving production problems is often a difficult task. To some extent, you need basic skills for problem analysis and structured working methods: you must be able (and willing) to carefully monitor each step, each check made, each test performed, and each single result achieved. Without this level of accuracy, you cannot draw conclusions quickly. Personal skills are also necessary: a troubleshooter must be able to cope with the pressure of having to solve a production problem immediately, sometimes while people are looking over his or her shoulder. The best troubleshooters are usually those developers who have extensive SAP knowledge, not only about ABAP development, but also about the functionality of the application, the customizing settings, and even SAP's technical basis.

This Section is devoted to several guidelines for problem solving, which are addressed via the main questions that you as a developer should ask yourself: Was anything changed just before the program failed? Is there a pattern in the way the error occurs? What signs can be associated with the incident?

What Has Changed?

A production incident usually doesn't occur completely out of the blue. There's always a reason why something goes wrong. Therefore, when determining the reason for a sudden ABAP problem, your first step should be to check what has changed since the last time the suspected ABAP code was used correctly. In a highly integrated system, this can be anything—even a minor change can lead to serious problems. But, when looking for and tracking changes, you should adhere to a certain order: initially, you should check changes in the ABAP code; next, check changes in the direct environment, that is, in other ABAP Workbench objects; then, check changes in the outer environment; and finally, check changes in how the code is used. Now, we'll discuss the last three reasons for changes in greater detail.

1. Changes in the direct environment

By changes in the direct environment of a development object, we mean changes in related Workbench objects. For example, changing the definition of a data element can lead to problems in all the ABAP programs that use it. Therefore, it does make sense to investigate all the transports that have recently been imported in the production environment, and check the interdependencies between the objects in those transports (see also Section 2.3).

If a problem can be solved only by restoring an old version[10] of a development object, SAP's version management functionality can help: the typical procedure is then to restore the old version in development, create a new transport, and import this transport in the production system, so that the situation that existed before the incident is recreated. This workaround ensures that the operation can continue as before; afterwards, the change that caused the problem can then be implemented again, but this time, more carefully.

---

10 Note that SAPscript and Smart Forms do not support version management.

2. Changes in the outer environment

Not every incident is necessarily caused by a change in an ABAP or a ABAP Dictionary object. It may also concern a change in customizing settings, master data, user settings, or even technical system parameters (consider the topics that were discussed in Section 4.4). All these factors can be relevant. Changes in customizing can be traced by checking imported customizing transports; changes in master data and user settings can be traced by checking their change documents; changes in the technical profiles of SAP application servers are visible via Transaction RZ10.

3. Changes in the use of the code

Finally, a production incident is not necessarily always caused by a tangible change in the object's environment; for example, a program can also cause errors simply because it is *used* differently for the first time (see Chapter 4). Remember that many programs contain potential problems (*time bombs*), which may not immediately, or even never, cause real production incidents.

Is There a Pattern in the Error?

The second approach to a production incident doesn't primarily focus on recent *changes*, but rather on the *circumstances* in which a problem occurs. The problems that are the most difficult to analyze are those that don't occur all the time. The best way to tackle these infrequent types of errors is to try and find a pattern. Knowing the specific circumstances in which an error occurs will make it easier to find the cause of the error. We have some suggestions that may help you to find a pattern:

▶ Is there a connection with preceding programs or transactions?
For example: "If program *x* runs in the same job as our program, the error occurs; if program *y* runs in the same job, everything works as usual."

▶ Is there a connection with the sequence of steps that are made in an online program?
For example: If a problem occurs only "after dynpro *9000* in transaction *x* has been called."

▶ Is there a connection with the time that the program runs?
For example: "If the program runs in the evening, the error occurs. Otherwise, it does not." Perhaps, other programs that are running in the evening cause the problem.

▶ Does the problem occur in every logon language? Perhaps there are missing descriptions (as in correctness, database views).

- Does the same problem occur on every desktop? Is there a relation with the SAP GUI version, or the Operation System running on the desktop?
- Does the problem occur independently of user settings such as decimal notation, date format, time zone, and parameter ID values?
- Is there a relationship with user authorizations? (Use Transaction SU53 to check this possibility.)
- Does the same problem also occur for other organizational entities in the SAP system?
  For example: The problem may only occur "for company code *1100*" or "for plant *2000.*"
- Are there any relations with customizing settings? Does the problem occur only for a specific order type, or one material type, etc.?
- Is there a relation with master data? Does the problem occur only for one specific customer, one material, one supplier, etc.?
- Does the problem occur in both dialog and background processing?

What Is the Real Cause?

The third basic approach is to try and look beyond the first signs of an error.

In practice, you may see that the visible sign of an incident isn't always directly related to its cause. What frequently happens when an unanticipated exception occurs in a program is that this doesn't immediately result in an error. Instead, the program may continue to process the wrong data for awhile, before eventually starting to behave strangely, or ending by displaying the wrong data, or ending with an error message or a runtime error (i.e., a program dump). Programmers often tend to look at the end of the chain of events only, where the final error was caused, whereas they should have attempted to trace the initial error in the chain instead.

An example of such a situation is the case in which a division by zero raises a runtime error and a program dump. What an inexperienced programmer may do with this error is prevent the program dump by catching the runtime error (for example, with a TRY...ENDTRY block as explained in Section 5.3.1). Although this will remove the sign of the error (the symptom), the cause of the error may still be there. What we recommend in this particular case is to investigate the division by zero to determine whether the presence of the value zero was caused by a deficiency in the code that was processed earlier.

One of the more notorious examples of trying to determine the origin of the problem occurs when a program doesn't anticipate exceptional return codes after processing a SELECT statement. If a specific row cannot be found in a database table and the program doesn't anticipate this exception, the work area will usually still contain its previous value. The severity of this problem depends on what happens next with the wrong data. The value may serve directly as output for a screen; it may also be used in a database update or an interface message or file, causing things to go wrong elsewhere.

Therefore, we strongly encourage you not to relax too soon after having solved a production problem. Besides, it may also be an extra motivation to add proper exception handling to each piece of ABAP code. This will help you to find the causes of problems more efficiently and prevent most production problems.

9.2.2 Correctness Incidents

In correctness incidents, something is usually inherently wrong with the data: the data that is displayed in a list, or the data to be updated in the database. In this section, we address signs, causes, and troubleshooting tools for three common correctness errors: incorrect data, database inconsistencies, and update cancellations.

Incorrect Data

Signs of incorrect data are, for example, descriptions that seem to repeat themselves or amounts that cannot be correct. Wrong data can be displayed in lists or on screens, or worse, updated in database tables or included in the interface data to be sent to another system.

In Chapter 3, we discussed several types of ABAP constructions that can lead to similar problems. Recall the incorrect use of an Open SQL statement, or the problems caused by limited user authorizations, or the danger of the ON CHANGE statement. However, above all, the most frequent cause of incorrect data is simply forgetting to include a statement to CLEAR or REFRESH data. This often goes hand-in-hand with another common example of short-sightedness—not anticipating exceptions such as return codes in Open SQL.

The best tool to help you detect the cause of correctness errors is the *Debugger*. It may be particularly difficult to do this if the program is complicated; for example, if it uses many form routines, functions and methods, and many different variables. The **Debugger Watchpoints** option (see Figure 9.26) enables you to automatically stop the program when the content of a field changes or gets a specific value.

Another helpful tool is the *Where Used List* in the ABAP editor. You could use this option to highlight where a specific field is being used in an ABAP program. This enables you to quickly trace all statements that change the contents of a particular variable.

Database Inconsistencies

A database inconsistency arises whenever the relation between data in database tables is disturbed. The relation between the keys of two tables can be defined very strictly in the ABAP Dictionary: as a foreign key relation of dependency type *key fields/candidates*. If you created various custom database tables, you should consider the relations between these tables, and perhaps also the relations with standard SAP tables.

Database inconsistencies often result from the improper processing of a *Logical Unit of Work* (LUW, see Section 3.5.2). In particular, the cause of database inconsistencies can be the wrong use of an explicit COMMIT WORK or ROLLBACK WORK command. For example, an erroneous update statement resulting in a return code other than '0' should almost always prompt the execution of a ROLLBACK WORK statement. If this statement is missing while other updates in the same LUW are implicitly committed, for example, when the execution of the program ends, this will lead to an inconsistency.

Another possible cause of database inconsistencies is the implicit commit or rollback handling. An implicit commit occurs between every dialog step. If a programmer does not take this into account, part of the database table updates are automatically committed after one dialog step and cannot be rolled back again. An implicit rollback is the result of a message of type 'A' (abend), whereas a message of type 'E' (error) does not lead to a rollback of database updates. If these message types are mixed up (used improperly), updates can either be rolled back or committed inadvertently.

Also in this situation, the Debugger is the optimal tool to find the cause of the error. Focus first on the update statements. The Debugger option **Breakpoint at • Statement** (see Figure 9.25) can help in this case.

Furthermore, the use of update statements can also be checked in the ABAP editor, or by using the *Code Inspector*. Still, the Debugger has the advantage that it also enables you to check the flow of the updates. Using the **Replace** option of the Debugger, you can deliberately introduce an error and check how the program responds to this error.

Once the correct LUW has been established, it usually isn't difficult to solve an update problem.

Update Cancelled

As we described in Chapter 3, updates in standard SAP programs are often executed in a special process mode called the *Update Task*. Processes in the Update

Task are triggered by calling function modules with the addition IN UPDATE TASK. You can also use this technique in customized ABAP programs.

A runtime error or a message of type 'A' (abnormal end) in the function module that is executed in an update process leads to the well known express message in Figure 9.40.

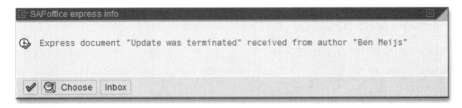

Figure 9.40 An Express Document as a Result of an Update Cancellation

There are two ways to find the cause of an update cancellation: Transaction SM13 to display the cancelled update requests (see Figure 9.41); and the **Update Debugging** option (see Figure 9.23) to trace the behavior of the Update Task function.

Update Requests

4 Update records found

Cln	User	Date	Time	TCode	Info		Status
100	RROOIJ	05/19/2004	11:56:00	ME22N			Error
100	RROOIJ	05/19/2004	11:55:20	ME22N			Error
100	BMEIJS	05/18/2004	16:31:36				Error
100	BMEIJS	05/18/2004	16:24:30	SE38			Error

Figure 9.41 An Overview of Cancelled Updates Via Transaction SM13

You can analyze the updates that have been cancelled by checking the interface data of the **Update Task** function, and viewing the message that led to the cancellation. Figure 9.41 displays other options, such as repeating the update or testing it. If the **Update Debugging** option is activated, the detailed behavior of the update function module can be analyzed.

However, be very careful when debugging update programs in a production environment: you probably don't want to process any update requests there. Therefore, it's preferable to try and reproduce the update error in a test environment, for example, by forcing erroneous data using the REPLACE option.

The most typical causes of update cancellations are:

▶ The primary key of the data to be inserted already exists.

▶ A unique secondary key of the data already exists. This can be the result of both an INSERT of a new table row and the UPDATE of an existing table row.

▶ The data to be updated or deleted doesn't exist.

▶ A statement that is not allowed in the **Update Task** is nevertheless found there; for example, CALL TRANSACTION.

Note that the first three problems can also be the result of inconsistencies in the interface data of the function module or function modules that form one LUW. To clarify this, we present two examples:

1. An internal table is used to insert various rows in a database table. However, the internal table contains duplicate lines. The INSERT command for the duplicate line will fail.

2. An entry is first deleted, and then updated again within the same LUW. Consequently, the UPDATE statement will fail.

9.2.3   Stability Incidents

In Chapter 4, we described all kinds of particular errors that are symptoms of unstable program behavior. Here, we'll examine the two most common and severe types of incidents: program dumps and technical error messages.

Dumps

A program dump should be approached differently depending on whether it is produced in dialog mode or in background mode. If a runtime error occurs in dialog mode, the corresponding program dump will immediately become visible. This has the advantage that the user can start debugging from there. However, for an end user, this doesn't make much sense—the typical end user doesn't have the authorization or the required knowledge to look into a program dump. Nevertheless, the information that the Debugger provides can be valuable. Therefore, we recommend that you try to reproduce the dump, preferably in a non-production system. If a background job has led to a runtime error, the job log will indicate that a program dump has been generated. (see Figure 9.42) This dump can be viewed using Transaction ST22 (see Figure 9.43).

Job Log Entries for /CTAC/R_STAB_DUMP_10_ERR

🗎 Long text 🗐 Previous page 🗐 Next page ⊞

Job log overview for job: /CTAC/R_STAB_DUMP_10_ERR

Date	Time	Message text	Message class	Message no.	Message type
06/09/2004	13:14:58	Job started	00	516	S
06/09/2004	13:14:58	Step 001 started (program /CTAC/R_STAB_DUMP_10_ERR, variant &0000000000000, user	00	550	S
06/09/2004	13:15:00	ABAP/4 processor: CREATE_OBJECT_CLASS_NOT_FOUND	00	671	A
06/09/2004	13:15:00	Job cancelled	00	518	A

Figure 9.42 Job Log of a Program That Led to a Runtime Error

Figure 9.43 An Overview of Dump Content

In most cases, the information provided by a program dump leaves little room for doubt: it usually points directly to the statement that caused the runtime error. A program dump delivers several types of useful information such as:

▶ The exact statement that caused the runtime error

▶ A code extract: the ABAP code lines immediately before and after the statement that caused the dump

▶ Hints for error analysis

▶ The exact contents of system variables and some program variables at the time of the dump

▶ The calls that were active when the dump was raised

Note that a dump can be the result of another basic problem, such as not properly anticipating an exceptional situation. Therefore, the program dump may well serve as a starting point for the search, but it cannot provide you with all the direct answers.

We've already mentioned that the Debugger is the most valuable tool that you can use to find the origin of a program dump. The **Act call stack** option (see Figure 9.28) in particular and the possibility to view the contents of all variables may provide valuable information on the exact circumstances in which the runtime error occurred.

A second useful source of information is the *System Log*, which you can view with Transaction SM21. The information provided in the System Log is useful in situations where a runtime error is the result of a problem that lies outside the program. Sometimes, the System Log provides information on a problem that occurred just before the dump. If the origin of a runtime error is a systemwide problem, then, other programs may also end in a program dump.

The third tool that you can use to investigate the general occurrence of runtime errors is the *Coverage Analyzer* (discussed earlier). This tool keeps a record of the number of runtime errors per form routine, function module, and so forth. Such information makes it less useful when you need to react instantaneously to incidents. However, it can be particularly appropriate for situations that require a more general approach to the stability of a SAP production system.

Error Messages

If an error message pops up in a production environment, finding its cause is not a real problem if the message is clear and directly related to the problem. Sometimes, however, tracking the cause of an error message is not such an easy task; for example, if a message is vaguely formulated. Imagine a program that was written years ago, which now suddenly starts to generate unfamiliar error messages. Chances are that no relevant documentation exists for this error message.

In this case, the most important question to ask yourself is "How can I use the Debugger as efficiently as possible?" What you should do is use the error message as a starting point for your investigation. Earlier, we described how you can start debugging from a pop-up screen (Figure 9.21). An alternative is to use the Debugger option **Breakpoint at • Statement** to set a dynamic breakpoint at the MESSAGE statement (Figure 9.25). If you use this option, the program will stop as soon as a MESSAGE statement is encountered.

9.2.4 Performance Problems

In contrast to stability and correctness incidents, performance *incidents* don't really exist, in the sense that they require immediate action. From that perspective, they don't really belong in this section about troubleshooting. If a program ends abruptly (a sign of unstable program behavior), or, if the information that a program generates is incorrect, the program usually won't be applied again until the problem has been resolved. Consequently, solving such problems will typically have a high priority. If, on the other hand, an ABAP program *performs* poorly, its functionality is still intact and immediate action isn't necessary.

However, there will always be a point where performance problems become unacceptable, and start to disrupt daily business processes; for example, when already loaded trucks have to wait for their customs forms, or when sales invoices aren't finalized in time, or management reports cannot be delivered, or end users no longer accept the long response times.

The difference between performance problems and real incidents is also visible in the approach that performance problems require, which is not typical for troubleshooting activities. Troubleshooting activities almost always must focus on one tiny detail, whereas the opposite is usually true for performance problems. Apart from programs that are executed exceptionally slowly, poor performance is often a systemwide phenomenon. Therefore, the associated problems require more of a top-down approach, whereas a typical incident requires a bottom-up approach. Now, we'll distinguish the tools necessary to evaluate overall system performance from those needed to evaluate program-specific performance.

Tools to Evaluate Overall System Performance

If slow performance is caused by the ABAP software, you should first analyze the abundance of performance data that SAP supplies. Many companies rely on the EarlyWatch and the EarlyWatch Alert services that SAP provides. Some companies rely on performance audits executed by others. But you can also analyze the performance data of a SAP system yourself with the *Workload Analysis* tool (Transaction ST03):

Figure 9.44 shows the main screen available in the Workload Analysis. The performance information displayed here has two dimensions: the type of task (in the column on the left), such as Background, Dialog, RFC, and Update; and the type of time, such as database time, CPU time, and Wait time.

Transaction ST03 supplies a lot more information that can be used to trace poorly performing development objects. All this information is related to a specified period of time: one day, or a week, or an entire month. The information provided includes data such as the top-40 of most time-consuming processes, the total and average response time per program, and the execution time of Remote Function Calls (RFCs). Note that interpreting all this information is not easy to do without having sufficient experience and background knowledge.

Workload in System CID

Instance	ctac1600_CID_00		First record	06/09/2004	00:00:33
Period	06/09/2004		Last record	06/09/2004	11:59:51
Task type	All		Time period	0 Day(s)	11:59:18

Times | Database | Roll information | Parts of response time | All data

Workload overview: Average time per step in ms

Task Type	# Steps	Ø Time	Ø CPU Time	Ø DB Time	Ø Time	Ø WaitTime	Ø Roll In~	Ø Roll Wait Time	Ø Load- + Gen. Time	Ø LockTime	Ø CPIC/RFC	Ø Time	Ø GUI Time
AutoABAP	144	159,911.5	2,711.8	211.9	0.0	0.1	5.3	0.0	80.5	1.1	179.4	0.0	0.0
Background	3,707	1,249.7	124.9	454.6	0.0	1.1	0.4	0.0	21.2	0.4	659.1	0.0	0.0
Buffer synchr.	360	21.1	0.6	14.1	0.0	1.1	0.0	0.0	0.0	0.0	0.0	0.0	0.0
Dialog	1,516	1,070.2	203.6	289.7	0.0	3.0	1.3	232.3	40.7	0.0	0.6	641.8	238.5
HTTP	135	20.1	3.5	4.9	0.0	3.3	0.0	0.0	2.1	0.0	0.0	0.0	0.0
RFC	74	377.4	206.2	94.3	0.0	2.5	0.5	0.7	7.0	0.1	0.0	0.0	0.0
Update	1	11,134.0	594.0	5,706.0	0.0	172.0	0.0	0.0	2,388.0	96.0	0.0	0.0	0.0

Figure 9.44 Example of Performance Information Supplied by Transaction ST03

In addition to the Workload Analysis, the *Coverage Analyzer* can also provide useful information about the overall system performance. It doesn't supply runtime figures, but it does offer some other valuable information: the number of times that a specific unit of ABAP code has been executed. On the basis of this information, you may decide, for example, to implement a relatively small performance improvement in a frequently used function module. Many small performance improvements can also have a significant effect.

Program Specific Performance Analysis

Performance improvement efforts should always be directed at the statements and procedures of a program that are responsible for the total runtime, and therefore have the largest impact on performance. Therefore, the goals of performance analysis are twofold: finding the problematic code, and proposing solutions to tackle the associated problem. In Chapter 7, we learned that the two main causes of performance problems within a program are inefficient use of Open SQL commands, and inefficient handling of internal tables. The Workload Analysis tool provides information that can help you choose the right tool to analyze performance problems. Remember the information that the top-40 response times can supply (see Figure 7.29 in Chapter 7).

More detailed information can be collected via the *Runtime Analysis* tool (Transaction SE30). If you can run this tool in a test system environment with a comparable amount of data as in the production system, or, if you can use this tool in the production system, you'll get a realistic indication of which part of the program has the largest impact on the program's total response time. The Runtime Analysis clearly distinguishes between database and program processing time (see Figure 9.45).

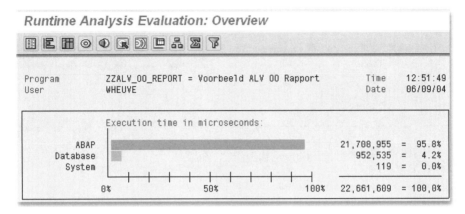

Figure 9.45 The Runtime Analysis Evaluation overview

Figure 9.45 shows that a large part of the response time for program zzalv_00_ report is caused by non-database activities (especially internal table handling). These are referred to by the term *ABAP*. Therefore, in this particular case, attempts to improve the performance should not be primarily aimed at the way in which the program performs its database handling.

If the database-handling activities of a program consume the larger part of the response time, we recommend that you focus first on SQL statements such as SELECT, INSERT, or IMPORT. Perhaps the performance checklist can add some useful tips. We'll deal with two particular performance issues in order to show you how to use the available tools: inefficient index usage, and identical SELECT statements that can be combined into one.

SQL Trace (Transaction ST05) is the optimal tool for investigating inefficient index usage. Figure 9.46 shows that in this example, database table VBAP is read (approached) via index 0, which is in fact its primary index.

Identical SELECT statements are individual SELECT statements that use the same WHERE clause on the same database table. These statements can often be combined into one statement using internal tables as a data buffer. This can improve performance considerably (see Section 7.3.3). A SQL Trace provides this information.

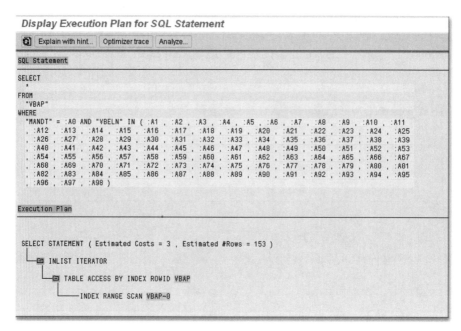

Figure 9.46 Display the Execution Plan for Reading Table VBAP

Summarized SQL Statements: Sorted by duration

Executions	Identical	Duration	Records	Time/exec	Rec/exec.	AvgTime/R.	MinTime/R.	Length	BfTp	TabType	Obj. name
10	90	643,966	120	64,397	12.0	5,366	1,588	436		TRANSP	S004
10	90	299,569	120	29,957	12.0	2,496	2,347	436		TRANSP	S004
2	0	104,132	1	52,066	0.5	104,132	89,077	88	gen	TRANSP	VARIT
6	0	79,035	6	13,173	1.0	13,173	6,486				DDNTF
2	0	57,367	2	28,684	1.0	28,684	27,983	20,092		TRANSP	D342L
2	0	37,812	2	18,906	1.0	18,906	8,178	20,072		TRANSP	D345T
3	0	31,831	2	10,610	0.7	15,916	2,074	2,972	cust	TRANSP	VARI
2	0	23,391	2	11,696	1.0	11,696	8,363	20,072		TRANSP	D346T
1	0	21,783	1	21,783	1.0	21,783	21,783	318	gen	TRANSP	DDFTX
1	0	16,971	0	16,971	0.0	16,971	16,971	121	sng	TRANSP	D347T
2	0	15,286	1	7,643	0.5	15,286	7,901	61	gen	TRANSP	VARIS
2	0	13,777	1	6,889	0.5	13,777	11,917	132	gen	TRANSP	VARID
6	0	13,039	6	2,173	1.0	2,173	1,114	94	sng	TRANSP	TFDIR
1	0	12,739	4	12,739	4.0	3,185	3,185	318	gen	TRANSP	DDFTX
2	50	3,228	0	1,614	0.0	3,228	1,739	137		TRANSP	DWINACTIV
2	50	2,492	2	1,246	1.0	1,246	1,135	170		VIEW	TRDIR
1	0	2,193	1	2,193	1.0	2,193	2,193	111	gen	TRANSP	TRDIRT
1	0	2,055	2	2,055	2.0	1,028	1,028	37	gen	TRANSP	USRBF2
1	0	1,545	1	1,545	1.0	1,545	1,545	171		VIEW	PROGDIR
57	35	1,382,211	274	24,249	4.8	5,045					

Figure 9.47 FIgure 9.47 The SQL Trace: Summarized SQL Statements

The menu option **Summarized SQL Statements** collects which SQL statements are identical. In Figure 9.47, the first line shows that ten identical SQL statements were performed on Table S004. There's also an option to get a summarized table overview. This shows you exactly which table access has the largest impact on runtime.

A second option for analyzing database performance is to use the *Runtime Analysis Evaluation* tables evaluation. This overview doesn't supply any information on inefficient index usage, however, the analysis file contains information on the database-handling time required per table and the number of table accesses. A high number of table accesses most probably points at `SELECT` loops or identical `SELECT` statements.

Runtime Analysis Evaluation: Tables

Tab./View	#Acces	Runtime	Class	Buffering
LTDXT	1	135,343	TRANSP	generic
BDSLOIO2	13	105,811	TRANSP	
VBAP	3	90,219	TRANSP	
BDSPHIO2	43	73,201	TRANSP	
MAKT	2	59,872	TRANSP	
VBEP	3	51,834	TRANSP	
LTDXD	3	44,930	TRANSP	generic
BDSLOIOT2	9	43,555	TRANSP	
VBAK	3	32,892	TRANSP	
KNA1	1	32,804	TRANSP	
T006A	1	31,020	TRANSP	generic
DDFTX	3	29,486	TRANSP	generic
LTDXS	1	29,099	TRANSP	generic
BDSPHF2	12	27,241	TRANSP	
DOKIL	4	26,593	TRANSP	partial
V_LTDX	3	24,953	VIEW	generic
VARID	24	23,739	TRANSP	generic

Figure 9.48 The Runtime Analysis: The Number of Accesses and Runtime of Database Table Handling in Runtime Analysis

For example, Figure 9.48 shows that table EKPO has been accessed 90 times and demanded a total runtime of almost 2 seconds.

A third, but somewhat less handy option is offered by the *Process Monitor* (Transaction SM50). During the execution of a program, this monitor displays the database table that the program is currently reading. If the same table name pops up repeatedly, you should initially focus on the database handling of this table.

If performance problems aren't caused by database handling, the next place to look is in the internal table handling, also via a *Runtime Analysis*. The detailed information that this tool provides enables you to find the exact statements that cause slow performance.

Runtime Analysis Evaluation: Internal Table Hit List

Int. tab.	No.	Gross	=	Net	Gross (%)	Net (%)	Program Name
IT_1147	3	166,727		130	0.7	0.0	CL_DD_DOCUMENT================CP
IT_381	5	135,523		150	0.6	0.0	SAPLSKBS
IT_955	5	134,749		253	0.6	0.0	SAPLSDCL
IT_902	3	113,701		190	0.5	0.0	SAPLSLVC_FULLSCREEN
IT_54	1	93,206		141	0.4	0.0	ZZALV_OO_REPORT
IT_246	88	69,792		12,258	0.3	0.1	SAPLSLVC
IT_56	1	60,261		210	0.3	0.0	ZZALV_OO_REPORT
IT_390	2	45,019		89	0.2	0.0	SAPLSKBS
IT_1058	6	43,216		482	0.2	0.0	SAPLSDCL
IT_936	6	39,538		309	0.2	0.0	SAPLBDS_METHODS
IT_437	5	34,424		227	0.2	0.0	SAPLSLVC
IT_435	20	34,376		2,000	0.2	0.0	SAPLSLVC
IT_1113	8	32,103		533	0.1	0.0	SAPLSDCL
IT_1533	1	31,413		12,342	0.1	0.1	CL_GUI_DATAMANAGER============CP
IT_115	5	29,136		61	0.1	0.0	CL_GUI_CONTAINER==============CP
IT_138	15	28,840		250	0.1	0.0	CL_GUI_CONTAINER==============CP
IT_67	1,485	26,288		23,414	0.1	0.1	SAPLOLEA
IT_1555	1	22,869		7,893	0.1	0.0	CL_GUI_DATAMANAGER============CP
IT_172	9	22,198		135	0.1	0.0	CL_GUI_CONTAINER==============CP
IT_233	2	20,407		2,525	0.1	0.0	CL_GUI_CONTROL================CP
IT_1413	6	19,746		530	0.1	0.0	SAPLSDCL
IT_922	3	19,025		182	0.1	0.0	SAPLBDS_CONNECTIONS

Figure 9.49 Runtime Analysis Evaluation: Internal Table Performance

Figure 9.49 shows which internal tables are processed by a program. Note that the names of the internal tables shown in this list are merely symbolic references. These are not the actual names used in the ABAP code. If necessary, however, you can directly jump from the overview to the ABAP code to find the real table names.

Column *Gross* in the overview represents the total processing time per internal table, that is, including the time required for the statements that are placed in-between the commands LOOP and ENDLOOP. The column *Net* depicts the response time that the LOOP statement requires. The net time will usually be more interesting than the gross time.

When attempting to solve internal table performance problems, you may be inspired by some of the recommendations provided in Section 7.4.3, or by consulting the performance checklist in Section 9.1.3 of this chapter.

9.3 Summary

As you may have noticed, we have adopted a different viewpoint in this chapter. While most of the other chapters in this book focus on guidelines to help you resolve specific programming problems, in Chapter 9, we focused on the tools that you can use to detect and analyze a host of ABAP programming deficiencies. First, we discussed testing approaches and tools that can help you during development. We hope that your ABAP developments can benefit from the general tips on testing, and that our brief description of colleague checks or peer reviews will encourage you to read more on the subject. If you're serious about implementing colleague checks, you can use the checklists provided here as a prototype, and extend these over time. In fact, these checklists succinctly summarize the contents of this book. We also recommended which tools are best suited for testing each particular aspect of technical quality.

In the second part of this chapter, we provided you with a basic approach for problem solving and gave you several tips on troubleshooting, namely, the optimal tools to use for each specific problem. Solving problems in SAP production systems will always remain an integral part of the developers work. However, you can be sure that the number of problems you encounter in your production systems will decrease considerably once you've adhered to the guidelines we recommend.

A   A Proposal for Naming Standards

Names of customer ABAP Dictionary objects and Workbench objects must be assigned to a customized namespace: in general, this means that names should start with y, z, or a specific customer namespace like /ctac/. See SAP OSS Note 16466 for a complete overview of the customer name ranges for every type of object that customers can create.

A.1   Program Internal Data

Data Types	Prefix	Name	Suffix Examples	Example
Internal standard table	ta_	Descriptive, if possible refer to TYPE	old new cur	ta_orders_new
Internal sorted table	ts_	Descriptive, if possible refer to TYPE	old new cur	ts_orders
Internal hashed table	th_	Descriptive, if possible refer to TYPE		th_customers
Ranges/Type Range of	ra_	Descriptive		ra_matnr
Work area for database and internal tables	wa_	Descriptive, if possible refer to TYPE		wa_mara
Structure (record)	st_	Descriptive, if possible refer to TYPE		st_sales_download
Table control	tc_	Reference to the screen number		tc_9000
Data reference	dr_	Descriptive, related to the data it will refer to		dr_datum
Reference variable	rf_	Descriptive, related to the class it refers to		rf_invoice
Other variables	tp_	Descriptive, if possible Refer to TYPE	_max _min _avg _cnt _sum _swi	tp_menge_avg

Data Types	Prefix	Name	Suffix Examples	Example
Select-options	so_	Refer to TYPE		so_matnr
Parameters	pa_	Descriptive, if possible refer to TYPE		pa_downl
Constant	co_	Descriptive		co_waers_company
Local Variable	l*			ltp_matnr
Statics	lst_	Descriptive, if possible refer to TYPE		lst_menge_cnt
Field-Symbols		Descriptive		<sortfield>
Types	ty_	Descriptive		ty_orderlist
Local Class	lcl_	Like global class, but starting with l		lcl_rectangle
Local Interface	lif_	Like global interface, but starting with l		lif_symbol

A.2 Formal Interface Parameters

	Prefix	Name	Example
Subroutine			
Using	u*	Refer to TYPE	utp_matnr uts_orders
Changing	c*	Refer to TYPE	ctp_calculationg
Tables	t*	Refer to TYPE	tta_orders
Methods			
Importing	i*	Refer to TYPE	itp_matnr
Exporting	e*	Refer to TYPE	eth_suppliers
Changing	c*	Refer to TYPE	cts_orders
Returning	r*	Refer to TYPE	rtp_found_swi
Functions			
Importing	i*	Refer to TYPE	itp_lifnr
Exporting	e*	Refer to TYPE	etp_menge_sum

	Prefix	Name	Example
Changing	c*	Refer to TYPE	cts_orders
Tables	t*		tta_orders

A.3   ABAP Dictionary Objects

If we don't have to indicate the specific standard used, we use <company choice>.

Object type	Name	Example
Database Table	<name space>+T+<company choice>	zt0001 ztorders
Database View	<name space>+V+<company choice>	zvvbakvbap zv_material
Structure	<name space>+S +<company choice>	zsordersin
Table Type	<name space> +<company choice>	zttsorders zmaterialtab
Domain	<name space>+<company choice>	zordnr
Data Element	<name space>+<company choice> Reference to used domain, possibly the same name is relation is 1:1	zordnr
Lock Object	e+<name space>+reference to base table	eztorder
Search Help	<name space> + reference to data that is searched for Note the relation between search help and database table or view name.	zsrchcust /ctac/h_type (refers to table /ctac/type)
Type Group	<name space> +<company choice>	/ctac/const01 ztgr01

A.4   ABAP Workbench Objects

If we don't have to indicate the specific standard used, we use <company choice>.

Object type	Name	Example
Report	<name space> +<company choice>	zorderoverview zrvr0001
Module Pool	<name space> +<company choice>	sapmz001

Object type	Name	Example
Include	<name space> +<company choice>	ziconstants01 mz001top
Function Group	<name space> +<company choice> Note that function group name is part of generated includes.	z001 zinfo
Class	<namespace>+<SAP class type prefix> +_description	zcl_rectangle /ctac/cx_nodata
Interface	<namespace>+if+_description	zif_figures
Transactions	<name space> +<company choice>	z001 zordlist
Package / Development Class	<name space> +<company choice>	zsd01
Messages	<name space> +<company choice>	zsd01

B   Example of an Exception Handling Class

```
*&---------------------------------------------------------------------*
*&  Include /CTAC/EXCHANDLING_NEW
*&---------------------------------------------------------------------*
*$*$ Company   : Ctac Nederland
*$*$ Author    : Ben Meijs
*$*$ Date      : April 2004
*$*$ SAP rel.  : 6.20
*$*$ Purpose   : Include containing an example for a Local Class that
*$*$             stores exception information in the Application Log.
*$*$             You can create your own Global Class based on this Local
*$*$             Class and adapt it to your standards.
*$*$
*$*$             This local class uses Application Log functions available
*$*$             as of Release 4.6. Check function modules starting with
*$*$             'BAL*' for more Application Log functions.
*$*$
*$*$             An Application Log can be viewed using Transaction SLG1.
*$*$
*$*$             You can create several instances of this class, for
*$*$             example, to distinguish between logs for end users and
*$*$             administrators.
*$*$             We used Object and Sub-object levels for this purpose.
*$*$             They are defined using Transaction SLG0.
*$*$
*$*$             Only one exception class (our own /ctac/cx_log_error) is
*$*$             raised and passed to the calling program using the
*$*$             RAISING interface parameter.
*$*$
*$*$             In future releases of Web AS, the method write_to_db can
*$*$             be moved to the destructor method.
*---------------------------------------------------------------------*
* CLASS LCL_EXCEPTION_HANDLER DEFINITION
*---------------------------------------------------------------------*
CLASS lcl_exception_handler DEFINITION.


*---------------------------------------------------------------------*
* PUBLIC SECTION
*---------------------------------------------------------------------*
  PUBLIC SECTION.


*---------------------------------------------------------------------*
* METHOD CONSTRUCTOR
*---------------------------------------------------------------------*
* Constructor importing object + subobject + External key for application
* logging
```

```
      METHODS constructor IMPORTING value(itp_object)     TYPE balobj_d
                                    value(itp_subobject) TYPE balsubobj
                                                         OPTIONAL
                                    value(itp_extnumber) TYPE balnrext
                                                         OPTIONAL
                        RAISING /ctac/cx_log_error.

*--------------------------------------------------------------------*
* METHOD MESSAGE_TO_APPLICATION_LOG
*--------------------------------------------------------------------*
* ADD one message to the open Application Log

    METHODS message_to_application_log
      IMPORTING value(itp_id)     TYPE symsgid
                value(itp_type)   TYPE symsgty
                value(itp_number) TYPE symsgno
                value(itp_msgv1)  TYPE symsgv OPTIONAL
                value(itp_msgv2)  TYPE symsgv OPTIONAL
                value(itp_msgv3)  TYPE symsgv OPTIONAL
                value(itp_msgv4)  TYPE symsgv OPTIONAL
                    RAISING /ctac/cx_log_error.

*--------------------------------------------------------------------*
* METHOD FREE_MESSAGE_TO_APPL_LOG
*--------------------------------------------------------------------*
* ADD a free-form message to the open Application Log.

    METHODS free_message_to_appl_log
      IMPORTING itp_msgty TYPE  symsgty
                itp_text  TYPE  string
        RAISING /ctac/cx_log_error.

*--------------------------------------------------------------------*
* METHOD WRITE_TO_DB
*--------------------------------------------------------------------*
* Write Application Log. This method should be in the destructor

    CLASS-METHODS write_to_db    RAISING /ctac/cx_log_error.

*--------------------------------------------------------------------*
* METHOD DISPLAY_DIRECT
*--------------------------------------------------------------------*
* Display the Application Log directly on the screen.
```

```
    CLASS-METHODS display_direct RAISING /ctac/cx_log_error.

*--------------------------------------------------------------------*
* PRIVATE SECTION
*--------------------------------------------------------------------*
  PRIVATE SECTION.

*--------------------------------------------------------------------*
* CONSTANTS
*--------------------------------------------------------------------*
* Boolean
    CONSTANTS: co_true    TYPE boolean VALUE 'X',
              co_false   TYPE boolean VALUE ' '.
*--------------------------------------------------------------------*
* DATA
*--------------------------------------------------------------------*

    DATA: tp_app_log     TYPE bal_s_log,
          tp_log_handle  TYPE balloghndl.

    DATA: tp_log_open    TYPE boolean.

    DATA: tp_msg         TYPE bal_s_msg .
* This static attribute contains all the available log-handles of
* all instances
    CLASS-DATA: ts_handle TYPE bal_t_logh.

ENDCLASS.                  "lcl_exception_handler DEFINITION

*--------------------------------------------------------------------*
* CLASS LCL_EXCEPTION_HANDLER IMPLEMENTATION
*--------------------------------------------------------------------*
CLASS lcl_exception_handler IMPLEMENTATION.

*--------------------------------------------------------------------*
* METHOD CONSTRUCTOR
*--------------------------------------------------------------------*
  METHOD constructor.

    tp_app_log-object     = itp_object.
    tp_app_log-subobject  = itp_subobject.
    tp_app_log-extnumber  = itp_extnumber.

    CALL FUNCTION 'BAL_LOG_CREATE'
      EXPORTING
        i_s_log              = tp_app_log
      IMPORTING
        e_log_handle         = tp_log_handle
      EXCEPTIONS
        log_header_inconsistent = 1
        OTHERS               = 2.
```

```
        IF sy-subrc <> 0.
          RAISE EXCEPTION TYPE /ctac/cx_log_error.
        ELSE.
* Add the log handle to the internal table that contains all
* instantiated log objects.
          INSERT  tp_log_handle INTO TABLE ts_handle.
          tp_log_open = co_true.
        ENDIF.

   ENDMETHOD.                       "constructor

*---------------------------------------------------------------*
* METHOD MESSAGE_TO_APPLICATION_LOG
*---------------------------------------------------------------*
   METHOD message_to_application_log.
      IF tp_log_open = co_true.
* This function adds one message to the log.
* Identical messages are not added.
         CLEAR tp_msg.
         tp_msg-msgty = itp_type.
         tp_msg-msgid = itp_id.
         tp_msg-msgno = itp_number.
         tp_msg-msgv1 = itp_msgv1.
         tp_msg-msgv2 = itp_msgv2.
         tp_msg-msgv3 = itp_msgv3.
         tp_msg-msgv4 = itp_msgv4.

* Other available fields
*MSGV1_SRC
*MSGV2_SRC
*MSGV3_SRC
*MSGV4_SRC
*DETLEVEL
*PROBCLASS
*ALSORT
*TIME_STMP

         CALL FUNCTION 'BAL_LOG_MSG_CUMULATE'
           EXPORTING
             i_log_handle            = tp_log_handle
             i_s_msg                 = tp_msg
             i_compare_attributes    = co_true
             i_compare_context       = co_true
             i_compare_parameters    = co_true
*       IMPORTING
*         E_S_MSG_HANDLE          =
*         E_MSG_WAS_LOGGED        =
*         E_MSG_WAS_DISPLAYED     =
           EXCEPTIONS
```

```abap
            log_not_found                = 1
            msg_inconsistent             = 2
            log_is_full                  = 3
            OTHERS                       = 4
                            .
      IF sy-subrc <> 0.
* The entry could not be added to the open log
        RAISE EXCEPTION TYPE /ctac/cx_log_error.
      ENDIF.
    ELSE.
* The log was not open
      RAISE EXCEPTION TYPE /ctac/cx_log_error.

    ENDIF.

  ENDMETHOD.                    "message_to_application_log
*-------------------------------------------------------------------*
* METHOD FREE_MESSAGE_TO_APPL_LOG
*-------------------------------------------------------------------*

  METHOD free_message_to_appl_log.
    DATA: ltp_text(255) TYPE c.
* Free form message text for application log
    IF tp_log_open = co_true.
      ltp_text = itp_text.
      CALL FUNCTION 'BAL_LOG_MSG_ADD_FREE_TEXT'
        EXPORTING
          i_log_handle               = tp_log_handle
          i_msgty                    = itp_msgty
*         I_PROBCLASS                = '4'
          i_text                     = ltp_text
*         I_S_CONTEXT                =
*         I_S_PARAMS                 =
*       IMPORTING
*         E_S_MSG_HANDLE             =
*         E_MSG_WAS_LOGGED           =
*         E_MSG_WAS_DISPLAYED        =
        EXCEPTIONS
          log_not_found              = 1
          msg_inconsistent           = 2
          log_is_full                = 3
          OTHERS                     = 4
                            .
      IF sy-subrc <> 0.
* The entry could not be added to the open log
        RAISE EXCEPTION TYPE /ctac/cx_log_error.
      ENDIF.
    ELSE.
* The log was not open
      RAISE EXCEPTION TYPE /ctac/cx_log_error.
```

```
      ENDIF.
    ENDMETHOD.                            "free_message_to_application_log


*----------------------------------------------------------------------*
* METHOD WRITE_TO_DB
*----------------------------------------------------------------------*
  METHOD write_to_db.
* This method saves all logfiles (one ore more object instances)
    IF   lines( ts_handle ) > 0.

      CALL FUNCTION 'BAL_DB_SAVE'
        EXPORTING
*        I_CLIENT              = SY-MANDT
*        I_IN_UPDATE_TASK      = ' '
          i_save_all            = 'X'
          i_t_log_handle        = ts_handle
*       IMPORTING
*        E_NEW_LOGNUMBERS      =
        EXCEPTIONS
          log_not_found         = 1
          save_not_allowed      = 2
          numbering_error       = 3
          OTHERS                = 4
          .
      IF sy-subrc <> 0.
* Save did not succeed
        RAISE EXCEPTION TYPE /ctac/cx_log_error.
      ENDIF.
    ELSE.
* Nothing to save
      RAISE EXCEPTION TYPE /ctac/cx_log_error.

    ENDIF.

  ENDMETHOD.                              "write_to_db
*----------------------------------------------------------------------*
* METHOD DISPLAY_DIRECT
*----------------------------------------------------------------------*

  METHOD display_direct.
* This method should only be executed if a SAPgui is active
    DATA: ltp_gui_active TYPE c.

    CALL FUNCTION 'GUI_IS_AVAILABLE'
      IMPORTING
        return = ltp_gui_active.

    IF ltp_gui_active = co_true.
```

```
        IF lines( ts_handle ) > 0.

          CALL FUNCTION 'BAL_DSP_LOG_DISPLAY'
            EXPORTING
*     I_S_DISPLAY_PROFILE          = tp_log_profile
              i_t_log_handle               = ts_handle
*     I_T_MSG_HANDLE               =
*     I_S_LOG_FILTER               =
*     I_S_MSG_FILTER               =
*     I_T_LOG_CONTEXT_FILTER       =
*     I_T_MSG_CONTEXT_FILTER       =
*     I_AMODAL                     = 'X'
* IMPORTING
*     E_S_EXIT_COMMAND             =
            EXCEPTIONS
              profile_inconsistent       = 1
              internal_error             = 2
              no_data_available          = 3
              no_authority               = 4
              OTHERS                     = 5
                      .

          IF sy-subrc <> 0.
* Display not possible
            RAISE EXCEPTION TYPE /ctac/cx_log_error.
          ENDIF.
        ELSE.
* No active SAPgui
          RAISE EXCEPTION TYPE /ctac/cx_log_error.
        ENDIF.
      ENDIF.
    ENDMETHOD.                    "display_direct
ENDCLASS.                    "lcl_exception_handler IMPLEMENTATION


REPORT  /ctac/appl_log_example           .
*&---------------------------------------------------------------------*
*$*$ Company  : Ctac Nederland
*$*$ Author   : Ben Meijs
*$*$ Date     : April 2004
*$*$ SAP rel. : 6.20
*$*$ Purpose  : This program contains an example of the following three
*$*$            subjects:
*$*$            1: Adding exceptions to the SAP Application Log
*$*$            2: Using Local Classes (include /ctac/exchandling_new)
*$*$            3  Using Class-Based Exception-Handling
*$*$
*$*$            In this example program, one exception leads to two
*$*$            entries in the Application Log:
*$*$            1: An entry for an End-User (Sub-object 'USER')
*$*$            2: An entry for an Administrator (Sub-object 'ADMIN')
```

```
*$*$            The Application Log object ('ZOBJ') and the two
*$*$            sub-objects are defined using Transaction 'SLGO'.
*$*$
*&--------------------------------------------------------------------*


*$*$----------------------------------------------------------------*
*$*$ Includes
*$*$----------------------------------------------------------------*
* Local class for using new Application Log.
INCLUDE /ctac/exchandling_new.


*$*$----------------------------------------------------------------*
*$*$ Constants
*$*$----------------------------------------------------------------*
* Constants with values for main object and sub-objects of the
* Application Log:

CONSTANTS : co_log_object TYPE balobj_d  VALUE 'ZOBJ',
            co_log_subusr TYPE balsubobj VALUE 'USER',
            co_log_subadm TYPE balsubobj VALUE 'ADMIN'.

CONSTANTS : co_msg_id     TYPE symsgid   VALUE '/ctac/bk',
            co_msg_tp_inf TYPE symsgty   VALUE 'I',
            co_msg_tp_err TYPE symsgty   VALUE 'E',
            co_msg_nr_def TYPE symsgno   VALUE '001'.
*$*$----------------------------------------------------------------*
*$*$ Data declarations
*$*$----------------------------------------------------------------*
* The Application Log can contain an external reference. In our example,
* we use a material number that cannot be found in table MARA.
DATA      : tp_extnumber  TYPE balnrext.

* Two Handlers for two exception objects. One for the USER and one for
* the DATA:
DATA      : rf_appl_lgusr TYPE REF TO lcl_exception_handler,
            rf_appl_lgadm TYPE REF TO lcl_exception_handler.

* Exception Classes. ('/ctac/cx_log_error' is a Ctac Exception-Class.
* You have to create your own Exception-class to replace this.
DATA      : rf_log_error  TYPE REF TO /ctac/cx_log_error,
            rf_sql_error  TYPE REF TO cx_sy_sql_error  ,
            rf_root       TYPE REF TO cx_root.

* Other variables to store extra information in the Application Log:
DATA      : tp_string     TYPE string,
            tp_repid      TYPE syrepid,
            tp_srcln      TYPE i,
            tp_msgv2      TYPE symsgv,
            tp_msgv3      TYPE symsgv,
            tp_msgv4      TYPE symsgv.
```

```
* Data for this example:
DATA      : wa_mara        TYPE mara.


*$*$------------------------------------------------------------------*
*$*$          S E L E C T I O N   S C R E E N                         *
*$*$------------------------------------------------------------------*
*$*$ Define your selection-criteria here.                             *
*$*$------------------------------------------------------------------*
* Parameter for this example
PARAMETERS: pa_matnr  TYPE matnr OBLIGATORY.


*$*$------------------------------------------------------------------*
*$*$          M A I N   P R O C E S S I N G                           *
*$*$------------------------------------------------------------------*
START-OF-SELECTION.
*
  TRY.
* This is just a piece of code in order to verify that everything works as
* planned.
      SELECT SINGLE * FROM mara INTO wa_mara
            WHERE matnr = pa_matnr.
      IF sy-subrc NE 0.
        RAISE EXCEPTION TYPE cx_sy_sql_error.
      ENDIF.

    CATCH cx_sy_sql_error INTO rf_sql_error.
* Store data in the Application Log.
      TRY.
* Store the material number.
          tp_extnumber = pa_matnr.
* Create log for the USER (Typically, this should be executed only once in
* your program! To simplify things, we inserted it here.)
          CREATE OBJECT rf_appl_lgusr
                EXPORTING itp_object    = co_log_object
                          itp_subobject = co_log_subusr
                          itp_extnumber = tp_extnumber.
* Create log for the ADMInistrator (Typically, this should be executed
* only once in your program!)
          CREATE OBJECT rf_appl_lgadm
                EXPORTING itp_object    = co_log_object
                          itp_subobject = co_log_subadm
                          itp_extnumber = tp_extnumber.
*
* Add 1 message to the log for the USER
          CALL METHOD rf_appl_lgusr->message_to_application_log
            EXPORTING
              itp_id   = co_msg_id
              itp_type = co_msg_tp_inf
```

```
          itp_number = co_msg_nr_def
          itp_msgv1  = 'Could not find material'(e01).

* Add 1 message to the log for the ADMInistrator.

* Get extra information from the Exception Object.
          tp_string = rf_sql_error->get_text( ).
          tp_msgv2 = tp_string.

          CALL METHOD rf_sql_error->get_source_position
            IMPORTING
              program_name = tp_repid      "Report Name
              source_line  = tp_srcln.     "Source Line Number

          tp_msgv3  = tp_repid.
* Write the source line number (Integer) to character string.
          WRITE tp_srcln TO tp_msgv4.
*

          CALL METHOD rf_appl_lgadm->message_to_application_log
            EXPORTING
              itp_id     = co_msg_id
              itp_type   = co_msg_tp_inf
              itp_number = co_msg_nr_def
* text-e02:            = 'Error SELECT SINGLE MARA for material
                            number'(e02)
              itp_msgv2 = tp_msgv2
              itp_msgv3 = tp_msgv3
              itp_msgv4 = tp_msgv4.

* Display both messages directly on the screen.
          CALL METHOD lcl_exception_handler=>display_direct( ).

* Store both messages in the database. (You should do this preferably only
* once at the end of the program. To simplify things, we inserted it here.)
          CALL METHOD lcl_exception_handler=>write_to_db.

* Adding data to the Application Log can lead to an exception.
        CATCH /ctac/cx_log_error INTO rf_log_error.
* Add your own error handling here.
* To simplify things, we just write the error on the screen.
          tp_string = rf_log_error->get_text( ).
          WRITE tp_string.
        CATCH cx_root            INTO rf_root.
* Add your own error handling here.
* To simplify things, we just write the error on the screen.
          tp_string = rf_root->get_text( ).
          WRITE tp_string.

    ENDTRY.
```

```
* Intercepting every other possible exception
    CATCH cx_root            INTO rf_root.
* Add your own error handling here.
* To simplify things, we just write the error on the screen.
      tp_string  = rf_root->get_text( ).
      WRITE tp_string.
  ENDTRY.
```

C   Template for an ALV Report

This appendix consists of a basic template that can be used for most of the *ABAP List Viewer (ALV) reports* that are required in a company. This template is based on several years of working with ALV reports in various companies. You should consider storing this template in the Reuse Library (Transaction SE83).

Copy this template and adapt the routines for selecting and processing the data. We recommend that you create a ABAP Dictionary structure that contains the fields to be displayed. This will provide an optimal integration for all existing ABAP Dictionary types, for example, documentation and layout formatting.

The ABAP code to be changed is indicated by '<<< DO CHANGE'.

```
REPORT  /ctac/alv_template.              " <<< DO CHANGE
*$*$-------------------------------------------------------------*
*$*$ Company  : Ctac Nederland
*$*$ Author   : Wouter Heuvelmans / Ben Meijs
*$*$ Date     : May 2004
*$*$ SAP rel. : 6.20
*$*$ Transport: <NR>
*$*$ Purpose  : Template For ALV Reports
*$*$            This template can be used as a basis for ALV Reports.
*$*$            After copying this template, you need to implement the
*$*$            following components:
*$*$            - Copy status STANDARD of function group SALV to the
*$*$              program and adjust the status to your needs
*$*$            - implement the selectionscreen as needed
*$*$            - implement subroutine A001_SELECTION
*$*$            - add the ALV structure with all displayfields to the
*$*$              Dictionary
*$*$            - adjust the TYPE-definition for
*$*$              - ta_list (ALV output table);
*$*$            - adjust the VALUE-declaration for the constants
*$*$            - co_struc = name of the DDIC ALV structure used
*$*$            - implement your own GUI functions in subroutine
*$*$              defined in constant CO_ROUT_UCOMM.
*$*$            - implement the headertexts in subroutine BUILD_COMMENT
*$*$            - if you need a second ALV list which is activated by
*$*$              one of your own GUI functions, you'll have to
*$*$              implement the following subroutines:
*$*$              * BUILD_SEC_LIST
*$*$              * DISPLAY_SEC_LIST
*$*$              * MODIFY_FIELDCAT_SEC
*$*$              * CHANGE_LAYOUT_SEC
*$*$
*$*$-------------------------------------------------------------*
```

```
*$*$--------------------------------------------------------------*
*$*$          M O D I F I C A T I O N S                          *
*$*$--------------------------------------------------------------*
*& Changed By :
*& Date       :
*& SAP rel.   :
*& Transport  :
*& Purpose    :
*&--------------------------------------------------------------*


*$*$--------------------------------------------------------------*
*$*$       G L O B A L   D A T A   D E C L A R A T I O N         *
*$*$--------------------------------------------------------------*


*$*$--------------------------------------------------------------*
*$*$ Type pool declarations
*$*$--------------------------------------------------------------*
TYPE-POOLS: slis,                "ALV types / constants
            sdydo,
            abap,                "ABAP reporting types / constants
            icon.                "Possible icons
*$*$--------------------------------------------------------------*
*-- Constants
*$*$--------------------------------------------------------------*
CONSTANTS:
  co_background_alv      TYPE  sdydo_key VALUE 'ALV_WALLPAPER',
  co_save                TYPE  c          VALUE 'A',
  co_msgty_inf           TYPE  symsgty    VALUE 'I'.
*--------------------------------------------------------------------*
* Constants for interactive functions of an ALV
*--------------------------------------------------------------------*
CONSTANTS:
  co_double_click        TYPE  syucomm   VALUE '&IC1',  "CHOOSE / F2
*--------------------------------------------------------------------*
* Customer interactive functions for the ALV
*--------------------------------------------------------------------*
  co_sec_list
     TYPE syucomm   VALUE 'SEC_LIST'.
"Secondary list
*--------------------------------------------------------------------*
* Names of the routines to be called dynamically from the ALV function
*--------------------------------------------------------------------*
CONSTANTS:
  co_rout_pf_stat        TYPE char30     VALUE 'R0_SET_PF_STATUS',
  co_rout_ucomm          TYPE char30     VALUE 'R1_PROCESS_USER_COMMAND',
  co_rout_top_of_page    TYPE char30     VALUE 'R2_SET_TOP_OF_PAGE',
  co_rout_html_top       TYPE char30     VALUE 'R3_SET_HTML_TOP_OF_PAGE',
  co_rout_html_end       TYPE char30     VALUE 'R4_SET_HTML_END_OF_LIST',
  co_rout_pf_stat_sec    TYPE char30     VALUE 'R5_SET_PF_STATUS_SEC',
  co_rout_ucomm_sec      TYPE char30     VALUE 'R6_PROCESS_UCOMM_SEC',
```

```
      co_rout_top_page_sec  TYPE char30    VALUE 'R7_SET_TOP_OF_PAGE_SEC'.

CONSTANTS:
  co_struc              TYPE tabname   VALUE '/CTAC/S_ALV_STRUCTURE',
  co_struc_sec          TYPE tabname   VALUE '/CTAC/S_ALV_STRUC_SEC'.
*$*$------------------------------------------------------------------*
*$*$ Data definitions
*$*$------------------------------------------------------------------*
*TYPES: <type>.


*$*$------------------------------------------------------------------*
*$*$ Data declarations
*-- Internal Tables
*$*$------------------------------------------------------------------*
*    TA_LIST is the internal table containing the data to be outputted
*    by ALV
*-------------------------------------------------------------------*
DATA: ta_list          TYPE TABLE OF /ctac/s_alv_structure.
*-------------------------------------------------------------------*
* Internal tables, needed for ALV formatting
*-------------------------------------------------------------------*
DATA: ta_comment       TYPE slis_t_listheader. "Top of page of the ALV


*$*$------------------------------------------------------------------*
*-- Work areas / records
*$*$------------------------------------------------------------------*
DATA:
  st_s_variant         TYPE disvariant,  "Display Variant (Ext. Use)
  st_s_var_usr         TYPE disvariant.


*$*$------------------------------------------------------------------*
*-- Temporary Fields / Variables
*$*$------------------------------------------------------------------*
DATA: tp_repid_this    TYPE syrepid.
*
*$*$------------------------------------------------------------------*
*$*$            S E L E C T I O N   S C R E E N                 *
*$*$------------------------------------------------------------------*
*$*$ Define your selection-criteria here                            *
*$*$------------------------------------------------------------------*
SELECTION-SCREEN: BEGIN OF BLOCK s01 WITH FRAME TITLE text-s01.
*SELECT-OPTIONS:   <so_sel01> FOR <table_field>.
*PARAMETERS:       <pa_parm1> TYPE <type>.
SELECTION-SCREEN: END OF BLOCK s01.


*$*$------------------------------------------------------------------*
*$*$ This block is meant for giving the user the possibility to      *
*$*$ define whether the output should be printed directly.          *
*$*$------------------------------------------------------------------*
SELECTION-SCREEN: BEGIN OF BLOCK immed WITH FRAME TITLE text-imm.
```

```
SELECTION-SCREEN: BEGIN OF LINE.
SELECTION-SCREEN: COMMENT 1(31) text-c01. " Output directly to printer?
PARAMETERS:      pa_print AS CHECKBOX.
SELECTION-SCREEN: END OF LINE.
SELECTION-SCREEN: END OF BLOCK immed.


*$*$-------------------------------------------------------------------*
*$*$ This block is meant for giving the user the possibility to        *
*$*$ choose an ALV variant on the selection-screen                     *
*$*$-------------------------------------------------------------------*
SELECTION-SCREEN: BEGIN OF BLOCK variant WITH FRAME TITLE text-var.
PARAMETERS:      pa_varia TYPE slis_vari.
SELECTION-SCREEN: END OF BLOCK variant.


*&-------------------------------------------------------------------*


*$*$-------------------------------------------------------------------*
*$*$           I N I T I A L I Z A T I O N                             *
*$*$-------------------------------------------------------------------*
*INITIALIZATION.


*$*$-------------------------------------------------------------------*
*$*$           A T   S E L E C T I O N   S C R E E N                   *
*$*$-------------------------------------------------------------------*
*-- Selection screen output
*AT SELECTION-SCREEN OUTPUT.

*-- Selection screen processing
AT SELECTION-SCREEN.

  PERFORM process_output_variant USING    pa_varia
                                 CHANGING st_s_variant
                                          st_s_var_usr.

AT SELECTION-SCREEN ON VALUE-REQUEST FOR pa_varia.
*-------------------------------------------------------------------*
* Handling possible values for the ALV Display Variant
*-------------------------------------------------------------------*

  PERFORM get_possible_variants CHANGING pa_varia
                                         st_s_variant
                                         st_s_var_usr.

*$*$-------------------------------------------------------------------*
*$*$           M A I N   P R O C E S S I N G                           *
*$*$-------------------------------------------------------------------*
START-OF-SELECTION.

  PERFORM init_report.
*-------------------------------------------------------------------*
* Select the data that is going to be displayed in the ALV
```

```
*------------------------------------------------------------------------*
  PERFORM select_data TABLES ta_list.

END-OF-SELECTION.
*------------------------------------------------------------------------*
* Finish the internal table that is going to be displayed in the ALV.
*------------------------------------------------------------------------*
  PERFORM process_data TABLES ta_list.
*------------------------------------------------------------------------*
* Call the correct function to display the ALV data.
*------------------------------------------------------------------------*
  PERFORM display_data TABLES ta_list.

*$*$--------------------------------------------------------------*
*$*$          F O R M    R O U T I N E S                          *
*$*$--------------------------------------------------------------*
*&----------------------------------------------------------------------*
*&      Form  init_report
*&----------------------------------------------------------------------*
*         One time actions that are required at this moment.
*----------------------------------------------------------------------*
FORM init_report .

  tp_repid_this = sy-repid. "or sy-cprog

ENDFORM.                    " init_report
*&----------------------------------------------------------------------*
*&      Form  select_data
*&----------------------------------------------------------------------*
*         Build internal table TA_LIST
*----------------------------------------------------------------------*
FORM select_data TABLES tta_list STRUCTURE /ctac/s_alv_structure.

*----------------------------------------------------------------------*
* For example, build the internal table from the purchase header database.
*----------------------------------------------------------------------*
*   SELECT * FROM  ekko
*           INTO TABLE tta_list
*           WHERE  ebeln IN so_ebeln.

ENDFORM.                    " select_data
*&----------------------------------------------------------------------*
*&      Form  process_data
*&----------------------------------------------------------------------*
*         Process the selected data so that it can be used in the ALV.
*----------------------------------------------------------------------*
FORM process_data TABLES tta_list STRUCTURE /ctac/s_alv_structure.

  SORT tta_list.
```

```
ENDFORM.                    " process_data
*&---------------------------------------------------------------------*
*&      Form  display_data
*&---------------------------------------------------------------------*
*       Prepare the ALV output.
*       Display output in ALV format.
*       If SAPGUI is available, the GRID will be displayed.
*       In other situations, the LIST will be displayed.
*---------------------------------------------------------------------*
FORM display_data TABLES tta_list STRUCTURE /ctac/s_alv_structure.

*---------------------------------------------------------------------*
* Comment:
* Define all data locally, except when you explicitly need it globally!
*---------------------------------------------------------------------*
  DATA: lta_fcat          TYPE slis_t_fieldcat_alv. "Field Catalog
  DATA: lta_extab         TYPE slis_t_extab.        "Excl. Functions
  DATA: lta_spec_groups   TYPE slis_t_sp_group_alv. "Spec. groups
  DATA: lta_sort_alv      TYPE slis_t_sortinfo_alv.
  DATA: lta_filter        TYPE slis_t_filter_alv.
  DATA: lta_events        TYPE slis_t_event.
  DATA: lta_event_exit    TYPE slis_t_event_exit.
  DATA: lta_alv_graphics  TYPE dtc_t_tc.
  DATA: lta_add_fieldcat  TYPE slis_t_add_fieldcat.
  DATA: lta_hyperlink     TYPE lvc_t_hype.

  DATA: lst_layout        TYPE slis_layout_alv,     "Layout Settings
        lst_is_print      TYPE slis_print_alv,
        lst_sel_hide      TYPE slis_sel_hide_alv,
        lst_exit_user     TYPE slis_exit_by_user.

  DATA: ltp_title         TYPE lvc_title,
        ltp_gui_active    TYPE boolean,
        ltp_tdline        TYPE tdline,
        ltp_reprep_id     TYPE slis_reprep_id,
        ltp_html_hght_top TYPE i,
        ltp_html_hght_end TYPE i,
        ltp_exit_caller(1) TYPE c.

*---------------------------------------------------------------------*
* First we build the field catalog.
* This internal table is required to determine which fields of the inter-
* nal table are to be displayed and how they should be displayed.
*---------------------------------------------------------------------*
  PERFORM build_fieldcatalog   USING co_struc
                               CHANGING lta_fcat[].
*---------------------------------------------------------------------*
* After building the field catalog (e.g., from a DDIC structure), we can
* modify these settings in the following subroutine.
```

```
*---------------------------------------------------------------*
  PERFORM modify_fieldcatalog    CHANGING lta_fcat[].
*---------------------------------------------------------------*
* Also, we can modify the layout settings.
*---------------------------------------------------------------*
  PERFORM change_layout_settings CHANGING lst_layout.


*---------------------------------------------------------------*
* Set title
*---------------------------------------------------------------*
  ltp_title = sy-title.


*---------------------------------------------------------------*
* Table ta_comment is used to display header information in the
* top-of-page of the ALV output.
*---------------------------------------------------------------*
  PERFORM build_comment CHANGING ta_comment[].


*---------------------------------------------------------------*
* Determine whether the report is executed within a SAPGUI environment.
* We need to know whether GUI-controls are accessible.
* If not, we use function module REUSE_ALV_LIST_DISPLAY (without
* controls) instead of function module REUSE_ALV_GRID_DISPLAY.
*---------------------------------------------------------------*
  CALL FUNCTION 'GUI_IS_AVAILABLE'
    IMPORTING
      return = ltp_gui_active.


*---------------------------------------------------------------*
* If we send the output directly to the printer, we can
* deactivate the GUI-setting and select the LIST-variant of the ALV.
*---------------------------------------------------------------*
  IF pa_print = abap_true.
    lst_is_print-print    = 'X'.
    CLEAR ltp_gui_active.
  ENDIF.

  IF ltp_gui_active = abap_true.
*---------------------------------------------------------------*
* GUI active -> Activate the ALV GRID (control enabled)
*---------------------------------------------------------------*
    CALL FUNCTION 'REUSE_ALV_GRID_DISPLAY'
      EXPORTING
        i_callback_program       = tp_repid_this
        i_callback_pf_status_set  = co_rout_pf_stat
        i_callback_user_command   = co_rout_ucomm
        i_callback_top_of_page    = co_rout_top_of_page
*        i_callback_html_top_of_page = co_rout_html_top    "
*        i_callback_html_end_of_list = co_rout_html_end    "
        i_background id           = co_background_alv
```

```abap
*          i_structure_name          = co_struc               "
           i_grid_title              = ltp_title
           is_layout                 = lst_layout
           it_fieldcat               = lta_fcat[]
*          it_excluding              = lta_extab[]            "
*          it_special_groups         = lta_spec_groups[]      "
*          it_sort                   = lta_sort_alv[]         "
*          it_filter                 = lta_filter[]           "
*          is_sel_hide               = lst_sel_hide           "
           i_default                 = abap_true
           i_save                    = co_save
           is_variant                = st_s_variant
*          it_events                 = lta_events[]           "
*          it_event_exit             = lta_event_exit[]       "
           is_print                  = lst_is_print
*          is_reprep_id              = ltp_reprep_id          "
*          i_screen_start_column     = 0                      "
*          i_screen_start_line       = 0                      "
*          i_screen_end_column       = 0                      "
*          i_screen_end_line         = 0                      "
*          it_alv_graphics           = lta_alv_graphics[]     "
*          it_add_fieldcat           = lta_add_fieldcat[]     "
*          it_hyperlink              = lta_hyperlink[]        "
*          i_html_height_top         = ltp_html_hght_top      "
*          i_html_height_end         = ltp_html_hght_end      "
*      IMPORTING                                              "
*          e_exit_caused_by_caller   = ltp_exit_caller        "
*          es_exit_caused_by_user    = lst_exit_user          "
       TABLES
         t_outtab                    = ta_list
       EXCEPTIONS
         program_error               = 1
         OTHERS                      = 2.
     IF sy-subrc <> 0.
       MESSAGE ID sy-msgid TYPE sy-msgty NUMBER sy-msgno
               WITH sy-msgv1 sy-msgv2 sy-msgv3 sy-msgv4.
     ENDIF.

   ELSE.
*--------------------------------------------------------------------*
* GUI not active -> ALV LIST displayed in Background.
* All parameters for interactive processing need not be supplied.
*--------------------------------------------------------------------*
     CALL FUNCTION 'REUSE_ALV_LIST_DISPLAY'
       EXPORTING
*        i_interface_check          = space                  "
*        i_bypassing_buffer         = space                  "
*        i_buffer_active            = space                  "
         i_callback_program         = tp_repid_this
*        i_callback_pf_status_set   = co_rout_pf_stat         "
```

```
*          i_callback_user_command = co_rout_ucomm          "
*          i_structure_name        = co_struc               "
           is_layout               = lst_layout
           it_fieldcat             = lta_fcat[]
*          it_excluding            = lta_extab[]             "
*          it_special_groups       = lta_spec_groups[]       "
*          it_sort                 = lta_sort_alv[]          "
*          it_filter               = lta_filter[]            "
*          is_sel_hide             = lst_sel_hide            "
           i_default               = abap_true
*          i_save                  = co_save                "
           is_variant              = st_s_variant
*          it_events               = lta_events[]            "
*          it_event_exit           = lta_event_exit[]        "
           is_print                = lst_is_print
*          is_reprep_id            = ltp_reprep_id           "
*          i_screen_start_column   = 0                       "
*          i_screen_start_line     = 0                       "
*          i_screen_end_column     = 0                       "
*          i_screen_end_line       = 0                       "
*        IMPORTING
*          e_exit_caused_by_caller = ltp_exit_caller         "
*          es_exit_caused_by_user  = lst_exit_user           "
         TABLES
           t_outtab                = tta_list
         EXCEPTIONS
           program_error           = 1
           OTHERS                  = 2.
       IF sy-subrc <> 0.
         MESSAGE ID sy-msgid TYPE sy-msgty NUMBER sy-msgno
                 WITH sy-msgv1 sy-msgv2 sy-msgv3 sy-msgv4.
       ENDIF.

     ENDIF.

ENDFORM.                    " display_data
*&---------------------------------------------------------------------*
*&      Form  get_possible_variants
*&---------------------------------------------------------------------*
*       Handle request for possible values on the output variant.
*----------------------------------------------------------------------*
FORM get_possible_variants CHANGING ctp_varia    TYPE slis_vari
                                    cst_s_variant TYPE disvariant
                                    cst_s_var_usr TYPE disvariant.

  DATA: ltp_exit(1)   TYPE c.

  PERFORM init_variant USING sy-repid
                   CHANGING cst_s_variant.
```

```
      CALL FUNCTION 'REUSE_ALV_VARIANT_F4'
        EXPORTING
          is_variant    = cst_s_variant
          i_save        = co_save
        IMPORTING
          e_exit        = ltp_exit
          es_variant    = cst_s_var_usr
        EXCEPTIONS
          not_found     = 1
          program_error = 2
          OTHERS        = 3.

    CASE sy-subrc.
      WHEN 0.
        IF ltp_exit = abap_false.
          ctp_varia = st_s_var_usr-variant.
        ENDIF.
      WHEN 1.
        MESSAGE ID sy-msgid TYPE co_msgty_inf  NUMBER sy-msgno
                WITH sy-msgv1 sy-msgv2 sy-msgv3 sy-msgv4.
      WHEN 2.
        MESSAGE ID sy-msgid TYPE co_msgty_inf  NUMBER sy-msgno
                WITH sy-msgv1 sy-msgv2 sy-msgv3 sy-msgv4.
      WHEN 3.
        MESSAGE ID sy-msgid TYPE co_msgty_inf  NUMBER sy-msgno
                WITH sy-msgv1 sy-msgv2 sy-msgv3 sy-msgv4.
    ENDCASE.

ENDFORM.                                 " get_possible_variants
*&---------------------------------------------------------------------*
*&      Form  init_variant
*&---------------------------------------------------------------------*
*       Initialize the output variant
*----------------------------------------------------------------------*
FORM init_variant USING    utp_repid_this TYPE syrepid
                  CHANGING cst_s_variant  TYPE disvariant.

  CLEAR cst_s_variant.
  cst_s_variant-report = utp_repid_this.

ENDFORM.                              " init_variant
*&---------------------------------------------------------------------*
*&      Form  r0_set_pf_status
*&---------------------------------------------------------------------*
*       If you need additional GUI functions, copy status STANDARD
*       from function group SALV and add your own functions to this sta-
*       tus. In this routine, you specify that you want to use your own
*       GUI status instead of the basic GUI status.
*----------------------------------------------------------------------*
```

```
*       -->UTA_EXTAB  text
*----------------------------------------------------------------------*
FORM r0_set_pf_status USING uta_extab TYPE slis_t_extab.   "#EC CALLED


*----------------------------------------------------------------------*
* Copy GUI status 'STANDARD' from functiongroup 'SALV'.
* After copy, reactivate function '&RNT_PREV' and place this function
* in the 1st position of the menu bar.
*----------------------------------------------------------------------*
  SET PF-STATUS 'STANDARD'.

ENDFORM.                     "R0_SET_PF_STATUS
*&---------------------------------------------------------------------*
*&      Form  r1_process_user_command
*&---------------------------------------------------------------------*
*       This routine deals with the "non-standard" GUI-functions.
*       It enables you to do the following:
*       - Double-click or click on a hotspotted field
*       - Implement your own GUI-functions
*       You'll find some predefined examples in this routine.
*----------------------------------------------------------------------*
FORM r1_process_user_command                             "#EC CALLED
    USING utp_ucomm    TYPE syucomm
          utp_selfield TYPE slis_selfield.

  DATA: lta_list_sec        TYPE TABLE OF /ctac/s_alv_struc_sec.

  DATA: ltp_repid           TYPE syrepid.

*  DATA: ltp_ebeln_num(10)   TYPE n.
*  DATA: ltp_ebeln           TYPE ebeln.
*  DATA: ltp_matnr           TYPE matnr.
*  DATA: ltp_matnr_char(18)  TYPE c.
*
*----------------------------------------------------------------------*
* Handle the specific user-commands.                                   *
*----------------------------------------------------------------------*
  CASE utp_ucomm.

*----------------------------------------------------------------------*
* Handle double click or hotspot on a specific field.                  *
* These are some examples                                              *
*----------------------------------------------------------------------*

    WHEN co_double_click.
      CASE utp_selfield-fieldname.

*        WHEN 'EBELN'.
*
*          ltp_ebeln_num = utp_selfield-value.
```

```
*              ltp_ebeln    = ltp_ebeln_num.
*              CALL FUNCTION 'MR_PO_DISPLAY'
*                   EXPORTING
*                        i_ebeln = ltp_ebeln.
*
*        WHEN 'LIFNR'.
*
*          SET PARAMETER ID 'LIF' FIELD utp_selfield-value.
*          CALL TRANSACTION 'MK03' AND SKIP FIRST SCREEN.
*
*        WHEN 'TABNAME'.
*
*          REFRESH bdcdata.
*          PERFORM bdc_dynpro USING 'SAPMSRD0'         '0102'.
*          PERFORM bdc_field  USING 'BDC_OKCODE'       '=SHOW'.
*          PERFORM bdc_field  USING 'RSRD1-TBMA'       abap_true.
*          PERFORM bdc_field  USING 'RSRD1-TBMA_VAL' utp_selfield-value.
*
*          CALL TRANSACTION 'SE11' USING bdcdata MODE 'E'.
*
      WHEN OTHERS.

    ENDCASE.

*---------------------------------------------------------------*
* Handle your own GUI functions here                            *
* For example, handle a secondary ALV List                      *
*---------------------------------------------------------------*

    WHEN co_sec_list.

      PERFORM build_sec_list   TABLES    lta_list_sec.
      PERFORM display_sec_list TABLES    lta_list_sec
                               CHANGING utp_selfield.

*---------------------------------------------------------------*
* Or some other GUI-functions                                   *
*---------------------------------------------------------------*

*    WHEN 'OKCODE_01'.
*      Actions for this okcode

    WHEN OTHERS.

  ENDCASE.

ENDFORM.                    "R1_PROCESS_USER_COMMAND
*---------------------------------------------------------------*
*      FORM R2_SET_TOP_OF_PAGE                                  *
*---------------------------------------------------------------*
*      Put the content of table TA_COMMENT on the top of the ALV *
*---------------------------------------------------------------*
```

```
FORM r2_set_top_of_page.                              "#EC CALLED

  CALL FUNCTION 'REUSE_ALV_COMMENTARY_WRITE'
    EXPORTING
      it_list_commentary = ta_comment
    EXCEPTIONS
      OTHERS             = 2.

  IF sy-subrc <> 0.
    MESSAGE ID sy-msgid TYPE sy-msgty NUMBER sy-msgno
            WITH sy-msgv1 sy-msgv2 sy-msgv3 sy-msgv4.
  ENDIF.

ENDFORM.                        "R2_SET_TOP_OF_PAGE

*&---------------------------------------------------------------------*
*&      Form  build_comment
*&---------------------------------------------------------------------*
*        Create the internal table that is going to be the TOP-OF-PAGE
*        of the ALV grid or list.
*----------------------------------------------------------------------*
FORM build_comment CHANGING cta_top_of_page TYPE slis_t_listheader.

  DATA: lwa_line TYPE slis_listheader.

  REFRESH cta_top_of_page.

*----------------------------------------------------------------------*
* LIST HEADING LINE: TYPE H
*----------------------------------------------------------------------*
  CLEAR lwa_line.
  lwa_line-typ  = 'H'.
*----------------------------------------------------------------------*
* LLINE-KEY:  NOT USED FOR THIS TYPE
*----------------------------------------------------------------------*
  lwa_line-info = text-100.
  APPEND lwa_line TO cta_top_of_page.

*----------------------------------------------------------------------*
* STATUS LINE: TYPE S
*----------------------------------------------------------------------*
  CLEAR lwa_line.
  lwa_line-typ  = 'S'.
  lwa_line-key  = text-101.
  lwa_line-info = text-102.
  APPEND lwa_line TO cta_top_of_page.
  lwa_line-key  = text-103.
  lwa_line-info = text-104.
  APPEND lwa_line TO cta_top_of_page.
```

```
*----------------------------------------------------------------*
* ACTION LINE: TYPE A
*----------------------------------------------------------------*
  CLEAR lwa_line.
  lwa_line-typ  = 'A'.
*----------------------------------------------------------------*
* LLINE-KEY:  NOT USED FOR THIS TYPE
*----------------------------------------------------------------*
  lwa_line-info = text-105.
  APPEND lwa_line TO cta_top_of_page.

ENDFORM.                    " build_comment
*&---------------------------------------------------------------*
*&      Form  build_fieldcatalog
*&---------------------------------------------------------------*
*       Build a field catalog from the DDIC structure specified.
*----------------------------------------------------------------*
FORM build_fieldcatalog    USING utp_struc TYPE tabname
                      CHANGING cta_fcat  TYPE slis_t_fieldcat_alv.


*----------------------------------------------------------------*
* Build a field catalog for ALV, based on a DDIC structure.
*----------------------------------------------------------------*
  CALL FUNCTION 'REUSE_ALV_FIELDCATALOG_MERGE'
    EXPORTING
      i_program_name        = tp_repid_this
      i_structure_name      = utp_struc
      i_bypassing_buffer    = abap_true
    CHANGING
      ct_fieldcat           = cta_fcat[]
    EXCEPTIONS
      inconsistent_interface = 1
      program_error         = 2
      OTHERS                = 3.

  IF sy-subrc <> 0.
    MESSAGE ID sy-msgid TYPE sy-msgty NUMBER sy-msgno
            WITH sy-msgv1 sy-msgv2 sy-msgv3 sy-msgv4.
  ENDIF.

ENDFORM.                    " build_fieldcatalog
*&---------------------------------------------------------------*
*&      Form  change_layout_settings
*&---------------------------------------------------------------*
*       Set some layout attributes.
*----------------------------------------------------------------*
FORM change_layout_settings  CHANGING cst_layout TYPE slis_layout_alv.


*----------------------------------------------------------------*
* Modify layout settings.
```

```
*---------------------------------------------------------------*
  cst_layout-zebra             = abap_true.
  cst_layout-colwidth_optimize = abap_true.

ENDFORM.                        " change_layout_settings
*&--------------------------------------------------------------*
*&      Form  modify_fieldcatalog
*&--------------------------------------------------------------*
*        Modify the field catalog for the primary list, if needed!
*        You can set attributes for every column in the ALV output by
*        selecting the fieldname belonging to the column.
*        For an overview of the attributes available, see the
*        online documentation of function module REUSE_ALV_GRID_DISPLAY.
*---------------------------------------------------------------*
FORM modify_fieldcatalog  CHANGING cta_fcat TYPE slis_t_fieldcat_alv.

  DATA: lwa_fcat             TYPE slis_fieldcat_alv.


*---------------------------------------------------------------*
* Modify the field catalog according to the requirements.
* Some examples are shown below.
*---------------------------------------------------------------*
  LOOP AT cta_fcat INTO lwa_fcat.
    CASE lwa_fcat-fieldname.
*      WHEN 'EBELN'.
*        lwa_fcat-key       = abap_true.
*        lwa_fcat-hotspot   = abap_true.
*        MODIFY cta_fcat FROM lwa_fcat.
*      WHEN 'BUKRS' OR 'EKORG' OR 'EKGRP' OR 'EBELP'.
*        lwa_fcat-key       = abap_true.
*        MODIFY cta_fcat FROM lwa_fcat.
*      WHEN 'LIFNR' or 'BELNR'.
*        lwa_fcat-hotspot   = abap_true.
*        MODIFY cta_fcat FROM lwa_fcat.
*      WHEN 'NETPR' OR 'DMBTR' OR 'MENGE'.
*        lwa_fcat-no_zero   = abap_true.
*        MODIFY cta_fcat FROM lwa_fcat.
*      WHEN 'ZGR_REQ' OR 'SHKZG'.
*        lwa_fcat-just      = 'C'.
*        MODIFY cta_fcat FROM lwa_fcat.
    WHEN OTHERS.
    ENDCASE.
  ENDLOOP.

ENDFORM.                        " modify_fieldcatalog
*&--------------------------------------------------------------*
*&      Form  modify_fieldcat_SEC
*&--------------------------------------------------------------*
*        Modify the field catalog for the secondary list, if needed!
*        As you could for the field catalog of the primary list, you
```

```
*           can set attributes for every column by selecting the corresponding
*           field name. Look at the examples.
*-----------------------------------------------------------------------*
FORM modify_fieldcat_sec  CHANGING cta_fcat TYPE slis_t_fieldcat_alv.

  DATA: lwa_fcat               TYPE slis_fieldcat_alv.

*-----------------------------------------------------------------------*
* Modify the field catalog according to the requirements.
* Some examples are shown below.
*-----------------------------------------------------------------------*
  LOOP AT cta_fcat INTO lwa_fcat.
    CASE lwa_fcat-fieldname.
*      WHEN 'EBELN'.
*        lwa_fcat-key       = abap_true.
*        lwa_fcat-hotspot   = abap_true.
*        MODIFY cta_fcat FROM lwa_fcat.
*      WHEN 'BUKRS' OR 'EKORG' OR 'EKGRP' OR 'EBELP'.
*        lwa_fcat-key       = abap_true.
*        MODIFY cta_fcat FROM lwa_fcat.
*      WHEN 'LIFNR' or 'BELNR'.
*        lwa_fcat-hotspot   = abap_true.
*        MODIFY cta_fcat FROM lwa_fcat.
*      WHEN 'NETPR' OR 'DMBTR' OR 'MENGE'.
*        lwa_fcat-no_zero   = abap_true.
*        MODIFY cta_fcat FROM lwa_fcat.
*      WHEN 'ZGR_REQ' OR 'SHKZG'.
*        lwa_fcat-just      = 'C'.
*        MODIFY cta_fcat FROM lwa_fcat.
      WHEN OTHERS.
    ENDCASE.
  ENDLOOP.

ENDFORM.                    " modify_fieldcat_sec
*&---------------------------------------------------------------------*
*&      Form  build_sec_list
*&---------------------------------------------------------------------*
*       Build internal table for second ALV list
*-----------------------------------------------------------------------*
FORM build_sec_list TABLES tta_list STRUCTURE /ctac/s_alv_struc_sec.

ENDFORM.                    " build_sec_list
*&---------------------------------------------------------------------*
*&      Form  display_sec_list
*&---------------------------------------------------------------------*
*       This form builds a second ALV list with another field catalog
*       based on a second DDIC-structure (change this name!!!)
*       Fill in the right structure name for constant CO_STRUC_SEC!
*         .
```

```
*--------------------------------------------------------------------*
FORM display_sec_list
    TABLES   tta_list     STRUCTURE /ctac/s_alv_struc_sec
    CHANGING ctp_selfield TYPE slis_selfield.

  DATA: lta_fcat          TYPE slis_t_fieldcat_alv.
  DATA: lta_sort_alv      TYPE slis_t_sortinfo_alv.

  DATA: lst_s_variant     TYPE disvariant,
        lst_layout        TYPE slis_layout_alv,
        lst_exit_by_user  TYPE slis_exit_by_user.

  DATA: lwa_fcat          TYPE slis_fieldcat_alv.

  PERFORM build_fieldcatalog         USING co_struc_sec
                                   CHANGING lta_fcat[].
  PERFORM modify_fieldcat_sec      CHANGING lta_fcat[].
  PERFORM change_layout_settings   CHANGING lst_layout.
  PERFORM init_variant               USING tp_repid_this
                                   CHANGING lst_s_variant.

  CALL FUNCTION 'REUSE_ALV_GRID_DISPLAY'
    EXPORTING
      i_callback_program       = tp_repid_this
      i_callback_pf_status_set = co_rout_pf_stat_sec
      i_callback_user_command  = co_rout_ucomm_sec
      i_callback_top_of_page   = co_rout_top_page_sec
      is_layout                = lst_layout
      it_fieldcat              = lta_fcat
      i_save                   = co_save
      is_variant               = lst_s_variant
      it_sort                  = lta_sort_alv
*     is_print                  = wa_is_print
    IMPORTING
      es_exit_caused_by_user   = lst_exit_by_user
    TABLES
      t_outtab                 = tta_list
    EXCEPTIONS
      program_error            = 1
      OTHERS                   = 2.
  IF sy-subrc <> 0.
    MESSAGE ID sy-msgid TYPE sy-msgty NUMBER sy-msgno
            WITH sy-msgv1 sy-msgv2 sy-msgv3 sy-msgv4.
  ENDIF.
*--------------------------------------------------------------------*
* If field wa_exit_by_user is filled, the user has indicated that he/she
* wants to quit.
* In that case, enter value 'X' in field utp_selfield_exit in order to
* cause the ALV function to stop and not return to the first ALV list
* shown.
```

```
*------------------------------------------------------------------*
  IF NOT 1st_exit_by_user IS INITIAL.
    ctp_selfield-exit = abap_true.
  ENDIF.

ENDFORM.                    " display_sec_list
*&-----------------------------------------------------------------*
*&      Form  set_sort_criteria
*&-----------------------------------------------------------------*
* Determine the sort order and/or the subtotalling of the basic list.
*------------------------------------------------------------------*
FORM set_sort_criteria  CHANGING cta_sort_alv TYPE slis_t_sortinfo_alv.

ENDFORM.                    " set_sort_criteria_sec
*&-----------------------------------------------------------------*
*&      Form  process_output_variant
*&-----------------------------------------------------------------*
*       Process the selected output variant
*------------------------------------------------------------------*
FORM process_output_variant USING    utp_varia      TYPE slis_vari
                            CHANGING cst_s_variant TYPE disvariant
                                     cst_s_var_usr TYPE disvariant.


*------------------------------------------------------------------*
* If display-variant entered on the selection-screen, we need to check
* whether this variant exists.
*------------------------------------------------------------------*
  IF NOT utp_varia IS INITIAL.

    MOVE: cst_s_variant TO cst_s_var_usr,
          sy-repid      TO cst_s_var_usr-report,
          utp_varia     TO cst_s_var_usr-variant.

    CALL FUNCTION 'REUSE_ALV_VARIANT_EXISTENCE'
      EXPORTING
        i_save        = co_save
      CHANGING
        cs_variant    = cst_s_var_usr
      EXCEPTIONS
        wrong_input   = 1
        not_found     = 2
        program_error = 3
        OTHERS        = 4.
    IF sy-subrc <> 0.
      CLEAR cst_s_variant.
    ELSE.
      cst_s_variant = cst_s_var_usr.
    ENDIF.
  ELSE.
    PERFORM init_variant USING    sy-repid
```

```
                CHANGING cst_s_variant.
  ENDIF.

ENDFORM.                    " process_output_variant
```

D Bibliography

Bresch, Stefan, Christian Fecht, and Christian Stork, "Write Smarter ABAP Programs with Less Effort: Manage Persistent Objects and Transactions with Object Services," *SAP Professional Journal*, January/February 2002.

Keller, Horst, and Sascha Krüger, *ABAP Objects: An Introduction to Programming SAP Applications*, SAP PRESS, 2001.

Keller, Horst, and Joachim Jacobitz, *ABAP Objects: The Official Reference*, SAP PRESS, 2003.

Keller, Horst, and Stefan Bresch, "Why Use ABAP Objects?" *SAPTechEd*, 2003, ABAP 256 (Abstract from Lecture, available via *sdn.SAP.com*).

Keller, Horst, and Jürgen Heymann, "Introducing ABAP Objects," *IntelligentERP*, Volume I, Number 3 1999.
(*www.intelligenterp.com/feature/archive/heymann.jhtml?_requestid=228970*)

Keller, Horst, and Holger Meinert, "Inheritance and Interfaces – Polymorphism in ABAP Objects," *IntelligentERP*, Volume 1, Number 4 1999.
(*www.intelligenterp.com/feature/archive/keller.jhtml?_requestid=229131*)

Kessler, Karl, Matthias Edinger, et al, "Controls Technology," *Workbench Edition*, 1999.

Schneider, Thomas, *SAP R/3 Performance Optimization: The Official SAP Guide*, SAP PRESS 2003.

On Performance

Kurka, Axel, "How Plausibility Checks Detect Bottlenecks in ABAP Programming," *SAP Insider*, January-March 2001.

Janssen, Susanne, and Werner Schwarz, "How to Build Optional Parallel Processing into Your Applications for Increased Throughput and Reduced Processing Time," *SAP Professional Journal*, Volume 4: Issue 2, March/April 2002.

Schwarz, Werner, "Performance Problems in ABAP Programs: How to Find Them," *SAP Professional Journal*, Volume 5: Issue 3, May/June 2003.

Schwarz, Werner, "Performance Problems in ABAP Programs: How to Fix Them," *SAP Professional Journal*, Volume 5: Issue 4, July/August 2003.

On Unicode-Enabling

Hansen, Christian, "How to Make Your ABAP Code Unicode-Enabled," *SAPTechEd*, 2003, ABAP 151 (Abstract from Lecture, available via *sdn.sap.com*).

Kessler, Karl, and Andreas Blumenthal, "ABAP 6.10: New Unicode-Enabling Features, Plus a Whole Lot More!" *SAP Insider*, July-September 2001.

On Stability and Correctness

Gebhardt, Boris, and Erik Sodke, "ABAP Troubleshooting," *SAPTechEd* 2003, ABAP 257 (Abstract from Lecture, available via *sdn.sap.com*).

Keller, Horst, and Christoph Stöck, "Steering Clear of the Top 10 Pitfalls Associated with ABAP Fundamental Operations and Data Types," *SAP Professional Journal*, Volume 3: Issue 4, July/August 2001.

Kurka, Axel, "Developer's Desk: ABAP Runtime Error—Prevention and Detection," *SAP Insider*, October–December 2000.

Sodtke, Erik, "An Integrated Approach to Troubleshooting Your ABAP Programs: Using Standard SAP *Check* Tools During Development and Testing," *SAP Professional Journal*, Volume 6: Issue 2, March/April 2004.

Other Subjects

Jenkins, David F., "Decrease Problem Determination Costs and Increase User Satisfaction with SAP Logging Solutions," *SAP Professional Journal*, Volume 4: Issue 5, September/October 2002.

Jenkins, David F. "Put Better Programs into Production in Less Time with Code Reviews: What They are, How to Conduct Them, and Why," *SAP Professional Journal*, Volume 5: Issue 4, July/August 2003.

Kessler, Karl, "New Features in SAP Web Application Server 6.40 for ABAP Developers," *SAP Insider*, January-March 2004.

Hansen, Dr. Christian, "Improve Testing by Tracing ABAP Program Execution: Take a Closer Look with the Coverage Analyzer," *SAP Professional Journal*, Volume 4: Issue 5, September/October 2002.

Kluger, Gerd, and Christoph Wedler, "A Programmer's Guide to the New Exception- Handling Concept in ABAP," *SAP Professional Journal*, Volume 4: Issue 5, September/October 2002.

Janz, Holger, and Rolf Hammer, "Shared Objects in ABAP," *SAPTechEd* 2003, ABAP 254 (Abstract from Lecture, available via *sdn.sap.com*).

There are many good books on Object Orientation. We found the following book to be very helpful in understanding its basic principles:

Eckel, Bruce, *Thinking in Java*, Second Edition, Prentice Hall 2000.
(The first chapter clearly describes the object-oriented paradigm.)

Other References

SAP Insider (*www.sapinsideronline.com*)

SAP Professional Journal (*www.sappro.com*)

SAP Developer Network (*sdn.sap.com*)

SAP Help Portal (*help.sap.com*)

Online documentation in SAP, notably Help on ABAP statements

Author Portraits

Ben Meijs is Product Manager of Application Development at Ctac. Ben is an expert in the field of the ABAP Development Workbench. Since 1989, he has amassed an extensive knowledge in SAP implementations, optimizations, upgrades, and application management. Since 1997, Ben has performed several audits on the quality of customized ABAP software, helping customers to improve technical quality issues raised in this book. Ben joined Ctac in 1995.

Ben is responsible for the overall contents of this book, in addition to coordinating the efforts of its contributors. In addition to writing and reviewing texts, he has been the main technical counterpart for Albert.

Albert Krouwels works for Ctac as a specialist in the field of Logistics and Production Planning. Having worked with most SAP releases from R/2 to R/3 Enterprise, he has extensive experience in the design of ABAP developments. He is experienced in all phases of the software lifecycle: implementation, optimization, and maintenance. Albert joined Ctac in 1995.

As the editor of this book, Albert ensured that the text was consistent throughout. His frequent questions "Why is this important? What is the point you are trying to make here?" helped to make this book a work of quality.

Wouter Heuvelmans works for Ctac as an expert in the field of the ABAP Development Workbench. He has 15 years of experience in this field. He joined Ctac in 1996, where he has worked in implementation and optimization projects, and specialized in auditing ABAP developments. He is also an established ABAP trainer for his colleagues and customers.

In addition to contributing to the contents of this book, Wouter is also responsible for all illustrations.

Ron Sommen is Product Manager of Integration Technology at Ctac. As a consultant, he has worked to develop applications in SAP R/3 with a focus on accessibility of R/3 for other systems and users. He specializes in EAI, XI, Web Applications, and Web services. Ron joined Ctac in 1997.

His knowledge of integration techniques and ABAP Objects has been integral to ensuring that the book is complete and up-to-date. His contributions to the text, his reviews and the ABAP code throughout this book have proved invaluable.

Ctac is a leading SAP Service Partner—the largest SAP reseller in the Netherlands and Special Expertise Partner for SAP-Enterprise Portals. More than 100 commercial and industrial organizations, business service providers, government institutions, and universities make up its customer base.

The company has been active as a consultancy organization since 1992. It has substantial functional and technical expertise that is focused entirely on SAP.

Ctac is listed on the Euronext Amsterdam Official Market and is included in the Euronext Next Economy segment.

Ctac provides SAP implementation and integration of SAP with other systems as well as support for SAP system upgrades and optimization. Ctac is proud to be Ramp-Up Partner for SAP NetWeaver as the sole local SAP partner.

Ctac specializes in SAP system management and counsels businesses on setting up and organizing SAP administration, which can range from partial to full system management outsourcing, depending on the customer's needs.

Index

I

Implicit Selection Conditions 82
implicit workarea 317
IMPORT FROM shared buffer 322
IN UPDATE TASK 207
Incorrect Data 443
INDEX 310
indexes 270
infostructures 283
inheritance 27
Inline documentation 45f.
INNER JOIN 298
inner joins 82
INSERT 272, 318
Instance 20, 126f.
Interactive Reporting 105
Interface Data 140
Interface Parameters 458
Interface Parameters of a Procedure 224
Interfaces 372
intermediate data 321
Internal Table Processing 309
Internal Table Type 319
Internal Tables 311
Internet Transaction Server 337
INTO 317
INTO CORRESPONDING FIELDS 302
INTO TABLE 302, 306
Invalid Data Type 173

J

Java 26
Job Log 447
JOIN 292, 297
Joins 82, 86

L

Legacy System Migration Workbench 59
list 352
local classes 22
local data 23
Lock Objects 130, 133
Locking 130
Logical Unit of Work 136, 138, 444

Logistics Information System 76
LOOP 110
LOOP AT 102

M

Maintainability 18, 331, 401, 403
MAX 307
Memory Concept 125
Menus 251
Message Handling 228
Messages 255, 264
method 126
methods 20, 341
Modal Window Functions 258
Modification Assistant 335
MODIFY 319
MODIFY LINE 202
Module Pool Programs 342
Multi-Application Landscape 65
Multi-System Landscape 52

N

namespace 69
Naming Conventions 337
Naming Standards 457
Native OS commands 190
Navigation 260
Nested Internal Table Processing 312
Nested SELECT 303
New Developments 379
Note Assistant 332
Note Browser 332

O

object 20, 25
object-orientation 20
offline development documentation 49
offset 153
ON CHANGE OF 98
one-system landscape 56
online documentation 47
ORDER BY 292
OSS Notes 332
outer join 83